EDWARD LEWIS **Bob**
Bartlett
of Alaska

EDWARD LEWIS Bob Bartlett of ALASKA

...a Life in Politics

CLAUS-M. NASKE

UNIVERSITY OF ALASKA PRESS
FAIRBANKS

FOR   Dinah A.

Natalia-Michelle Nau-geak

Nathanial-Michael Noah

Introduction

This is the story of a love affair between a man called Bob and the land he wanted recognized as the forty-ninth state. This affair consumed his adult life as he moved from Alaska to Washington, D.C. and back again countless times. He kept a dignified pace: walking with others in the same easy way on the floor of the Senate as he did on the streets of Fairbanks; finding friends in Washington for the new state as easily as he made friends among the voters of Alaska. With grace, he led Alaska to statehood.

WILLIAM C. FOSTER

Legislative Assistant to Senator Bartlett

Acknowledgements

This book grew out of a volume dealing with Alaska's struggle for statehood, which I initially prepared as a doctoral dissertation. While researching and writing that volume, I became intrigued with the career of E. L. "Bob" Bartlett.

Senator Bartlett died in 1968. A couple of years later I met his widow. We became good friends, and many hours spent in conversation gave me invaluable insights into her husband's career.

The efforts of state Senator John Butrovich enabled me to take the time off from my teaching duties to devote the needed energies to this undertaking. For this opportunity I am most grateful to Alaska's senior legislator.

Relatives, friends, and associates of Bartlett graciously granted long hours of interviews. I am indebted to the following individuals for their substantial contributions: Forbes Baker, Frank Barr, Doris Ann Riley Bartlett, Vide M. Bartlett, Frank Barton, Joan Bowers, John M. Cornman, Mary Lee Council, Dr. Don Dafoe, Justice John Dimond, former Alaska Governor William A. Egan, Joseph FitzGerald, William Foster, Charley Geis, Will Goding, Charles Herbert, Katherine Hurley, Joseph P. Josephson, Fred Lorden, Mary A. Nordale, Susie Bartlett Peterson, Dr. Irwin Silverman, Margery Smith, Paul Solka, Doris Stewart, Judge Tom Stewart, George Sundborg, Sister Marie Therese, Hugh and Madge Wade, and Ray Ward.

Archivists and librarians of the Elmer E. Rasmuson Library of the University of Alaska in Fairbanks, the National Archives in Washington, D. C., and the Federal Records Center in Suitland, Maryland have given me immeasurable assistance over the years, and I am grateful to them. I am particularly grateful to Renee Jaussaud of the National Archives for always cheerfully sharing her Alaskan expertise with me, and to Renee Blahuta of the University of Alaska Archives for her help in finding a way through the voluminous Bartlett papers.

A wonderfully cooperative group of women typed and retyped this manuscript. My deep thanks are expressed to Kathleen Aamodt, Judith Smith, Mary Hayes, and Susan Hoffman. I also want to thank Dr. Robert Carlson, the Director of the university's Institute of Water Resources, and Charles Hartman, its executive officer, who gave encouragement and staff support throughout.

I am particularly grateful to Marian Tompkins for efforts far beyond the call of duty. She speedily and cheerfully typed the final version of this manuscript.

My good friend and colleague, Dr. William R. Hunt, read, edited, and reread the manuscript in its various stages. In addition, we had long conversations about

Bob Bartlett in particular and the nature of biography in general while doing our daily noon jogging along the Parks Highway. I am most grateful for his assistance.

I also want to thank my friend and colleague, Thomas A. Morehouse of the Institute of Social and Economic Research, for his many valuable suggestions. I am particularly grateful to George Sundborg and Lianne Forney for their superb editorial skills.

I asked numerous friends to read the manuscript and make suggestions. I appreciate the efforts of Robert N. DeArmond, Gary Holthaus, David M. Hickok, Mary A. Nordale, Jim and Sheila Nordale, Joe LaRocca, Kent Sturgis, Fred Pratt, Senator John Butrovich and Ann Swift.

Richard B. Engen, the director of state libraries and museums, was helpful in many ways. I appreciate his contribution. At a crucial stage, Billy Bob Allen extended a helping hand. It came in the nick of time, and I am grateful to him. Gerald E. Bowkett, director of the University of Alaska Press, was of great assistance with proofreading and supervision of the production processes.

Long ago my friend and mentor, David H. Stratton, shared his skills with me for which I am grateful. Dinah Ariss Naske helped, on various occasions, with skillful editing suggestions and encouragement.

Preface

In his lifetime Bob Bartlett was a member of a number of public institutions: the federal bureaucracy, the House of Representatives, and finally the United States Senate. Bartlett first arrived in Washington shortly after Franklin D. Roosevelt had been inaugurated as the thirty-second president of the United States. Bartlett's public career spanned a part of the New Deal, World War II, the Cold War, the Truman Presidency, the Korean War, the Eisenhower years, the New Frontier of John F. Kennedy, the Vietnam War, the civil rights revolution, and the Great Society of Lyndon B. Johnson.

This diversity of historical circumstances and public institutions were the context of Bob Bartlett's public life, and in juxtaposition with it they provide an opportunity for understanding the interplay between personality and institutions in America. Bartlett's character, his methods of acquiring and maintaining public office, his use of power, and his personal strengths and weaknesses can be viewed in different contexts, providing an invaluable look at the dynamics of public office and the changing structure of the American political system during his lifetime.

On another scale, Bob Bartlett's story provides a view of the changing nature of American life in twentieth-century Alaska. The territory in which Bartlett grew to manhood was far different from the one he represented in Congress as a delegate. The North of his youth was remote, primitive, and unimportant to the well-being of the rest of the nation.

The Second World War dramatically changed Alaska and its relationship to the United States as a whole. The North became a keystone in America's defense system. Massive military spending transformed Alaska's economy from one based on the seasonal extraction of gold and the harvest of fish and furs to one dependent on federal spending. No longer was Alaska so remote and inaccessible. Now a highway linked the territory with the forty-eight states, and scheduled air service brought Alaska within hours of the heart of the nation.

Representing Alaska as a delegate was a burdensome task. As the territory's only elected representative in the nation's capital, Bartlett had to perform duties shared in every state by two United States senators and a minimum of one representative. He had to act as a go-between for residents of the territory and the numerous federal agencies and bureaus operating in Alaska. He also had to keep up with any House or Senate measures affecting his territory, even those affecting it indirectly or by exclusion. Bartlett soon found that it was far easier to learn what Alaskans wanted than to provide it.

He had no vote nor any political leverage. He could only hope to educate members of Congress about Alaska, its problems, needs, and promises, and persuade them to vote as he would have done.

Throughout his life, Bartlett believed that Alaska's many problems would be solved and its needs provided by economic expansion and population growth. He was firmly convinced that it was the responsibility of the federal government to help Alaska achieve economic stability. Both as a delegate and a United States senator, Bartlett used his considerable energies and talents in prodding Congress and the executive departments into fulfilling their responsibilities to Alaska.

Statehood signaled multitudinous changes in the great land, among them a significant population increase and the further urbanization of the state. As more and more citizens chose Alaska as a place of permanent residence, development objectives were aimed at providing the amenities of modern life. This was a pronounced change from the territorial days when a relatively small, largely nonresident population exploited Alaska's fish and mineral resources and spent the profits outside the territory.

Alaska's economy also changed significantly. It moved away from one based primarily on federal spending to one reliant, once again, on the extraction of natural resources, this time oil and gas.

The formation of the Alaska Federation of Natives, the assertion of aboriginal land claims in the 1960s, and the discovery of the Prudhoe Bay oil field in 1968 indicated that great forces of change were in operation.

Once again forces outside Alaska shaped the fate of the state. When Bartlett died in December of 1968, the pioneer Alaska of his youth had already disappeared. The tenor of politics had changed as well. Whereas Bartlett had relied on his many friends and personal contacts throughout Alaska in his ten uniformly successful election and reelection campaigns, "Madison Avenue" had come to the state in the slick and professional campaign waged by Mike Gravel for the U.S. Senate. The age of mass-media campaigning had arrived.

This biography is based primarily on the rich Bartlett papers that he donated to the University of Alaska. These papers are housed at the archives on the Fairbanks campus. It is also based on inverviews with many of Bartlett's relatives, friends, and associates. These ranged from a Juneau neighbor, retired in Sequim, Washington to a boyhood friend in Casa Grande, Arizona to a former federal official now living in New Jersey to numerous friends and associates, both in Washington, D.C. and Alaska. His wife and daughters offered invaluable recollections and insights.

Undoubtedly, there remain many untapped sources of information about this unusual man. His circle of friends and associates was so wide that it was not possible to contact all of them and still complete this work in a timely fashion.

Contents

CHAPTER 1

Family and Youth

B OB BARTLETT'S FAMILY ORIGINS have been obscured by the passage of time, and it is not clear whether, when his ancestors first arrived in the New World, they came as solid citizens in search of larger economic opportunities or as rogues barely ahead of the law. Whatever the reasons, they settled in New England and apparently acclimatized rapidly. It is reported that some of the Bartlett ancestors fought as officers in the Revolutionary War and that one member of the family participated actively in the War of 1812.

In the early nineteenth century, one branch of the family migrated to Texas, where its members raised cattle and horses, maintained livery stables, and operated stage coaches. It also appears likely that one or more men of the Texas branch of the Bartlett family married Indian women.

Ed Bartlett, Bob's father, and Ed's three brothers and a sister were born in Texas. The boys followed construction work and freighting. They left Texas and moved slowly north and west to Washington Territory. In Seattle the brothers established a freighting business and were known for the long mule teams they employed. They often delivered freight to various parts of British Columbia.

When gold was discovered in the Klondike, the Bartlett brothers, together with many others, were drawn to the new Eldorado which held out promises of larger economic opportunities. In the late 1890s the Bartlett brothers left Seattle behind, and by early 1898 they were in business in Skagway, packing freight over White Pass to Lake Bennett. Soon thereafter they left Skagway and opened their freighting business in the raw, bustling, and prosperous center of the new mining operations, Dawson City. It was not an attractive place. Along the river front for half a mile, boats of every size and description lined the bank. Mules, pack horses, and men floundered along in the muddy streets. The Bartlett brothers located their storage, commission, and freighting business on Third Street.

Bob Bartlett's mother, Ida Florence Doverspike, was born in Putneyville, Armstrong County, Pennsylvania, the daughter of Lewis and Lavina (Gumbert) Doverspike, on January 4, 1863. Her family moved to Mount Pleasant, Minnesota in 1865 and two years later to Wisconsin, where the family established its home. Ida Florence, the oldest of six children, went to grade school in Nelson and to high school in Alma. She was graduated and taught school in Buffalo County for about three years. At age twenty-nine or thirty, she went to Marysville, California to visit a friend. After about a year, she left California and visited relatives near Mount Vernon, Washington. Soon thereafter Ida decided to try her luck in the far north. She went to Seattle and booked passage on one of the many steamers bound for Skagway, where she spent the winter. In the spring of 1898 she went over White Pass and then down the Yukon River in a journey which included a harrowing passage through Miles Canyon. She arrived in Dawson, Yukon Territory, in the latter part of June 1898. Employed as a cook for various gold-mining outfits in Dawson, she eventually worked for the Bartlett brothers. Having met in Skagway the previous year, she and Ed Bartlett decided to throw their lot together and were married in Dawson in the spring of 1899. Shortly after the wedding, she went to San Francisco. The couple's first child, Doris, was born there.

Some time after Ida Bartlett's return from San Francisco, Ed decided to leave declining Dawson for young and vigorous Fairbanks, where he established himself as a freighter just outside of town on Goldstream Creek. Ida Bartlett departed Dawson for Seattle ahead of her husband in 1903. Her son, Edward Lewis, was born in Seattle on April 20, 1904. Four-year-old Doris, for reasons of her own, refused to address her brother by his given name and instead called him "Bob," a name which was destined to stick with him. In 1905 Ida Bartlett returned north with her two children and joined her husband on Goldstream.[1]

Bob Bartlett and slight, red-haired, brown-eyed Vide Marie Gaustad, one day to be his wife, grew up together in Fairbanks. Her parents had moved there from Hunker Creek, Yukon Territory, in 1905 in search of better economic opportunities. Vide, "the most beautiful girl Fairbanks ever produced," according to Forbes Baker, lived on Cleary Creek, some twenty miles north of Fairbanks. There her father, O. P. Gaustad, mined on claims 4 and 2 above Cleary Creek and eventually bought into claim 10 below Cleary which proved to be a very rich mine.[2]

The mining camp of Cleary was a busy one in those days, with many stores, cabins, and bars, and the big Grand Hotel, among others. For a little girl, the mining camp was an ever changing and interesting place in which to live. As in all such camps, single men predominated, although there were a few families. Dr. Danforth, a physician who maintained an office at Chatanika, some eight miles from Cleary, regularly rode his pinto horse into camp to hold clinic. A peddler, Doc Stearns, drove a horse and wagon and sold notions, including hair dyes, to his clientele. To advertise the dyes, he often changed the color of his own hair. Big Erik Nelson drove a stagecoach in the summer and a double-ender sled in the winter. Gravel paths connected the mines with each other, and much visiting occurred between the families. Community gatherings for festivities such as Christmas took place in the two-story Arctic Brotherhood Hall. Participants brought along food for the various celebrations, and the few children amused themselves by climbing hand over hand on ropes which hung from the rafters.

Although Cleary was a simple mining camp, the ladies of the settlement wore long dresses, gloves, and hats with plumes. While some of the little girls sported coveralls, dresses were well nigh mandatory for all, even on such outings as berry-picking on the hillsides. Vide's mother, Mrs. Lou Gaustad, made most of Vide's clothing, which consisted of long underwear, heavy stockings and felt boots, heavy dresses and coats (the latter made out of blankets lined with rabbit fur), gloves, and appropriate headwear.[3]

After Vide's father had bought into claim 10 below Cleary Creek, he did very well financially, and the family left Alaska in 1910 with the intention to retire and "live forever in *the glory of* Southern California." Her father invested his "poke" in an orange grove. But Alaska was in their blood, and the Gaustads did not stay quite a year, returning north in 1911. Gaustad invested the rest of his fortune again in claim 10 below Cleary and resumed mining with his partner, Tony Troseth.

In the meantime, in 1908, Ida Bartlett, together with her two children, again went "outside" to Seattle, where Doris, her daughter, who required medical attention not available in Fairbanks, attended the second grade. The next year Ida and her offspring moved to Wisconsin, where her family lived. They returned to Fairbanks in 1911 and rented the big Marshall Irwin house in town. At that point the Gaustads and the Bartletts became neighbors, and the children played together. Soon, however, Vide and her mother moved into another area of town, while her father continued mining at claim 10 below Cleary Creek.

While Cleary was a raw mining camp, the Fairbanks in which Bob Bartlett grew up already had become a modest town. And, like any other of the northern gold rush settlements, it was an unusual place because of the harsh climate and the conglomeration of people who constituted its citizenry. Fairbanks, like other Alaskan settlements in those days, was an isolated place. To reach the nearest portal to the outside world entailed an eight-day trip by horse and sleigh over a primitive trail to Valdez, where a steamer could be taken to Seattle. One could also leave Fairbanks by traveling down the Tanana and Yukon rivers to Saint Michael and there transfer to an ocean-going vessel for the trip "outside."

Fairbanks was named after a U.S. senator from Indiana who later became vice-president of the United States. It was built on the banks of the Chena River, which drained into the turbulent Tanana River just four miles behind the town. Front Street followed the contours of the Chena. It was lined with false-fronted business houses constructed from locally sawn green lumber. Opposite these, on the bank of the river, stood numerous warehouses on piles, where steamers tied up just below the bridge and discharged their cargoes.

In 1911 Front Street and Second and Third avenues constituted the business core of the town. Spreading out beyond these stood the many low log houses in which most residents lived. Most of the saloons were on Front Street, while the shops were located on Second and Third avenues and along Cushman, the main street bisecting the avenues.

Economically, Fairbanks depended on the miners who worked the rich placer deposits of the Tanana Valley. All others — traders, grocers, butchers, hardware merchants, dry-goods dealers, lawyers, saloon keepers, restaurant keepers, bakers, cleaners, gamblers, prostitutes — depended for their livelihood on the labors of these men.

Although Fairbanks had begun its economic decline in 1912, earlier prosperity had endowed the town with electricity, and the core of the town enjoyed steam heating and city water as well. There were various churches, two hospitals, a city hall, and the big, boxy, two-story olive-green federal courthouse on Second Avenue, while the post office was located in the Northern Commercial Company building. In addition, there were numerous newspapers and a city police force. A number of physicians and dentists took care of health problems.[4]

The many diggings at the creeks outside Fairbanks were connected to the town by the Tanana Valley Railroad, a narrow-gauge carrier with forty-five miles of track. The railroad operated every day of the year, a spectacular achievement, considering its mediocre equipment and the added fact that the temperatures along the line ranged from $-65°F$ in winter to $+88°F$ or more in summer. Besides supplying the operations at the creeks, the railroad also lured the miners into town by offering special weekend round-trip rates from the creeks on festive occasions, such as dances.[5]

Luckily for Fairbanks, prospectors found gold deposits at such places as Iditarod and Ruby as the Tanana Valley placer deposits declined; and Fairbanks soon became a supply center, particularly of heavy machinery, for the outlying mining districts. Not only trade, however, but other economic activities helped support Fairbanks. A number of federal agricultural experiment stations had been operating in Alaska for varying periods of time, among them one in the Tanana Valley since the turn of the century. In time homesteaders around Fairbanks developed farms and raised hardy vegetables, grains, and hay for the many draft horses. Dairies supplied the town with milk, while a fellow known as "Short and Dirty" was one of several enterprising potato farmers. John Charley, a native of Switzerland and an expert gardener, even successfully developed a hardy variety of strawberries, while Harry Badger, a real estate man, cultivated the new variety and became the town's strawberry king. Three men operated greenhouses and offered ripe tomatoes, green peppers, lettuce, cucumbers, and small green onions for sale early in the spring to Fairbanksans starved for fresh greens after a winter of canned vegetables, potatoes, root vegetables, and dried fruit. Without doubt, agriculture helped support the town's frail economy.[6]

It was the climate that dominated the town's life and gave it a certain regularity and rhythm. Just before freeze-up in October, the last boats arrived and quickly departed again for Saint Michael, at the mouth of the Yukon River. Individuals who had decided to winter "outside" bid farewell to their friends, while the last cargoes were hurriedly unloaded at the warehouses. As the days grew shorter and the temperature dropped, slush ice formed on the river, snow fell and covered the country, and soon the river was frozen from shore to shore.

Like most other houses, the Bartlett one was small, with a living-dining room, kitchen, bedrooms, and an attached woodshed-storage room, which also contained the privy. Charley Geis, one of Bob Bartlett's boyhood friends, remembers that the garbage man also emptied the "honey buckets" on certain nights of the week. All houses contained the indispensable Cole Airtight Heater, which consumed prodigious amounts of four-foot lengths of spruce and birchwood, while the kitchens were equipped with big wood ranges which burned fourteen-inch pieces of wood. With low ceilings, storm windows, and three feet of earth banked against the outside walls, the houses were snug and warm. Perishables, such as root vegetables, potatoes, and canned goods, were stored in the cellar, while meat and fish were kept frozen in the storage shed.

Some houses had a water well and hand pump in the kitchen sink, which drained into a bucket. The water, however, was heavily mineralized and hardly usable. Fairbanksans, therefore, depended on their two watermen, who delivered spring water with their tank wagons or sleighs, depending on the season. Before delivery the men looked at the blue or yellow cards in the windows, which indicated two or four buckets. They then filled five-gallon oil cans fitted with wire handles, hooked them onto wooden yokes, and carried in the water. During the winters a stove along the tank on the sleigh kept the water from freezing.

M.C. Smith was the proprietor of a large icehouse located just off Front Street. Smith staked out an area on the frozen Chena River, where he cut fifty-pound blocks of ice that he stored in sawdust. These blocks, which were sold in the summer, had other uses besides cooling food and drink. Fairbanksans thawed them and used the softer water for washing clothes.[7]

Fairbanks children walked to attend their school, a big and relatively modern building, housing both grade and high schools. Located at Eighth and Cushman, it boasted its own heating plant and contained very comfortable and good-sized classrooms. Grade school children occupied the first story, while high school students had the second floor. Miss Henrietta Mirick and Miss Margaret Carpenter came as summer tourists and remained as teachers for years, until 1921.

Mrs. John Kelly instilled the fundamentals of Palmer penmanship into a school generation of Fairbanksans, while Miss Margaret Keenan ably supervised the town's educational establishment and kept order among her flock as well.[8]

School children stood in awe of the bravery of peace officer Pat O'Connor, a bear of a man. One day, a mentally deranged fellow suddenly appeared in one of the schoolrooms with a five-gallon can of gasoline, threatening to explode it and kill everyone. The teacher talked the man out of his plan, whereupon he fled to his cabin. Pat O'Connor, hastily summoned, followed him there and demanded admittance, but the man shouted that he would shoot anyone who came near him. O'Connor "broke open the door amid blazing gunfire from within and took his man."[9]

School let out early in the afternoon, but by December, daylight hours were so short that the children walked to and from school in darkness. Temperatures dipped to −40°F, and sometimes even to −50°F or −60°F, although January, the coldest month, averaged −10°F to −20°F. On very cold days, ice fog covered the little town, obscuring buildings and fur-clad people alike.

After school many children hooked their sleds behind horse-drawn delivery sleds and let themselves be pulled all over town. Although the drivers frowned upon this practice, this did not stop the youngsters. "We had snow fights," recalls Charley Geis. "We used wash-boiler lids for shields. We would have fights with kids from another part of town. We used to pick up the hard clots of snow from the streets" to use as ammunition.[10]

Fairbanks youngsters looked forward to Friday nights when Dick Thorn, the theater proprietor, provided free movies for the children. And when conditions were right, there was ice-skating on the Chena River below the bridge in front of town. Often idle miners, bachelors, watched the children and helped with the skate buckles and even kept fires going on the river's bank so the skaters could warm themselves from time to time. In a town with a predominantly bachelor male population, children were loved and spoiled, and most families had a trapper or miner friend who became a member and visited on most holidays.[11]

During the long winter there were other diversions. One of these was mail day, usually on Thursdays. When school was dismissed, the children hurried out of the building in order to see the stage come in, usually about 3:30 P.M. If they were lucky, they heard the bells first and then saw the sleigh, pulled by four horses, emerge from the Valdez Trail, the town's lifeline to the south. Loaded with fur-clad passengers, mail, and cargo, particularly "over-the-ice eggs," the stage was a welcome sight to all Fairbanksans.

The Northern Commercial Company, the town's leading grocery and merchandise store, also operated the power plant that contained the "six o'clock whistle" and the fire siren. The whistle set the schedule for Fairbanks life. A piercing blast at six in the morning woke the citizens, and at seven it sounded again to get them off to work or school. At noon it called for lunch, and at 6:00 P.M. it announced the end of the working day. It reminded the children of their curfew at 9:00 P.M. in the winter and an hour later in the summer. The steam whistle also announced important events in the life of the little community, such as congressional passage of the Alaska Railroad bill in March 1914 and the end of World War I on a bitterly cold night in November 1918.

When the Northern Commercial Company siren blew, it "was an eerie thing . . . it set you on edge, it was a terrific siren. The siren would blow first and you would know there was a fire and then" the regular six o'clock whistle blew. The number of blasts of the whistle designated the location of the fire.[12]

Fairbanks children soon became aware that there were two towns: the one of families and homes, school and church attendance, and visits to the library; and the other, of the saloons and the "Line." Between these existed a cigar store, where men congregated to play pool and solo in the back part, while others sat in chairs in the front part, open to the street, and watched passing pedestrians through a big window. Here they smoked, talked, and read old newspapers from the "outside." Professional men as well as miners and workers patronized the cigar store. Miners particularly spent much of their waking hours there waiting for the mining season to open again. There was also the Tanana Club, located right above the Fairbanks Buffet, a sort of gentlemen's club with large easy chairs, a private bar, solo and poker games, and even a steward.[13]

In the very center of town, beginning at Fourth and Cushman and extending downstream a couple of blocks, was the red-light district, known as the Line or the Row. Surrounded by a high board fence, it had gates on both ends, one on Cushman Street and the other on Barnette. There was a door through which customers went into the Line. Delivery rigs went through the gates. One old-timer stated that "those girls never mixed in society. They would never go to dances or anything like that. They minded their own business, and they were protected by the police, examined by physicians, and therefore the incidence of venereal disease was low. They performed a duty, a job." Reputedly some girls even staked financially troubled miners from time to time. Some married, "and they were very successful marriages for the most part. Those girls made good wives."[14]

All Fairbanksans looked forward to spring. By February the sun returned, and by April the snow was rapidly melting. Layers of clothing were shed, and rubber boots became a necessity as streets turned to mud. In May majestic Canadian geese, sandhill cranes, and many other migratory birds stopped there on their way to breeding grounds in the north. Attending school, then as now, must have been difficult for pupils who had to sit in warm classrooms while the eaves dripped and the sky was blue and the sun was already hot. It was a time for sledding and snowball fights, while mothers attempted to dry wet shoes and clothing and complained about the mud being tracked into the houses. With the last snow, the dog teams of trappers who had spent the winter in the woods came into town laden with furs, the products of the season's labors.[15]

With the arrival of May, all waited for the breakup of the river ice. The men prepared for the event by using as many horses as possible to pull the superstructure of the bridge across the Chena River off its pilings and up the street. The outgoing ice ripped the pilings out each year, and patiently the barge pile driver replaced them, working from the Garden Island side opposite Fairbanks.[16]

It was the fire siren and the six o'clock whistle that announced the ice was going. School closed to allow pupils to witness the spectacle of large ice jams being raised on edge, piled upon others, tumbling down the river. Sometimes there were ice jams which had to be blasted loose.

All citizens read the bulletins posted on the front of the yellow United States Signal Corps telegraph office on Cushman Street announcing breakups elsewhere. When the ice had finally gone out at Dawson, the first downriver steamer was soon to be expected. Its arrival meant the delivery of packages, magazines, papers, and catalog mail orders, all bulky items which had not been carried over the Valdez Trail during the winter. By the time the first boat arrived sometime in May, all the birches in the Tanana Valley had turned a soft green and the weather had become very warm. In May countless mosquitoes also appeared, which helped to make life difficult in the north. Most houses had screened-in porches, and everybody burned Buhach, an evil-smelling chemical designed to drive off these pests. Working outside while planting numerable vegetable gardens, Fairbanksans wore headnets or applied thick layers of Citronella. Townspeople went on picnics, on outings, and to ball games. They played tennis and attended the plays put on by traveling stock companies from the "States."[17]

Fairbanks was, and still is, a great baseball town. Numerous teams played on the dirt diamond at Weeks Field, which also featured a good grandstand. On the longest day of the year, June 21, all of Fairbanks celebrated. Beginning in the evening after work, festivities continued all night. There was a parade containing the floats and flags of all the clubs and lodges, especially the Pioneers, Pioneer Women, and the Native Sons and Daughters of the Golden North. A band played, and the parade ended in the ball park, to be followed by the midnight ball game. After that, many went to the dance, which lasted all through the night.[18]

Most Sundays saw full schedules that pitted baseball teams from the various lodges, such as the Arctic Brotherhood and the Eagles, against each other as well as against teams sponsored by local merchants. Fairbanksans, in short, although they might not have made the major leagues, were enthusiastic players then and now. Awestruck Fairbanks youngsters believed fairly, if unreasonably, that "no player could ever have lived with the dynamic power in his bat possessed by. . . Ed Stroecker," who later became president of the First National Bank of Fairbanks. Well remembered was that "one fearful day for the opposing team when Ed Stroecker, in three successive times at bat, hit the ball so hard and so far that on each occasion it was lost in the farther reaches of the outfield . . ." George Parks, later to be governor of Alaska, was a catcher and probably "was more important in that capacity to his youthful admirers than he could possibly have been in his later role of Alaska's chief executive." The boys had their own teams, the Rip Van Winkles and the Tampas, each sporting their own colors in their homemade suits. Bob Bartlett, however, did not distinguish himself on the diamond, because he was never especially athletic.[19]

As Bob was growing up in Fairbanks, the town's economic condition was slowly deteriorating. When World War I broke out in 1914, high wages and better opportunities lured many Alaskans "outside." These were lean years, when the territory's economic and population growth, never spectacular except during the gold stampedes, came to a standstill. Census statistics between 1910 and 1920 showed a drop of 9,320 in population.[20] While Fairbanks still had a population of some 3,400 in 1910, by 1920 it had dwindled to little more than 1,100 souls. Charley Geis recalls that it was "a very tough time in Fairbanks—people just about existing, and that is all." The Alaska Road Commission hired a few men in the summertime, and construction of the Alaska Railroad helped a little, but economically the times were tough.[21]

Under those conditions Fairbanksans tried their best to survive. Ed Bartlett owned horses, solid draft animals which he used in his freighting, mail contracting, and mining ventures. Bob Bartlett always remembered the time when his father bought "two huge bays, just brought in from Valdez and each weighing a solid ton." His father "counted out for their payment in the kitchen . . . of their home solid gold pieces, $1,000 in $20 gold coins." Up to that time Bob had not thought it possible that anyone could have so much money.[22]

To a boy's mind, however, untroubled by economic worries, the Tanana Valley was one of limitless horizons, with "the Chena a great river, the Tanana a mighty river, and the Yukon the most majestic stream flowing anywhere." The paper birch, in their summer green and autumnal yellow, were as beautiful then as now. The air was clear, and far across the Tanana River loomed the snow-clad mountains of the Alaska Range, among them North America's tallest peak, Mount McKinley. The rolling hills surrounding the little town offered an abundance of wild berries in the summer, while the valleys sheltered moose. To the north of town, thousands of caribou passed on their annual migration as they had done for centuries, while sloughs and ponds abounded with waterfowl. Salmon, on their long journey to their spawning grounds, came up the Yukon, Tanana, and Chena rivers. Alaska's interior indeed enjoyed a certain isolation and solitude broken only by the lively river traffic during the ice-free season, which extended from approximately the middle of May to the beginning of October.

Although there was not much money in town, it was still not difficult for youngsters to obtain some change. Charley Geis remembers: "We go out and pick up a dozen beer bottles and sell them to the soda pop outfit there. We get two bits a dozen. We'd sell whiskey flasks in the early days before prohibition. We pick up half a dozen or a dozen whiskey flasks and sell them to the saloons for six bits a dozen." This gave the boys enough money to go to the clubhouse above the Eagle's Hall after school and play pool for an hour or two. On other occasions Bob Bartlett and his three inseparable friends, Clarence Burglin, Clifford Smith, and Charley Geis, would visit the old Nordale Hotel on First Avenue, "and they had a bunch of pool tables down there, and us kids used to go down there and play." The fee for playing pool downtown was based on an hourly rate, and it was not very expensive.

In high school the boys had casual dates whom they took mostly "to a picture show." During the winter season there also were public and high school dances which afforded pleasure and diversion.[23]

When prohibition went into effect in 1918, a number of bootleggers appeared in Fairbanks. A Belgian by the name of Arthur Van Dam operated a speakeasy, and the high school youths visited his place from time to time to drink beer. The bootleggers also made white mule: "It was white. They did not color it with anything. It came out white. Some of it was pretty good and some of it was terrible . . .did not get distilled right. . .actually would kill a person if you got too much of it." Some of the bootleg whiskey apparently was of high quality: "It was aged, and made way out of Fairbanks, mostly. Nobody knew where they [the bootleggers] had their secret places, where they had their stills." One of the best of these stills was located at Chena Hot Springs, where the proprietors produced excellent whiskey. Delivered into town to a distributor, it would readily find its way to the thirsty consumer. The marshal's office was fairly lenient about enforcing the prohibition laws. As long "as fellows did not flaunt it and [were not] selling it openly, they did not make a big issue. They knew people wanted it."[24]

As did others working in seasonal jobs, the Bartlett family had money when Ed worked. During the off-season, economic conditions could be rough. Money, however, was needed to pay inordinate medical expenses. Bob had badly crossed eyes which required a number of costly operations. Bob later remembered the first of these performed without an anesthetic, with him seated in a chair "with his eyes propped open with metal sticks" during the operation. He dug the fingers of one hand right into the bone during that operation and carried the scar all of his life.[25]

Then there was the ever present reality of his older sister Doris' poor health. Long ailing, she took a turn for the worse in 1915, which required her again to journey to the Mayo Clinic in Rochester, Minnesota, this time for an operation. Early in 1916 her mother and brother joined her in Long Beach, California, where she had been sent for recuperation. Too weak from long years of illness, she died there in April 1917 and was buried in Seattle, Washington the same month. Ida Bartlett attempted to console her husband, writing to him that "she is better off, her troubles and trials are over. But we are selfish and want her. I think it is for ourselves we mourn." Bob, she continued, stayed "in the house by me all of the time. He don't feel well I think, it is because he is feeling so bad about Doris."[26] The death of his sister apparently made a deep and lasting impression on Bob. After the funeral he and his mother once again returned north to Fairbanks, where Bob entered the eighth grade in the fall of 1917.

In the meantime, O.P. Gaustad, Vide's father, won one of the two territorial Senate seats from the Fourth Judicial Division in the 1914 election. He went to Juneau to take his seat when the second biennial territorial legislature met in the spring of 1915. In 1916 Gaustad joined the rush for the new Livengood mining district, leaving behind his mining operations at Cleary Creek. He established himself in the little settlement of Brooks. Gaustad acquired a tramline which ran from the west fork of the Tolovana River, the end of water navigation, to Brooks. He also operated a sawmill, a grocery store, and acted as United States postmaster. During these years Vide and her mother continued to live in Fairbanks but spent their summers in Brooks. It was then a lively settlement of approximately one thousand people, where "the moonshine ran faster than the waters in the creeks," and thousands of dollars changed ownership in the course of many poker games. For a young girl, the open and boisterous atmosphere of Brooks was exhilarating.[27]

During the school terms Bob and Vide attended school together. Although Bob was an above-average student, his ninth grade teacher reprimanded him for whispering too much and reminded him that he was capable of better work. In the tenth grade his teacher observed that his desk was untidy, he wasted time, and he incited others to mischief. His academic work, however, was good.[28]

During the summers Bob worked. Generally he helped his father with the freighting business, hauling wood for the Northern Commercial Company or ore from the Joe Quigley mine in the Kantishna mining area near Mt. McKinley. He also helped in road building at Birch Lake, some fifty or so miles south of Fairbanks on the Richardson Trail. Once his employer sent him some twenty miles south from Birch Lake to Munson's Roadhouse to help with road emergency repairs. Nothing seemed as luxurious to a boy as to live "in a real roadhouse with all expenses paid and to subsist so grandly at the Munson table." On many occasions he was "almost rendered incapacitated by too liberal attention to blueberries which, in huge dishes, were placed at the table at every meal."[29]

One summer his father mined on Eagle Creek in the Circle district. Since this was before the construction of the Steese Highway, the Bartlett wagon train had to hew its own way over the rough trail, with six teams to haul supplies for a summer's mining activities. The distance between Fairbanks and Eagle Creek amounted to just over one hundred miles and took approximately ten days. Some days were very hard, and progress was tedious. One "Captain" Cunningham served as cook. Like many a sourdough, or Alaskan old-timer, Cap was well-read and both willing and prepared to debate fluently on any imaginable issue. "In addition to his somewhat dubious culinary attainments, Cap was a layman physician of self-acknowledged merit, and to such youngsters as Wilbur Jewell and Bob, it was a constant struggle to keep Cap from administering. . .the strange herbs and barks which seemed to be such a vital part of his medicine chest." Ed Bartlett, in his son's eyes, was an acknowledged master at handling horses. Con Whalley ranked next in skill to Ed Bartlett. He had been the reinsman of the twenty-horse teams which had carried ore from the fabled mines of Colorado and other western states. He appeared wise and kind and gentle to Bob. A mystery, however, surrounded the man. He never removed his hat, and nobody ever discovered what he covered so zealously.[30]

During that same summer Ed Bartlett told his son to hike the ten or so miles to Miller House for some needed groceries. As an afterthought, Ed added that Bob might pick up some tobacco for the men. Addicted to nicotine, they were in desperate need of replenishment. Bob picked up the groceries and, on the spur of the moment, decided that the best way to break the tobacco habit was to be without the weed. He shouldered his groceries, hiked the ten miles back to the mine, and reported that he thought it best for the men's own good not to obtain the tobacco. The smokers responded swiftly to this reform effort, and within five minutes Bob had started again for Miller House — in somewhat of a hurry this time and with very strong voices urging him on. At that very moment, Bob Bartlett resolved against active participation in tobacco reform and felt even more certain of that decision after he had completed two twenty-mile hikes in the one day.[31]

Cleanup time followed the summer's work. This consisted of washing the gold from the pay dirt which the men had been digging out and piling up all summer long. Cleanup produced the "somewhat less than princely sum of $80," which induced Ed Bartlett to leave hurriedly and make arrangements with a successful mine operator, Tom Aiken, to haul his ore from the mine to Roosevelt on the Kantishna River. The men Ed Bartlett had employed for the summer left as well, and Bob and his mother stayed behind to pack and transport the gear into Fairbanks. They departed with the single remaining team. On the way down the Chatanika their horses strayed, and it took Bob three days to find them again. Their food supply had already run out, and they lived on flour and Eagle Brand

sweetened, condensed milk. Thirteen miles out of Chatanika, their wagon got
stuck in the shifting sand of the Chatanika River, so Bob and his mother abandoned it and returned to Fairbanks on horseback.[32]

Ed Bartlett, whose financial position fluctuated with his business fortune, while
flush with money, bought one of the first Ford motor cars for his son. One summer
Bob went into business as a taxi driver and hauled miners from the creeks into
town. And since he also knew "where the places [speakeasies] would be around
town," Bob, if asked, drove eager miners to where they could slake their thirst.[33]

In 1921 Bob left high school before breakup to help his father with his work of
ore freighting in the Kantishna. He boarded the railroad at Kobe (renamed Rex in
a burst of xenophobia during World War II) and went into the Kantishna with the
mail carrier and his dog team. The carrier fitted him with a pair of snowshoes with
which Bob made no progress at all. In order to catch up with the dogs, he took off
the unfamiliar shoes and ran in the soft snow. After his arrival at the camp, his
father drew him aside and told him that "under duress of necessity, Henry Crook,
a teamster, had been coerced into cooking" after the regular man had quit. Henry,
although a good teamster, was an absolute failure as a cook. Bob took over the
cooking the very next morning but failed to please. The crew rebelled against his
first breakfast, because the hotcakes were served to them half cooked, and the
young chef lost his job.[34]

Bob had left behind a number of incompletes at school when he joined his
father early in the spring. French was the subject which gave him the most trouble.
He relied on Vide to send him her French assignments, which he copied and then
sent to school. His teacher, Constance L. Edmunds, acknowledged the receipt
of two lessons in June 1921 and even sent some note paper, because he had no
other source of supply.[35]

While Bob had been struggling with French, Vide's father had run unsuccessfully for a second term in the territorial Senate. The Gaustad marriage, never very
good, deteriorated further. Gaustad, accustomed to the social and political atmosphere of Juneau, could not face returning to the Livengood mining district.
Instead, he went to California, sold a ranch he had acquired in 1910, and lived
high for a time.[36]

Vide and her mother remained in Fairbanks, where Vide attended high school.
She and Bob dated occasionally. In the fall of 1921 Lou Gaustad sold enough
personal goods to buy tickets, and she and her daughter left for Los Angeles to
join the errant paterfamilias.[37]

Bob Bartlett, "pretty keen" about Vide, decided to accompany her as far as
Chitina. From Chitina the three then took the train to Cordova where Vide and
her mother were to board a boat for the "outside." Fall storms, however, delayed
the arrival of the steamer for two weeks. Since the trail from Chitina to the Valdez

Trail was closed by then, the only way Bob could return to Fairbanks was by boat to Valdez and then back to Fairbanks over the year-round maintained trail. But, reluctant to leave Vide, he decided instead to sail south with the Gaustads. On the steamer journey from Cordova to San Francisco, Bob booked passage back to Valdez. He returned to Fairbanks for his senior year of high school and was graduated on May 31, 1922, with twelve other students. Vide attended Hollywood High School in Los Angeles and received her diploma the same year. In the fall of 1922 she enrolled at the University of California, Los Angeles, and Bob began studying at the University of Washington in Seattle. He enjoyed some of his courses, particularly one taught by English professor Vernon L. Parrington, author of the outstanding multi-volume intellectual history, *Main Currents in American Thought*. The discipline of university study did not appeal to Bob, although he stuck it out that first year. In the spring of 1923 he booked passage on a steamer for the voyage north. With him on the northbound steamer was Fairbanks high school teacher and aviator Carl Ben Eielson, with his pride and joy, a crated airplane. Back in Fairbanks, Bob enrolled at the Alaska Agricultural College and School of Mines [later to become the University of Alaska] for a few courses, despite his dislike of university life.[38]

During the summer of 1924 he worked as a reporter for the *Fairbanks Daily News-Miner*, the lone survivor of more than a score of newspapers which had at one time or another existed in Fairbanks. The Fairbanks economy was slack, because World War I, with its inflation, had dealt a severe blow to gold miners in the Tanana Valley, where the high-grade placers had already been exhausted. Many dwellings were deserted, and a large number of buildings in the business district were sold to meet delinquent taxes.

But Fairbanksans were optimistic and hoped for better days ahead. Colorful William Fentress Thompson, majority stockholder, editor, and manager since 1908 of the *Fairbanks Daily News-Miner,* who was variously known as "Wrong Font," "Colonel," or simply "W. F." Thompson, showed his faith in the city's future by continuing to publish a daily newspaper even though the town boasted hardly more than a thousand residents. As a cub reporter, Bob Bartlett learned the rudiments of journalism, but other lures attracted him more. He quit the *News-Miner* in 1925, and in the fall of that year he journeyed south, accompanied by his mother, to enroll at the University of California, Los Angeles. He took Spanish, among other courses, and received a failing grade at the end of the term. Discouraged, and with money running low, the Bartletts returned to Fairbanks.[39]

On a cold and clear January day in 1926, Bob Bartlett once again went to work as a reporter for the *Fairbanks Daily News-Miner*. "Wrong Font" Thompson, in failing health, died in 1927, and Hjalmer Nordale took over the position of editor. Economic prospects for Fairbanks brightened at about the same time, because the

United States Smelting, Mining and Refining Company of Boston, also referred to as the Fairbanks Exploration Company, had bought much placer gold-mining ground on the creeks outside of town and some property in the city for an administration building. It now had five dredges operational, and many Fairbanksans once again went to work.

Hjalmer Nordale, the new editor, decided to move the newspaper to a location with more floor space. It was no easy task, however, hauling the heavy presses, folder, make-up stones, linotype machines, and numerous cases of type. Adolph Olson, who owned a huge team of Clydesdales, together with the whole newspaper crew, accomplished the task without too many mishaps. Linotype operator Forbes L. Baker later recalled that it was during the move that Bob Bartlett proved himself in journalism by creating news three days ahead of time so it could be put in type to use during the moving period. Furthermore, unlike many reporters and editors who are hard to work for, "kind of skittish, in fact a lot of them . . . blame you for a lot of mistakes . . . ," Bob Bartlett always was "very, very considerate," Baker recalls. Not only that, Bartlett also had a wonderful personality: "He knew just about everybody. He had a tremendous memory; he might not remember a man's last name, but always knew his correct first name or nickname." Forbes Baker and Bartlett became friends, and over a number of years, the older man taught Bartlett how to set type.[40]

In 1929 Austin E. "Cap" Lathrop, Alaska's lone large-scale entrepreneur, purchased the newspaper. Shortly afterwards he brought in Bernard M. "Bernie" Stone, a New Zealander and veteran newspaperman, as editor. Stone, however, proved to be much more adept with the spoken than the written word. Furthermore, editor Stone, a hard drinker, thrived on white mule and habitually hid some of his booze in the newspaper's paper stockroom. One morning, raging with thirst, Stone stormed through the glass front door of the plant without unlocking it and made a beeline for the bottle. Much to his dismay, he could not find it. The irate and suspicious Stone accused Bartlett of having taken it. Bartlett denied any wrongdoing. After some hot words had passed, the editor went to the front office and, noticing the broken door for the first time, angrily demanded to know "who in the hell" had broken it. No wonder that most of the labor of supplying copy for the paper fell on Bob Bartlett, who felt overworked and underpaid.[41]

Bartlett scrambled every day to fill the paper's news columns. Wire service news in those days was sketchy, and its use determined costs. Local events had to make up the bulk of the newsworthy items and fill the paper. The young reporter's rounds were not limited to news gathering, as he had to collect advertising from businessmen on his tours around town as well. His job was no sinecure, but it gave him the opportunity to acquire skills which were to stand him in good stead in later years. Though he was always a good writer, journalism sharpened his style and taught him to evaluate and describe quickly many different situations and events. In addition, he covered many occurrences which were of worldwide interest for the Associated Press. Among these stories were the record-setting polar flight of Hubert Wilkins and Carl Ben Eielson from Barrow to Spitzbergen and the international search for Eielson and his mechanic, Earl Borland, after they were lost on a flight to Siberia.

While Bob Bartlett had attended a number of universities and colleges for various periods of time and finally had chosen journalism as a career, Vide Gaustad had been graduated from U.C.L.A. with a bachelor's degree and a teaching certificate for junior high school. But teaching jobs were scarce, and Vide was glad to get a twenty-dollar-a-week job as a reporter working for a small newspaper near Seattle. Vide abandoned journalism eagerly when an Alaskan friend offered her a teaching position at Wrangell, a small community in southeastern Alaska. She assumed her teaching duties in Wrangell but became ill with rheumatic fever during the school term. Lying on a mattress in the open back of a coal truck, she was taken to the little local hospital and spent the next four months there.[42]

Vide left Wrangell for Spokane to recuperate at her Aunt Rose Logan's home. Back on her feet again, she went to Seattle early in 1929 and enrolled for some graduate courses at the University of Washington that spring and summer. While attending school, she met and dated a young law student from Hoquiam. At the end of the summer, she took a job as a reporter with a newspaper in Aberdeen to be near the young man. The job was of short duration, because within a few weeks she had accepted a teaching job in the little lumbering community of Pe Ell, on the border between Pacific and Lewis counties.[43]

Vide assumed her teaching duties in the fall, while Bob continued working as a reporter on the *News-Miner*. It was a successful year for both, professionally as well as personally. In that Great Depression fall of 1929, however, neither Bob nor Vide had any idea what changes the following year would bring to their lives.

CHAPTER **2**

Courtship and Marriage

BOB AND VIDE HAD known each other for a long time. They had carried on a sporadic courtship over the years. Bob had proposed marriage on numerous occasions, particularly while Vide attended U.C.L.A. She liked Bob well enough, but marriage held no great appeal to her just then. Beautiful, vivacious, and flirtatious, she thoroughly enjoyed life in the States, which offered opportunities and amenities unknown in Fairbanks.

Bob had persisted in his courtship, and with each proposal he sent the same diamond ring. In her sorority house at the U.C.L.A. campus, Vide's sorority sisters were amused over periodic arrivals of a little box containing the ring. As regularly as it arrived, she returned it.

Bob's chance to present his case directly came when she was teaching in Pe Ell. He wheedled an assignment to escort a number of Alaskan prisoners to McNeil Island Federal Penitentiary near Tacoma, Washington. He also had to make certain that the recovered body of famed aviator Carl Ben Eielson was shipped from Seattle to his home in Hatton, North Dakota. Eielson had disappeared on a flight to the American trading ship, the three-masted *Nanuk,* icebound off the Siberian village of North Cape.

Bob quickly discharged his duties and then visited Vide in Pe Ell. Although dating Oscar Kalenius, a football player at the University of Washington, Vide was happy to see Bartlett again.[1]

The next few weeks sped by too quickly. Although originally Bob was to have returned to Alaska shortly after he had completed his assignment in Seattle, he gained extra time after accidentally meeting his employer, the redoubtable Alaskan capitalist "Cap" Lathrop, in Seattle. Lathrop, who had a reputation as a tyrannical employer, had sympathy for his young reporter and advanced the love-struck Bartlett one hundred dollars. This enabled him to stay with friends in Seattle and to visit in Pe Ell a few more times, attempting to persuade Vide to become his bride. Bartlett had definitely made up his mind to marry Vide.

On April 20, 1939, Bartlett celebrated his twenty-sixth birthday. He felt dissatisfied and uncertain about what he wanted to do with his life. Having attended three universities sporadically and recognizing that he never would adjust to the required mental discipline, he had finally quit college and given up hope of obtaining a degree. Over the years he had slowly drifted into newspaper work, but he was aware that he occupied a dead-end job as a reporter at the *Fairbanks Daily News-Miner*.

The life of a bachelor no longer appealed to him. He realized that his life lacked firm direction and purpose. Bob felt that his twenty-sixth birthday was a milestone of sorts. He desperately wanted to establish roots and perhaps build a career in journalism. Above all, he loved Vide Gaustad. Marriage, he realized, represented the type of stability for which he longed.

Reflecting on their first meeting in Pe Ell, Bob wrote: "Honestly, Vide, I never thought it would come to this again. Always I knew I would love you forever, but never did I think love could flare up again like this."

A few days later in Seattle he wrote: "Vide, dearest Vide, until I saw you last night, I did not know how strong my love had maintained itself through the years. Like you, I too have many times, perhaps, felt there were others I loved better than you." Bob confessed that "there has always been since '26 a girl I liked a whole lot, but now I know no other can be set before you."

Back in Seattle he wrote that he was only "a few short hours away," and yet "the length of the world [lies] behind us. When did I last look into your face and know you were near? Was it today or the better season that lies behind?" The hours spent together, he assured her, counted "among the most happy and the most miserable of my life."

Vide shared his happiness and misery, torn, as she was, between the entreaties of Bob Bartlett and of Oscar Kalenius. Bob reminded Vide that he had traveled some four thousand miles to see her. He advised her to take a few days off from teaching in order to spend some time with him "while I am patiently near . . . and close to you." Bob assured Vide that he would, with whatever "means in my power. . .try to win you." He remembered "the motions of your hands, your manner of speech, and a hundred other endearing things. . . ." He confessed: "Lord, Vide, you're in my thoughts all the time, sleeping, it seems, as well as waking. Sometimes those thoughts are all to the good and sometimes they are not—because I know there's a long trail ahead yet before, if ever, I shall win you."

Bob wondered aloud what the future might hold for him in Fairbanks: "I don't have much faith in the gentleman [Cap Lathrop] who owns my services and no great desire to work for him too long." He confessed to Vide that he was "just praying that the prospecting my dad did may have turned out all right," but he doubted it, because his father would probably already have notified him in Seattle to negotiate the purchase of additional needed equipment if that were indeed the case. Perhaps, he reasoned optimistically, "something may turn up yet."

Uncertain of his persuasive powers, he reminded Vide that he was aware that handsome Oscar, the football star, was still his rival. Apparently Bob had always been conscious of shortcomings in his physical appearance. He wished that he "too could be handsome and all the rest of it, for your sake if nothing else, but it's a little late now to do anything about it." Bob confessed that he felt the "handicap keenly enough," but added that there was "no use crying about it, and that feeling of mental superiority you spoke of does act as a sedative in a good many instances."

Vide hesitated in spite of Bob's entreaties. She was not emotionally ready to marry. Perhaps it was a reluctance to return to the isolation of Fairbanks or an uncertainty about her own feelings which made her hesitate. She needed time to think and sort out her confused emotions, so she rather sharply informed Bob that she wanted to be alone for awhile. He reacted with the hypersensitivity of a man in love: "Vide: Has the good departed out of you? What are you trying to do? Have I done you hurt that you should do this thing to me? Who talked to me this morning over the phone? Not you, assuredly. . . Long ago, I thought my soul never again could be seared, and now it is more open and raw than ever before. . . Where have I wronged you? I cannot comprehend what has happened."

Bob promised to see Vide before he returned to Alaska. The suspicion that Vide "went from me to another and turned from me" tortured him and left a scar "that knows no healing." In desperation he asked her, what "have I done to you, darling? Have I done you hurt that you should do this thing to me? [What of] all the years ahead of us—the perfect trust that knew no breaking—the ceremony without a word—the kisses that sealed our love—are these, too, vanished, dear heart? O little Vide, who is so muddled in her thinking!" Believe not, "my sweetheart," he assured Vide, "that you belong to any other!"

Bob wished the return of "the old jealousy of mine. . .so I could hate someone." Yet that feeling had vanished forever. "Now, when this has come to me, I am all frantic, but way down in the inner part of me there is understanding and I know you are mine." But if Vide loved the "boy in Aberdeen," Bob urged her to marry Kalenius: "Don't make him unhappy too." However, he did caution Vide that "you'll soon know in your heart of hearts that you love me. . . ." He optimistically boasted that one day he would become a famous writer, "because I know what there is in me to say and I know how I want to say it." Yet marry Oscar anyway, he suggested, and "have three kids, and be content. Live in your little city, which you would never do with me." As for himself, Bob only wanted "the wild places of this world, and before I'm done I shall see them all. Your shows, your street cars, your cement, your noise, don't entrance me at all. . . ."

And yet Bob's longing to see the world was more imaginary than real. Desperately in love, he wanted only to marry Vide. She had accused him of just wanting a home. "You are the only person in all this world, excepting my mother, I'd make a home for," he told her.

Bob found it very difficult to return to Alaska, because nothing definite had been settled between them. He alternated between depression and hope. "I'm dreadfully sick and tired of Alaska," he wrote to Vide, "and cannot stay there much longer." Yet he had to go back to his Fairbanks job, because he was out of funds. Depressed, he wrote to her: "To be frank with you now, I can't see why you would have me around at all. If I had any money, or was handsome, or had position, or any of these, there might be some excuse." Or was it perhaps possible "that you love my love for you?. . . Do you understand what I mean?" He was determined to wait for her, "but if your happiness lies elsewhere, then I'll be happy to know you are content." Bob now had to return north, and before boarding the *Northwestern* for Alaska, he wrote to Vide: "The sound of your voice and the feel of your soft cool flesh have vanished, and this is the nearest we can be. The past is dead; the future can take care of itself; but the present is glorious and sadness comes only from having to depart from you Vide, darling; you've done something queer to me. I can't explain it exactly but feel different all over and have more confidence and more faith. . . ."

All too soon the ship would sail, and Bob would have to confront "solid realities" once again. "Well, not quite that," he mused to Vide, "for there are glorious dreams to treasure and — perhaps, would you have me say — glorious dreams to look forward to. . ." Bob worried that "it was hard for you at Pe Ell in a way, because you are up against that inevitable proposition of small-town talk." Bob reassured an apparently worried Vide that "no matter what anyone says, let me tell you that you never need worry about me drinking. If we were out together and wanted to, that would be different; but as for me 'coming home swacked' — that would be absolutely out of the question."

At last the *Northwestern* set sail for Alaska. Parting was difficult: "You've brought me contentment, Vide, a contentment I never knew before. You are my world, my being, my all." Bob almost missed the ship waiting for a letter from Vide, writing that "by the time you have read this, I'll be listening to the thud of the ship's engines." Despite the unsettled nature of their relationship, he wrote: "I go back happy. I never knew so much living could be compressed into the few hours we've seen each other in the last three weeks. They've had their stormy periods, but as I look back, I remember we never uttered one harsh word to each other." Bob hoped to win Vide as his bride, "and if ever I can win you, I'll count myself the luckiest of men. When you said no wedding ceremony was needed, I believe you said the truth; it seems to me now you are a very part of me."

The next day on board ship, Bob was depressed. "Outbound for Alaska once more," he wrote, "and this time there will be no happiness in reaching home." The one month "outside," he confessed, had been a crowded yet wonderful one but perhaps had not been easy for Vide, because it had "unsettled your life where it was settled." Bob felt he had done "all that I could do to bind us together . . . distance removes me from the active lists." Vide had promised Bob not to see Oscar Kalenius again, for she had perhaps already realized that he would play no further role in her life.

A future in Fairbanks, Bob conceded to Vide, looked bleak indeed. He felt "no more anxious to go back north than you [do], but I see no way out right now." He asked Vide, in her travels around the state of Washington, to keep her eyes open for a newspaper business for sale "that wouldn't require too much of a down payment and could be built up."

As the ship approached Seward, Bob recalled the many times he had traveled back to Alaska, writing to Vide and seeking her love, always wondering if this time it would be different. "The first few days out," he confessed, "I didn't miss you so intensely as I do now. It seems as if we had always been together and that this absence somehow is wrong."

With Vide very much on his mind, Bob boarded the Alaska Railroad at Seward to return to Fairbanks and his job of reporter. Two letters from Vide awaited him on his arrival. They put him "on top of the world" as nothing ever had: "I've been sneaking off all day to read them over and over again. Can it be that after all this time we've hit one another's stride at last? It seems as though there is a spiritual bond between us, that we now move as one and look to the same end."

Vide had finally accepted the much-traveled diamond ring. Bob was exuberant. "Vide, darling," he wrote, "you can't want any more attention [than that which] I want to give you. I want to dedicate the whole of my life to the giving of it. I want so to hold you close again and forever, to hear the sound of your voice, to have you near and around me." Bob urged: "Honey, come to me—let us not fight any longer against the happiness that should be ours. It seems that I will never be happy until I have seen you again, kissed you again. The days drag out their weary length and here, where all my life I have lived, I am troubled and alone." Life was too short to live "on our memories of high spots." Bob concluded that the continuous separations were too hard: "Let's try the game together now that we know it's going to be a winning game. I cannot love you more perfectly, Vide, but I can wish that you were close on this lonely night with all the beauty and understanding and good that is you."

A few days later Bob railed against Alaska's isolation: "That's the crime of this country, this burning away of the years that mean so much, the years during which life could flame. To spend them here, isolated and hopeless, is a sorry sin." Bob was lonely and felt as if "we had been separated after having been together for years." He confided to Vide that "over and over I ponder what you said up in my room that other Saturday night — 'we're really married already.' Maybe I haven't any right at all, but I do feel as if we were and that it is up to me now to protect and care for you."

Vide was obviously reluctant to move back to Alaska on a permanent basis. She was too well aware of the many disadvantages of life in the North, among them seasonal unemployment, lack of cultural opportunities, and severe weather. All of this bothered her. Bob agreed: "When you spoke against the country, I could understand your attitude in one way, and in another I couldn't. But coming back I got that side of it too, I think, and that's why I wrote you that even if you did come up, I wouldn't want or wouldn't let you stay long. 'Life's too short' is a terrible, trite saying but applicable here."

Reflecting particularly on the Fairbanks weather, Bob noted that "here it is May 9 and the ice has just gone out, and only a few nights ago it was freezing." Summer was too short, for in August there would be light frosts, hard ones in September, and "by October the old grind has started again." Winters, Bob reflected, were too "desperately long" and there was "too much suffering. Everyone is wishing his life away—continually wishing spring would come, with the realization that once it has come, it is practically time for winter again." Continuous association with the same people, he continued, without a chance to get away, was "bound to sour" people, no matter how close they might be to each other. And "except for a few old-timers who know no better, everyone is looking prayerfully forward to the day when he can go Outside to stay," or at least for a short visit. The "interior," moreover, held little economic promise for the future: "Business is worse right now and has been worse all winter than for the years past. Of course I can say that doesn't affect me and that my job still lasts, but no one has given me a written guarantee that my job is going to last forever." As an afterthought, Bob added that if his job were indeed guaranteed for a lifetime, "I'd go out and shoot myself."

In spite of this, Bob still hoped that Vide would come "up to this country I curse so wholeheartedly. But if I honestly thought that you would have to stay for any length of time, I believe I could say forget me right now and let the past be the past." Bob ventured that Vide might even get to like Fairbanks again for a few months: "You would have a chance to get out in the open you don't have there and lots of other things."

Bob was clearly uncertain about Vide's intentions. He complained to her that the uncertainty about the course of future events made this "the hardest period I have put in in my life, and would be the hardest waiting even if I knew positively you were coming. I feel like I am fighting the battle of my life but that my gloves are leaden and my hands can't reach out and do what the mind tells them to. It's a horrible handicap, dear heart, and I would never have left when I did if it hadn't been absolutely necessary."

By midsummer of 1930 Vide had definitely succumbed to Bob's courting and decided that "it was time to quit playing around." They would meet each other in Valdez and marry there in August. Before going north for her wedding, Vide visited her mother in Los Angeles who was much relieved that her daughter had "finally settled on Bob."

Vide boarded the *Yukon* in Seattle for the trip to Valdez, afraid to let anybody know that she was getting married, because in those days people used to play tricks on prospective brides and bridegrooms. On board she met a charming, handsome, and cultured young bachelor, Robert Marshall, later to gain fame for his conservationist viewpoints and writings, particularly his book *Arctic Village,* about the little mining settlement of Wiseman in the southern foothills of the Brooks Range. The two became well acquainted during the long voyage, and Marshall, obviously smitten with Vide, told her "about everything, his whole life story." Young and flirtatious, Vide did not discourage him and kept her engagement a secret. When they finally pulled into Valdez on the afternoon of August 14, 1930, Marshall, who was continuing on to Seward, told Vide to be sure to get acquainted with his good friend Bob Bartlett, a young reporter, in Fairbanks. Marshall found that his recommendation was accepted when he learned that Bartlett waited at dockside for Vide and that the two would get married the same day.

At 7:30 that evening, Vide, attired in a beautiful chiffon gown in soft tones of blue, became the wife of Bob Bartlett. The Reverend Michael J.Kippenbrock married the couple in the Episcopal Church, while territorial Senator and Mrs. Anthony J. Dimond, old friends of Vide's family, witnessed the ceremony.

The young couple departed Valdez immediately on the Richardson Highway for Tonsina Lodge, where they planned to spend the night. Bob's dilapidated Page car, however, broke down just outside of town, forcing them to spend the night in Valdez.

Early in the morning of August 15, the Bartletts started for Fairbanks once more. The trip was considerably slower than intended because of repeated tire punctures. At Salcha, a roadhouse close to Fairbanks, Bob's mother and Mr. and Mrs. Clarence Burglin met the young couple on the afternoon of August 17 and escorted them to town, where they rented the Whitney house on First Avenue. The *News-Miner* reported that "our 'Bob' returns with bride" and commented that the wedding "marked the culmination of a delightful romance which was begun during the High School days of the young couple here in Fairbanks."

CHAPTER 3

Bob Bartlett Enters Politics

I T WAS NOT LONG BEFORE the effects of the Great Depression were felt in Alaska. Prices paid for fish and copper, the territory's two chief commodities, declined. This drop, in turn, led to a curtailment of their production, and many Alaskans found themselves out of work. The work force in the fishing industries, for example, dropped from 29,283 in 1929 to 12,695 in 1933, with an accompanying cut in wages. In the same time span, the value of fish products declined from $50,795,819 to $32,121,588. Likewise, imports of goods and supplies from the continental United States to Alaska dwindled from 350,193 tons in 1929 to 240,379 tons in 1933, while exports from Alaska for the same period, consisting mainly of fish products, minerals, and furs, shrank from 449,944 tons to 260,138 tons. Government employment in the territory was cut back proportionately.[1]

The economic outlook was bleak in April 1932 when Alaskans chose their delegates to the national party conventions. The Republican delegation left the territory pledged to the renomination of President Herbert Hoover, while the Democrats generally supported the nomination of Governor Franklin D. Roosevelt of New York for president.

There was also a territorial primary election to choose candidates to run for election as Alaska's delegate to the U.S. Congress. Republican James Wickersham, who had returned from political retirement in 1930 to regain his old seat, was unopposed as his party's nominee for a second term. As Alaskan stringer for the *New York Times*, Bob Bartlett characterized the Republican candidate as an affable politician of the old school, who, although more than seventy-five years old, was still vigorous and quick of wit. He had been his party's mainspring since 1908 and had made a name for himself, not only as a controversial politician, but as a scholar of Alaskan history as well. When Wickersham had made his political comeback in 1930, the Republican leadership had not been unanimous in welcoming him back. Indeed, peace was restored solely on the understanding that Wickersham serve only one more term to round out his career. To their obvious dismay, the leadership discovered in 1932 that two years had proven too brief a time span for the rounding-out process, and the old warrior showed no signs of retiring. To make matters worse, his record in Congress in the previous two years had been rather lackluster. The widespread disaffection among Republicans with Wickersham, Bartlett reported, promised a lively contest between him and his Democratic opponent.

The three-cornered race for the Democratic nomination to the position involved territorial Senator Anthony J. Dimond of Valdez and George B. Grigsby and A. H. Ziegler, both of Ketchikan. Democrats selected the senator to be the Democratic standard-bearer in the general election. Dimond was a longtime Democrat. The territorial senatorship had been virtually forced upon him. An injury in his youth had cut short Dimond's prospecting days, whereupon he read law, and "his fine abilities . . . advanced him to the topmost flight of Alaska's legal talent." Dimond's excellent reputation made him the most formidable candidate the Democrats had fielded in years. Although the Democrats were hopelessly outnumbered along party lines, the outlook for victory appeared bright if they could overcome the Republican Indian vote in southeastern Alaska and win the confidence, and hopefully the votes, of the sourdoughs. Political forecasting in Alaska was hazardous, Bartlett conceded, yet he nevertheless predicted that Dimond would be elected.[2] Anthony J. Dimond read the prediction in the *New York Times* as well as in various Alaskan papers and liked what he read. He went on to win in the Democratic landslide in the fall of 1932, just as predicted. Although Bartlett did not know it then, it was partially on the basis of this article that Dimond was to hire the young man as his secretary in 1933.

In the meantime, Bartlett's working conditions at the *News-Miner* deteriorated. Editor Stone became even more difficult to work for and drank more heavily than before, keeping a bottle in the bottom drawer of his desk all the time. Bob wrote the paper, including the editorials, practically by himself. Those not produced by him were bought from the wire services. Bartlett was discouraged with his job and seriously considered going to Tanana and taking a contract for wood cutting during the winter, which would have brought more money than was yielded by his work for the paper.

To Vide, this looked serious indeed. She did not cherish at all the idea of going out into the bush for the winter. As an alternative, she suggested that "after all, a delegate has to have a secretary," and that Bob should apply. Startled by the idea, he did just that.[3] Dimond hired the young reporter, delighted to have a man of Bartlett's talents and knowledge of Alaska fill a position which, in those days, combined the duties of administrative assistant, legislative assistant, and general factotum. In addition, Dimond knew Vide and her family well and, as noted, had been a witness at the young couple's marriage in Valdez in 1930.

New vistas of life in far-away Washington, D. C. opened for the Bartletts. Most immediate, however, was the problem of financing the trip. A sale of all negotiable items partially solved the problem. Among the items which went on the block was a bedspread which brought the magnificent sum of three dollars.[4]

Vide left Fairbanks ahead of her husband in February 1933 to visit her mother in Los Angeles. Travel "outside" in those days involved a train trip to Seward and a lengthy steamship voyage to Seattle, then train journeys of varying lengths from there to the travelers' destinations.

Bob had another three weeks' work in Fairbanks before joining his wife in Los Angeles for the train trip to Washington. Time passed far too slowly to suit him. In the meantime, his father was about to haul a ton of freight to his mining venture at Independence Creek in the Circle district in preparation for the season's work. Bob worried that the mining work might prove too strenuous for his elderly parents, but their general good health eased his concern. He shared his parents' high hope that "Independence will pan out in a big way."

Bob soon became impatient because he had not received any mail from his wife. He reminded her that she had promised to wire immediately upon her arrival in Los Angeles. "What's the matter?" he inquired, teasingly adding that perhaps her silence could be explained because "she might have taken to the tall timber with a Swede, or Finn, or Norwegian." His replacement at the *News-Miner,* Bob told Vide, had already arrived. David B. Tewksbury, "an elderly man, short and . . . rather stout," was waiting to occupy "this old familiar desk and this chair, fitted to every contour of the part of me it should fit . . . ."[5]

In the meantime, on March 4, 1933, Roosevelt took the oath of office as the thirty-second president of the United States. In his inaugural address he reassured his countrymen that he would do all in his power to alleviate the miseries of the Great Depression. A day later the new president summoned the seventy-third Congress to convene in special session on March 9. Invoking powers granted by the Trading with the Enemy Act of 1917, Roosevelt prepared a proclamation, effective March 6, declaring a four-day national banking holiday which would suspend all transactions in the Federal Reserve and other banks, trust companies, credit unions, and building and loan associations.[6]

Back in Fairbanks, Bartlett was finally ready to leave for the nation's capital, but the banking holiday barred his access to his accumulated funds. Desperate, Bob called on his friends to lend him the money. Milo Hajdukovich, an old trader from Upper Clearwater, having a full "poke," advanced him the funds. After an uneventful voyage, Bartlett joined his wife in Los Angeles.

At the end of March, the Bartletts left Los Angeles for Washington via New Orleans. Remembering the advice that his friend John A. McIntosh of Fairbanks had given him, Bob purchased just one berth on the transcontinental railroad, because he had been led to believe that two could sleep in a berth as easily as one. It was a mistake. It was hot, the one berth was far too small for both, and they had to sleep in shifts on the long journey.[7]

They arrived in the nation's capital at the beginning of April. Getting off the train at Union Station, they stepped outside and saw the capitol looming directly in front of them, seemingly close enough to touch. Years later Vide recalled that "it was the greatest thrill … either of us had ever had before."[8]

They had to find a place to rent immediately. They remembered that Dr. Charles Bunnell, the president of the University of Alaska, who frequently visited Washington, had recommended that they stay at the centrally located, clean, and reasonably priced Harrington Hotel. The university president was a thrifty man, as Bob and Vide quickly discovered. The Harrington was a very cheap place indeed. It would do until they found something more suitable. That same day Bob went to Dimond's office to announce his arrival and get started in his job. At the hotel that night, he and Vide pored over the rental ads. The next day Vide inspected a number of places. For a couple living on a salary of $250 per month, most were too expensive and were unattractive to boot. She finally settled on a small place in the Bond Apartment House and moved in the same day. They stayed there for a couple of months, sharing the place with innumerable and very active cockroaches. They then moved into a one-bedroom apartment close to Capitol Hill. This allowed Bob to walk to work and come home for lunch, which saved scarce dollars.[9]

The Bartletts had arrived in time to witness, at least in part, the heady atmosphere of President Roosevelt's famous Hundred Days, beginning March 9, when Congress cheered into law the Emergency Banking Act, and ending on June 16, with passage of the National Industrial Recovery Act. Between these two dates, the chief executive continually unveiled new programs and displayed rare imagination and energy. Before an exhausted Congress finally adjourned on June 16, 1933, the president had delivered ten major speeches, fashioned a new foreign policy, presided over press conferences and cabinet meetings twice a week, taken the country off the gold standard, sent fifteen messages to Congress, and guided through the House and Senate thirteen pieces of legislation. These included insurance for all bank deposits, refinancing of home mortgages, authorization for nearly four billion dollars in federal relief, legalization of beer, and creation of the Civilian Conservation Corps, the Agricultural Adjustment Administration, and the Tennessee Valley Authority.[10]

The first action of the unfolding New Deal which benefitted Alaska directly was a presidential order in September 1933 that increased the price of gold from $20.67 to $35.00 per ounce. Although production did not increase for another two years, it helped to revitalize the mining industry. In 1933 the value of Alaska's gold production had amounted to $9,701,000. In 1934 it had already climbed to $16,007,000. Although part of the increase reflected monetary inflation, the price increase had been a real stimulus to the gold-mining industry. Alaska's economy picked up everywhere, aided by small and large projects of enduring value sponsored and financed by the Public Works Administration and Works Progress Administration. Among other projects, these included a hotel at the entrance of Mount McKinley National Park, schools, fire stations, paved streets, and playgrounds.[11]

Bartlett found the work in Dimond's office exciting and exhausting. He quickly learned congressional politics and recognized the limitations inherent in the voteless position of the delegate from Alaska in Congress. He found that the delegate had the enormous task of scanning every piece of legislation to determine if Alaska was included or excluded. When, as so often happened, Alaska was excluded, strenuous lobbying was required to attempt to include the territory. Too often, the efforts proved to be fruitless, as when Dimond appeared before the House Subcommittee on Appropriations for the Interior Department on December 20, 1933, and pointed out that Alaska's natives had been receiving only one-third as much federal aid of any kind as the Indians in the States. Dimond inserted a detailed comparison of expenditures into the record of the appropriations committee hearings. Even though the chairman of the subcommittee, Congressman Edward T. Taylor of Colorado, recognized that school repairs were much costlier in Alaska than elsewhere, the committee recommended no changes.[12]

Time passed quickly in Dimond's office. No day was quite like the preceding one, yet the Bartletts, contrary to their expectations, soon realized that they were terribly homesick for Alaska. They wanted to return north when and if the chance for a job allowed them to do so.

On February 7, 1934, their first child, Doris Ann, was born in Washington. They wanted to raise their child in the North, and their desire to return to Alaska therefore intensified. The Roosevelt administration extended the Federal Housing Administration to Alaska, and Bob's opportunity arose when the job of assistant territorial director opened up in Juneau. He applied successfully, and in November 1934 the Bartletts left the nation's capital. Vide and Doris Ann went to Los Angeles to visit with her mother, while Bob went by train to Seattle and by steamship to Valdez, from where he flew to a reunion with his parents in Fairbanks. While Vide remained in Los Angeles, Bob spent that Christmas in Fairbanks, proceeding south to Juneau early in 1935 to assume his duties under Federal Housing Administration director John E. Pegues. Wiring his wife on February 6, 1935, he instructed her to "extend to our daughter my heartiest congratulations and all due wishes for her future happiness even if subject uninteresting to her. Let her have her cake and eat it too."[13]

Despite the euphoric feeling of having returned "home," it soon became apparent to Bob that the Juneau office of the Federal Housing Administration, with nine employees, was vastly overstaffed. "There are nine of us all told," he related to his wife, "and, honest to God, nothing to do but sit around on our fannies." The organization, he felt, would not be abandoned for another couple of years, however, "and that is all that concerns us now."[14]

Soon after, Vide and her daughter left Los Angeles and joined Bob in Alaska's rainy capital of Juneau.

The year 1935 turned out to be a difficult one for both Bob and Vide. They did not enjoy the gray, windy, moist climate of southeastern Alaska. To make matters worse, the Bartletts rented a place outside town on the Glacier Highway and were inconvenienced by a lack of transportation. Vide felt stranded, isolated, and lonely. As the year slipped by, the lower-ranking employees of the Federal Housing Administration were laid off. It was an uneasy time.

On August 29, 1935, a telegram from Clarence Burglin, an old family friend in Fairbanks, jarred the Bartlett family: "Your dad felt fine and worked all day yesterday. Apparently died of stroke at five this morning."[15] Bob left immediately for Fairbanks to comfort his mother and settle his father's affairs. He learned that his father had awakened early in the morning and had complained of a burning sensation in his chest. He took some soda, lying down on the bed again, and "in a split second it was all over. Surely it must have been too swift for him to realize the adventure was upon him." Bob added that he had not looked at his father's body, and "I am not going to."

The funeral was a simple one, conducted according to the rites of the Pioneers of Alaska, and burial took place in Seattle some time later. His mother, he told Vide, was "holding up well, as I knew she would. It is tough, but she is going to make the grade."[16] Several weeks after his father's death, his mother returned to Independence Creek to supervise the cleanup and close down the mining operation for the winter.

Within a couple of weeks, Bob returned to his job in Juneau and then accompanied his mother to the burial in Seattle in October 1935. The two returned to Juneau at the end of October, and Mrs. Ida Bartlett spent the winter with her son's family in the territorial capital. In the spring of 1936 Bob Bartlett resigned his position as assistant territorial director of the Federal Housing Administration, after he had decided in family council to take over his parent's mining operation at Independence Creek.

Mining Days

AFTER THE DECISION had been made to take over the operation of the Independence Creek mine, the Bartlett family left Juneau in the spring of 1936 and arrived in Fairbanks on April Fool's day, a cold, windy, and overcast day. They arrived on the train and were met by many friends. Yet, to Vide, it was not only cold but very disheartening as well to be back in Fairbanks, having left it with such high hopes for a new life just three short years earlier.[1]

Bob probably had not intended to follow a career in mining, although he always had been aware of his father's activities and ambitions. Roughhewn Ed Bartlett had spent his life freighting and gold mining, and his son had actively helped in these endeavors while attending high school in Fairbanks.

Like many men who chose the North, Ed Bartlett was an optimist, a man who rarely gave up hope or who was easily discouraged. For him, there always existed new opportunities, a new and brighter tomorrow.

While Ed Bartlett was daring and adventurous, his wife Ida was cautious and wanted to pile dollar upon dollar in order to have a cushion and security for old age. Ed Bartlett, however, always harbored schemes which, he confidently felt, would bring him a fortune. He also was certain that he could talk his wife out of the family savings and borrow the remainder that he would need to launch yet another enterprise. Ed Bartlett, together with his brother Al, had been in the freighting business in Dawson, Yukon Territory, where he had amassed a small fortune and then lost it again.

In the late 1920s Ed Bartlett had acquired a gold-mining claim on Eagle Creek in the Circle mining district. The operation went bankrupt. Undeterred, Ed freighted again, made some money, and persuaded his wife to sell her property on an island not too far from Seattle and sink the proceeds into yet another mining claim. This one was on Independence Creek near Miller House, also in the Circle mining district. Ed continued freighting during the winters, but mined during the summers.[2] At the time of his death, Ed was still working the Independence Creek claim with moderate success.

When Bob Bartlett arrived in Fairbanks on that windy and cold day in April 1936, his mind probably wandered back to a September day in 1933 when, while serving as Delegate Anthony J. Dimond's secretary in far-off Washington, D.C., he had received a jubilant telegram from his father. It stated that cleanup had yielded 70½ ounces "after splashing ten minutes per hour for twelve days. Still splashing. Ground is good, all payments on ground have been made. Prospects for winter good financially."[3] Most likely, Bob had rejoiced over his father's luck, hoping that he finally had struck it rich.

While on the train platform in Fairbanks on that April day in 1936, Bob undoubtedly thought of the mining season ahead of him and hoped that Independence Creek would live up to its name and make his little family financially independent. The immediate concern, however, was to find a place in town for Vide and Doris Ann, who had been dangerously ill with pneumonia and who was still too weak to travel. As soon as his family was settled, he and his mother impatiently left for Independence Creek to prepare for the coming mining season.[4]

Independence Creek was one of several gold-bearing creeks, including Mammoth, Mastadon, Harrison, and Porcupine, in the vicinity of Miller House on the Steese Highway north of Fairbanks. The Circle mining district had been opened up in 1893 when partners Pitka and Sorresco discovered gold on Birch Creek. Miners drifted into the area, and in 1896 Fritz Miller and Casper Ellingen built Miller Roadhouse to accommodate them. It soon became a regular point of call for freighters and stagedrivers operating between Fairbanks and the Circle district. It also became the supply center for the various placer mining operations in the vicinity. In 1935 M.F. Miller [no relation to Fritz Miller], an old sourdough originally from Kentucky, and his wife took over as owners-operators of the roadhouse.[5]

By the time Bob and his mother were preparing for the upcoming season, placer mining had changed substantially from earlier and simpler days. The typical gold-bearing stream was small, sometimes only a few yards wide, while the flats through which it wound might be a half mile or more in width. The shallow creeks wound between sparsely wooded, rounded hills and often originated above timberline. Typically, gold was found in the streambed gravels, a distance of anywhere between fifteen and one hundred feet below the overburden. In the old days, miners built a wood fire at the site of the shaft, some distance laterally from the streambed, and slowly excavated the thawed ground down to the bedrock. If a paystreak had been found, a miner would usually excavate the ancient streambed laterally. The thawed gravel was lifted to the surface in buckets and heaped beside the diggings in conical mounds to await spring cleanup.

Wherever underground or drift mining was practiced, these mounds grew all winter. With the spring thaw and the availability of water, the miner shoveled the gravel into a sluice box through which water was flowing. The heavy gold remained in the riffles of the box as the lighter materials were washed away.[6]

By 1936, however, hydraulic giants had long since replaced the slow wood fires. Cold water shot out of a nozzle at tremendous force and washed away the overburden, or muck. A bulldozer was used to stack gravel tailings, which eventually were sluiced for the gold.

Bob and his mother took a bush plane to Circle. They then had to walk to the mine, some forty miles away. It was a more than strenuous experience for Bob, who claimed, in jest, that he hadn't walked "that far all his life put together." Very tired, they arrived at the mine, where they found deep snow on the ground. While his mother prepared the bunkhouses for the work crew, Bob and Ray Wrede, who had worked for his father and had stayed to become his foreman, dug ditches to establish a drainage pattern. It was hard work, and Bob lost twenty pounds in as many days.

Time passed quickly in preparatory work. Vide and her daughter finally arrived in Circle Hot Springs in Vic Ross' bush plane, "one put together with baling wire," on a bright, clear, warm, and sunny day, so typical of interior Alaska in early spring. Snow still covered the ground when the two, together with Doris Ann's cocker spaniel Toto, established themselves in a cabin behind the Circle Hot Springs Hotel. During the summer Jimmy Nordale, age four, the son of a Fairbanks friend, joined them.

While Bob and his crew worked at the mine, Vide took care of the children at the hot springs. As soon as the road became passable, she often drove to the mine in the family pickup truck for visits. Bob and the work crew came to the hot springs for baths on weekends. The crew generally consisted of eight men working three eight-hour shifts daily.

Summers in Alaska's interior, however, are all too short and soon turn into fall. By the end of September, the birches have turned a brilliant yellow. Waning daylight and the first snows at the beginning of October herald the arrival of winter once more. Bob had done well financially that first mining season but thought that he could do much better if he had modern equipment. Therefore, much of the profits of that first year went into the purchase of machinery.

Bob intended to move to Fairbanks for the 1936–37 winter. After they had closed the operation for the season, the crew dispersed, and Bob and Vide moved to town, where Bob once again went to work for the *Fairbanks Daily News-Miner.* Soon, however, he received a job as an information service representative with the Social Security System territorial office in Juneau.[7] When Bob went to Juneau to assume his new duties, the Bartletts, financially hard-pressed, decided that Vide and Doris Ann would spend the winter at Circle Hot Springs, because it was cheaper living there than in town.

Lonely for his family, Bob resigned his job in May 1937 and went north once more to resume mining for the season. Vide, Doris Ann, and Mary Nordale, young Jimmy's sister, moved into a new two-story house at the hot springs.

New equipment, Bob soon found, did not necessarily increase profits, because the equipment frequently broke down. It was Vide who drove the 160 miles between Circle Hot Springs and Fairbanks often that summer to get replacement parts at the Northern Commercial Company.

Uncooperative weather was another difficulty that stood in the way of sudden riches. Water is a necessity in hydraulic mining. The penstock has to be kept full in order to operate the hydraulic giant. Yet the rain clouds that summer never seemed to empty on Independence but, instead, dumped their waters on Harrison Creek, just over the divide, where Ray Hamilton mined. Still, the summer was good enough to enable Bob to pay for the equipment and also to make a small profit.

It was a good summer for Doris Ann and Mary Nordale as well. Although she was then a small child, Doris Ann remembers men working and white tents at Independence. Her father would take her for rides on the Caterpillar tractor and let her think that she was operating the monstrous machine. Doris Ann also recalls the big, open pool at the hot springs and the chained sled dogs as being especially dangerous for children. She remembers one occasion when a number of horses broke out of their stable and crazily stampeded through the little settlement, trampling her sled in the process. Through it all, her cocker spaniel Toto was the constant companion of the two girls.[8]

At the beginning of that fall, territorial Governor John W. Troy offered Bob the position of executive secretary of the Alaska Planning Council in Juneau. Bob went directly to Juneau, but Vide and Doris Ann spent some time in Fairbanks, joining him later in the territorial capital. In the meantime, however, a potential conflict had arisen in Juneau. On April 28, 1937, Governor Troy had appointed Bartlett a member and first chairman of Alaska's Unemployment Compensation Commission. The position carried no salary but did pay a per diem of ten dollars plus expenses for the infrequent meetings. In order to avoid any conflict, Bob resigned his Alaska Planning Council position effective November 9, 1937. Bob and his wife and daughter then went to Seattle and planned, like many others who worked seasonally in Alaska, to winter "outside" in style.[9]

When spring came, Bob and his mother returned north for yet another mining season. Vide and Doris Ann stayed behind in Seattle. Although they had lived well that winter, money now was in short supply. It turned out to be a difficult summer for Vide, who had a total of eighty dollars per month, forty dollars of which went for rent payment. It turned out to be a difficult summer for Bob as well, because not only was he lonely for his family, but that season finished the pay streak at the mine.

Bob and his mother arrived at Independence Creek in late April, and on May 1 he reported that snowdrifts were deep and that it was still snowing intermittently. "It may be a hungry summer," Bob warned Vide, and although "It's beautiful here . . .I can't gain the proper enthusiasm." Despite the snow, the men accomplished a great deal of work. Before Bob's arrival, Ray Wrede and Johnny Frasca already had yarded out ten cords of wood. Together, the three men put up another seventy cords of wood.[10]

The weather, however, changed for the worse, and for two days the men sat out a blizzard playing bridge in the bunkhouse. Impatiently, Bob declared that he wished "fall were here, with all my heart I do—but maybe it wouldn't be well to see too many cleanups ahead."[11] Three days later, with work still slow because of the inclement weather, Bob wrote to Vide from the bunkhouse, where there was about a foot of ice under his bed. May, he observed sarcastically, seemed to be off to a good start, and "I can say it's only five months or so until we are reunited—and that doesn't seem too long for this once, but never again."[12] As the weather warmed, Bob's spirits lifted, and he exulted: "The sun rides high on this May evening of glory, and the world is good. On such a day as this there is no lovelier spot in the world for me. Mountains and sun and snow, all blended into what nature ought to be. And past the tent, the first waters of spring rushing by tell of the green to come. Perhaps the sunbeam that strikes through the window shines too on you and Doris Ann, wherever you are this day. As ephemeral as the sunbeam is the wave of my thought projected out to you, my dear ones."

On a more plaintive note, Bob acknowledged that airmail service had been inaugurated between Juneau and Fairbanks but complained that everyone with the exception of him had received letters on the first trip. He chided Vide that if his memory did not deceive him "two, or maybe three [letters] went to you southbound on the inaugural flight." On the cheerful side, the cook was a very good one and had served big, rare juicy steaks that night. Hopeful on a full stomach, Bob asked, "Prosperity, where can you be found?"[13] Bob apparently also felt that he would have to lead his work crew a little more firmly, for he confided to Vide that "this establishment is going to be run more for the benefit of the Bartletts henceforth and less for the benefit of the men. It will be a proposition of eight good hours of work—or down the creek."

On May 10 Bob received a letter from Vide. It made his day. Vide had told him that she was lonely for him but recognized that he was a realist and not one to be bothered with sentimentality. Not so, Bob protested, because "for you two, everything is and all my thoughts and longings are for you." Life alone was hard, he stated, and asked whether Vide realized that "we have actually lived together only slightly more than two years of the last four." Writing too much of love merely brought up too many memories and made him "desperate with longing." Bob concluded that he could not much longer endure these continual separations, "for we have not world enough or time."[14] He wished to find "a nugget as big as a house this summer" so that they could "buy a small newspaper and live the life we were cut out for, instead of running around pretending to be a miner, when it's all pseudo with a capital P." Furthermore, there were too many mosquitoes in the ditch, he told his wife, and they were of the large variety, but perhaps not as large as those legendary ones in the Koyukuk which "could stand flatfooted and f— a turkey."

What about conditions in the camp? Well, his mother was in the "reclining chair after doing washing and reading; boys are in bunkhouse gassing; cook stirring up her sourdough against the coming of morning." In short, he wrote, "God's in His heaven and all's right with the world."

In a more serious vein, Bob realized that he needed "at least one more good season, now that the tractor bill is so large . . . ." He concluded, however, that everything was bound to work out in the end, for "we must have a guiding star in the offing somewhere, else we should have been in the poorhouse long ago."[15]

From economics, Bob's thoughts turned to the community of people working in the Circle district. The favorite pastime among his fellow miners consisted of criticizing one another for being lazy. Bob had no doubt that he was called lazy by the crew and by all others in the Circle camp: "Maybe they are right. That has been worrying me this spring, and I find myself seeking justification for not especially caring about the 'bull' work. That seeking is a bad sign." Mining was not his line of work, he continued, because "all my instincts are against moving a shovel up and down. In my opinion, persistent use of such a tool should be, and most commonly is, reserved for the duller-witted of the human race."

Everyone constantly was being "branded with that common iron" of laziness: "The storekeepers, Taylor and Miller, are ipso facto lazy, because they do not even pretend to wield a pick and shovel. They are quite beyond the pale and are in contempt. Ray Hamilton is lazy because he reads in the winter time. Leo McKinnon is suspect because he clerks at times. Happily, he has recovered his sense and will work in a mine this summer. Bob Bartlett is even much worse than Ray Hamilton because he doesn't even pretend to do much in the summer." Office work, Bob mused, offered variety, while "the monotony of this type of work [mining] would drive me mad." And, after all, he concluded, the rewards of "the exponents of the lusty muscle" were nothing more than an average wage of between $600 and $800 a year and the necessity of starting every spring in debt. The short season and paltry income did not make for a life-style to which he cared to aspire.[16]

On May 15 Bob awakened to a "world full of soft, wet snow," so sloppy that work ceased for awhile. He observed that the sparrows were back on the messhouse porch demanding scraps, and a weasel "hides a panful of gingersnaps between the two mattresses of the cook's bed." It was a windy day, and "everyone coaxes everyone else to go to Miller House for news and possible mail. No one goes." There was boredom all around, Bob related, with the men "in a fever of sharpening their pocket knives . . . and talking mining and women. 'The prettiest whores in the world are in Truckee, California.' 'No, they're not. Why, I remember. . .' and away they go."

In the afternoon the weather cleared. Work resumed when the men began laying the pipe. Soon there "was a desperate call for a piece of blocking the thickness of three red hairs from a certain part of a necessarily redhaired woman's anatomy." What a crew they were, Bob observed dryly, for soon another of the men "breaks wind and a match is lighted to determine if an explosion will result." It did not, and work continued.[17]

On May 21 Bob complained about the "drop-in-for-eating company," which consisted mostly of young fellows looking for work. They had little money and were appalled by roadhouse meal prices, obviously having assumed that mining camps were at least good for a free meal. It was an expensive proposition for the operator, because it cost fifty cents and more to feed each one of them. In addition to the cost, it also made more work for the temperamental cook. Yet despite this, Bob concluded that he was a soft touch and did not, as he threatened to do on numerous occasions, hang out a price schedule.[18]

There was still no mail from his wife on May 23. Bob had received the last letter from Vide some twenty-four days earlier. He anxiously asked: "Are you there, Vide? Where are you? You have had time, since last I heard, to secrete yourself in the heart of Africa—although it might be difficult to do that on account of your daughter's willingness to let all know where and how she is." The day before, he related, he had gone to the hot springs and "topping the rise, I forgot for a moment, and my heart sang within me—and then reality came down once more, and it was only a hotel and a group of cabins. A haircut, a bath and home again . . . ." Mail, he told Vide, was to arrive on May 24, and "young lady, if there isn't a whole flock of letters from you, I'm going to let forth a yell that can be heard in California. That's a good thought to leave you with."[19]

Finally, at 10:30 A.M. on Memorial Day, mining started officially at Independence Creek, "when a giant is lifted to send a stream of gravel into the boxes." It was an early start, eight days earlier than ever before, and below the boxes there was a huge field of ice, although the cut was free. There had been an abundance of water until the early part of the previous week, but then the weather suddenly had turned very cold and the water flow had slowed to a trickle, just enough for one nozzle. The day before, however, Bob related, there had been a couple of stiff showers, and the water had come up a lot. Yet the outlook for mining was none too good. A water shortage threatened because most of the snow in the hills had already thawed. He would have to "buck frozen ground right from the outset," which would slow operations considerably. To get an early start that year, Bob had begun work with a bigger crew than ever before, which, of course, added to his expenses. In addition, there were $3,000 in loans which had to be repaid by October 1, 1938. The tractor had broken several times, and the repair bill had come to $1,500. Bob advised Vide to be careful with whatever money she had left, because "there may be none to replace it when it is gone. I say these things not to alarm you," he concluded, but merely "so you'll know there is real need at this time for cautious spending."[20]

By June 10 Bob's worst fears seemed to be confirmed, because there had been no precipitation. If it did not rain very soon, he concluded, "we'll have to close 'er up." It was not the economic uncertainty alone which preyed on his mind, but, perhaps even more, the loneliness, "these eternal separations [which made his] soul grow weary. If you only knew how much I really loved you," he concluded.[21]

On June 24 Bob wrote Vide that once again the bulldozer needed repairs, which included welding, a spring that cost $80, new cutting edges for $120, and "various bolts, nuts and other parts, many $$$. Bolts falling to the left and bolts falling to the right. But no cat, no mining." The money for these repairs had to be spent, albeit reluctantly. As if this news were not bad enough, the runoffs after the recent rains had been the fastest yet, and water now stood at a low ebb. The cut which the Bartlett crew was working was panning worse than any other since Bob had begun mining. The rock simply refused to yield gold in significant quantities. The Berry dredge had cleaned up the previous day, he continued, and had yielded a total of $5,000, the worst ever. As to the time for the Bartlett cleanup, no guess was possible at that time. "Play close to your belly," he advised Vide, "I smell bad news ahead."[22]

Not only did Bob worry about family finances, but mining as a way of life dissatisfied and depressed him. He saw no future in such a life and dreaded repeating his parents' lives. He wrote: "Our life during the past couple of years or so, it has occurred to me, there has been a close parallel between our lives and those of my father and mother. He was so much away from home or in the aggregate, mother was so much away from Alaska that he never had a real opportunity to know his children or to enjoy home life. I cannot face such a prospect with equanimity. I do not imagine such a condition to eventuate, but after all, I have been, as I said to you before, with Doris Ann scarcely more than half her life. And the future, as it is now cast, what chance does it offer? Here in the summer, Outside in the winter if all goes well. Half and half."

As their wedding anniversary, August 14, drew near, Bob reproached himself for having failed to be the "kind of a husband I should have wished myself to be." Why is it, he asked his wife, "that not even marriage, which brings human beings closer together than anything else, can at all times bring about a clear understanding, one of the other?" Answering his own question, Bob stated that it was "futile to write this way, since it results in nothing." If, however, he could but tell Vide "that after eight years my love for you is stronger than ever," he would be quite content.[23]

By the end of July, the lack of water had forced Bob to close down most of the mining operations, except for some stripping. It had been a dreadful summer, Bob confided to his wife, and "all confidence in myself. . .all feelings of being on top of the wave, have vanished." He had no money, could not call a single dollar his own. The separation had been terrible, and he sensed that people thought that "you have hauled out for good and neither they nor I could blame you for that." He had, he stated, tried to write to her about his fears, but every time he started, it had been as if a wall suddenly had been erected, and most of the letters had been destroyed. Whatever the future brought, however brutalized he had become by the mining life, he could not "forget the raptures of these splendid years. You are, you shall remain, and you have been my all, no matter how things turn out."[24]

The economic picture brightened when rains started to fall in early August, since it enabled the resumption of mining operations. The Bartlett mine had just bought a "big and bright red and formidable-appearing" water pump, because without it any kind of mining would "have been a fantastic dream." Practically coincident with the water pump's arrival, it started to rain, and "how it has fallen! Result: There is now more water in the creek than at any other time this year, including the so-called spring runoff. More than can be used." Bob jestingly suggested that the Circle mining district take up a collection to reimburse the Bartletts for the water pump, "for sure as fate, if it hadn't been here, there would have been no water."[25]

In addition to the arrival of water, letters from Vide also helped Bob to overcome his depression. By August 19 he reported that he had become very optimistic about everything, a change he attributed entirely to her letters. He also stated that, much to his satisfaction, "the drinking problem is a thing of the past for some little time in the future."[26]

It rained hard on the night of August 1, and by the morning of August 2, rain had changed to snow, and it was blowing hard. The temperature at 8 A.M. stood at +35°F. Bob reported that when he ran outside to get some water for the messhouse, the wind cut through to the bone. But cold or not, the long-awaited water had arrived, and with a decent cleanup, there was hope for some profits. If Vide could manage with her remaining funds until the first of September, everything would be all right then.²⁷

By August 10 the weather again had become "warm and soft, even the nights are warm. The last two nights, the moon, all round and huge and yellow, has been briefly visible and it makes the heart grow tender in immemorial fashion." The work was going well, Bob stated, and the ground was yielding over forty cents per cubic foot of dirt, in contrast to less than twenty-five cents the previous year. It looked good, but still "I don't know how I am going to get $20,000 out of it" to pay all the bills.

Saturday night, August 14, 1938, would mark the end of eight years of marriage for the Bartletts. Bob wrote to Vide:

Yet we are one: your gracious condescension Granted, and grants, the loveliness I crave. One, in the perfect sense of Eastern mention, Gold and the Bracelet, Water and the Wave.

Your Husband
Bob²⁸

On the practical side, with the prospect of some money in store, Bob worried about providing for Doris Ann's future. He asked Vide to look around in Seattle for some investment firm which "would sell one share of Alaska Juneau [Gold Mining Company] at a time. We must, for Doris Ann's education, start a systematic program of saving. One share of Alaska Juneau a month would do the trick. It is just as safe as a bank, and the money would double in ten years, or about that, instead of every thirty or forty years as in endowment insurance."²⁹

Despite brightened prospects for a decent cleanup, in 1938 Bob had come to realize that he did not want to mine for a living for the rest of his life. He also realized that Independence Creek had almost yielded its maximum return for the labor and capital invested. As early as July, while in Fairbanks, he had seen and briefly talked to Delegate Dimond: "I didn't talk to him about Washington but will next time. I am sure nothing could be done until Eckles [Dimond's secretary at that time] leaves, and there seems to be no prospect of that."³⁰ In Fairbanks again at the end of August, Bob and 'Cap' Lathrop had sat next to one another at breakfast, "and something tells me if I tried that I might go places on the *News-Miner*. But, frankly, I hate to think of even trying."³¹

The mining season of 1938 finally ended in the late fall on a financially more cheerful note than Bob had anticipated. He was satisfied. He had broken even and knew that Independence Creek had yielded her best. When he joined his wife in Seattle in November 1938, he was at loose ends, casting about for opportunities. He definitely knew that 1938 had been his last mining season.

CHAPTER 5

Secretary of Alaska

O N AN OVERCAST, RAINY November day, Bob Bartlett joined his wife in Seattle. After a financially meager mining season, Bob's first concern was to find employment which would enable him to support his family. He investigated the possibilities of a position with the United States Census Bureau, suggested to him by Delegate Dimond. But before he was able to pursue the lead seriously, Edward W. "Ned" Griffin, the secretary of Alaska, died of a heart attack while making a speech.

The death of Griffin and the ensuing vacancy at Juneau prompted a number of Alaskans to apply for the position, which, despite its impressive title, contained few responsibilities. It consisted principally of being the "Keeper of the Territorial Seal" and acting as governor when the chief executive was absent from the territory. To fill this position, Delegate Dimond recommended the appointment of James J. Connors, the collector of customs for Alaska; territorial legislators from the Third Judicial District supported the candidacy of Herbert W. Brown, the mayor of Anchorage; and Governor John W. Troy championed E.L. "Bob" Bartlett, whom he considered to be "young, energetic, well-balanced, possessed of considerable experience in governmental administrative matters." Other applicants for the vacancy were civil engineer Victor C. Rivers of Anchorage and M.E. Monagle, a Juneau attorney. Of all the contestants for the job, Bartlett prevailed, and President Roosevelt appointed him secretary of Alaska effective February 2, 1939, for a four-year term.[1]

The appointment brought a period of modest economic security which the Bartletts had previously lacked. Bob left his wife in Seattle and arrived in Juneau at the end of January 1939 to assume the duties of his office. Writing to Vide, he noted that "I'm going to enjoy Juneau more than ever before." He added, however, that "politics isn't especially down my alley, but I feel we can really be happy for two or four years."[2]

After Bartlett's arrival in Juneau, Governor Troy arranged an official reception for the new secretary of Alaska. Bartlett, who had known the governor for some years and was aware of Troy's failing health, still must have been shocked at the extent of physical deterioration which had taken place since he had last seen him. Bartlett soon found that the governor apparently had been unable to carry out fully the functions of his office. The task had gradually been assumed by Harry G. Watson, secretary for both Governor Troy and, before that, for Troy's predecessor, Governor George A. Parks.

It soon became clear that Governor Troy was not only in ill health but in legal troubles as well. Government officials contracting for goods or services involving the expenditure of public funds were required to sign an oath of disinterestedness, disavowing any personal interest in, or profit from, the contemplated transaction. Troy had signed such an oath for printing done for the territorial government by the *Daily Alaska Empire,* which he owned. This was a criminal offense. Everyone knew that the governor owned the paper and that it had received government printing contracts for years.[3]

Bartlett and others were certain that Troy had unwittingly signed the printed oath together with other materials which Watson had put on his desk or had taken to the hospital on one of the governor's many stays there. Watson, in fact, had become acting governor whenever Troy was absent due to poor health, a duty normally assumed by the secretary of Alaska. Watson even physically occupied the governor's office in Troy's absence. With a new and energetic secretary of Alaska on the job, it was no wonder that Bartlett and Watson soon came to ideological blows over their respective responsibilities and jurisdictions. Bartlett immediately made it clear that he intended to be an active secretary of Alaska. Vide later recalled that "Harry was pretty upset with Bob. Their relationship wasn't warm."[4]

Soon the Department of the Interior investigated the governor's office and found, among other things, that Harry Watson was using an official department car for his personal pleasure. The Department of the Interior examiners uncovered various other irregularities, and Governor Troy was finally given the choice of resigning or facing criminal prosecution. Troy resigned his office for reasons of health. Ernest Gruening, the director of the Division of Territories and Island Possessions in the Department of the Interior, indicated that the attorney general of the United States had decided that because "of the technical nature of the alleged violation and the extenuating circumstances . . . together with the fact that Mr. Troy had resigned" as governor, no prosecution would be conducted.[5]

President Roosevelt filled the vacancy created by the resignation of Governor Troy by appointing Gruening as the new chief executive. This appointment was made despite the objections of many Alaskans who would have preferred a resident for the position. While in his post in the Department of the Interior, Gruening, a bright, aggressive, and abrasive administrator, had come into conflict not only with his supervisor, Secretary of the Interior Harold L. Ickes, but also with Rexford Guy Tugwell, a member of Roosevelt's "brain trust," who was setting up Puerto Rican development programs. Gruening headed the Puerto Rican Reconstruction Administration and soon came into conflict with Tugwell's plans. At that point the president apparently decided that, in order to restore harmony, Gruening would have to be promoted up and out.

Before the new governor arrived in Alaska and was sworn into his new office in December 1939, events took place in Europe which ultimately were to affect Alaska drastically. On September 1, 1939, German armies invaded Poland. England and France, which had guaranteed Poland's integrity, declared war on Germany on September 3. The Second World War had begun. Still, Alaskans and other Americans generally felt remote from European events. Living in Juneau at that time, Vide remembers that "we just couldn't believe that this was happening in Europe and it was going to do something to us."[6]

Poland quickly collapsed, and during the night of May 9, 1940, German armies surged toward France across the frontiers of Belgium, Holland, and Luxembourg. On June 23, 1940, France collapsed and signed an armistice with Germany. That night in Juneau, Vide had gone to a community dance. People were nervous by then, because the military news from Europe had been consistently gloomy. Individuals had been trying to pick up shortwave broadcasts on their radio sets. Vide recalls that about midnight "the music stopped and the announcement came [of the signing of the armistice] and we all vanished like lemmings . . . I'll always remember all of us pouring out of that building, leaving the orchestra sitting there, and going home . . . We just couldn't put up a front anymore, we were all just thoroughly scared . . . probably because we thought we were going to get it."[7]

Worse was to come. But in the meantime Gruening had taken over the governor's office in an energetic fashion. On the very first day, the chief executive proposed to Bob Bartlett that he assume a considerable share of the work in the governor's office.[8] Bartlett agreed to do so, and thus began a long-lasting relationship between these temperamentally very different men. Gruening was bright, urbane, polished, and Harvard educated—a man who already had behind him a successful career as a journalist, editor, and government bureaucrat and administrator. Bartlett was equally bright, but he was also folksy—a college dropout who had tried his hand at journalism, gold mining, and now administration. It soon became clear that they worked well together. The next four and a half years proved to be fruitful ones for the two men, who shared a similar liberal political outlook, if not working style. Gruening, the senior, furnished the intellectual leadership. Bartlett, although he had earlier stated that politics was not "especially down [his] alley," learned quickly and soon became a consummate politician, often smoothing political feathers ruffled by Gruening's bulldozer approach to men and issues. In addition, he gained valuable administrative experience when serving, sometimes for months on end, as acting governor, while Gruening spent much of his time in Washington lobbying for Alaskan causes. Furthermore, a great deal of travel in his official capacity across the breadth and length of Alaska enabled Bartlett to acquire an intimate knowledge of the territory and to become acquainted with many of its citizens.

In the meantime the war in Europe went from bad to worse. The United States became ever more deeply involved. Public opinion polls revealed that the rest of the country was worried primarily about European developments. However, Americans living on the West Coast, including Alaskans, were not much interested in the threat of Naziism but were "ready to take on the Japanese any time."[9]

Alaska's delegate in Congress, Tony Dimond, had recognized Japan as a threat to America's security as early as 1933 and had asked Congress for military airfields, planes, and army garrisons. He reiterated his warnings over the years and, in 1937, told his House colleagues that Japanese fishermen, ostensibly fishing off Alaska's coast, were actually disguised military personnel seeking information on the depth, defenses, and landmarks of Alaska's harbors.[10] Congress responded slowly, but in 1940, construction of a score of military installations, stretching from Dutch Harbor to Kodiak Island and from Sitka to Anchorage and Fairbanks, got under way.

Suspicions and uncertainties about Japanese intentions were laid to rest on Sunday morning, December 7, 1941. In Alaska, Tom Gardiner, a Juneau resident, called Governor Gruening with the news of the Japanese attack on Honolulu and Manila, which he had picked up listening to Seattle's radio station KIRO. By noon Juneau radio station KINY broadcast details of the attack. That evening a civil defense committee met in the city hall and arranged for a blackout for the following night.[11] Vide recalls that it was difficult to find material to cover the windows. The Bartletts were lucky because they had oversized blankets which had been used at the Independence Creek mine and which just about covered the large windows. B. Frank Heintzleman, the Juneau-based head of the U.S. Forest Service in Alaska, organized the civil defense effort. It had been rumored that the Japanese were planning air attacks on various Alaskan coastal cities, but bad weather all along the coast apparently prevented such raids, if indeed they had been planned at all.[12]

As part of emergency preparations, families were told what rations they would need and what type of clothing should be handy in case of evacuation. Several mine tunnels around town, including some of the Alaska Juneau Gold Mining Company, were designated as air raid shelters.[13]

Since officials expected a severe curtailment of transportation to Alaska, they suggested that residents buy foodstuffs to the limit of their financial ability and cache the supplies. At Bob's urging, Vide stored an "outfit" of groceries, which included all the peanut oil she could buy, some four gallons. George Brothers Grocery Store offered a case of pimentos which she bought. There were seventy-one cans, she remembers, and she was "a little horrified" at that time, but, within the year, every grocery store in town called and made trades for cans of pimentos.[14]

There were many scares, and rumors circulated freely. Residents saw, or imagined they saw, the periscopes of Japanese submarines near Juneau. At another time, rumor had it that the enemy was between Juneau and Sitka. Many Juneau residents panicked, among them the Bartletts. Fearing an imminent occupation of the town, Bob called his wife and told her to get ready to leave quickly. They did, together with others, and went outside Juneau to the beach. The men left the women and children and returned to Juneau. Then all was silence. Vide thought, "There's something going on. I figured the Japs have come, Juneau gone, that's all there's to it." To pass the time the women played bridge. Among Vide's partners was the wife of the weather bureau man, "a very quiet, little mousey woman, seemingly without much sense of humor." While playing one evening and worrying about how close the enemy was, that little woman spoke up. She said, "Well, you know, I think when it comes right down to it, the Japs come in and they rape the women and kill the men. That's what the Russians did to the Aleuts, and I think the only thing a person can do is let them rape and enjoy it. It's the end anyway." That broke the tension, and on the third day the men came out to the beach with the news that it all had been a false alarm. After only a few such scares, life went on much the same as ever.[15]

The government's role, however, expanded greatly during the war. As the governor and his staff listened to President Roosevelt's "Day of Infamy" speech on Monday, December 8, 1941, asking for a declaration of war, all realized how militarily unprepared Alaska was. As Japanese conquests in the Pacific area expanded, it also became clear that Alaska would probably become an enemy target. The expected Japanese attack occurred on June 3, 1942, when the enemy bombed Dutch Harbor and occupied the Aleutian Islands of Attu and Kiska. By that time, war had already tremendously accelerated the pace of life in Alaska. Now massive military operations began, and the military bases, under construction since 1940, were hurried to completion.

The Japanese naval threat also forced a swift decision for an alternate to the sea route to Alaska. An Alaskan highway link had been in the talking stage since 1930. Now, under the pressure of defense needs, work began in 1942 on a pioneer road from Dawson Creek, B.C. to Big Delta, Alaska. The U.S. Army Engineers were to construct the pioneer road. A permanent road would be built by the Public Roads Administration under the general direction of the army engineers.

Under often harsh weather conditions and over extremely difficult terrain, seven engineer regiments, aided by forty-seven contractors, worked toward each other from various points along the route. They finished the pioneer road exactly nine months and six days after the start of construction.[16]

Acting Governor Bartlett left Juneau on November 17 for the formal ribbon-cutting ceremony, which was to take place on November 20, 1942, at Soldier's Summit above Kluane Lake, Yukon Territory. Bartlett was accompanied by former Governor Parks, M.D. Williams of the Public Roads Administration, Major Carl Scheibner, who had been assigned to the governor's office to help organize a territorial guard, Lieutenant Warren Caro of the Coast Guard, and reporter Bill Carter of the Juneau *Daily Alaska Empire.* Getting to Skagway turned out to be more of a problem than anticipated. The group boarded a coast guard boat at Auke Bay for the trip to Skagway. "It was about 50 feet long and many times in the next 25 hours we wished it had been a 200 footer," because a violent storm raged in Lynn Canal that made the little boat pitch and roll. The group finally arrived in Skagway and there boarded the White Pass and Yukon Railroad, "or as some of the trainmen prefer to put it, 'wait patiently and you will ride,'" for the trip to Whitehorse. There they were met by Captain Richard Neuberger, later to be elected a U.S. senator from Oregon, and were lodged in the army barracks, which were so new, Bartlett observed, that the water had not yet been turned on.

They stayed overnight, and the next morning Bartlett, his group, and a number of feature writers and photographers set out for Kluane Lake. After traveling for six and a half hours, the group camped for the night in another collection of new quonset huts. Early the next morning the group was off for Soldier's Summit, where the ribbon was to be cut. It was a beautiful spot, with the lake close on one side and sizable hills ringed by much higher mountains on the other side. The thermometer hovered around $-30°F$ under a thin winter sun. The soldiers had started two big bonfires to warm the dignitaries until the ceremonies commenced. Then Bob Bartlett for the United States and Ian Mackenzie for Canada each took one blade of a pair of gold scissors and "cut, or rather gnawed," the red, white, and blue silk ribbon which opened the Alcan (Alaska-Canada Military Highway). Shortly thereafter, the first truck, the Fairbanks Freight, rolled north to that city.[17]

Along with such improvements as the Alcan, war also brought its fair share of absurdities. Among these was army censorship of mail destined for Alaska. Residents who subscribed to papers and magazines soon found large excisions in most issues. Pages of the *Seattle Post Intelligencer,* for instance, which contained official navy pictures of Dutch Harbor, had been cut out before the paper was sent. Russell H. Peters, the managing editor of the *Post Intelligencer,* complained to officials that it seemed utterly fantastic to spend thousands of dollars maintaining the morale of troops in Alaska and then supplying them with papers that looked "as if they had been run through a meat grinder." On another occasion a registrant with the Fairbanks draft board had moved to the continental United States and later wrote that he was moving again. He asked that mail be sent to him in care of the United States Army Engineers at his new location. The censor had cut out the name of that new place, and the board consequently lost track of a potential soldier.[18]

Worse yet, some four hundred clerks in Seattle working for the censorship office opened private mail coming to and from the territory and excerpted information they considered important to national security. This material was made potentially available to some thirty government agencies. Eventually after some complicated maneuvering, censorship stopped, and the Seattle branch of the Office of War Censorship closed.[19]

There were other war-related activities in Alaska. In the fall of 1942 President Roosevelt, by executive order, established the Alaska War Council, composed of senior representatives of various federal agencies in Alaska. Gruening was named chairman. The council was to establish a working relationship with the military services in the territory.[20]

In early August 1942 the council met and considered a variety of problems, among them censorship, traveling restrictions imposed on residents, and the civilian supply problem. The council heard complaints that liquor had been shipped to Alaska to the exclusion of other items. It was Bartlett's task to go to Seattle and investigate. He reported that no priority had been given to liquor. The War Shipping Administration had instructed its agent, Alaska Steamship Company, not to carry liquor until all other foodstuffs were loaded first. The army, however, reserved a great deal of space and shipped large quantities of beer. Bartlett felt that drinking was a problem in Alaska but one that was understandable, with so many soldiers, sailors, and construction workers in the North and with so few recreational opportunities for them.[21]

The army sometimes undertook projects which astounded Alaskan government officials. The Alaska War Council, for example, learned that the military planned to build a base at Excursion Inlet, some seventy miles northwest of Juneau. It was to serve as an assembly point for troops and supplies which would then proceed under convoy to the Aleutians to expel the Japanese. Gruening and Bartlett inspected the site, a small inlet graced by a cannery. There were no facilities—all had to be built from scratch. Juneau had docks, a water supply, and electricity, and the army could save itself considerable effort and money by locating the base there. Gruening contacted General John L. DeWitt and pointed out the folly of building at the proposed site. The general replied that he had already signed the order and that he never reversed any of his decisions. Long before construction was completed, the Japanese had been driven out of Attu and had evacuated Kiska. The $25 million spent had been wasted, yet construction continued. After the base was finished, German prisoners of war were brought there, all the facilities were dismantled, and the salvaged materials were shipped elsewhere.[22]

Throughout this period Bartlett participated fully in the work of the chief executive's office. It was an exciting and satisfying time for him. His assignments took him to practically every part of Alaska, and his work enabled him to acquire substantial administrative experience. He progressed socially as well. Governor Gruening often entertained visiting dignitaries in the mansion and always invited the secretary and his wife for these occasions, where they met many Washington figures of importance. Adding to Bartlett's happiness was the birth of another daughter, who was christened Susie, on December 9, 1940.

Looking back to his mining days, Bartlett realized that he had accomplished a great deal. Still, he felt restless. On April 20, 1942, he had celebrated his thirty-eighth birthday and was, as Vide recalled, rather anxious about approaching the age of forty. Vide called it the "never, never age—too old to be drafted, and yet too young not to be in the war . . . ." In any event, Bob determined to make a serious effort to get into the armed forces. He did not want to be left out of what he considered to be the biggest thing that had happened so far in his lifetime. On the practical side, he also knew that once the war ended, a military service record would be almost a prerequisite for a public service career.[23]

A suitable opportunity offered itself early in the spring of 1943, when the army advertised for candidates for the military government division of the provost marshal general's office. The army intended to create a specialists' reserve for future use in the military government of hostile areas to be occupied by the armed forces. Those selected were to be appointed to the Officers Reserve Corps and were to carry an inactive status, without pay, until actually needed. Before the call to active duty, the candidates were to attend the army school of military government in Charlottesville, Virginia for four months. This was an opportunity to serve and to utilize his skills at the same time, Bartlett felt, and he asked Delegate Dimond and Governor Gruening to write the necessary recommendations to speed along the bureaucratic process.[24]

Bob himself left no stone unturned and communicated with various military authorities. Soon he had filled out the necessary forms in triplicate and was brusquely notified that his qualifications would be carefully reviewed. He was "particularly requested to make no further inquiry by telephone or letter to this or any other War Department Office. . . ." The army obviously resented congressional intervention and made it clear that they would call when and if they needed Bartlett.[25]

While army bureaucratic procedures ground on, Governor Gruening attempted to have Bartlett commissioned as an officer and stationed with the Selective Service headquarters in Alaska. The governor wrote to General Lewis B. Hershey, the director of the Selective Service System, that while Bartlett would be missed as secretary of Alaska, "he is so eager to go that I see no justification for not doing everything possible to further his desire." There was one complication, however, and that was that Bartlett, although fully qualified, could not be commissioned for appointment to the Selective Service without prior military service. The secretary of war had declined repeatedly to make exceptions, but a person could try nonetheless.[26]

Together with the proper forms, the army also required a physical examination, about which Bob was leery. He knew that his eyes were bad, one nearsighted and the other farsighted. He was overweight and had high blood pressure. Yet he and his friend Hugh Wade, another federal official, were determined to pass the physical examination, because "they both felt that they had to go to war or bust." The evening before the physical, a sympathetic friend who was an army physician gave both men some pills that would lower the blood pressure and slow the heartbeat. He warned both "not to walk fast, and if there were steps, to walk very slowly up the steps." They passed the physical, if barely.[27] Triumphantly they informed Delegate Dimond that both were "almost perfect specimens of manhood physically" — a fact now "part and parcel" of the army's records. They added, however, that they had been "quite well acquainted with the army physician and he spent probably more time than he does on average cases to reassure himself as to the physical merits of these two aging men." Both asserted that their intentions were honorable and decent and that they both wanted very much to serve. Anything Dimond could do would be appreciated.[28]

With that hurdle out of the way, Bartlett discovered that the army would not consider his application complete until his employer, the Division of Territories and Island Possessions and the Department of the Interior, gave the necessary permission for his release. In due time, Bob obtained the required clearance, although the assistant director of the division informed him that she hoped his bad eyes would keep him out of the military. She acknowledged his eagerness to join the army but found it "hard to see all of the good people lining up to be shot at."

With the division's clearance in his pocket, Bob Bartlett became optimistic and could practically see himself in major's uniform administering conquered territories. The optimism was of short duration, however, because Secretary of the Interior Harold L. Ickes informed him that the permission had been a mistake. Bartlett was needed as secretary of Alaska, a position in which he was making greater contribution to the war than he would in the army. After much maneuvering and the intercession of friends, Secretary Ickes finally relented and agreed to release Bartlett to enter military service.[29]

On September 21 Bob Bartlett received the long-awaited commission — as captain in the specialist reserve. It was a shock, because he had confidently expected the grade of major, particularly after having read of a New York City

Department of Sanitation employee who had been taken from a forty-eight-dollars-a-week job and made a major in the AMGOT (Allied Military Government of Occupied Territory). It was a disappointment and a dilemma, for Bob knew that acceptance meant a decrease of his salary from $5,600 per year to $3,984. It would also cost him money to maintain himself away from home. He did not believe "there would possibly be enough left over for the folks and, desperately as I want to get into this, I cannot let them go hungry." Again Dimond and Gruening attempted to help. Gruening especially was enraged when he remembered "some of the relatively worthless or unqualified people from Alaska who have received commissions as lieutenant colonels and majors." Both Dimond and Gruening recommended strongly that Bartlett be commissioned as a lieutenant colonel. It was not to be. In mid-October 1943, Bob declined the offer of a captaincy. It was a hard thing to do, he confided to his friend Don W. Hagerty, but he could not deprive his family. Bob resigned himself to the fact that his contribution to the war effort was to be on the home front.[30]

All wars eventually wind down. After the expulsion of the Japanese and their evacuation of Kiska in 1943, and particularly after American naval victories in the Pacific, the United States position improved spectacularly. This relieved the pressure for the rapid completion of the Alaska Highway. New specifications for the highway, no longer the main supply road, were drawn up.

Beginning in 1943, military activities in Alaska were reduced. From a high of 150,000 men in November 1943, military personnel of the Alaska department had fallen to 50,000 by March 1945.[31]

The war had been a sobering experience for Bob Bartlett. It had given him direction and experience. He had learned a lot under the forceful intellectual leadership of Governor Gruening. Bartlett had considerably matured and now was ready to strike out on his own.

1944

ARTLETT REALIZED THAT the war and its attendant changes offered many options and opportunities. By late 1943 his reappointment as secretary of Alaska at the end of his term, in early 1944, seemed certain. Bartlett had enjoyed his work but also had become aware of the frustrations of public office. He had hoped, he confided to Tony Dimond, that liberal Alaskans would have backed Governor Gruening in his farsighted plans. Instead, many had joined forces with the reactionaries just because they disliked Gruening or because they feared that his questioning of territorial and municipal affairs would upset long-established relationships.

Gruening had soon found that Alaska's tax system was hopelessly inadequate. He felt it essential to present the next legislature with a modest revenue system for the territory. But that legislature rejected all proposals, including needed social and educational legislation. It also successfully put down every tax-reform measure that would have affected absentee economic interests. The lobbyists for these interests had been very successful once again. The sixteenth biennial territorial legislature, convening in January 1943, did as little that was constructive as the 1941 session.[1]

Bartlett was discouraged. He was shocked by the widely expressed anti-Semitism that was directed against the governor because he was Jewish. James Denis, the liquor enforcement officer for the territory, had expressed this particular prejudice, and it was far too prevalent. "We have," Denis had written, "a Kike governor in this territory that is trying to run the whole country." Many Alaskans did not share these anti-Semitic sentiments but simply disliked the New Deal and its attending reforms. To them, Governor Gruening represented all they loathed in the Roosevelt administration.[2]

Gruening already was well aware that reforms were hard to accomplish, and Bartlett, under Gruening's tutelage, quickly came to share the governor's knowledge. In short, Bartlett found too many of his fellow citizens who were serving their own ends rather than the common good, and he found that public office frustrated him. But he also discovered that the rare victories were elating.

Bartlett considered buying a small newspaper in an Alaskan community, some-thing he had hoped for in the prewar years, and giving up public office altogether. Such a new direction required serious consideration first, because he knew that each option chosen would necessarily close off many others. At the age of thirty-nine, two distinctly separate careers beckoned him. He dreaded making a decision that would force him to commit himself, although he knew that he soon had to make a choice. What he did not know at that point was that Governor Gruening would make a choice for him—one that would, in effect, shove him into elected public office.

Late in 1943 Delegate Dimond made it known unofficially that he would not seek reelection, and he and Governor Gruening suggested that Bartlett seek the position. Dimond had worked in Washington for twelve hard years and wanted to return home. In addition, he had always wanted to cap his career with a judgeship. The possibility of obtaining one presented itself when the Department of Justice refused to reappoint Simon Hellenthal, the federal judge for Alaska's Third Judicial Division, with headquarters in Anchorage. Dimond's retirement plans suited Governor Gruening because the two men, although on cordial terms, were not particularly in accord politically. Gruening had remarked that "while an extremely valuable member of the House in many ways, Dimond is frequently at odds with the Department of the Interior on matters of policy," and that was bound to be disadvantageous to Alaska.[3]

Gruening pressed Bartlett to seek the office of delegate. Besides genuinely liking and respecting his junior partner, Gruening also knew that he would be able to work much better with Bartlett than with any other man in that position. Bartlett was typically indecisive. He had thought about the possibility of running but had many reservations. He told the governor that no one minded "going up in the world . . . and fill[ing] the highest position which the people of Alaska have in their power to offer." On reflection, Bartlett added that he, "no less than any fellow . . . would be willing to wear the toga in a very statesmanlike manner."

There were, however, many obstacles to overcome before he could seriously consider filing for the position. Bartlett assumed that numerous Alaskan politi-cians would oppose his candidacy, among them Oscar Olson, the territorial treasurer; Walter Sharpe, the director of the Unemployment Compensation Commission; Henry Roden, the attorney general; and Allen Shattuck, a legislator and Juneau insurance agency proprietor. Bartlett also lacked money for a cam-paign and, furthermore, had never seriously considered himself as a candidate for elected office. He felt unable to assess his chances for waging a successful cam-paign realistically.

If he actually decided to run and if the Department of the Interior accepted his resignation as secretary of Alaska, it would owe him his pay for some sixty days of accumulated leave. A resignation coinciding with the filing deadline in February, Bartlett reasoned, would carry him through the primaries. The Department of the Interior, he hoped, might want to hold the secretaryship open until his fate in the primaries had been decided. If defeated, Bartlett suggested, he could well be reappointed. "There would be a howl," he expected, "but this is cold-blooded politics and I must say that I believe the department should be willing to go this length in order to ward off the seating of a delegate who could be very unfriendly."[4]

As far as Bartlett was concerned, the perfect solution to his problem was for Dimond to file in regular fashion pending the judgeship. Nobody in the Democratic party would file against him — nobody except Bartlett, who would file ten minutes before closing time. Dimond subsequently would accept the judgeship, and Bartlett would be the unanimous choice of the Democratic party. Such a scenario, Bartlett was convinced, would assure him of victories in both the primary and the general election. Bartlett admitted that he "was enough of a lowlife politician to think of [this] perfect out, but Tony would not subscribe to it and I would not have him do it because it is not in harmony with the way he does things."[5] Dimond's rejection of that plan absolved Bartlett once more of having to make a difficult decision.

Nevertheless, by the end of December 1943, plans for the Bartlett candidacy had progressed further. Should he choose to run, the Department of the Interior had tacitly agreed to accept the secretary's resignation, pay him two months' accumulated leave, and hold the secretaryship open pending his nomination for the delegateship.[6]

At this juncture, however, Dimond was not ready to announce his retirement nor Bartlett his candidacy. It was Governor Gruening who gave both men the necessary push. The governor, never one to hesitate, leaked news of Dimond's impending retirement to various associates in Alaska and Washington. At the same time, Gruening highly recommended to Secretary Ickes the delegate's appointment as a federal judge. He assured his superior that Alaskans would approve universally of Dimond. The governor also urged Bartlett to run, because his one supreme desire for Alaska was "to do my darndest to get you elected delegate."[7]

On January 17, 1944, Delegate Dimond officially announced that he did not intend to seek reelection. The *Fairbanks Daily News-Miner,* which carried the story, stated that there were rumors that Dimond would replace Judge Simon Hellenthal in Anchorage.[8] Bartlett announced his candidacy for the delegateship the very next day, reasoning that this would create "a feeling in the minds of the public that so far as Tony was concerned he was stepping aside for me." Dimond unwittingly obliged Bartlett. Gruening, who was in Washington at that point, visited Dimond and urged him to endorse Bartlett. The delegate refused, stating that "I'm not going to support him until he files [for the office], because I don't want to be influential in Bob's making a decision that is going to affect so much of his life." Gruening wanted to push Bartlett, so he phoned Dimond a few days later, stating that Bartlett had filed. Dimond then immediately sent a telegram in which he publicly endorsed Bartlett, stating, in part, that "your outstanding fitness for that office. . .makes me the more content to leave an office in which I have for so many years enjoyed an era of good will in serving the people of Alaska, knowing that they will have an opportunity to elect one of your qualifications." The truth was that Barlett had not filed as yet. When Dimond discovered this, he was extremely upset. Gruening was pleased that his candidate was all but committed, but Bartlett, although the die had been cast, was still indecisive.[9]

Despite Bartlett's being all but committed, he was beset by doubts and insecurities, understandable in a failed miner who, for the first time in his life, occupied a secure position. Bartlett simply lacked self-confidence, and although he had made some noise, he had not filed his papers of candidacy. He did not know who his opponents would be in the primary. Serving as secretary of Alaska, he felt, was a very satisfying experience, and there appeared to be a good possibility that Congress would increase his salary within a short time. Furthermore, the possibility of leaving Juneau distressed him, for "during the last several days [that city] has seemed a grander place than ever before." In his anxiety Bartlett turned to his friend Hugh Wade, then a federal employee in Washington, D.C., and asked him to exert his influence and have Delegate Dimond reconsider his decision to leave the delegateship. Nervously, Bartlett wrote that "I would give my entire fortune if he would," forgetting that he had no fortune in the first place.[10]

Unaware of Gruening's role in obtaining the support that Dimond had extended, Bartlett telegraphed the governor, who was then on a trip in New Mexico. Bartlett wanted "to clear up any misunderstanding which may exist. . .I have not filed but merely announced intention of doing so; anything done to date is not irrevocable." To Hugh Wade, Bartlett confided that he was in an uncomfortable position "with one foot in and one foot out." In a further maneuver, he had persuaded the territorial commissioner of mines, B.D. Stewart, his next-door neighbor, to fill out a sworn declaration of candidacy for the delegateship and to give him the original. If Bartlett decided to back out of the race at the last minute, Stewart's candidacy would give him the perfect excuse—he would not run against a friend.[11]

When President Roosevelt nominated Dimond for the judgeship on January 24, 1944, this should have been the signal for Bartlett to file without hesitation for the delegateship. He had seven days until the deadline of February 1 to make up his mind.[12] Yet his ambiguity and anxiety persisted, and he described himself as being in a dither. He did not have "the yen I ought to have to get to Washington," and thoughts of urban congestion gave him "the willies."[13]

As the day of decision drew near, Bartlett's friends in Juneau and elsewhere in the territory increasingly urged him to file. Vide, however, opposed his candidacy, remembering that when Bob had worked as Dimond's secretary in Washington, D.C., he had not been fond of that city nor of the work. Money was another consideration. They did not have much in their savings account, did not own their house, and Vide could not see how they would finance their trip to Washington if Bob won the delegateship. The whole proposition, she thought, was absolutely crazy. Vide and her friends Katherine Nordale and Stella Young asked him not to file. Perhaps Vide feared that, if elected, Bob would not be able to handle the Washington job. Katherine Nordale "was kind of ambivalent about the thing, because she just knew Bob very well, and Bob was drinking at the time and gambling, and she wasn't confident that he could really follow through on it. Yet she knew his value," and she was unimpressed with the other candidates. "She was concerned about what would happen to the family if he did, and yet she was concerned about what would happen to Alaska if he didn't." Above all, she felt very strongly that Bob was the logical successor to Dimond and, most importantly, "that the most intelligent, most capable people Alaska could send back to Congress should go." Bob Bartlett certainly was one of these.[14]

A number of Bartlett's friends closeted themselves with the reluctant candidate and attempted to convince him to file. The struggle before the filing deadline, Bartlett confided to a friend, was terrific. "Prime movers in this plot to foil me in political ambitions," he asserted, were Vide and her friends. "Several times during the day I almost had to let them have it on the chin, principally, I suppose, because every time they uttered a word they were reflecting my own sentiments." As the 5 P.M. filing deadline approached, Governor Gruening "turned on the heat in a big way." To Bartlett's surprise, Gruening grabbed the telephone and called the secretary of the interior, who agreed to hold the secretary job open in case Bartlett lost in the primary.[15]

Close to the magic hour, Vide received "a call from the boys" to come and confer. She didn't want to, but she did so anyway—and "sat down very obstreperous and obnoxious." Many of Bob's Juneau friends had crowded into his office. They explained to her why they felt Bob had to file for the position. As far as Vide was concerned, lawyer Joe Kehoe's reasoning finally clinched the case for her husband's filing. Bob, Joe told her, "announced months ago. He's been in all the newspapers, he's got support in practically every town in Alaska, people are geared to support him, they want him. [He would be doing] a great disservice to all of these people, all over Alaska, who have organized to support him in the primaries; and win, lose, or draw, he will be doing a really dastardly act if he doesn't file at least." Although Kehoe, in his enthusiasm, had surely exaggerated Bartlett's territory-wide support, Bob finally filed a few minutes before the closing time. From that moment, he was in the race in earnest.[16]

In addition to Bartlett, three other well-known Alaskan Democrats announced their intention of running for the delegateship. Henry Roden, a Swiss-born, naturalized American citizen, was a sourdough who had mined and prospected on the Yukon and Tanana rivers. He had served several times as a member of the territorial legislature, including the first one in 1913. He was a self-taught lawyer whom Judge James Wickersham had admitted to the Alaska bar. He was Alaska's attorney general and, in his late sixties, was the oldest of the candidates. Many people, including Governor Gruening, considered Roden to be Bartlett's most formidable opponent. Gruening stated that Roden would be backed by the vested interests, canning and mining, "and will of course remain in office throughout the campaign, continuing not only to draw his salary, but also using the travel funds of his office for campaign purposes."

Also opposing Bartlett was A.H. Ziegler, a well-to-do Ketchikan attorney. He was fifty-four years old and had come to Alaska in 1913. Admitted to the Alaska bar in 1915, he practiced law in Juneau with Z.R. Cheney, then the territory's Democratic national committeeman. World War I had disrupted his career. He had served in the United States Navy until he was discharged in 1919, whereupon he had settled in Ketchikan. Ziegler had often been a lobbyist for the liquor interests during the sessions of the legislature, and he could expect substantial financial support from that quarter.

The Republicans fielded L.V. Ray, a former territorial senator and a prominent Seward attorney. Gruening thought that to have Alaska represented by any one of these three in Congress would be a terrible step backwards.[17]

In comparison with his primary opponents, Bartlett faced an uphill struggle. He would have to raise every cent to pay for travel around the territory, which was extremely costly. He would also need to raise funds for at least one circular letter to the voters, for posters, for stenographic aid, for telegrams, and for radio and newspaper advertising. Gruening gave the Bartlett campaign a lift during a trip around Alaska in which he raised $3,500. In those days that was a tidy sum with which to start a campaign.[18]

Campaigning in Alaska was difficult and expensive because of the territory's tremendous size, varied regions and climates, and poorly developed transportation system. In the 1940s, four of Alaska's seven cities with populations of one thousand or more were on all-year ocean routes, while two were located on the Alaska Railroad line. Nome, with no land access, was accessible by water transportation only during the summer months. At that time, Alaska could boast of little more than two thousand miles of roads suitable for automobile and truck traffic. Although the Alaska-Canada Military Highway linking the north with the continental United States had been built, the highway was not opened to civilian traffic until 1948, so Alaskans relied primarily on the airplane for their transportation needs.

The vastness of the country can be illustrated by noting the distances between various places. From Ketchikan to Seward via ocean steamer, for example, is approximately 1,100 miles; from Seward to Anchorage on the Alaska Railroad is 114 miles; and from there to Fairbanks is 356 miles. The distance by river steamer from Nenana to Saint Michael at the mouth of the Yukon River on the Bering Sea is 900 miles. Using Fairbanks as the base from which he campaigned, Bartlett had to travel 100 miles by air to reach Circle Hot Springs, 190 miles to Wiseman, and 700 miles to Nome.

Above all, Alaska was, and is, sparsely settled. In 1944 it had a population of 185,000, some 104,000 of whom were members of the military forces; or, put another way, Alaska had a population density of 0.3 persons per square mile. This compared with an estimated 44.3 persons per square mile for the United States as a whole and 22.6 persons per square mile for the far west. The mountain states, the most sparsely populated region in the continental United States, had an estimated population of 5.9 persons per square mile.

With these facts in mind, it was no wonder that Bartlett economized whenever possible.

Bartlett formally launched his primary campaign on February 8 in Wrangell, where he spoke at a one-dollar-a-plate dinner held by the Wrangell Statehood Club. This organization, led by Lew Williams, Bartlett's eventual successor as secretary of Alaska, only recently had been established to sponsor discussions on statehood. Bartlett believed in statehood, probably having been persuaded by Dimond's advocacy of it. Bartlett made that issue his campaign theme, labeling the existing system of government "outmoded and inefficient and only a stop-gap between territory-hood and statehood." He acknowledged that statehood would cost more money but asserted that it could be afforded by "taxing some of the millions of dollars which are now going out of the territory without returning one cent in revenue."[19] Only statehood, he argued, could bring full citizenship to all Alaskans and eliminate the excessive control the federal bureaucracy exercised. Enough revenues would be generated to pay for the added costs of self-government, he confidently predicted. Bartlett promised to do his utmost in Congress to achieve that goal.[20]

The statehood theme was to dominate Bartlett's life for years to come. In the course of his primary race, however, he also dealt with post-World War II adjustments, economic problems, and opportunities in Alaska. "On the stump" or over the radio, Bartlett reminded his listeners again and again that the Second World War had wrought changes far more drastic than those that had occurred during the gold rush days. The war had brought a more complete road system, airports, a telephone system that linked Alaska to Canada and to the continental United States, and a highway which did the same. Furthermore, the territory enjoyed increased aids to navigation and a pipeline to bring cheaper fuel north. "A century of ordinary, peacetime appropriation," Bartlett continued, would never have given them "all these benefits."[21]

Despite these windfalls, however, much remained to be done, Bartlett told his listeners. Tuberculosis ran rampant, and perhaps some of the excellent army hospitals built during the war could pass to territorial ownership and furnish some of the needed facilities to combat the dread disease.

Bartlett was concerned with local problems and addressed himself to these in the various communities he visited. Juneau, Douglas, and the Gastineau Channel faced a crisis. The Alaska Juneau Gold Mine had closed, the Juneau Lumber Company had burned, and the city and its surrounding areas were left with only the territorial and federal governments as sources of employment. Bartlett pledged himself to an eight-point program for the Juneau area, which included resisting any attempts to diminish the importance and functions of the city as the territory's capital. It also advocated the development of the tourist industry.[22]

Bartlett assured worried citizens of Seward that the Department of the Interior had no intention of abandoning the southern section of the Alaska Railroad, since it had been built to aid in the development of all of central Alaska. Furthermore, the department would do everything possible to help in the construction of a road to Anchorage.[23]

It was not easy for Bartlett to give speeches before an audience. According to Katherine Nordale, "he was an absolutely lousy public speaker at the time. Excellent choice of words, terribly self-conscious about speaking, and absolutely convinced that the minor speech impediment that he had precluded him from speaking intelligently to a large group of people." Here is where Nordale was able to help. She had studied drama and speech in college and offered to coach her friend. Amid mounting tensions, she undertook to give Bob speech lessons. Bartlett was resistant to these lessons, but she was determined that he was going to learn. And learn he did, becoming a tolerable public speaker.[24]

The governor helped Bartlett with advice and, more concretely, through his contacts with various individuals throughout Alaska. By March 17 Gruening reported that "on the whole, the picture appears to me to be increasingly favorable," since Roden, the more formidable of Bartlett's two opponents, was slipping. Ziegler seemed to be gaining, but he did not have the territory-wide support that Roden had. A few days later he reported that "Henry Roden seems to be getting confused. He evidently thinks he is campaigning against me, which is splendid—I hope he keeps it up."

A great deal of work remained to be done before the primary, Gruening reminded Bartlett. The governor warned him that the opposition undoubtedly would have a key man or woman in each community to bring out the local votes— and "you must be sure to have the same and be able to count on more than one person."

Above all, he advised Bartlett, it was particularly important to visit and see as many places and people as possible, since "there is nothing like having a community see a candidate; it is important for this campaign and for the future." For example, Dimond had visited the little town of Seldovia — and with wonderful results. Seldovia had produced a total of 127 votes in the September 1940 election. Dimond had received 102 of those votes, so "that would seem to be worth going after," Gruening concluded.

The governor also expressed his concern over reports that Bartlett was making statehood the chief issue of the campaign. However strongly "you may feel about statehood, and I share your view, that I feel is not the issue in this campaign and stressing it may be used to your disadvantage." The really important issue, Gruening felt, was who "is going to be most effective in providing for Alaska's needs for the balance of the war and in the important postwar years to come."[25]

Throughout his campaign, Bartlett had to contend with accusations of being a Gruening man or a Dimond man. Bartlett pointed out that he had worked with Gruening for over four years and considered him a brilliant and distinguished citizen of Alaska. The governor's support pleased him, although he had not always agreed with Gruening. He did not, Bartlett emphatically stated, belong to that group of politicians who, in attempting to gain public office, blasted the governor, an activity which they obviously regarded as popular and helpful to their cause.[26]

Bartlett proudly admitted being a Dimond man, explaining that Dimond had been a splendid delegate who had worked hard and accomplished a great deal. Bartlett was honored to have Dimond's endorsement as the candidate "best equipped to take his place."[27] Gruening and Dimond were two well-known politicians who had been Bartlett's mentors and who had made his bid for political office possible; and Bartlett knew that he had more to gain than lose from his association with them.

Henry Roden campaigned vigorously and pointed with pride to his territorial legislative record, which showed that he had supported every progressive measure and had consistently opposed many that were calculated to retard progress. In addition, Roden aligned himself with the working man, maintaining that he knew what it meant to pull a sled by the back of the neck, sink shafts, work in drifts, and hustle a payroll. Roden's philosophy was summed up in the slogan, "The greatest good for the greatest number, from Ketchikan to Kotzebue." Roden usually concluded his campaign speeches by pointing out that if "experience, industry, courage, determination, and knowledge of the Territory, and a thorough understanding of her peoples' problems counted for anything, I feel I am qual- ified." Bartlett and Roden often campaigned together and after their appearances sometimes joined each other for a meal or a cup of coffee and kidded each other on the similarity of their speeches.[28]

A. H. Ziegler also campaigned effectively. Like Roden, he had served several terms in the territorial legislature and had always been the top vote-getter in southeastern Alaska. Ziegler maintained that he had supported all progressive legislation and had opposed special privileges. Ziegler hedged on statehood: he wanted first to "find out what we're talking about" and then ask the electorate what it thought. He accused Bartlett of being the governor's man and stated that, as an Alaskan, he resented the "intrusion and interferences of appointees from the 'outside,' who are really carpetbaggers." This was considered a cutting argument among Alaskans, most of whom were born somewhere "outside" but took great pride in the number of years they had spent in Alaska. Last but not least, Ziegler observed, not only did Bartlett lack qualifications for the delegateship, but "it would be a pity to turn the affairs [of the territory] over to the Governor and his clique."[29] This was, of course, an effective argument for those who disliked New Dealer Gruening and still considered him an outsider.

As the campaign moved along, Bartlett traveled extensively throughout Alaska, generally hitching rides and staying with friends to save money. He had handbills printed in large quantities and distributed widely throughout the territory. The words may have varied, but the message was always essentially the same: "Vote for E. L. 'Bob' Bartlett, Primary Election April 25, 1944. Forty years of age, Alaska Resident for 39 years, Miner, Newspaperman, Two Years' Experience in the National Capital as Secretary to Delegate Dimond, Secretary of Alaska for last five years, Democratic Candidate for Delegate to Congress, endorsed by 'Tony' Di- mond," or "Young, Progressive E.L. (Bob) Bartlett for Delegate to Congress (Subject to Democratic Primary, April 25, 1944), an Alaskan for Alaska."[30]

Printing and mailing expenses strained Bartlett's budget. Although he ran the campaign from his house with the help of many family friends, money became increasingly scarce. The women in the governor's office also helped with the campaign in their free time, writing thank-you notes and stuffing envelopes. According to Katie Hurley, "We all went out to Vide's and helped. In fact, we were doing some letters in the office. EG [Ernest Gruening] told us we could do it, but it really wasn't supposed to be done . . . if anyone was walking through there—and we had reporters going through there all the time—why the girls had to be pretty foxy about what they were doing. Most of the time, however, we went over to Bob's house." In time a few contributions trickled in, and occasionally, Vide recalls, "somebody would give you fifty dollars. . .called 'walking around money.'" Vide's mother came from California and helped take care of the two Bartlett children, Doris Ann, nine years old, and Susie, who was four. Although not affluent, Mrs. Gaustad contributed her share to the maintenance of the household.[31]

Bartlett's friends cheered his campaign efforts whenever he was in town but were chagrined at his speeches. They were "just terrible. [They] all just cringed because. . .he was just not a speaker. He was a wonderful one-to-one person," and he could write well. "I was not as critical then as I would be now," one of his friends stated, "but I can remember everybody just talking about that [his speeches] and wondering." Luckily, speechmaking was not a requirement in Alaskan politics in those days, and Bartlett had an astounding number of people working for him because they liked him for what he was.[32]

Well-wishers wrote and lifted Bartlett's spirit. Mary Lee Council, Delegate Dimond's secretary, wrote that "we all are pulling and praying for you and are rubbing wood and doing all the things that fulfill good wishes for someone we like so much."[33] U.S. Commissioner Everett E. Smith from Haines wholeheartedly agreed with Bartlett's statehood stand as one endorsed by all "people who are natural born Alaskans and have the interests of our country at heart. . .too long has Alaska, with her boundless natural resources, been denied development by the fact that we are more or less controlled by a few selfish interests."

Noel C. Ross of Beaver contributed $100 toward the election of "the right man for the job, the only man running who knows the country, the people, and who is not a bureaucratic-minded authoritarian."

John Wiese, a Cordova fisherman, beat the drum for Bartlett in that community by telling his fellow workers that the candidate was not tied to any special interest group. Wiese suddenly realized, however, that his approach had been too negative. When he talked with Red Carlson, the chairman of the Cordova Fishermen's Political Welfare Committee, Carlson had been noncommittal until Wiese told him that Bob Bartlett had been Delegate Dimond's secretary at about the same time that Carlson had been in Washington, D.C. to testify at some Alaskan fisheries hearings. Carlson immediately perked up, remembering how helpful Bartlett had been to the visiting Alaskans, and launched into the following monologue: "For Kris sake, you mean to tell me you're talking about that young fellow used to be Tony's Number One Man! ... Why the Hell didn't you say so long ago. Gawdam it, man, here I been settin' for a couple of weeks not knowing who you're talkin' about and I coulda been out blackjacking a few of those numb-skulls into learning his name and knowin' like I know that he's okay! I'll tell 'em, by gawd, how he tried his damndest to help us out several years ago when we needed friends, and by gawd they'll vote for him if I have to skin 'em alive and bring their pelts in and vote 'em for 'em. I'm gonna do some campaign'n for that guy."[34]

By April 25, primary election day, the issues had been discussed. Bartlett spent the day in Juneau and cast his vote. When the returns started to come in, it soon became apparent that he had won the cherished Democratic nomination. He had swept the territory, carrying all judicial divisions. Among the major cities in which he had won were Juneau, Skagway, Wrangell, Petersburg, Anchorage, Fairbanks, Cordova, Valdez, Homer, and Kodiak. Roden, his nearest opponent, had won in Sitka, Haines, and Nome. Ziegler had carried his home town of Ketchikan and neighboring Metlakatla. In Ketchikan he had received 379 votes to Bartlett's 340, and in Metlakatla the vote was 75 to 36. When all the votes had been tallied, they showed Bartlett with 3,610, Roden with 1,845, and Ziegler with 1,793. The sparse numbers indicated the importance of waging a personal campaign, the need for travel, and the value of vocal and supportive partisans in various communities.

Bartlett exulted that it had been a "glorious victory everywhere." To his mentor, Dimond, he confided that "spitefully enough, it made me very happy to see Z. [Ziegler] run third. I could have taken a licking from Henry Roden with perfect equanimity but the other would have been hard to bear." While Bartlett respected Roden as a man and an opponent, he had little regard for Ziegler.[35]

After the euphoria of victory had died down, Bartlett had to confront the task of waging yet another campaign, this time against Anchorage attorney John Manders, the Republican standard-bearer. The first task at hand, however, consisted of writing hundreds upon hundreds of thank-you letters to friends throughout the territory and to appeal for further support and funds in the general election.

The notes that the Bartletts and many of their Juneau friends wrote were suited to individuals in different localities. These were as personal as a letter of that kind could be. Bob Bartlett had, over the years, kept a booklet of names and addresses of people he had met. With each name he had included some specific information, such as business associations, hobbies, size of family, and names of children. His letter to Miss Jessie M. Howard, the U.S. Commissioner of Ophir, Alaska was typical. Bartlett reminded Miss Howard that he had interviewed her several times while he was a reporter for the *Fairbanks Daily News-Miner* in the early 1930s. Although Bartlett had noticed by the primary election returns that Miss Howard was a registered Republican, he still appealed for her support in the general election. As an old-time Alaskan, Bartlett concluded, he was very familiar with territorial problems and would represent her well in Congress.[36]

Bartlett also reminded his potential supporters that campaigning was expensive. He thanked U.S. Marshal Paul Herring of Kodiak for all the help he had already rendered. Bartlett intended to campaign in Kodiak, "but it all depends on the way the campaign funds roll in."[37]

Contributions did arrive, but they were not enough to cover expenses. As they had done during the primary, Bartlett's friends helped to run the campaign from the candidate's house. Included were Bartlett's oldest daughter Doris Ann and her friend Mary Nordale. The two girls folded and stamped hundreds of letters, and Mary's brother Jim and other children posted Bartlett notices throughout Juneau.[38]

While the Juneau headquarters hummed with activity, Bartlett traveled throughout Alaska by boat, car, and plane, as much as limited financial resources permitted. The campaign for the general election did not get under way in earnest until August 1944. By that time the military command had lifted all travel restrictions within Alaska, with the exception of the Aleutian Islands.

With war still raging in Europe and the Pacific, however, even such an important process as the election of a delegate was relegated to newspaper back pages. The headlines instead recorded the progress of the war. On August 1, 1944, Alaskans learned that "Yank Forces Surge Into Brittany; Reds, Poles Open Battle for Warsaw; and MacArthur Takes Vogelkap, Final New Guinea Area."[39] On August 8 headlines proclaimed that "Paris Only 100 Miles Ahead of Driving Yanks," while on August 14 "100,000 Nazis Doomed in France, 'Waterloo' Shapes for German Army."[40] In the meantime, Democrats in Juneau had created a Bartlett-for-delegate club and had selected Judge William A. Holzheimer to lead the group.[41]

Bartlett's Republican opponent had also started his campaign. Manders demanded home rule for the territory and pledged that he would work to free Alaska from bureaucratic domination and the heavy hand of conservation, which had so long stymied territorial development. The Republican suggested that Alaskans be informed on statehood so that they could evaluate any future congressional enabling act. Manders believed that Congress had been remiss in its responsibilities toward Alaska. He felt that Congress should grant Alaskans the right to elect their own governor; extend the federal highway act to the North; reduce freight rates on the federally owned and operated Alaska Railroad; build adequate roads and small boat harbors; open the Kenai Peninsula for agricultural settlement; liberalize federal conservation programs; and pass appropriate legislation for the protection and well-being of Alaska's natives.[42]

In his travels through the territory, the Republican candidate—as all candidates of every political persuasion everywhere — essentially repeated the same campaign speech, adding a few variations to suit the particular localities. In Juneau, for example, Manders severely criticized Secretary of the Interior Harold Ickes for creating vast native reservations. Preserving large areas for the use and occupancy of Alaskan natives had become a possibility in 1936 when Congress extended the Indian Reorganization Act (the Wheeler-Howard Act) of 1934 to Alaska. Under its provisions the Department of the Interior could establish reservations for Eskimos and Indians in Alaska. White and native Alaskans quickly criticized the measure. Non-natives feared that even more land than already reserved would be locked up, preventing the development of resources and the growth of Alaska's economy. Natives, knowledgeable of reservations in the continental United States, also feared that they would be confined to small areas with limited resources. Despite substantial controversy, the secretary of the Interior created seven reservations between 1941 and 1946. The largest, which included the villages of Venetie, Arctic Village, Kachik, and Christian Village, encompassed 1,408,000 acres, while the smallest, Unalakleet, contained a mere 870 acres.[43] Manders claimed that some "90 percent of the Territory of Alaska is being held in reserve" and predicted that at the present rate of withdrawals, it would rise to 96 percent within a few months. Under continued Democratic rule, he said, Alaska would soon be known as the lost frontier rather than as the last frontier. He accused the Department of the Interior of "shutting [the] door to Alaska" and concluded that only an "open door policy" would enable Alaska to participate in the expected postwar economic development.[44]

Bartlett responded to the whole issue of reservations and Indian claims. Individuals throughout Alaska had urged him to denounce the claims and everyone having anything to do with them. Bartlett had refused to do so, because he believed that treating the matter as a partisan political issue would not solve it. Furthermore, "the facts available were insufficient to support anything but a snap judgment, and to come out for either side would have been similar to arriving at a decision in a law case without consideration of the evidence." As a delegate, Bartlett intended to oppose "with all the vigor at [his] command, the creation of a wholesale system of reservations for exclusive use or benefit of the native race in southeastern or any other part of Alaska." Bartlett pledged to take those claims into "a competent court of jurisdiction so that the Indian people may receive just compensation in whatever amount they have been damaged." The candidate also promised to work for "the granting of [fish] trap sites in selected Indian localities so their economic lot may be bettered."[45]

Rather than criticizing the federal government and, by implication, the Democratic party, Bartlett maintained that the federal government would play an important role in Alaska's postwar economic development — one that would be advantageous to Alaskans. Alaska had benefited from a growing road network, aviation facilities, and other construction projects, as well as by an increased population. "We are growing up," Bartlett maintained, "and because we are, one of the principal tasks of the next Delegate will be to renew the fight to convince Congress that we have reached the stage where we are entitled to more voice in our affairs. Certainly there would be no more appropriate time to give us real home rule than at the conclusion of a great war which is being fought to preserve the democratic ideal."[46]

During much of the campaign, Bartlett's wife accompanied him. A. H. Ziegler, a Bartlett opponent in the primary, originated the practice by taking his young and beautiful wife along in his travels. Vide recalls that "never before had anybody seen a wife as a campaigner. It was the man; it wasn't his family or his wife. But there was this lovely . . . wife going along with him every place and meeting everybody and this was bringing women out to some of the campaign orations. . . and this really threw a bombshell" into traditional campaign practices.[47] At that time Vide did not foresee that this practice of the Zieglers, combined with her own inclinations, would change her life radically and, in time, make her an expert campaigner in her husband's behalf.

Vide started her new career as a campaigner when Bob received a campaign contribution of $1,000 from Keith Capper, the owner of the garishly decorated but highly successful Lido Gardens nightclub in Anchorage. Capper attached one stipulation to his contribution: Bartlett was to take Vide along on the campaign trail. "Well, a thousand dollars," Vide remembers, "good God, that was a lot of money." Bartlett sent for Vide while he was in Anchorage. On her arrival the Lido Gardens hosted a big campaign party for the Bartlett team. Then the two were off to Valdez by bus. They campaigned at every bus stop along the route. On the return trip the Bartletts hitched a ride from Valdez to Copper Center and again made numerous stops at the roadhouses along the way. At one point torrential rains turned the Richardson Highway into a quagmire, and it looked as if the campaigners would be marooned in Copper Center. Fortunately, Al Ghezzi, an old friend and construction contractor, came by in his truck. He rescued the Bartletts and drove them north through the mud to Birch Lake. Luck was with them, for the weather cleared, and they were able to return to Fairbanks without further incidents.[48]

In Fairbanks the Bartletts generally campaigned separately, a pattern they were to follow for years. Time was always too short and there were many people to see— too many to do justice to old friends. Campaigning separately, however, they could contact more people. Vide's personality made her an effective campaigner. The *News-Miner* admiringly described her as "spontaneously witty, just folksy and completely frank."[49] Much more self-confident than Bob, she felt very much at ease among old-time Alaskans like herself and talked easily to large groups. Another contribution in the amount of $1,000 from Jimmy "Fortune" Ryan of Montana, whose family had become wealthy from copper mining, enabled Vide to accompany her husband on a number of other campaign trips in the fall of 1944.[50]

The last few weeks of the campaign rushed by, with Alaskans equally interested in the momentous military events unfolding in faroff Europe and the territorial political battle between Bartlett and Manders for the delegateship.

The Bartletts spent election day in Juneau. Friends and well-wishers tramped in and out of the house on Calhoun Avenue all day long and late into the night. The early returns looked very good, and it soon became evident that Bartlett would be Alaska's next delegate in Congress. Euphoria reigned among the members of the Bartlett crowd in Juneau, and they celebrated victory with a big party. Official returns showed 7,255 votes for Bartlett and 3,763 for Manders.[51]

For Bob, victory meant that many uncertainties lay ahead. The euphoria had died down, and, now faced with success, Bartlett was still perplexed. He did not know "where to go from there and he went into a kind of emotional tailspin." He once again drank hard and gambled excessively. By the time he left for Washington, the little money the family had was gone. It was not long, however, before Bartlett regained his equilibrium and launched his career as delegate from Alaska. Vide and the children joined him in Washington in the spring of 1945.[52]

CHAPTER 7

The Early Years in Congress

E ARLY IN 1938 a husky young man of average height and large frame drove into Fairbanks from the Circle country where he mined gold. He stopped at the Northern Commercial Caterpillar department and bought a replacement spring for his D-5 Caterpillar tractor. Burke Riley, the clerk, located the part, and the customer then asked him to help carry it to his truck, which proved to be some three blocks away. "By the time we got the 200-pound spring to the truck, the truck bed looked ten feet high," Riley remembers. He then asked to whom the spring was to be billed. Send the bill to me, the young man stated and then introduced himself as Bob Bartlett. "Even then," Riley recalls, "the name was familiar. I remarked that he must be the one who'd been in Washington with Tony Dimond. He nodded, and that in turn prompted my asking why would anyone give up a soft touch like Washington to pack a 200-pound spring across Fairbanks." Bartlett replied, "That had been easy since Washington was too much like hard work."[1]

To a certain extent, that assessment was a realistic one, at least as far as Bartlett's own reaction toward life in Washington was concerned. Although widely known as a warm, congenial, and friendly fellow, he had not had a reputation as a disciplined hard worker. Indeed, when he had faced difficult and sustained work as Delegate Dimond's secretary in Washington, he had quit and returned to Alaska. But with his involvement with Governor Gruening in the administration of the territory, Bartlett's reputation quickly changed.[2]

Arriving in Washington after his election to the delegateship, Bartlett quickly became known for his industry and accomplishments. In fact, he became addicted to his work, to the exclusion of practically all else. While living in Juneau, he had gone fishing with his friend Hugh Wade from time to time, and that had been the extent of his outside interests. Now in Washington he had no hobbies, took no vacations, and quickly became a workaholic.

According to Vide, Bob would "leave early in the morning and get home late at night, and this was the story of his life. He really was a morning person, he was up early, usually at five A.M., and he would take the first bus he could get over to the Capitol and he claimed he could do his best work, his best thinking [then.]" He went to work six days a week and labored approximately twelve hours a day. Usually on Sundays he would read the morning paper, drink several cups of coffee, and then announce, "I think I'll just run down to the office for a little while and do a little dictating." He would be gone for most of the day.

Such a schedule did not permit much of a family life. For example, when Bartlett's eight-year-old daughter Susie went to Alaska with Vide in 1948, a territorial trooper drove them from place to place where Bartlett had cam- paigned. Susie called the trooper "daddy" because he was with them daily over an extended period of time.

The children must have resented their father's work schedule, Vide surmises: "All Congressmen's children are a little half-baked, they can't help but be." That life-style was perhaps hardest on their older daughter, Doris Ann, then eleven years of age. Susie, on the other hand, was five years old when they arrived in Washington. She grew up in the city "and was probably not conscious of the fact that she didn't have a father around, because from the time she was born he was immersed." Clearly, the life in politics Bartlett had chosen foreclosed a close family life. It was an occupational hazard.[3]

The war was not over yet when Bartlett arrived in Washington. He was, an associate recalled, "almost like a country boy," feeling his way around Congress and quickly discovering the parsimonious mood among his colleagues for every- thing but the war effort. His office staff was small. It consisted of Mary Lee Council, who had worked for Dimond, and Margery Neil, a daughter of the pioneer Goding family of Skagway, who subsequently married a Washington newspaperman and became Margery Smith. The two could handle the work without difficulty, because "there wasn't that much work. It didn't really accelerate till about 1947 and 1948, and it wasn't because Bob wasn't active in trying to get legislation through." Congress was preoccupied with war and postwar problems.[4]

As his predecessor had been, Bartlett was appointed to serve on eight House committees, among them Indian affairs, merchant marine and fisheries, mines and mining, public lands and territories. The last one in particular was very important, because in some ways it exercised functions over the territory equiva- lent to that of a city council.

Following Tony Dimond's lead, Bartlett continued to seek relief through private bills for various individuals and companies which had suffered losses through the negligence or carelessness of federal agencies. Not only was this kind of private legislation difficult and time-consuming, but successful passage required the delegate to maintain excellent relationships with key committee chairmen and members in both houses, as well as with top-level bureaucrats. Bartlett made friends easily and was well liked. That helped matters immensely. Still, the two examples which follow demonstrate just how involved it was to get the scores of such measures which he sponsored through Congress. The saga of H.R. 802, for the relief of the Alaska Native Brotherhood of Sitka, and the case of Mike Clipper, a fisherman, are typical of the torturous course of such private legislation.

The case of H.R. 802 began early in the spring of 1942, when the Alaska Native Brotherhood (ANB), Camp Number 1, of Sitka agreed to let the Alaska Territorial Guard use the ANB Hall for their drill exercises. No charges were to be assessed, but some time later the city's mayor suggested that the ANB be paid fifty dollars per month for electricity and janitorial services. The ANB received two such payments. At that point, the armed forces stationed at Fort Ray also asked and received permission from the ANB to use the hall. The army agreed to pay all light and fuel bills. Apparently the ANB also understood that the army would carry insurance on the building.

The army, it turned out, monopolized the building from early morning until late at night, every day of the week. The ANB, in effect, had been driven out of its own building.

On January 13, 1943, army personnel had been playing basketball in the ANB hall. They had left at 9:30 P.M., after which two guards extinguished the fire in the heating stove and locked the building. A fire subsequently started in the main room on the ground floor, but because of the blackout arrangements, passersby did not notice the flames inside. The fire burned long enough to reach and shatter the front window in the upper room. Flames escaping through the broken window melted the lead shield of a phone cable, causing a short circuit which set off the fire alarm at 10:15 P.M. Before it was extinguished, the fire had done extensive damage to the interior of the building, estimated at $6,500, including the destruction of lots of equipment.

Appeals by the ANB to the army at Fort Ray to repair the building were unavailing. Consequently, the burned-out building stood empty from January 13 to December 25, 1943, at which point the ANB decided to do the repairs itself, because the community needed the facility. By early January 1944, the building was in use once again.[5]

At that point Leslie Yaw, the superintendent of Sheldon Jackson School in Sitka, on behalf of the native organization, turned for help to Delegate Dimond. Dimond introduced legislation to compensate the Sitka ANB for damages suffered in the amount of $6,500, but he warned Sitkans that there was no way of knowing when Congress would act on the bill.[6]

On November 21, 1944, the War Department finally submitted an unfavorable report on the measure, opposing an award for $6,500 but agreeing to a $6,000 settlement, the amount estimated as sufficient by the army. The War Department claimed that the fire was not caused in whole or in part by any fault or negligence on the part of any member of the armed forces. The army admitted, however, that soldiers had been careless in the use of the building by neglecting to honor the "No Smoking" signs, and although a $6,000 award was "slightly excessive," the War Department was willing to compromise on that sum.[7]

Bartlett had been elected delegate in 1944, and on January 3, 1945, he reintroduced Dimond's bill asking, as the War Department had suggested, for a compensation of $6,000 for the Sitka ANB. The House passed Bartlett's measure on March 20, 1945, and soon thereafter the Senate did likewise. On July 3, 1945, the president signed the measure into law. Five months later, some three years after the fire, the Sitka ANB finally received the check for $6,000.[8]

The case of Mike Clipper, a fisherman, is another example of justice long delayed but finally achieved. It begins in the summer of 1942, when the army employed Clipper as rigger and stevedore at Cold Bay in the Aleutian Islands. Lacking living quarters, the army agreed that he could live on his boat until suitable quarters were built. He tied his boat to the wharf and lived on it until September 20, 1942, when a big storm approached. Two navy tenders, the *Howkan* and *Minnehaha*, which were also tied up along the wharf, were poorly secured and lacked watchmen. The line of the *Howkan* eventually broke, and the tender drifted towards rocks in the channel. At this point the officers in charge ordered Clipper to assist the navy in overtaking the *Howkan* and securing her. Clipper protested and stated that his own boat was endangered. The officers assured him that someone would look after his boat. In the evening, Clipper discovered, much to his dismay, that the storm had tossed his *Dora* onto sandbars. Clipper had lost his boat, the *Dora*, valued at $6,700. It had been his principal source of income. Clipper complained to the navy and army, seeking compensation.[9]

The navy quickly disavowed any responsibility for the loss of the *Dora* "inasmuch as you were employed by the army at the time the loss occurred." The navy advised "that you write the Commanding General, Alaskan Department, with regard to this matter."[10]

Clipper next turned for help to Seward attorney L. V. Ray, who, in turn, contacted Delegate Bartlett and asked for advice. Bartlett decided that the army should settle the matter, and he drafted a private bill to compensate Clipper for his loss. However, Congress did not act on his measure that year. In June 1946 Clipper, unaware of Bartlett's bill, wrote to the delegate, telling him that "i seen Mr. Antony Diman i ast hiem a bout if i could get any thing for the Loss of boat mr. diman advise me to write to you sir and he told me if any thing that could be done that you are in a posison to help me iam all timear in alaska i am old sea farin man and fishr man all i had to depen on for my Leving as my boat to make Leving for me salfe which to bear from sir sincerely yours Mike Clipper." The crudely composed plea to Bartlett expressed Clipper's plight quite adequately.[11]

On January 2, 1948, the Department of the Army finally informed the chairman of the House Committee on the Judiciary that there would be no objection to the passage of Bartlett's private bill if the amount of compensation were scaled down from $6,700 to $3,700, which the army asserted was the true loss figure. Bartlett introduced a new measure with the revised amount on January 3, 1949. The bill passed both houses and became law in 1949. It authorized the secretary of the Treasury to pay Clipper the specified amount of the award, with the stipulation that no more than ten percent of the total be paid in lawyer's fees.[12]

The ANB and the Clipper measures both dealt with minor grievances, but they are typical of the tasks that occupied a significant proportion of the delegate's time. Both required large doses of legwork, exertion, and persuasive lobbying before the pieces of legislation were passed.

In addition to bills such as these, there were many Alaskan housekeeping measures which required congressional approval. These included items as diverse as the protection of fisheries, the sale of a parcel of land to the Catholic bishop of the territory, the authorization for the construction of a hospital for the insane, and permission for municipalities and public utility districts to issue bonds.

As were his predecessors, Bartlett was very much aware of the limitations which the Organic Act of 1912 had placed on the territorial legislature. It was forbidden to alter, amend, or repeal any laws passed by Congress establishing the executive and judicial departments. The federally appointed governor was given veto power, and Congress could repeal any act of the territorial legislature. The legislature was forbidden to pass any law interfering with the primary disposal of the soil, which prevented it from doing anything about the land laws that had already proved to be unworkable. The legislature could not alter the system of license taxes on business and trade imposed by Congress in the Alaska Criminal Code Act of 1899. It also was forbidden to alter the Nelson Act of January 1905, which provided for the allocation of the revenues from the business and trade license taxes for roads, schools, and the care of the insane.[13] The territorial legislature could not regulate the rate of interest on money; could not incorporate cities, towns, or villages; could not change or amend the charter of any town, city, or village; and could not pass laws affecting divorces. Perhaps more galling than all else, the federal government retained control over Alaska's game, fish, and fur seal resources.[14]

Attempts to amend the Organic Act of 1912 had proven unsuccessful. Every previous delegate in Congress, most Alaskan legislators, each of the men who had served as the state's governor, as well as many organizations throughout Alaska had urged Congress since 1912 to increase the territory's autonomy, but no extension of the powers of self-government were ever obtained.

Nevertheless, Bartlett followed in his predecessors' footsteps and attempted to have the Organic Act of 1912 amended and revised. To this end, in almost every session between 1945 and 1955, he introduced measures for an elective as well as resident governor and secretary of Alaska. By 1955 he realized the futility of the situation and discontinued submitting such bills.

In 1945 territorial representative Stanley J. McCutcheon of Anchorage introduced a memorial that passed the territorial House but not the Senate. It called for many changes in the Organic Act of 1912. Governor Gruening urged Bartlett to try to have Congress pass such an amended organic act for Alaska. "Public opinion will support [the amendments]," he asserted, and "the point of it is that we may not get statehood for several years, but if these changes can be made they would help us definitely in the direction of self-government."[15]

By early summer of 1945, Bartlett had asked for, and had received, a draft measure revising the Civil Government Act of 1900 and the Organic Act of 1912. Although Bartlett liked the draft, he was disturbed that no provisions were made for turning natural resource management over to the territory. One of the important provisions called on the federal government to turn over all income taxes collected in Alaska to the territorial government. Bartlett did not think that the federal government would ever accept such a scheme, and even if it did, he wondered if it would be "altogether desirable, because once we had this golden flow, would we ever be able to accept statehood?"[16] Bartlett circulated the draft widely among friends and acquaintances, asking for comments and suggestions. He received many, yet he was still uncertain whether he should introduce the measure. He worried that passage might signal to Congress that Alaska's governmental status had been clarified and improved, and as such be "highly damaging to our statehood aspirations."[17]

By late fall of 1945 Bartlett still had not decided whether to introduce the measure. Several members of the House Committee on Territories had told him "that to amend the Organic Act at this time would be to postpone indefinitely statehood for the Territory." On the other hand, Congressman Hardin Peterson, the chairman of the committee, urged Bartlett to introduce the revised organic act "so as to have something for discussion." Bartlett and Gruening finally decided to drop the measure for the time being in anticipation of the territory-wide referendum planned for 1946. If the vote was positive, Alaskans would be interested only in statehood. If the vote was negative, Bartlett then would introduce the revised organic act.[18]

While Bartlett was slowly finding his way in Washington, momentous events were occurring elsewhere. By spring of 1945 it was evident that the war in Europe would soon end. President Roosevelt, who had been ailing for some time, died on April 12, 1945, and Vice-President Harry S. Truman succeeded him. The news of the president's death caught Bartlett, like most Americans, by surprise. Bob, Vide, and Mary Lee Council were working in the office when the news first reached them about 6 P.M. "We all said in one breath, 'I don't believe it.'" Then there was a rush to the radio and the sad news was confirmed. "I think everyone felt a very keen personal loss," Council observed. The three speculated on the effect the president's death would have on the United States and on the world. The atmosphere in Washington was very subdued, and "poor Truman gets scrutinized for every move he makes, including every time he mops his brow."[19]

Early in 1945 Bartlett appeared before the House for the first time in what was to become an annual ritual, namely the defense of the Alaskan items in the Department of the Interior budget. Bartlett pointed out that "in a unique sense we are dependent upon what Congress does or fails to do for us by means of this supply bill." He briefly mentioned the functions that the various agencies within the department performed in Alaska. In addition, he pointed out that the Alaska Road Commission and the Alaska Railroad employed a sizable number of territorial residents. Alaska, Bartlett maintained, had become an important link in America's defense network, and now national and even international attention focused on the North. Bartlett predicted a rush of settlers to Alaska. He concluded that as long as the federal government so totally dominated territorial activities, Alaskans had to turn to Washington for help; yet "we shall do so with no sense of diffidence, no feeling we are requesting something to which we are not altogether entitled."[20]

In the meantime, the war in Europe ended when Germany surrendered unconditionally on May 8, 1945. At the end of May Bartlett traveled to Europe on an inspection trip as a member of the Committee on Military Affairs. It was his first trip overseas. Bartlett wrote his observations as the army transport plane crossed the Atlantic Ocean: "We were flying towards the rising sun almost as soon as it had set in the northern sky. There was a very brief period of darkness and then — Ireland. It was first a dark patch and then could be distinguished more clearly. To this eye it appeared much like the country around Point Barrow at first—a myriad of lakes—and then more settled. Before too long—it is never long with the four motors of the C-54—we were flying over Belfast and then across the Irish Sea to England. It was like a story book picture — all neat and checker-boarded and green. At 1:15 A.M. May 31, thirteen hours to the minute from the take-off, we landed at the American airport [near London]." But, unhappily, "because the globe rotates or because of some other reason sufficiently explored by science, it was not 1:15 at all but 7:15 A.M. The English use double daylight saving, which would indicate they are twice as foolish as we are."

From the airport the congressional group drove twenty-eight miles to London: "Everything one had read about England at once leaped to life. The winding, narrow streets, the hedges, the roadside inns, the bicycles in great number, the two decker busses—all these were at once instantly present."

All was new and different for Bartlett. His group was billeted at the Cumberland Hotel across from Hyde Park, "which, contrary to any thought I may have had, is huge and extends for blocks and blocks." Above the huge bathtub in his hotel room was a bell for the chambermaid: "I refrained from ringing it while in the tub. The bath towels could be used for sheets or blankets. They are big enough." Bartlett and committee members traveled to Southhampton and Newport in Wales, where they inspected American installations. Bartlett found the climate to be much like Juneau's, with a lot of rain, and the country to be wonderfully green. "Have seen two possibly pretty women," he reported, "but suspect both were Americans. Women incredibly homely, a judgment given by all of us old rascals."

English rations were very slim, he observed, and "we are living by comparison in super-abundance." From England the party flew to Cherbourg. "One trouble is natives speak French," Bartlett commented. They visited "Omaha Beach", one of the locations where the Allies had landed in 1944. From France the party traveled to Bremen in devastated Germany, as well as to various other towns. They visited Paris and then returned to the United States. For Bartlett it had been an intensely interesting, if sometimes confusing, visit.[21]

Back from overseas, Bartlett lunged once again into his work. Unlike his predecessor, however, he could not get visitors out of his office. Margery Smith recalls that they "would come in and they'd start chatting and Bob would let them ramble on and on." Dimond had been more adept: "Tony would listen a gracious amount of time to goodness knows what kind of malarkey—but if people have come that far you have to give them the time of day. But then after they'd been there a proper time he just got up and walked over to them and thanked them deeply for giving him the advantage for having their thinking on the subject."[22]

The first two years Bartlett spent "learning the atmosphere of Capitol Hill. He was never discourteous to anyone. He was adored by the charwomen, the elevator operators, the committee staffs." He saw his function, in part, as one of obtaining federal monies for the territory. "It was just an established way of life" that congressional committees routinely reviewed Alaskan appropriation requests but automatically gave the same amount which had been given the previous year. For Bartlett, that was not good enough. "He was a marvel at telling the story as it was," Smith remembers. "He could point to the direct need" for a particular request.[23]

Like most members of Congress, Bartlett did not draft his own bills. To staff members, "Bob would express his aim, or what he was trying to achieve, over cups of coffee. . . . Various committee staffs drafted the bills, would come in and have a jam session with Bob, he'd pick their brains, and he would direct their thinking around so that they were thinking the way he wanted them to think. He was a genius at that, but he knew his subjects, he knew them thoroughly. He had a knack for putting his finger on the crux of a matter that was absolutely fantastic. He got to know the quirks and the idiosyncrasies of every member of any committee on which he served." Not having a vote himself, Bartlett quickly learned that the only way to achieve anything was to know the influential people very well and then state and develop a case adequately and quickly.[24]

One of these influential individuals was Congressman Mike Kirwan of Ohio. Margery Smith recalls "Mike hadn't gone beyond the third or fifth grade. He had been a railroad engineer. He got to Congress and stayed, and he got to be in a position of power. Bob would come into the committee with his requests for the Alaska funds and Mike would say, 'This is going to be off the record.' Mike had a lot of demands for Army-Navy football tickets so he would say to Bob, 'How many tickets this year?' And Bob would say, 'Will eight help, sir?' And Mike would say, 'That's just fine,' and then they would go back on the record and deal with the requests." In Mike Kirwan's committee there rarely was any discussion about the justification or merit of the monies Bartlett requested. "Mike would practically rap the gavel and say, 'That's O.K., that's O.K.' He just went like that year after year."[25]

Aided by his friendly and unpretentious personality and his knowledge of how Congress worked, Bartlett quickly became a very successful delegate. After Congress had adjourned in the fall of 1947, he was able to report that twelve measures he had introduced had passed both houses and had been signed into law by the president. A thirteenth still awaited the chief executive's signature. In fact, aside from legislation sponsored by committee chairmen, Bartlett was the author of more successful bills than any single member of the House or Senate. Bartlett's bills ranged from one allowing a nonprofit interdenominational corporation to purchase some thirty-five acres for use as a recreational camp for youngsters to one which directed that 37.5 percent of all monies received from the sales, royalties, or rentals of Alaska's public lands support the territory's public education and roads.[26]

Bartlett's constituency expected him to deal effectively with the federal government and to work for increased federal expenditures. The delegate was successful in meeting these expectations of his constituency, who returned him to Congress every two years.

Campaigns and Elections

HEN BARTLETT FIRST SOUGHT elective office in 1944, Alaskan politicians played on a small stage before a limited audience. Candidates personally knew most of their constituents, with whom they shared similar work experiences and life-styles. Political issues were mostly local, and whenever national concerns intruded, politicans and their constituents interpreted these in the context of their implications for the North.

As Alaska's delegate in Congress, Bartlett spoke for a territory that had the nation's smallest population and largest land area. As the territory's sole representative, his work load at any time was very large indeed. To get the work done, he had to spend most of his time in Washington. An Alaskan visit required a ten-thousand-mile round trip, with six time zone changes each way, in addition to many more thousands of miles of travel within Alaska itself.

The position of delegate was an important one, since the federal government controlled more than 97 percent of the territory's land area, contributed millions of dollars to the Alaskan economy, and also employed a sizable segment of Alaska's working force. Alaska clearly was a bureaucrat's dream, for nowhere else under the U.S. flag had the federal government such a grip on the lives of American citizens. Cutting a tree, building a house, harvesting wild game and fish, or going into business, Alaskans found that bureaucrats were on hand to issue regulations. Alaskans therefore needed an energetic delegate as their Washington spokesman, somebody who promoted territorial interests in the Congress, the executive branch, and the federal bureaucracy.

Although he was a non-voting member of the House of Representatives, Bartlett, like his colleagues, still had to run for reelection every second year. During his campaigns Bartlett traveled extensively within Alaska and met and talked with large and small groups of residents. His speeches were informal and focused on local problems and issues. Increasingly, he could point to his accomplishments in Congress which included private bills for the relief of numerous constituents, increased federal appropriations for various Alaskan projects, and

75

major public measures which had become law, such as the Alaska Mental Health Enabling Act of 1956. Candidates, and particularly Bartlett, were supported more on the basis of friendship than of party membership, because the small population allowed candidates to become acquainted with, or at least meet, most voters.

A certain informality also characterized northern politics. Governor Gruening, for example, was startled because Alaskans merely dropped in and expected to see the governor without delay. When Gruening traveled around Alaska, "callers seldom bothered even to announce themselves or to knock before they entered [his] room, and it might be any time of the night or day." Gruening resignedly observed that "it was all part of the natural democracy of the time and place."[1]

Calling a politician an outsider could spell defeat. Bartlett was a sourdough, or old-timer, a fact he was careful to reiterate over the years and impress upon his constituents. When campaigning in Alaska, Bartlett dressed for the occasion in his "suit"—a wool shirt with several pockets, an ivory string tie, and some sort of baggy pants that gave him the proper rumpled appearance.

Bartlett was considerably cheered when his political mentor, Judge Dimond, reported to him at the end of his first year in office that Alaskans appreciated the delegate's work, that he was "strong and popular and [could] be reelected without difficulty in 1946." Dimond speculated that Bartlett probably would not want to be a candidate in 1948, but he was wrong. He had become an astute student of Congress. The delegate had found his life's work.

Bartlett's Republican opponent in 1946 was Almer J. Peterson, an Anchorage attorney. Peterson had replaced L.V. Ray, a Seward attorney who had been a candidate and had suddenly died.[2]

After accompanying Secretary of the Interior Julius Krug on an inspection trip to Alaska in the summer of 1946, Bartlett stayed behind to campaign against Peterson. In mid-September he reported to Vide that "the old man is becoming weary; so weary he finds it increasingly difficult to write letters by the time each busy day is done." The Republicans were well organized and working hard, while the Democrats were "confronted by our usual state of disorganization." From Anchorage, Bartlett and territorial senator Steve McCutcheon flew to Seldovia, Homer, and Bristol Bay for campaign appearances. In Fairbanks next, Bartlett reported that the town thoroughly depressed him: "It is miserable. Despite all the money that has floated around, houses are unpainted and look gloomy and run down; dust is everywhere."[3]

There were few issues in the campaign. Bartlett pointed to his "flawless record as our present delegate to Congress." He stated that he had been educated at the universities of Alaska and Washington—but did not add that he had spent a total of three semesters at both institutions. The delegate criticized the U.S. Fish and Wildlife Service for its neglect of Alaska's game resources. In the fall of 1930, for example, the caribou herd south of Fairbanks on the Richardson Highway had numbered 500,000 animals. At the time of Bartlett's 1946 campaign, the Fish and Wildlife Service estimated that there were only about 100,000 in the whole territory. Alaskans needed to manage their own fish and game resources to reverse the trend, he asserted.[4]

By early October the delegate felt that he was "a cinch. The only place where a contrary opinion was expressed was at Anchorage." Acquaintances believed Bartlett would have to work very hard to win there. Other people told Bartlett that his opponent would not win but that the Republicans were having Peterson run merely to build up a good vote which would be helpful to a stronger candidate in 1948. Bartlett was "on the wagon," he assured Vide, "so you don't have to worry about that angle this time and no desire either, so maybe there is no right to take any credit."[5]

Campaigning without his wife was a lonely business, he confided: "I surely am anxious to see you. It must be love. Must be. Even after 16 years. Make me awful mad now if some airplane south bound would lose a wing."[6]

A few days later, Bartlett had virtually lost his voice due to his many speaking engagements. He considered that a terrific handicap for "a politician in the closing days of a campaign." In southeastern Alaska at the time, Bartlett flew from town to town, Juneau to Hoonah, Pelican to Sitka, back to Juneau, then Petersburg, Kake, Wrangell and Ketchikan. By October 5, Bartlett calculated that he had spent a total of 96.5 hours in airplanes.

The polls opened on Tuesday, October 8. Bartlett was in Juneau. "Eleven A.M. in Juneau; 9 A.M. in Fairbanks and Anchorage; 8 A.M. and the polls just opening in Nome. Hurray! I have my campaign suit on, a sure sign of victory. I have a big breakfast under my belt . . . the terrific rains of yesterday have ceased. It is a Bartlett day," he exulted. "It's in the bag. No reservations. An outright prediction." He was correct, receiving 11,516 votes to Peterson's 4,868, or a respectable 70 percent of the votes cast for delegate. Bartlett had received $4,590 in contributions, $287.32 of which had been spent on advertisements in newspapers and on two radio addresses.[7]

Two years pass quickly when having to face reelection during the second year. In 1948 Delegate Bartlett stressed his abilities to divert federal monies to Alaskan programs. The delegate prepared careful summaries of the various federal programs that aided each of Alaska's four judicial divisions. In the First Judicial Division, these programs ranged from a $716,000 deficiency appropriation to meet the higher construction costs of the 200-bed sanitarium at Mount Edgecumbe on Japonski Island near Sitka to federal cooperation in the operation of the Ketchikan Fishery Laboratory. In the Second Judicial Division, Congress had authorized the construction of a seawall at Nome to protect that community from tidal storms and had appropriated $14,600,000 to the Department of the Navy for continuation of exploratory work on Naval Petroleum Reserve Number 4 for another three years. For the Third Judicial Division, Bartlett listed projects ranging from an $8,000,000 international airport at Anchorage to $11,370,000 for construction of the Turnagain Arm Road that joined Anchorage to the Kenai Peninsula. For the Fourth Judicial Divison, he pointed out the $950,000 for the construction of a geophysical institute at the University of Alaska in Fairbanks, the $2,250,000 for surfacing the first seventy miles of the Richardson Highway south of Fairbanks, and the expenditure of millions of military dollars at Ladd and Eielson airfields. Territorial voters expressed their confidence in Bartlett by giving him 79 percent of the total votes cast for delegate. He received 17,520 votes, while his Republican rival, R.H. Stock, an Anchorage contractor, received 4,789 votes.[8]

On January 6,1950, Bartlett again filed for reelection to his job. And again he decided to make federal appropriations, coupled with the pending statehood bill, a keystone of his campaign. From January until the election on October 10, Alaskan papers carried items outlining congressional generosity toward Alaska. At the end of May, for instance, voters learned that, under the statehood measure then pending before the Senate, the proposed State of Alaska would be authorized to select twenty million acres of land. In July Bartlett announced that Congress had earmarked an unprecedented $215,093,304 for the territory.[9] There were other benefits, such as a fifth United States district judge and monies for the construction of a hydroelectric plant at Eklutna near Anchorage. All these benefits, voters could understand, were traceable to their delegate's hard work.

In September Bartlett opened his campaign in Nome. He estimated that his chances for reelection were very good indeed. "The people are most friendly," and it looked like "a shoo-in." Nome residents always responded well to him, and Bartlett considered it good luck to begin his campaigns in that town.[10]

Bartlett traveled widely that fall. From Fairbanks he flew to McGrath and Bethel, where he was met at the airfield by friends. They all adjourned to the roadhouse for dinner. After dinner a community meeting took place in the schoolhouse. After having been a reporter," Bartlett stated, "I fail to understand why anyone goes to such a meeting voluntarily." From Bethel, weather permitting, he intended to visit Holy Cross, Nulato, Galena, Ruby, Tanana, Manley Hot Springs, and Nenana and then return to Fairbanks. He got stuck in Ruby because of foul weather. Privately, the river towns depressed him: "Uniformly they are down at the heels even when it would seem unnecessary for them to be". But Bartlett felt no need to lecture the few residents of these villages about this point of view.[11]

By the middle of September, the constant movement had tired the delegate. "Once more in the air," he told his wife. "The succession of takeoffs and landings is beginning to seem endless. Maybe I am getting a bit tired." Bush flying was also dangerous, as stories of spectacular crashes often reminded him. Flying from Kotzebue to Fairbanks, "we first passed over Anvil Mountain five miles from Nome, where last Saturday a Douglas plane crashed in a fog killing all aboard — the pilot, his wife, copilot and a passenger. The flier and his wife leave a year-old baby in Fairbanks." While flying to Nome, the weather turned foul, and the pilot had to make an instrument landing. With the crash fresh in his mind, Bartlett protested that he did not like instrument landings.

There were endless rounds of visiting. He was lonely for his family, and ready to go home, but four weeks remained in the campaign. Contributions had been very slow in coming, "the leanest year ever," although the territorial Democratic Central committee paid for his transportation. Fatigue induced a measure of depression. At this point Bartlett was ready to forego the biennial rounds: "I've had it. And for no special reason."

To add to his dejection, there were other tragedies. One involved George McNabb, a young Fairbanks attorney, who owned a float plane that both he and his wife piloted. Just after landing on the river, a girl stepped out on a pontoon to help, and the propeller decapitated her.[12] In another instance, the campaign party had just taken off from McGrath when they saw the wreckage of a float plane. It had crashed just that morning, in a dense fog, killing both flyers. In addition, "a soldier fell from a boat in front of town and was drowned day before yesterday. Two people went crazy yesterday. So there has been no lack of excitement," Bartlett concluded, "most of it tragic."[13]

A few days before the general election, the *Anchorage Daily Times* stated that Bartlett, the incumbent, was favored heavily over his Republican opponent, Almer J. Peterson. The Republican, however, was putting up a good fight. For the first time in years, the "white" and "black" factions of the Republican party were cooperating. Albert White, the controversial Republican boss of Juneau and Monrovia, California, was aggressively leading their drive. He accused the Democrats of having harbored "corruption, malfeasance, and misfeasance" in office. Democrats replied that they had initiated actions to oust accused officials. Despite these accusations against Democrats, the voters responded to Bartlett's appeal once more. He defeated Peterson for a second time with 13,588 to 5,138 votes, or approximately 73 percent of the total vote cast for delegate.[14]

CHAPTER

Surviving the 1952 Republican Landslide

THROUGHOUT THE NATION, and in Alaska as well, the Democrats had been in control since 1932. Any group that long at the helm develops a certain arrogance of power and a concomitant sloppiness in governmental performance. Added to this were revelations about the inevitable corruption and bribery in high places. In addition, the White House had been performing in a stumbling manner. Taken together with the widespread frustration with the continuing war in Korea and Red-menace hysteria, Democratic aspirants for elective office knew they would have difficulties at the polls in 1952.

The power-starved Republicans exhibited increasing irresponsibility, losing the faith of an electorate which had rejected it in five straight presidential elections. The minority party was determined at all costs to discredit the Democrats. Exposing wrongdoing and incompetence was its duty, but the Republicans' savage attacks on Secretary of State Dean Acheson and Secretary of Defense General George C. Marshall, honorable and decent men, were quite another matter.

Bob Bartlett observed all the acrimony from close to its source in Washington. He sensed the mood of the country, which demanded change. He listened to the "old guard" wing of the Republican party categorizing the Democrats into criminals, traitors, cowards; incompetents who always blundered into war; and effete who lacked sufficient vigor to invade China and conquer it. In normal times, politicians who differ usually tolerate one another. But these were not normal times, and by the fall of 1951 the oratorical thrust had driven a deep schism between the parties and the individuals who represented them.

Bartlett had spent two months in Alaska in the fall of 1951. There he had felt the same deepening schism between the parties. Obviously next year's election would be a difficult one. Bartlett had never taken any election for granted, but he realized that 1952 would require extraordinary efforts to survive the expected Republican landslide.

It was a conservative Democrat who fired the first salvo of the campaign on October 11, 1951. Neil F. Moore, the auditor of Alaska, asked the delegate to make an accounting of some fifteen thousand dollars of Alaska Statehood Committee funds that had been at Bartlett's disposal. Moore related that several rumors had been circulating in Alaska pertaining to these monies. One of these alleged that Bartlett had turned over five thousand dollars to the financially hard-pressed editor and publisher of the pro-statehood *Ketchikan Alaska Chronicle.* Chief among the rumor-mongers was Jim Beard, the editor of the *Daily Alaska Empire* of Juneau, long critical of the Gruening administration in Alaska and of Bartlett's performance in Washington. Committee members quickly realized that Moore intended to embarrass, and perhaps even discredit, not only Delegate Bartlett but the Alaska Statehood Committee as well. Several Alaska Statehood Committee members, therefore, decided to play along and "perhaps needle these rumor-mongers to the point where they will be publishing this rumor as an established fact. After we get them out on a limb it will be very simple to cut it off." Presumably, once fiction had been published as fact, the statehood committee or the delegate might sue the *Daily Alaska Empire* for defamation of character.[1]

Bartlett reacted angrily to Moore's allegations. Clearly they were politically inspired and "so obviously designed to hurt my reputation and that of Mr. William L. Baker (the Ketchican publisher)" that he "did what any self-respecting man would have done—I told Moore. . .to go jump in the lake." That advice, however momentarily satisfying it may have been to Bartlett, did not end the matter. Various newspapers picked up the allegations, and the dispute between the auditor and the delegate dogged Bartlett for more than a year. It also became something of a campaign issue.[2]

One bright spot in the coming election was that, for the first time since 1944, no Democrat opposed Bartlett in the April primary. In December 1951 the delegate and his Republican adversary, Bob Reeve, an Anchorage Republican who was also unopposed, announced their candidacies for the delegateship.

Destitute and sick, Reeve had arrived in the little town of Valdez in 1932. The thirty-year-old had already lived an adventurous life. Among other exploits, he had participated in World War I, had served in the Chinese Maritime Customs Service on the Yangtze and Hai rivers out of Shanghai and Tientsin, and had flown the mails for Pan American-Grace Airways in South America. In Alaska Reeve became known for his daring glacier landings in the Prince William Sound area. He was also famous as the man who, in 1948, had shot the world's largest-recorded known bear, a record not toppled until 1953. Reeve eventually became the founder and owner of Reeve Aleutian Airways and several other businesses in Anchorage. Popular throughout Alaska, well financed, and with easy access to air transportation, Reeve appeared to be a formidable opponent. Bartlett soon convinced himself that Reeve, "a nonpolitical creature," had decided to oppose the delegate "solely from a desire to exact revenge," because Reeve had been "embittered at me ever since I refused to urge that boat service to the Westward be discontinued so that he could carry mail (and freight and express too!) on his airplanes."[3]

There appeared to be great sentiment for change at the local and territorial levels in Alaska, and Bartlett was visibly nervous. He admitted that most of his previous opponents had been severely handicapped by the fact that they were well known in their own communities but not elsewhere. This always had given Bartlett a tremendous head start and an advantage. Nineteen fifty-two would be different.[4]

There was no doubt that Reeve was a likeable fellow in his own crusty fashion, respected by Alaska's fraternity of commercial and bush pilots and admired by the sourdoughs for killing the biggest bear. Bartlett comforted himself, however, by reasoning that at least the Alaskan aviation industry itself would not support his adversary, because Washington connections would put Reeve, as head of an operating airline, at a substantial competitive advantage. As for the affection of the sourdoughs — Bartlett would give his opponent a run for his money on that score.[5]

Early in that year Reeve looked like a winner. He had entered politics as a shining knight, "untouched by intercession in or connected with any of the burning political issues of past years." The delegate consoled himself that his opponent's armor would eventually be "dented and dirtied." Reeve would soon "have to declare himself — and specifically — on the issues." At that point, undoubtedly, Reeve would please some Alaskans and antagonize others. Taking a stand on issues always created divisions. "It would be nice and sweet and simple if he [Reeve] could run on a platform with such laudable planks as doubling the price of gold. His discovery will be that those generalities will not suffice."

Reeve started campaigning early in the year. Bartlett was in Washington, watching his opponent's moves and soliciting intelligence and advice on strategy from his many Alaskan friends. Frank Barr, an Alaska Airlines pilot and an old friend who had flown the delegate into many bush communities in previous elections, reported that what most impressed him about Reeve was the candidate's ability "to murder the King's English, his dissatisfaction with the administration under which he made all his money, and his ignorance of what you have been doing in Washington." But Reeve had started early and was spending some of "his money to convince the people that he is the ideal man for the job. If you haven't got the money," Barr advised the delegate, "then you better spend some time. Remember I still have my own airplane and am not too decrepit to fly. . . ."[6]

From Juneau Vernon M. Metcalfe advised Bartlett that a Reeve campaign appearance in that city had not gone too well. Reeve had read a monotonous speech woodenly. The Republicans had recorded it for posterity but now were apparently not too sure that "they want posterity to hear same . . . I think it is a shame that the Territory will be deprived of hearing this epic."

Metcalfe reported that the adversary press and "De Armond are raising their usual brand of hell" about the five thousand dollars of statehood committee money which Bartlett allegedly had transferred to Willam Baker. Metcalfe was referring to Robert N. De Armond, conservative Juneau newspaperman and historian, who had authored a widely distributed column entitled "A Northern Notebook." De Armond had begun to refer to the delegate as Seattle-born Edward Lewis "No Audits" Bartlett, Governor Gruening's Washington bird dog. Bartlett felt uncomfortable at being tied too closely to Ernest Gruening. Although the two were good friends and often agreed on issues, the governor had made many enemies in Alaska over the years—and these Bartlett was unwilling to share. But it was the reference to being Seattle-born that most enraged Bartlett. He prided himself in being a sourdough, a true Alaskan. To be branded as an outsider could be a real political disadvantage with Alaska's parochial voters.[7]

Soon the *Daily Alaska Empire* of Juneau, although nominally a Democratic paper, endorsed Bob Reeve for the delegateship and continued to criticize Bartlett and the Gruening administration. The governor considered this a sign that, for the first time in months, things were looking up, because "the Empire hasn't picked a winner in years. Its support of Reeve will be a kiss of death." Gruening thought that Bartlett could feel reasonably confident of election. He scathingly described Jim Beard, who managed the paper for its owner, Mrs. Helen Troy Monsen, as "the pimp in the journalistic whorehouse of which Helen is the madam."[8]

The *Empire* criticized the delegate's record at length. The editor asked why Bartlett planned to introduce a bill that would eliminate fish traps in Alaskan waters over a five-year period. Did Bartlett merely want publicity? Perhaps the delegate intended to destroy Alaska's major industry. Without traps, maintained the *Empire*, salmon in the can would soon be in the same price bracket as caviar, truffles, and hummingbird's tongues. The editor suggested that in Bartlett's "spare time, when he isn't pushing statehood or some of Gruening's brainstorms," he should represent the people who had elected him. As far as the editor was able to determine, Bartlett had miserably failed Alaska's 130,000 residents.[9]

Bartlett did not have to answer the criticisms, because his friends did so for him. Kenneth Bowman, a southeastern Alaskan Democrat, reminded Monsen that Democrats had unanimously requested that the delegate introduce legislation abolishing fish traps. Bowman accused Monsen of having aligned herself with selfish forces "which have primarily their self-perpetuation at heart, and not the economic development and welfare of Alaska or its resources." In the past, Bowman reminded Monsen, he had defended the paper and its role of critic. Unfortunately, he felt that the editorial policy of the *Empire* now reflected the national trend of Taft Republicans, maligning and defaming the Democratic party, its members, and office holders—and that could not be considered Democratic under any circumstances. Bowman concluded that "there is very little line of demarcation between ultra-conservatism and Fascism, Naziism, and the now encroaching menace of Communism. Remember," he cautioned, "these three ISMS showed no consideration for the popular will of the people."[10]

The Republican party in Alaska made a determined effort to discredit Bartlett, and Republican themes for the campaign took shape rapidly. Republicans told audiences that, although Bartlett had pushed for federal expenditures in Alaska, these monies had gone into various socialistic schemes, "[without a] dime for positive and absolute development of Alaska or business and industry." Fishermen were being told that the delegate had "deliberately. played around with the antifishtrap bill by not pushing it in committee" and by not working for its support among members of Congress. The proposed elective-governor bill, the Republicans claimed, had been shelved by Bartlett in part to perpetuate Governor Ernest Gruening in office. They also declared that the statehood bills Bartlett had introduced did not confer enough land on the proposed state nor convey adequate controls over Alaska's resources. Reeve hammered home the idea that Americans had to return to free enterprise, that creeping socialism had to be destroyed.[11]

Such talk certainly appealed to many Alaskan newcomers voting there for the first time and to those people "with twelve-year-old mentalities. . . ." Republicans, said Gruening, solicited both categories of voters.[12]

In his widely read column, De Armond attacked Bartlett and the "Gruening branch" of the Democratic party in Alaska for their many shortcomings. Don't be fooled by the Democrats' cry of smear tactics, he warned, because such complaints were only to distract voters. "And the sorry crew of candidates the Gruening gang is running for office," De Armond stated, "come from the dregs of both parties." The big issue of the campaign concerned the fifteen thousand dollars of taxpayers' money which had been sent to Washington some years ago "to be dished out by the delegate in Congress. . ." in furtherance of statehood. Bartlett refused an audit, although he had previously stated that "he had all of the figures down in his little black book." De Armond recalled that earlier Bartlett had insisted that public officials should have "the very brightest lights" turned on them. "All that is wanted," De Armond concluded, "is a measly little two candlepower light on one account book for a few minutes."[13]

Basically the Republicans promised to do the same things the Democrats had been doing for so long—only better and more efficiently. They appealed to those who disliked the changes Alaska had been experiencing, and they fretted about the increasing bureaucracy, the growing budget, the demands for more governmental services, and the prospect of Alaska statehood.

Yet Bob Reeve did not share such concerns. He urged Alaskan voters to elect an old-time bush pilot, business leader, and employer. He would "help cure our present difficulties. They are many, and a strong and fearless fighter and producer can lick them by an honest approach and a strong-willed determination." Reeve alluded to many problems, including fishing and land controversies, the need for roads and better schools, the improvement of opportunities for Alaska's natives, the development of Alaskan lands and minerals, better care for the old and needy, and the development of a good statehood bill that the people could accept with confidence. "Free enterprise," Reeve continuously reminded his audiences, "had made Alaska and pulled us out of the doldrums many times in the past." Reeve asked that voters "elect a man who has helped build Alaska with his own hands and blood and sweat and knows the bad along with the good." This down-to-earth approach typified Reeve's election efforts.[14]

In a series of Jefferson–Jackson Day banquets, Governor Gruening answered Republican charges of "creeping or leaping socialism." Gruening declared that if Reeve really did oppose government subsidy or assistance as he claimed, he showed himself to be something of a hypocrite: "This loud-voiced campaigner . . . has not mentioned that to his success as a private enterpriser the federal government in the last four years has contributed — not loaned, but paid — over half a million dollars in air mail subsidies. That isn't creeping or even leaping socialism . . . that would be 'flying socialism.'" Gruening had not heard that Reeve had refused "any of this dough, or offered to turn it back!" Why didn't Reeve practice what he preached? Gruening concluded that Reeve was "just another fellow, who, down at the heels and out at the elbows when he came to Alaska at the end of the Republican era twenty years ago, has been made prosperous by Democratic policies."[15]

When Alaskans trooped to the polls in the open Alaska primary on April 30, 1952, they set a new turn-out record. Republicans polled so many votes that observers gave them a good chance of electing most of their ticket in the October general election. Although receiving more votes than Reeve, Bartlett's leading margin was slim. The delegate was discouraged: "What set me back on my heels was not the fact that I received a terrific thumping in Juneau, Reeve's lead there being almost enough to overcome the plurality I had rolled up in the entire Fourth Division; what dismayed me was that in Ketchikan I barely squeaked through and in Sitka, which has been a veritable Democratic fortress, I was kicked right in the teeth."[16]

The Democrats had taken a most dreadful shellacking. In a postelection analysis of the primary, most Bartlett advisers agreed that Reeve had campaigned effectively, working hard and spending liberally. Voters had expressed a desire for change rather than a concern for the issues, which had involved the level of federal spending in Alaska and the delegate's record in Washington as Alaska's watchdog. Bartlett's running battle with auditor Moore over the fifteen thousand dollars in statehood funds had unsettled the voters. Many of them apparently suspected corruption in the handling of the statehood funds, and publicity about Democratic corruption at the national level had not helped the situation. Bartlett's active backing of Democratic sourdough Bobby Sheldon against Moore and his attacks on Moore had backfired, because voters viewed Moore as "the honest little guy who fears no one and is willing to take on the big boys," in Bartlett's view.

Appointments of inept candidates to territorial positions also had damaged the Democrats. Furthermore, Alaska, despite its physical size, constituted a relatively small community where waste and inefficiency could personally be observed and criticized. Any state or federal agency in New York, for example, could be employing a hundred more people than necessary, and millions of citizens would not know the difference. Territorial or federal employees in Juneau doing their shopping during business hours were noticed and resented by taxpayers.[17]

Democratic campaign conduct had been flawed. Although Governor Gruening's speeches at Jefferson-Jackson day banquets in various Alaskan communities that spring had been generally well received, the affair in Juneau had been disastrous. Gruening's speech and the banquet were preceded by hefty drinking in the Bubble Room of the Baranof Hotel and in Secretary of Alaska Joseph W. Kehoe's private apartment. Both the secretary and his wife had appeared at the banquet "completely plastered." J. Gerald Williams, the territorial attorney general, seemed "to have fallen off the wagon with a boom, after maintaining a dry status for some months. . . ." In any event, he "made a star-spangled Jackass of himself." Peter Wood, the master of ceremonies, "was in little better state." Worse yet, some of the proceedings had been broadcast over the radio, where amazed listeners heard the booing of the drunk attorney general and the master of ceremonies' reprimand: "Shut up, you damn fools, you are on the air." One listener had observed that, although this had been a dinner honoring the memories of Thomas Jefferson and Andrew Jackson, it had sounded on the radio like New Year's eve at Duffy's Tavern. All this had left a sour taste with the voters.[18]

The Democrats had committed many blunders, and the Republican press had been quick to capitalize on these and feed the suspicions of the Alaskan electorate. Whatever else the outcome of the primary may have done, it certainly convinced Bartlett "to get on his horse and walk, trot, canter, and gallop very energetically" during the remainder of the campaign.[19]

While still in Washington, Bartlett formulated a campaign strategy. He would build a political organization in the territory and collect a sizeable war chest so he could spend freely on advertising of all kinds. But, most importantly, he decided to conduct an aggressive campaign and to concede nothing to partisan charges.[20]

The delegate arrived in Alaska in July, bringing with him folders of statements his opponent had made in Alaska's settlements and towns. Many were contradictory, and Bartlett intended to use this material. He anticipated finding an unfavorable political situation but one which could be redeemed through hard work. It was far worse than he had expected. Stopping in Wrangell, Bartlett found that nobody on the street except the town's Catholic priest would even speak to him: "To my surprise and shock and even horror, I discovered that my channels of communication, good as I had believed them to be, had not conveyed to me the full measure of the political right-about face on the part of the public. I sensed at once that not only the general Democratic ticket was in danger, but that I too might be counted among the casualties." In the face of these realities, Bartlett decided to campaign extensively in the sparsely populated Second Judicial Division, where Nome was the focal town, and to do the same in the Third Judicial Division, where Anchorage was the main population center. He expected to lose heavily in southeastern Alaska, but if his strategy worked, his winning margins in the second and fourth divisions would offset his losses in the third and first.[21]

Bartlett waged his campaign on a broad front. A friend and sympathizer had donated the use of a plane piloted by Frank Barr, an old friend and political associate. This allowed the delegate to visit most settlements along Alaska's major rivers. Bartlett's Washington staff had prepared a campaign newsletter summarizing the delegate's congressional accomplishments, which they mass mailed. The delegate also left copies of it liberally along the trail of his campaign.[22]

Bartlett's first priority was to repair the damage done by his dispute with auditor Moore. The delegate reviewed the history of the issue, pointing out that the territorial legislature had created a bipartisan statehood committee in 1949, which had transferred fifteen thousand dollars to the delegate to further the cause of statehood. All accounting of these funds was to be made to the Alaska Statehood Committee and not to the auditor. Although the statehood committee books were available during the 1951 territorial audit, Bartlett emphasized the auditor had made no attempt at an audit. Obviously Moore had not found the time "ripe for politicking" just then; it was the auditor's current reelection campaign which had prompted hints of corruption.[23]

Bartlett sensed increasing voter hostility toward the Democrats. For the first time, he was encountering real opposition, and it scared him and his family and associates. The campaign was affecting his wife and his daughters. It created a spectre in their minds of job loss and unemployment. Everybody was upset. Bartlett had become very vulnerable: "All of a sudden there was this real possibility that for no good reason Bob would be defeated."[24]

Wherever Bartlett went he repeated his account of the controversy with auditor

Moore, but he focussed mainly on his congressional work and accomplishments in behalf of Alaska. These achievements were many. Ever since 1942, for example, various federal agencies represented in Alaska had paid a 25 percent cost-of-living allowance for personnel stationed in the territory, to offset the high cost of living. In 1945 the War Department had objected, proposing to pay this differential only to those employees hired in the continental United States and assigned to the territory. Bartlett's objections had killed this War Department proposal, and in 1948 an executive order had provided for the payment of a cost-of-living allowance, not to exceed 25 percent of base pay, to all federal employees stationed outside the continental United States. In addition, the Civil Service Commission was directed to make annual surveys determining whether these payments were justified and what the rate should be. Each year since 1948, the delegate had appeared before the Civil Service Commission to argue for the continuation of these payments. As late as 1951 a proposal had been made again to deny the differential pay to resident federal employees. A long and hard battle had ensued, finally resulting in the continuation of these payments.[25]

Land disposal, utilization, and acquisition had always been important to Alaskans. Since 1945 the delegate had steered measures through Congress simplifying the means of gaining use or ownership of public lands. Among them was the extension of the Small Tract Act to Alaska in 1945, which allowed acquisition of five-acre parcels; in 1949 it permitted the purchase of tracts of up to 160 acres; and since 1948 it had allowed Alaskan natives to hold unrestricted deeds to townsites. Another measure enabled World War II veterans to apply their military service credits toward occupancy requirements for homesites and homesteads.[26]

Much to Bartlett's surprise, national and international problems did not play a role in the campaign. Only one voter asked a question about the Korean War. Alaskans were intensely interested only in local and territorial issues.

Piloted by Barr, Bartlett and a number of territorial Senate and House candidates visited many communities in the Fourth and Second judicial divisions. Bartlett's *Pilgrim,* a slow, rugged, single-engine eleven-seater plane, landed at Akiak, Aniak, Sleetmute, Tanana, Alakanak, Barrow, Kivalina, Noatak and other villages, where Bartlett and his associates made their pitch. The candidates and voters would all gather in the little community hall or somebody's big cabin. Barr recalls "the weather, which was always bad in the fall. A couple of times we had to stay over two nights in a place. Of course, we'd have a second meeting and try to think of something different to say. This is difficult, because the poor politician, he has what he wants to say and he says it in this village and the next village and the next village until he gets damn tired of hearing himself say the same thing over and over again."

Bartlett got along well with Alaska's natives. He had taken great interest in issues affecting their livelihood, and in "every village we landed they all greeted him like an old friend."

What impressed Barr again and again over the years was Bartlett's "down-to-earth and simple" style. Neither a good speaker nor one who ever used flowery language, he nevertheless captured the attention of his audience, mainly "because he talked about things that were vital to you." People felt that "he was one of the bunch. But he never overflowed, he was not forward. He was not a 'hail-fellow-well-met.' He was just somebody that you'd start talking to, and you just felt comfortable with him right away. He certainly wasn't a picture of a politician, backslapper type. . . ."[27]

Meanwhile, Bob Reeve visited many Alaskan communities in a DC-3, often making wild and reckless charges against Bartlett. In Anchorage Reeve accused Bartlett of being asleep while an aluminum plant that had been proposed for the Taiya River near Skagway was located in Canada instead. He also claimed that "I am paying my campaign expenses out of my own pocket, money I honestly earned regardless of my so-called subsidies. I will not accept any contributions from anybody—I am a free man. That's a heck of a lot more than Bartlett and Gruening will be doing when they start running around on the government payroll, at the taxpayer's expense, trying to beat me. And remember this, I am not in this for Bob Reeve—I am in this speaking for and representing 130,000 outraged, disgusted residents of Alaska. I represent everyone in Alaska. . .even. . .the socialistic New Dealers, to the extent that I can help save them from the crash that is coming if they continue to accept the folly of their false leadership and adherence to the principles of 'Government supreme' and 'the people subordinate!'"

At Seward Reeve told his audience that Alaska's GOP candidates could not be bought, implying that the Democratic hopefuls were for sale. At Palmer he accused Bartlett of having condoned large federal land withdrawals. "What does he think Alaskan people are—a bunch of saps?" Reeve asked. "They used to burn people at the stake for less than this." In an advertisement Reeve charged that "my opponent passively submits to imports of cheap Russian furs caught with slave labor that ruins our trapping, trading industry."[28]

Reeve accused Bartlett and the Democratic administration of conspiring to defraud the American people in the December 1951 tripartite fishing conference among the United States, Canada, and Japan. Reeve claimed that not only were there no restrictions on Japanese fishing activities in Alaskan waters, but the conference had been a "bald-faced sellout and handout of Alaskan resources," following the "deliberate squandering and dissipation of our people's money that has been indulged in by our socialistic New Deal administration." Reeve mused that perhaps General Douglas MacArthur had been dismissed by President Truman and Secretary of State Dean Acheson because he refused to accede to

Japanese demands. "What has Bartlett done about protecting Alaska's interest in the North Pacific Ocean and the Gulf of Alaska and the Bering Sea and Bristol Bay?" he asked, and he answered that Bartlett had done nothing. "Your present delegate was asleep at the switch, as usual. Burning at the stake is outmoded. But in October we can certainly burn him at the polls."[29]

Reeve made many other charges, holding Bartlett particularly to blame for the federal abandonment of a small airfield at Nome and of the Aleutian bases. This, Reeve reasoned with startling logic, had led to the Korean War, and Bartlett was responsible. Actually, the military had closed the Aleutian bases and the Nome air base for reasons of economy and had centered Alaskan defenses around Fairbanks and Anchorage. With the Korean War, the military reversed that decision, thereby defusing the thrust of Reeve's argument.[30]

Throughout the campaign Reeve's managers carefully avoided public debate between their candidate and Delegate Bartlett, since they were aware that Reeve was a hothead who got worked up easily and who could make some wild and foolish allegations. Despite the managers' efforts, a debate did occur.

In late September both candidates happened to be in Juneau at the Baranof Hotel. One night Reeve was showing his famous bear movie in the Gold Room of the hotel. While the lights were out, one of the bellboys, who had been hired by a Bartlett supporter, passed through the darkened room and left Bartlett literature with each movie viewer. When Reeve discovered this, he went wild and blamed the delegate, who actually had no knowledge of the event. While Bartlett was bathing early the next morning, Reeve banged on the delegate's door. He demanded that Bartlett come out immediately. The delegate recognized his opponent's voice, but because he was still in the tub, he told Reeve to return a bit later. Reeve returned in a few minutes and received the same reply. Bartlett told his opponent to go downstairs to the lobby and compose himself, and Bartlett would meet him there soon. They met. Reeve was furious about the campaign literature event of the previous night and demanded a debate — something his absent managers had carefully avoided during the entire campaign. Reeve wanted to debate Bartlett in Fairbanks within a week. The delegate declined, because he had a previous engagement in Anchorage on the specified night. Reeve thereupon went to the phone, returning with the suggestion of Wasilla as a debating site, probably on his advisors' hope that this little village would attract a small crowd and no press coverage.[31] Bartlett accepted the challenge.

Both candidates took the same plane to Anchorage. During the flight Bartlett made notes for the debate: "Once in a while I would steal a glance at Bob Reeve in the rear of the plane and every time I did so I almost fainted. He was talking with other passengers or reading magazines. I felt that surely he must be loaded for me and I didn't feel too comfortable about the whole thing."[32]

Landing in Anchorage, Bartlett was greeted by Vide and by Steve and Phyllis McCutcheon, friends and fellow Democrats, who drove the Bartletts to Wasilla. A tremendous crowd had assembled, including representatives from all of the Anchorage newspapers and from radio stations, who taped the debate.[33]

Reeve orginally had wanted to limit the debate to the fishing treaty and to Bartlett's fitness as delegate. Bartlett demurred, convinced that all relevant issues should be discussed. Bartlett opened the debate. As he — a liberal, New Deal Democrat — saw the issues, they consisted primarily of the role the Democratic party had played in Alaska. The voters would have to judge whether or not the party had performed adequately in the past and whether its platform and programs gave reasonable assurances of continuing policies that would increase Alaska's population, better its economy, properly utilize its rich resources, and generally promote the common welfare.[34]

Bartlett reminded his listeners of the tremendous job that had confronted the Democratic party when it had taken office in the depth of the Great Depression twenty years earlier. Since then, the federal government had appropriated some $1.3 billion for various Alaska projects — and he had played an important part in securing those monies. Alaska had been fortified militarily and made secure from attack. Many improvements had taken place in Alaska since 1933, and the delegate listed and discussed them. These ranged from airports, roads, and housing to a hydroelectric power plant at Eklutna, all of which encouraged "a more stable population, a happier population, and paved the way for the entry of private enterprise." The territorial Democrats, Bartlett reminded his listeners, work in unison with a Democratic team in Washington: "Acting on your mandates, this team revised our chaotic, outdated tax system. You insisted on more schools, more airports, more medical care, more help for our old-timers . . . and our territorial administration heeded your demands."[35]

Point by point, Bartlett disposed of charges Reeve had been making around Alaska. The matter of Russian fur importation, he told his audience, was a phony issue, because appropriate legislation had barred imports since January 5, 1952.[36]

An allegation also had been made that Bartlett had been unable to get Alaskan measures through the Congress. Not so, the delegate refuted. From 1945 through 1952, Bartlett had authored and Congress had passed some sixty-one bills, more measures signed into law than could be claimed by any other member of Congress[37]

Bob Reeve had his turn, and it soon became apparent why his managers had opposed a debate. While Bartlett settled back on the platform and read a newspaper, ostentatiously turning the pages from time to time, Reeve launched into an ungrammatical and occasionally incoherent attack on the delegate.

"I have listened with great interest to the pious declarations of my opponent on all these accomplishments of his in these eight years that he has been in Congress, and I am glad to hear that he had done something," Reeve began. Reeve's rebuttal was all downhill from there. "First, we have fish traps. It's been on the Democratic party to get rid of fish traps here ever since I came to the territory." Nothing had been accomplished. "Slopful politicians, delegates back there, they don't take care of that bill." Where had Bartlett been while the federal government was committing sundry sins against Alaska? Reeve asked. "Where has he been. . .I don't know, he must have been around there 'cause he's been drawing his pay regular." One heard a lot of fancy talk about Bartlett, he continued, "how he got the Alcoa Pulp Company of America in Alaska, which had been cancelled." Reeve added that Alaska still had not attained statehood: "Not one single improvement in our statehood, electing our own governor or anything, and this bill that they tried to get a few of them for the purpose of being United States Senators. That bill would have made us surrounded by government reservations."[38]

Reeve had just returned from southeastern Alaska where "I talked with thousands of our native population and my colleagues down there. He is going down there on a trip, and I advised them not to stay too long because they might lynch him down there for some of the things he has promised them for which they have never produced." Reeve professed not to worry about Bartlett's future after the election on October 14, because "I know that he can get a job as a lobbyist for fish traps anytime he wants or a job as an ambassador to Imperial Japan."[39]

Laughter greeted Reeve's last remarks, which prompted the moderator to observe that "this is getting serious."[40]

Bartlett laid his newspapers aside and again deftly disposed of Reeve's arguments and charges. He reminded his opponent that Judge James Wickersham, a Republican and the third delegate to have represented Alaska in Congress, had tried to have the fisheries transferred to Alaskan control — as had all delegates since then — to no avail. Only statehood, he observed, would bring about control over the fisheries. Alcoa, not Alcoa Pulp, but the aluminum company people, had come to Alaska to look the place over. "My opponent said Alcoa Pulp," Bartlett mildly observed, "but I think he's a little misinformed there."[41]

The moderator thanked Bartlett, who sat down and resumed his reading of the newspaper. The moderator then asked, "Brother Reeve, have you got anything to say yet?" Reeve now was on the defensive, starting with an explanation of the $230,000 annual federal subsidy that his airline received. The money, he claimed, "is given me as a trustee to that airline to furnish the best scheduled service in Alaska of any of them, and we furnish that down the Aleutian Islands."[42]

The debate ended. Clearly it had been an important event. It had given the Alaskans an opportunity to compare the two candidates. Bartlett's supporters lost no opportunity to broadcast the debate before the election. There is little doubt that Reeve's inept performance at Wasilla was a factor that cost him the election.

When Alaska's citizens went to the polls on October 14, 1952, they elected twenty Republicans and four Democrats to represent them in the territorial House. Eleven Republicans and five Democrats won Senate seats. Bartlett was among the handful of Democrats who survived the Republican sweep. Although he carried all four judicial divisions, he won the election by the smallest margin of his political career — 14,219 votes to 10,893, or 57 percent.[43]

In the November elections the Republicans won nationwide. The Republican team of Dwight D. Eisenhower and Richard M. Nixon gained the nation's top elective offices. In the congressional elections Americans chose 221 Republicans and 213 Democrats to serve in the House of Representatives. Forty-eight Republicans and forty-seven Democrats composed the Senate, as well as one independent, Wayne Morse of Oregon.[44]

Several factors accounted for the Democratic defeat nationally. The doubts, fears, and frustrations stemming from the stalemated Korean War, the Communist spy trials, the revelations of corruption in the federal government, rising prices and taxes all contributed to a strong wish for change in leadership. The Republican congressional victory margin had been narrow, only three more seats than the 218 needed for control of the House, and a bare one-seat margin in the Senate. Americans undoubtedly remembered the Depression and were unwilling to see a reversal of the social and economic gains of the Democratic years.

Perhaps Democratic losses in Alaska also could be explained by the strong desire for change. Bartlett's recitation of the many real improvements in Alaskan life over the years had fallen mostly on deaf ears, since many territorial residents had come north after the war and had no interest or knowledge of the old Alaska. These newcomers did not care whether the federal government had done little or much in the old days. New residents saw only the present deficiencies and needs rather than the very real accomplishments that had been made. In their home states they had been accustomed to running water, adequate sewage facilities, and paved roads — all in short supply in Alaska. The new Alaskans resented having their children attend school on a split-shift basis because of inadequate facilities. In short, they were frustrated because of the many needs not yet being met. They were not about to praise anyone for those improvements that had been made; rather, they simply wanted government to act — and act now — on the problems that still remained. Feeling that the Democrats had not responded fast enough, they chose Republicans, who by and large had promised to do the same things the Democrats had done. And like most Alaskans, new or old, they probably preferred the expenditure of federal to local dollars and felt that such federal funds had not been forthcoming enough under the Democrats.

The campaign had badly scared Bartlett and his family and friends. Winning easily every two years between 1944 and 1950, he suddenly had become vulnerable. For his wife and daughters, the campaign had been a shattering experience, because it had evoked the haunting spectre of unemployment and uncertainty for the head of the family. Bartlett knew that he had made significant achievements but that much remained to be done. He had slowly advanced the statehood movement, both in Alaska and in Congress. The idea that "somebody else would come in who wouldn't, could not do the same thing, couldn't work toward statehood in the same way he could, couldn't make this inch-by-inch progress toward statehood" simply appalled the delegate. Although he had never taken a campaign for granted before 1952, every one after 1952 contained real elements of fear that "something awful would happen that would result in his defeat and upset the statehood struggle."[45]

It is unclear what had motivated Reeve, a political novice, to run against Bartlett that year. Perhaps it was loyalty to the Republican party and indications that 1952 might be a Republican year. Friends felt that "if he'd just kept his mouth shut about political issues, as well as bears, he'd have won." Reeve was good-natured about his defeat: "My pals told me they'd watched me in politics and in the airline business— and I had better stay in the airline business!" Reeve agreed with that assessment. He probably was relieved at his defeat, because as one observer in the Bartlett camp put it, he "wouldn't have known what to put down first had he hit Washington. Really and truly."[46]

CHAPTER 10

The Last Campaigns for Delegate

N 1954 BARTLETT FOUND THAT THE REPUBLICANS had selected Mrs. Barbara Dimock, wife of an Anchorage insurance man, to oppose him. Running for office for the first time in 1952, she had polled more votes than any other Anchorage Republican for the territorial House. Dimock reportedly was good-looking, with lots of vitality and verve. Although she was not a particularly formidable opponent, Bartlett was uneasy about even running in the Democratic primary — only to face her later — for a variety of reasons. Foremost among them was that the Republican administration had allocated little federal monies for Alaskan programs. Bartlett feared that it would be said that all their woes had come about because of the fact that Alaska had a Democratic delegate in a Republican administration. The delegate also felt that the natives and the fishermen no longer solidly supported him — the natives because of failure to make any progress with their claims, and the fishermen because of continued federal mismanagement of the fishery resources. Bartlett suspected that, under the circumstances, almost any Republican could defeat him. For the first and last time in his career, he wondered whether to run again. Being a methodical man, he listed the reasons for and against his candidacy.

His reasons for running were:

1. that it was his duty to lead the Democratic party to victory;
2. that his accumulated Washington experience could be put to increasingly better use for the territory;
3. that somebody might be elected holding views detrimental to Alaska;
4. that his delegateship, for better or for worse, had become his livelihood;
5. that the particular Republicans now controlling Alaska might otherwise be able to expand their influence;
6. that there seemed to be no one else in the Democratic camp who might win.

His reasons against running were:

1. that inevitably and unconsciously, a delegate grows away from his constituency by staying in Washington too long;

2. that he had fulfilled whatever obligations there were to the Alaskan Democratic party by running in 1952 when the outlook was bleak;
3. that, rather than possibly be defeated, it was better to retire while still the champ, making a comeback easier;
4. that certain elements in the Democratic party, particularly in Anchorage, opposed his continuation in office;
5. that, at this point, he was still young enough to start a new career;
6. that Vide wanted him to quit. She had had enough.[1]

Bartlett's soul-searching had been thorough, but in the end he decided to run again. He loved his work, his friends supported him, he was effective as Alaska's spokesman in Washington, and political office, despite the uncertainties, had grown on him. Moreover, he had been in Congress for almost a full decade, "and offhand," he confessed, "I don't know where I would turn for employment." Therefore, "for good or ill, I intend to file again."[2]

Between the fall of 1953 and the April primary in 1954, Bartlett's many friends showered him with advice. This was particularly so after Neil T. Moore, the auditor of Alaska and Bartlett's long-time nemesis, filed against him in the Democratic primary. Rumor had it that the Republicans were attempting to force Ray Beach, a veteran Juneau political hanger-on, to abandon his plan to file against Dimock on the Republican ticket. Leaving Dimock unopposed would enable Republican voters to support Democrat Moore in the primary, which would thereby knock out Bartlett and allow Dimock to win against Moore in the general election. Despite this possibility, territorial legislator Bill Egan of Valdez assured Bartlett that all was well, that he would receive a big vote throughout the territory: "Remember, Bob, YOU are the man Alaskans have confidence in, and you are going to be in office just as long as you wish to be. You don't have to listen to some of these so-called calamity alarmists who care more for their own welfare than they care about anyone else."[3]

Bartlett did extremely well on primary day, running up a lead of more than six to one against Moore in early returns. Dimock, the Republican nominee, attracted only a fraction of Bartlett's vote. Better yet, Bartlett's early vote total was twice the size of the vote for all other candidates in both parties. It was a gratifying victory, particularly since the delegate had feuded with Moore for a number of years. George Sundborg reported that the territorial auditor "is crushed. Goes around shaking his head and saying 'I just can't understand it,'" which prompted an unsympathetic commentator to remark that "when you're the welterweight champion [Moore], no matter how good you are, you just don't take on the heavyweight champ."[4] In view of the vote totals, the assessment made good sense, for Bartlett had received 7,604 to Moore's 388 votes.

Bartlett was mightily pleased that he had won such a decisive primary victory despite the fact that he had not campaigned in Alaska at all. Congress had been in session, forcing him to stay in Washington, D.C. Campaigning in the primary, Bartlett had mused, might be a liability rather than an asset. The delegate recalled that he had visited Barrow each summer in the past, years before there had even been a voting precinct there. He had continued visiting Barrow and had campaigned there in 1950. In spite of that, Almer J. Peterson, his 1950 opponent, had carried the town by three votes — and the fellow had not bothered to visit Barrow at all!

Bartlett also wondered why voters chose one candidate over another. One constituent had explained her reasoning to him after the 1952 election. Although she had found it hard to do so, this particular voter stated, she nevertheless had cast her vote for Bartlett. "At Seldovia you were dreadfully long-winded and didn't have anything to say. I didn't think I could ever vote for you. Then Bob Reeve [the Republican candidate] came over. He was worse than you. I didn't believe it was possible. I had to vote for you." That, Bartlett summarized, was the profile of a loyal constituent.[5]

Bartlett was delighted to run against Dimock. Admiring busty women, "he thought she was one of the best endowed women of all time. He kept hoping that they might share the same platform," but that did not happen. Bartlett's campaign against Dimock revolved around the Alaska mental health measure, the statehood struggle, and the various Alaskan bills that had been enacted into law during the last two years. Bartlett had been successful in having twenty-three measures signed into law, nine public-sponsored bills and fourteen private measures.[6]

In late September Bartlett led a ten-day swing through the Third Judicial Division with the candidates for the territorial legislature. Bartlett was exuberant, stating that "the tide was running. You can feel the difference in attitude compared with 1952."

The Democrats did indeed sweep back into office after their 1952 defeat. The Republican cause was undoubtedly hurt by the split between the young insurgents led by Walter J. Hickel, an Anchorage contractor, and the "old guard" under the leadership of Albert White. Bartlett trounced Dimock 19,916 to 7,083 votes, receiving 74 percent of the total votes cast for delegate.[7]

Although Bartlett hesitated again in 1956, he need not have been worried. He was opposed in the primary by fellow Juneau Democrat Peter Wood, a real estate dealer. Politically ambitious, Wood earlier had told Bartlett that he considered himself a "super-pol" and had intimated that he would run some day. He would be elected, he believed, "when I amass that fortune which, though infantile, is growing. It's extremely difficult to screw the public vigorously in real estate for a living and seek their indulgence spasmodically at the polls. But I am gaining, and if I ever get spending money it will be a three-ring circus." He may not have had the hoped-for fortune, but he did run in 1956—and Bartlett beat him 16,710 votes to 2,324 votes in the primary.[8]

The Republicans fought a hard and bitter campaign against Bartlett in the general election. Their candidate, Byron C. Gillam, a Fairbanks supermarket operator and former Seward merchant, sharply attacked Bartlett. He called on Congress to reduce federal income taxes in Alaska. A series of cartoons showing Bartlett snoozing on the job, ignoring the pleas of jailed children, guzzling liquor, grinding out legislation for his favored friends, and protecting fish traps were typical of the sour campaign. Although he was "on the wagon," the charge of "swigging booze" alarmed Bartlett.

Republicans also reminded voters that Gruening was Bartlett's friend and that the delegate had helped the former govenor find temporary employment with the Alaska Statehood Committee. The Republicans falsely charged that "Ernie Gruening from Washington-way came back to Alaska to make some hay. He spoke to the folks at the Constitutional Convention. There is just one thing he forgot to mention—that's the five thousand dollars he got for his talk. Let's vote Republican." Actually, the five-thousand-dollar fee was the sum Gruening had earned as researcher and consultant for the Alaska Statehood Committee. Another familiar Republican charge was that "Bartlett was the mouthpiece, Gruening was the boss. But Congress cried corruption, and statehood's what we lost. Vote Republican."

It all was to no avail. Bartlett carried the day again, defeating Gillam 18,934 votes to 9,332, receiving 65 percent of the total votes cast for delegate.[9]

Bartlett's repeated reelection to the office of delegate demonstrated not only that he had become a skillful political campaigner, but also that he had acquired an aura of political invincibility with the Alaskan electorate. The important Alaskan newspapers always showed Bartlett to be heavily favored over whatever challenger ran against him. That must have been discouraging for his opponents, and it certainly contributed to the delegate's electoral success, since voters like to be on the winning side. Bartlett also had the human touch, the ability to sense what his constituents wanted. The average voter, whether a construction worker, lumberjack, fisherman, or town or village dweller, liked to listen to Bartlett person to person. He had humor and warmth, and he concentrated on local issues that were of concern to his listeners. They felt that the delegate would represent them well— and he did. As a result, the voters time and again displayed their approval at the polls, making most of Bartlett's elections shoo-ins.

CHAPTER **11**

The Long Journey
to Morningside

BOB BARTLETT HAD many friends throughout Alaska. Each one undoubtedly
remembers a particular bill the delegate put through Congress—perhaps
a private measure for the relief of a specific individual, or a bill benefitting
a community or the territory. Since it is impracticable to chronicle each
legislative achievement, a history of two measures, each chosen for its general
importance to Alaska, may illustrate the legislative process and show the role
Bartlett played. The measures selected for this purpose are the Alaska mental
health bill and, in the next two chapters, the achievement of statehood.

In territorial days, it was said that there were three sides to Alaska—inside,
outside, and Morningside. "Inside" meant Alaska, "outside" the rest of the world,
and "Morningside" the institution near Portland, Oregon where those unfortunate Alaskans who went insane in the great land were incarcerated.

Jokes about Morningside had amused Alaskans over the years. These did not
reflect cruelty or cynicism but rather provided a light relief to a dark problem
besetting all communities—the care and treatment of the mentally ill. In more
reflective moods Alaskans realized that the problem was serious and that, like
many Alaskan problems, it was exaggerated by the isolation, distances, and high
construction costs that they suffered.

It was largely because of the Klondike gold discovery in Canada's Yukon Territory and the resulting influx of argonauts into Alaska that Congress at last decided
to enact legislation that would meet some of the territory's most crucial needs.
Among these pieces of legislation was the criminal code of 1899, which made
provisions for the mentally ill. Before its passage, only those Alaskans who had
become mentally ill while serving prison sentences could receive treatment in a
mental institution. Under the new code, which became law on June 6, 1900, a jury
could find a defendant not guilty on grounds of insanity. In such a case, if the court
found that nonconfinement endangered the public peace or safety, it had to
commit the individual to any lunatic asylum authorized by the United States. The
section of the code dealing with the civilian insane also contained a provision for

Alaska's governor to advertise for and review bids and, in behalf of the United States, contract from year to year "with the responsible asylum or sanitarium west of the main range of the Rocky Mountains submitting the lowest bid for the care and custody of persons legally adjudged insane" in the territory. The secretary of the Interior had to approve the contract, under which the federal government assumed all transportation and maintenance costs.

In January 1901, Alaska's governor John Brady signed a contract with the Oregon State Insane Asylum at Salem. The contract was renewed in 1902 and 1903. Because of overcrowding, however, the Salem institution refused to accept Alaskan patients after January 15, 1904. At this point Dr. Henry Waldo Coe, the founder of Mount Tabor Nervous Sanitarium near Portland, Oregon offered to care for them. In that same year congressional action enabled the Department of the Interior to eliminate yearly renewals and to award a five-year contract to Dr. Coe. From then on, until the passage of the Alaska Mental Health Enabling Act in 1956, Alaskan patients received treatment at the Portland institution, to which Dr. Coe had given the name Morningside.[1]

Alaskans welcomed legislation that would provide care and treatment of the insane, but they resented the fact that patients were maintained in an institution located outside the territory. Accordingly, in 1910 James Wickersham, Alaska's delegate in Congress, attempted to persuade his colleagues to build a federal mental institution in southeastern Alaska. The House Committee on Territories and the governor of Alaska, however, refused to endorse the delegate's bill because of the cost involved, the dreary climate of southeastern Alaska, and the fact that the insane could be accommodated elsewhere. Congress, as a matter of fact, considered it economically and medically unwise to treat the insane in an institution located in Alaska. Therefore, when it conferred territorial status in 1912, it refused to extend authority over the mentally ill to Alaskans.[2]

Dissatisfaction with the situation, however, continued to exist in Alaska. Despite the financial burdens which a mental institution in the territory would impose on Alaska's slender tax base, many Alaskans insisted that it was both humane and therapeutic to keep patients in a territorial institution where they could be visited by friends and relatives.

Not surprisingly, therefore, territorial delegates continued their periodic attempts to persuade Congress to grant authority over the mentally ill to Alaska. On July 15, 1935, Delegate Anthony J. Dimond introduced a measure (H.R. 8849) which would have enabled the secretary of the Interior to "locate, establish, construct, equip, and operate a hospital for the insane of Alaska. . . ." Igloo Number 1 of the Pioneers of Alaska in Nome applauded the delegate's efforts and observed that the "farming out" of the insane was inhumane, abominable, and an incentive to human greed and avarice. Edward Cannon, an ex-Alaskan living in

Seattle, congratulated Dimond and remarked that with an honest psychiatrist heading such an institution, it "will stop a lot of railroading [of patients] on frame-ups by crooked territorial appointees who wanted to settle their revenges in this way."[3]

Dimond's bill failed to pass. Undeterred, he again introduced a mental health measure (H.R. 1555) in 1937. Progress of sorts was made when Secretary of the Interior Harold L. Ickes reported on the measure. After briefly reviewing the legal basis for treating Alaska's mentally ill, Ickes stated that it was "conceivable that despite proper treatment at a reasonable figure, public sentiment aroused by a law requiring the insane to be delivered to the lowest responsible bidder would seriously interfere with both Government and the contracting institution in the discharge of their obligations to the patients." Above all, urged the secretary, "place the whole thing beyond the profit motive."[4] However valid the recommendations, the proposed legislation did not receive the approval of the Bureau of the Budget and therefore was doomed to failure.

Again in 1940 and in 1941, Delegate Dimond introduced legislation to remedy the mental health situation in Alaska, but Secretary Ickes, although assuring Dimond he realized the need for action, counseled him to postpone further efforts until the war had ended.[5]

After winning election in 1944, Delegate Bartlett continued his predecessor's efforts. Bartlett found that commitment procedures had not changed in over thirty years. The only way in which a mentally ill or retarded person could receive hospital care was to be declared "an insane person at Large" in a court hearing before a jury of six adult male residents and a United States commissioner, after a warrant had been issued for the detention of the individual. Although the accused was usually defended by a lawyer, in these hearings the person often was held in local jails while waiting for a hearing or for transportation to the hospital, because other facilities were not available. Some individuals arrived at Morningside without ever having been examined by a physician, much less a psychiatrist. No person or his family could request care in the hospital program without going through the court hearing. Children as well as adults had to endure the same procedure, whether they were mentally ill or merely retarded. In addition, numbers of patients who were committed to Morningside died a few hours after admission because they had not received proper medical care while in detention, while waiting for transportation, or while en route to Oregon.[6]

Not long after Bartlett had begun his duties, Congressman Homer Angell of Oregon introduced a measure to construct a facility in Portland that was to take care of Alaska's mentally ill as well as Oregon's. Congressman Hugh De Lacy of Washington submitted a similar measure to construct a facility near Seattle. Bartlett immediately found himself in a potentially embarrassing situation. Angell was one of Alaska's staunchest friends on the House Committee on Territories, and Bartlett did not intend to alienate the man. But he realized that building permanent facilities in the States that were designed to accommodate Alaskan patients would jeopardize the eventual establishment of comprehensive mental health facilities in the territory. Bartlett sounded out committee members and concluded that the chances for passage of any mental health bill were slim. For the record, he introduced his own carefully worded measure to construct a hospital for the insane of Alaska.[7] As Bartlett had expected, the various measures did not even receive a hearing. But when the bill was introduced again in 1947, he at least gained supporters.

The Alaskan mental health problem now advanced to the stage where it merited a study. Numerous members of Congress had been made aware of the revolution the Second World War had wrought in Alaska. Many wartime defense workers had chosen to remain in Alaska after the war, resulting in a population increase of 77.4 percent between 1940 and 1950, from 72,524 to 128,643 inhabitants.[8] The war had also resulted in a sharpened awareness of the problem of mental illness. Between 1940 and 1950 some 654 Alaskan mentally ill were admitted to Morningside Hospital, while a maximum of 355 Alaskans were patients at the hospital in any single year between 1940 and 1950. Federal appropriations for Alaskan patients had also increased from $208,840 in 1940 to $534,900 in 1950.[9]

After extensive consultation with various executive departments and the Alaska commissioner of health, the Department of the Interior in July 1949 decided to survey the problem. A team of experts, headed by Dr. Winfred Overholser, director of St. Elizabeth's Hospital, a large federal mental institution in Washington, D.C., traveled north. After first inspecting Morningside Hospital, they spent three weeks in Alaska, visiting towns from Ketchikan to Kotzebue.

The experts listened to testimony from Alaskans familiar with the territory's mental health problems. Anthony J. Dimond, Anchorage district judge and former delegate in Congress from Alaska, spoke to them. He objected on principle to the contract system for the care of the mentally ill. Dimond reminded his listeners that, as delegate, he had introduced several mental health measures for Alaska, without success, and that at one time he had received a commitment from President Franklin D. Roosevelt for several million dollars for an Alaskan mental institution. Nothing had come of all these efforts. Dimond said that he appreciated the first scientific inquiry in Alaska dealing with mental health problems. He hoped that the effort would "result in great aid and benefit to all who are here who are 'Touched,' as they used to say in the ancient days, 'with the finger of God' and who are not entirely responsible in some ways for what they say and do."[10]

William B. Healy, a deputy U.S. marshal for Alaska's Third Judicial Division, described the handling of persons suspected of being insane: his office served the arrest warrant and took the suspect into custody; the commissioner's court held a hearing; if the Court found the individual insane, he was committed and held in confinement. In most of the insanity proceedings, Healy stated, the accused was charged with the crime of being an insane person. The criminal aspect disturbed Marshal Healy, because "in most instances our people are mentally ill. They need medical attention. We have to confine them in jail. We have no other alternative. We confine them as though they were a criminal, when, in fact, they need care and attention." Transporting the mentally ill individual was yet another problem, since the person was treated as a criminal during that procedure as well. It was difficult for the guards and "a very severe shock . . . and detrimental to the patient their having to be put on a boat and placed in a straightjacket for eight days, maybe, getting them to Seattle, juggling them on the train and getting them to Morningside." Air transportation to Morningside required only two days, but airlines could refuse to carry insane prisoners at any time, the marshal stated, and nowhere in Alaska could prisoners be properly cared for while in confinement awaiting transportation. In short, Healy concluded, the marshals ought to get out of the business of handling these patients altogether.[11]

Throughout their trip, the experts heard of the urgent need for more humane and less public procedures for hospitalizing Alaska's mentally ill and retarded. Over and over again the team listened to the objections to the contract care of mental patients in proprietary institutions, which existed nowhere else in the United States.

At the conclusion of their trip, the experts recommended that a sound, long-range program for the care of Alaska's mental patients be initiated at the earliest possible date. This included the construction by the federal government of a readily expandable 350-bed hospital to be located in central Alaska and of a 50-bed treatment center at Mount Edgecumbe Health and Educational Center at Sitka. They also recommended that other Alaskan hospitals provide for emergency care of mentally ill individuals; that the mental health program in the territorial Department of Health be greatly enlarged; and that an agreement be worked out with the territorial government to take over and operate the facilities after their completion. In addition to these long-range recommendations, the team also advocated immediate changes, such as the development of a comprehensive mental health program under the territorial Department of Health.[12]

In the meantime, Delegate Bartlett had mobilized Alaskan churches, nurses' associations, physicians, and others interested in mental health reform. These groups bombarded Congress with pleas for favorable consideration of Bartlett's Alaska mental health measure, which formulated procedures for the hospitalization of the territory's mentally ill and also included the establishment of a hospital. But the Bartlett measure died on July 2, 1952, when Congressman Angell, who lived in Portland, home of Morningside Hospital, objected to the bill.[13]

Undeterred, Bartlett, early in 1953, introduced yet another mental health measure at the opening of the new Congress. This time the bill did not get out of the subcommittee, but heightened interest in reform led the departments of the Interior, Defense, and Health, Education, and Welfare (HEW) to sponsor a comprehensive survey by four experts from the Pittsburgh Graduate School of Public Health. In 1954 this survey was enlarged with the addition of still another team of professionals, who evaluated Morningside Hospital and health conditions in general in Alaska. Their findings about mental health care essentially agreed with those of the 1949 survey group. They characterized the admission proce- dures to hospital care as "comparable to the apprehension and commitment of a criminal" and, underlining their words, as "archaic, cruel, inhumane and essen- tially barbaric."[14]

Early in 1954 three mental health measures confronted lawmakers: Bartlett's bill from 1953, Pennsylvania Congressman John P. Taylor's new measure in the House, and Nebraska Senator Hugh Butler's bill in the Senate. Both House bills had been drafted in the Department of the Interior, Bartlett's with the assistance of psychiatric specialists, in response to the 1949 Overholser report. The chief difference between the two House measures consisted of a clause in the Taylor bill which provided that the federal government "shall never appropriate more money for the care of Alaska's mentally ill than it did in fiscal year 1954," some $798,600. It also provided that the contract between the Department of the Interior and Morningside Hospital would remain in force until its expiration in 1958. Bartlett privately objected to the provision that would freeze federal ap- propriations at the 1954 level because he was fearful that the territorial govern- ment would be unable to make up the differences in subsequent years. Bartlett voiced his reservations to the executive session of the subcommittee considering the Taylor bill but was overruled; and on May 24, 1954, the House Committee on Interior and Insular Affairs favorably reported the Taylor bill.

Bartlett had also communicated his fears to the territorial commissioner of health, Dr. C. Earl Albrecht, who was leading the Alaskan supporters of mental health reform. Although Bartlett had pledged him to silence, Albrecht apparently related Bartlett's worries to the *Ketchikan Alaska Chronicle,* which reported the delegate's "grave concern at the chances of passage" of Taylor's bill. Taylor angrily let Bartlett know that the only danger that might prevent early enactment of his Alaska mental health bill was Bartlett's objection to the $798,000 ceiling on federal appropriations. Bartlett was furious at Albrecht for his breach of confidence.[15]

On June 7, 1954, Congressman John Byrnes, an opponent of the Alaska legisla- tion, asked unanimous consent that the Taylor bill be passed over without prejudice, whereupon the author asked, and was granted, unanimous consent to remove the bill from the consent calendar. Shortly before the bill was called, Bartlett had seated himself next to Taylor, who apparently thought he was going to raise an objection. Taylor was ready to rise and ask that the bill be stricken from the calendar "so he could seek a rule for it, and [he] was so wound up that he did not notice" when Byrnes, and not Bartlett, made the objection. Bartlett subsequently noticed that the *Congressional Record* of June 7 omitted mention of Byrnes' action. He speculated that this deletion had been made so that there would be no permanent record of Republican opposition to the legislation.[16]

On July 6 the House passed the Taylor measure and sent it to the Senate. Bartlett did not express adamant opposition to the Senate version, but he did caution that he doubted the territorial government could pay the full costs of a mental health program within a year, despite the grant of 200,000 acres of land to help defray expenses. He urged the Senate committee to defer action on the measure and to pass a bill that would only revise commitment procedures. The delegate acted cautiously in his testimony before the senators because he had been warned "by a friend that it was very ardently desired by some that I express outright opposition to the bill; if that were done. . .political capital would be made of this against me in the forthcoming campaign." Presumably, a Republican governor and legislature in Alaska would accuse Bartlett of opposition to a reform measure widely desired by all segments of the Alaskan population.[17]

The Senate Committee on Interior and Insular Affairs favorably reported the amended Taylor bill to the full Senate on August 13. The measure provided for the voluntary hospitalization of mentally ill individuals. It also provided for a procedure for hospitalization upon court order, which contained all possible safeguards for the patient. Any patient refused discharge from a hospital would be entitled to a judicial hearing, and any patient hospitalized as the result of a judicial hearing could appeal the decision to Alaska's territorial district court. The new procedures were to replace the criminal lunacy proceedings that had remained unchanged since 1905.[18]

Although the Alaska mental health measure was approved by the insular affairs committee, when the bill finally came up in the full Senate, it was passed over. Bartlett's opposition to some of its specific provisions effectively killed the measure in that session. The delegate had been unhappy with a Senate amendment requiring Alaska to assume financial responsibility for the institutional care of those committed after April 1, 1955. He had also opposed the continuation of the Morningside contract until 1959. Bartlett, although approving of the concept of territorial financial responsibility, still believed that complete hearings should be held on the subject in 1955. The delegate's stand put him in opposition with the territorial Board of Health, led by the energetic Dr. Albrecht. Bartlett, who customarily attempted to achieve consensus and broad support for the resolution of important issues, felt that he had been undermined by the Board of Health's endorsement of the Senate version. Barbara Dimock, his Republican opponent in the 1954 delegate race, used the incumbent's opposition as a campaign issue. Bartlett easily retained his seat.[19]

Early in the new session of Congress, Delegate Bartlett and Representative Edith Green of Oregon introduced legislation modernizing commitment procedures. They presented separate bills providing for the construction of a hospital for Alaska's mentally ill. Shortly thereafter, Senator Richard Neuberger of Oregon, an old Bartlett friend, introduced similar legislation in the Senate. Morningside Hospital had served a useful role during Alaska's frontier era and was operating under responsible and conscientious owners, Neuberger observed, but the contract system of caring for the mentally ill was fundamentally wrong, cruel, and archaic. On earlier occasions, the senator continued, members of Oregon's congressional delegation had used their influence to block changes in the treatment of Alaska's mentally ill because Morningside Hospital had provided a valuable local payroll in Portland. "I renounce any such consideration," Neuberger concluded, "knowing that the humane and upright people of Oregon join me in this stand."[20]

With so many bills in the hopper, the Subcommittee on Territorial and Insular Affairs of the House Committee on Interior and Insular Affairs appointed a special subcommittee for inspecting Morningside Hospital in Portland. Subcommittee members, including Delegate Bartlett, spent April 7, 1955, at the hospital. There they learned from the testimony of Wayne W. Coe, owner and manager, and his son Henry W. Coe, general manager of the sanitarium company operating the hospital, that 1904 was the first time that the Department of the Interior had asked the hospital to take care, temporarily, of a few Alaskan mental patients. The temporary arrangement had become permanent. The latest contract between Morningside and the Department of the Interior had become effective on July 1, 1953, and was to run until June 30, 1958. The federal government had agreed to pay a base rate of $184 per patient per month, to be adjusted semiannually for inflation. Between 1904 and 1955, some 2,784 Alaskan patients had received care at Morningside. During this period the hospital population had remained fairly constant—between 330 to 360 patients per year—with discharge and death rates closely related to admission rates.[21]

The subcommittee counsel and members were bothered by Alaskan territorial commitment procedures. They learned that most patients arrived accompanied by a marshal or a matron, sometimes with a relative or friend as well, but that generally they came without any type of clinical history or diagnostic records. No transcripts of Alaskan commitment hearings were made. In a typical case, when hospital personnel contacted the commissioner who had committed a particular patient, they found that he knew as little about the case as they did. The commissioner reported that he had flown to an isolated village during a snowstorm, held the hearing, and took the patient out within a matter of half an hour or so.[22]

Between April 21 and July 8, 1955, the subcommittee held sporadic hearings in Washington, D.C. They heard and questioned closely some thirteen witnesses from the various executive departments.

By the middle of May, the departments of the Interior and Health, Education, and Welfare had submitted their proposed amendments in the form of a substitute measure, which had received the blessing of the Bureau of the Budget. Alaska's governor, B. Frank Heintzleman, endorsed the bill as providing, for the first time, a badly needed integrated and comprehensive program for the treatment of the mentally ill of the territory. Outlining the main points now incorporated in the new measure, Delegate Bartlett told a joint committee of the territorial legislature in February that there "was unanimity among the members. . .that the approach would be agreeable to the Alaska Legislature."[23] The delegate felt that the measure under discussion was an excellent one. Most witnesses favored the new bill, with the exception of Wayne and Henry Coe, who were fighting for their economic survival.[24]

While hearings were being held in Washington, territorial residents followed the congressional action on the mental health measure through occasional reports in the newspapers. While the Coes were on the stand, for example, the *Anchorage Daily Times* described for its readers how Wayne W. Coe, the sole owner of Morningside Hospital, had reaped a fortune from treating the territory's mentally ill. From 1936 to 1953 his company had shown a net return after taxes of $671,696.43. And since, as the sole owner, Mr. Coe had set his own salary during that period—a salary ranging from $23,000 to $30,000 per year — his total return for the seventeen years had amounted to $1,115,196.43. That, the paper concluded, was one way to make a million dollars and perhaps "be well on the way to a second or third million," because it was not known how much profit Coe had realized between 1904 and 1935.[25]

If Alaskan papers were unfriendly towards the Coes, the Coes at least found an ally in Congressman A.L. Miller of Nebraska, who lavishly praised the medical care administered at Morningside. Nevertheless, he favored passage of a bill that would revise commitment procedures as well as grant Alaska 500,000 acres of land to help the territory establish a mental health program. He adamantly opposed a proposal for a $6.5 million federal appropriation for the construction of mental health facilities in Alaska.[26]

Throughout the deliberations Delegate Bartlett clarified various aspects of the measure for subcommittee members. He attempted, often unsuccessfully, to ward off crippling amendments, such as one which earmarked income for the land grant, raised to one million acres by an amendment by Congressman Miller, for mental health purposes only.

In the final subcommittee vote, eleven Republicans voted against the measure while thirteen Democrats and one Republican voted in favor of it. Bitter debate had developed over the proposed grant of $6.5 million for the construction of Alaskan mental health facilities. Congressman Miller had wanted to cut the proposed appropriation in half but had withdrawn that amendment in favor of one which would have forced Alaska to match the construction appropriation dollar for dollar. Bartlett and his fellow subcommittee Democrats had successfully resisted this amendment, primarily because no preliminary discussions had been held on the matter. Miller had responded by calling Bartlett stubborn and blaming him for the slow progress of a variety of Alaska legislation.[27]

On July 8, 1955, the subcommittee reported the amended Alaska mental health measure to the full committee. In turn, the committee reported it to the full House on July 25, 1955.[28]

It soon became apparent that the Senate would not hold hearings on the Alaska mental health measure. There was also substantial doubt that the House Rules Committee would consider a request for a rule at this time, because the leadership had decided to clear for action only those bills which possessed national importance. Friends of the Alaska measure, therefore, decided to wait until 1956 for the final push in Congress. Bartlett optimistically predicted that the Alaska mental health bill would become law in 1956.[29]

In the meantime, the House Subcommittee on Territorial and Insular Affairs journeyed to Alaska to hear testimony and investigate any matters within its jurisdiction. Delegate Bartlett accompanied the subcommittee and at times presided over the hearings. For twenty-two days in September 1955, the subcommittee traveled widely throughout the territory, visiting eighteen communities, from Barrow to King Salmon and Kodiak to Ketchikan. Of the many residents testifying on a wide range of problems, approximately forty addressed themselves to the mental health program. The new bill before Congress, introduced by Representative Edith Green of Oregon, found wide support in Alaska.

Subcommittee members heard the U.S. attorney for the Fourth Judicial Division, Theodore F. Stevens, voice his criticism of the commitment procedures. Although greatly respecting the process of trial by jury, Stevens doubted jury judgments in insanity cases. Often, Stevens commented, insane individuals appeared extremely lucid on the witness stand at a sanity hearing, while perfectly normal individuals often got nervous and fidgety. The U.S. attorney told of having been cautioned in advance about one insane man who would appear very lucid and clear in his testimony and "that we should allow him to continue . . . as long as he wanted because he would reach the peak of his development and then slide quickly. It was well over an hour, probably into two hours, before that happened. But when it did happen, it was very spectacular. The gentleman took off his shoe and began reading a poem about the Statue of Liberty and gave us a political speech and a couple of other things."[30] Normally, however, no such advance warning was given, Stevens concluded, and sanity hearings usually took no more than twenty minutes. In short, there was considerable room for error.

In the hearings Bartlett went to the crux of the opposition issue by asking witnesses whether or not Alaska could assume the mental health obligation. Typical of the answers given were those of Byron Gillam and the Reverend George Boileau, S.J., of Fairbanks. Both denied any intention to secure further federal aid and Boileau asserted that given "a foothold ... we will walk ourselves."[31] Mrs. Richard Stryker of Anchorage perhaps summed up Alaskan opinions of the mental health bill best when stating that "whether Morningside is good, bad, or indifferent, the Alaskan people should be able to have control over their own mentally ill; they know what is required. It is closest to them. In my mind it is completely ridiculous that the Congress of the United States should have to worry about something that the Alaskans are perfectly capable of taking care of themselves. Morningside. . .is quite often brought up to draw attention away from the mental health bill itself, and it irritates me thoroughly when it happens."[32]

In Fairbanks Bartlett alerted Governor Heintzleman to the probability that Alaska would be required to match the construction funds on a dollar-for-dollar basis. Heintzleman was certain that Alaska would be unable to raise the necessary funds. In any event, the governor believed that constructing hospital facilities was a federal responsibility, since the territory would be "doing just about all we could be expected to do in picking up more and more of the check every year to take care of these people."[33]

A tired subcommittee returned from its travels in October 1955. Members had heard testimony and recommendations on many Alaskan matters. Best of all, they had gained an appreciation of its physical vastness and special problems.

Early in January 1956 the House of Representatives struggled to its collective feet and by unanimous voice vote passed the Alaska Mental Health Enabling Act. The congressmen were blissfully unaware that they had just set into motion a panic among a segment of the political right wing.

The panic itself began on January 25, 1956, with the appearance of an unsigned article in the obscure *Register* of Santa Ana, California, entitled "Now — Siberia, U.S.A." Expanded copies of the article were mailed out widely from Los Angeles by the California chapter of the right-wing Minute Women of the U.S.A. The article defined the Alaska mental health bill as a vicious measure that was a cover for an infamous scheme to establish in Alaska "our own version of the Siberia slave camps run by the Russian government." The one million acres, or slightly more than 1,562 square miles, granted to Alaska for the hospitalization and care of the mentally ill there was an enormous area on which innumerable individuals could be detained; and the definition of mental illness was so broad, the article charged, "as to include anything from dandruff, headaches, toothaches, or fallen arches." The article raised the fear that the legislation would, in fact, "place every resident of the United States at the mercy of the whims and fancies of any person with whom they might have a disagreement, causing a charge of 'mental illness' to be lodged against them, with immediate deportation to Siberia, U.S.A.!"[34] George Orwell had indeed been correct in his novel—only 1984 had arrived early.

Other right-wing groups and activists quickly joined the swelling protest against the Alaska mental health bill. Among many others were the Concordians of North Hollywood, California; the Tarrant County Medical Society of Fort Worth, Texas; the Association of American Physicians and Surgeons; Dr. George A. Snyder, a physician of Hollywood, California; Mervin K. Hart, the president of the National Economic Council, Inc., of New York; and Dan Smoot, a radio commentator in Dallas, Texas.

The country was flooded with wild, frantic newspaper articles, bulletins, and scare sheets, all in response to the ill-informed article with the catchy slogan "Siberia, U.S.A." that had appeared in the *Register*. Patriotic groups and other organizations, as well as the usual smattering of individuals on the lunatic fringe, picked up the slogan and elaborated on it. In general, they all believed that the mental health bill proposed to establish a political concentration camp of one million acres in the frozen arctic wastes of Alaska. Leaflets and pamphlets, mailed en masse and passed from hand to hand, warned patriots of the grisly future in store for them if they dared to be politically independent on the local level: if you were anti-United Nations, anti-UNESCO (United Nations Educational, Scientific, and Cultural Organization), against fluoridation, or in favor of the Bricker amendment; if you voiced Christian principles too loudly at Parent-Teacher Association meetings; if you expressed your disapproval of Bertrand Russell's philosophy; "they" would get you. "They" would probably arrest you in the middle of the night, Soviet style, find you guilty of mental illness, and hustle you off to faraway Alaska, separated from family and friends, where you would end your days as an inmate of "Siberia, U.S.A."[35]

As were other members of Congress, Bartlett was startled and nonplussed by the large volume of mail in opposition to the Alaska mental health measure. At the end of January the delegate urged Senator Henry M. Jackson of Washington to schedule Senate hearings quickly to clear up misunderstandings and apprehensions. "Some of these letter writers," Bartlett related, "are under the impression that the million acres would constitute a huge stockade in which insane persons will be turned loose, and a lot of other nonsense" as well. Some of the mail from California alleged that Dr. Overholser, who had testified in favor of the Alaska bill, had ties through his professional group to the World Health Organization (WHO). "WHO is affiliated with UNESCO," Bartlett concluded, "so it follows as a matter of simple logic [to these right-wing individuals] that the Alaska mental health bill is a communist enterprise."[36]

A few days later Bartlett exclaimed that letters were arriving "in such numbers and contain such marvelously strange statements that no man or group of men could hope to follow them all." Perhaps, the delegate argued, what was required more than enactment of the Alaska mental health bill were "huge grants of government funds to train without delay whole regiments of psychiatrists. They are badly needed. The campaign against the Alaska mental health act proves this." What we are dealing with, Bartlett concluded, are large numbers of "psychoceramics," in short, crackpots.[37]

On February 20, February 21, and again on March 5, 1956, the Senate Subcommittee on Territorial and Insular Affairs held hearings on the Alaska mental health bills. The Eisenhower administration supported the legislation, as did the overwhelming majority of witnesses who testified.

Senator Neuberger probably summarized best the reasons for support when he indicated that common humanitarian instincts dictated that Alaska's mentally ill be treated in the territory instead of shipped far away to Oregon. When first coming to the Senate about a year earlier, Neuberger stated, "I was informed that the only real chance that there would be for such legislation was that if a member of the Congress from Oregon would take the lead in sponsoring it." That situation existed, Neuberger continued, "because for approximately half a century a private hospital in my home community of Portland has been the official agency for caring for Alaska's mentally ill. Unless a member from the Oregon congressional delegation took the lead," other members of the Congress might be reluctant to pass a bill which would result in the wiping out or diminution of a payroll of an operating facility in the State of Oregon." Subsequently, he and Representative Green had taken the lead.[38]

Opponents of the Alaska mental health measure earnestly advised the senators that H.R. 6376 was an internationalist plot, a Communist scheme, and/or a plan to subvert the Constitution of the United States.

Mrs. Stephanie Williams, president of the American Public Relations Forum, Inc., of Burbank, California, was spokeswoman for her group of approximately one hundred members. She repeated the allegation that mentally ill from other states would be shipped to Alaska for incarceration in mental institutions if the measure passed. Williams rambled somewhat incoherently, discussing mental health bills in other states as well as dissecting the Alaska measure paragraph by paragraph. She told the senators that "before the United Nations Charter was signed, an alien could not own land in this country. They may do so now, and there is nothing to prevent Russia from buying a whole million acres or renting it for leasing," presumably to house American mentally ill. Throughout her confused presentation, the senators listened patiently. At the end of her testimony, Senator Alan Bible of Nevada, who chaired the hearing, thanked Mrs. Williams, telling her that "we are very happy to have had you with us [and] your remarks in analyzing the bill will receive the careful consideration of the committee."[39]

Mrs. Leigh F. Burkland of Van Nuys, California, the author of "Siberia, U.S.A.," objected to the definition of mental illness. "What is mental health?" she asked. "By whose standards can we decide one person is normal and another not?" She claimed that supporters of the Bricker amendment, as well as people opposing the United Nations of UNESCO, had been accused of having paranoiac tendencies.

John Kasper, a bookseller from Merchantville, New Jersey, told the senators that Ezra Pound, whom he considered America's greatest living poet, had been incarcerated in St. Elizabeth's Hospital, even without the passage of H.R. 6376. And, Kasper contended, Pound was sane, "one of the most brilliant men who has ever lived. You will find him surrounded by raving lunatics." Kasper identified Alaska as being "practically the furthest reach of the country." He claimed that psychiatry was a Jewish plot, since it had begun with Sigmund Freud and, therefore, "almost 100 percent of all psychiatric therapy is Jewish . . ."[40]

Thousands of conservative and right-wing Americans believed that sinister forces were fashioning a program of national brainwashing. They maintained that section 119, particularly subparagraph (c), of the mental health measure would permit the government to dispatch political dissenters and other citizens of any state to an Alaskan Siberia. To demonstrate that it could happen in America, another pair of witnesses, Charles and George Finn, dubbed the "terrible Finn twins" by Bartlett, told their tale of woe. They claimed that the government had illegally seized a surplus plane they had earlier purchased from the Federal Security Agency. They thereupon had executed a citizen's arrest of a United States attorney in Los Angeles. Consequently, they were indicted for interfering with an official in pursuit of his duties and were sentenced to a year in jail. However, upon recommendation of the judge, the Finns, without benefit of a psychiatric examination, were sent to a federal insane asylum in Springfield, Missouri and confined in a ward for the criminally insane. After a thirty-five-day hunger strike and the intervention of Senator William Langer, they were released.[41]

Dr. James A. Franklin, Jr., president of the Memphis chapter of "We, the People," opposed the legislation because he believed it to be a plot to socialize medicine in America. Retired Brigadier General Herbert C. Holdridge, a one-time vice-presidential candidate on the Prohibition ticket, also opposed H.R.

6376, believing it to be a Roman Catholic conspiracy aimed at establishing, "under the guise of humanitarianism . . . the horrors of a Siberian prison camp coupled with the horrors of a snake pit insane asylum."[42]

The hearings closed on March 25, 1956. The American political lunatic fringe had inundated Congress with letters, telegrams, and pamphlets in opposition to the Alaska mental health bill. Two senators told Bartlett that they had received more mail and telegrams against H.R. 6376 than on any subject since their arrival in the Senate. One had counted five thousand letters and wires in opposition to it. The delegate had tried to "hold off those who would prevent our Mental Health Act from becoming law . . . who would do to Alaska what Alaskans don't want done to Alaska and who don't want Alaskans to do the things they should be permitted to do." Bartlett admitted being "a bit confused after the onslaught of the Patriotic Women of the U.S.A., the Minute Women of the U.S.A., Inc., and ever so many others who have attacked the Mental Health Act."[43]

There were bright spots. The Coes apparently had realized that some sort of Alaska mental health measure was certain to pass. Giving up their previous opposition, they supported the Alaska bill before the Senate subcommittee, much to the surprise of Bartlett, who remarked that he had been regrettably unaware of this communality of interest. Morningside Hospital, the Coes told the delegate, unfortunately had been used as "an emotional whipping boy" over the years. It was important, they said, to go on with the business of caring for the mentally ill in the best possible fashion.[44]

It was the suggestion of Senator Barry Goldwater of Arizona that eventually broke the logjam. Since controversy had raged over Title I of the bill, which dealt with commitment procedures, Goldwater proposed to strike that title, leaving it to the Alaskan territorial legislature to draw up the necessary mental health legislation, just as many of the states in the continental United States had done. On May 15 the full Senate committee adopted the Goldwater amendment, and on June 7 the Senate passed the abbreviated version of the Alaska Mental Health Enabling Act by unanimous vote. On June 14 the House disagreed with the Senate version of the mental health bill and requested a conference, and on July 2 the conferees agreed to the Senate version of H.R. 6376.[45]

On July 20, 1956, the House took up the question. Congressman Miller, no friend of the territory, offered a motion to recommit the measure. The motion was ruled out of order, because the Senate already had adopted the conference report. On July 28, 1956, President Eisenhower signed the bill into law. At last the fight had been won.

The history of this legislation illustrates the familiar elements of opposition to Alaska measures—the fear of added expense to the federal government, the lack of understanding of Alaskan logistics, the reluctance to grant lands to the territory, and the resistance of various special-interest groups. In this case, the words "mental health" had come to be looked upon suspiciously by conservative and right-wing Americans who were alarmed over the vast pretensions of modern psychiatry, the ever increasing accumulation of data which showed the growth of mental illness in twentieth-century America, and the concomitant extension of local, state, and federal mental health programs. Bartlett generally had trouble enough, but he had almost despaired when the issue became involved in the emotionalism of an alleged conspiracy on the part of the federal government to create a vast prison camp for political undesirables in the icy wastes of Alaska. In the end, however, reason had prevailed, and the mental health bill cleared Congress.

1 Bartlett Brothers freighting outfit, Dawson, Yukon Territory, at the turn of the century.

2 Ed Bartlett, front left, and two of his brothers, Al and Mike. The three brothers owned a freighting business, first in Seattle, then in Alaska. Eventually each went his own way.

3 Ida Florence and Ed Bartlett, Bob's parents. Klondike pioneers, they met in Skagway in 1897 and were married in Dawson in the spring of 1899.

3

2

1

5

6

7

4 Ed Bartlett raised oats to feed his
   horses. Here he stands in his field at
   Golden, Alaska.

5 Bob Bartlett, about four years old.

6 Doris Bartlett, Bob's sister, who died as
   a young child.

7 Vide Gaustad, Bob's future wife, at
   her father's mine, No. 10 Below Cleary
   Creek, 20 miles north of Fairbanks,
   Alaska.

8 Vide Gaustad's graduation picture
   from Hollywood High School, 1922.   8

4

9 Bob Bartlett in the early 1930s.

10 Bartlett and pioneer Alaskan bush pilot Carl Ben Eielson, 1920s.

11 Bartlett and his mother at their Independence Mine in the Circle District, probably 1936.

12 Alaska's Territorial Delegate Anthony J. Dimond and his political protege Bob Bartlett.

13 Bartlett's first political campaign, 1944.

A Resident of Alaska for 39 Years—Fourth
Division for Over 30 Years!

VOTE FOR

E. L. [Bob] Bartlett

Democratic Candidate for

Delegate to Congress

Primary Election, April 25, 1944
Endorsed by Delegate Dimond

13

9

18

14

14 In May 1945, Bartlett (second from right) traveled to defeated Germany on an inspection trip as a member of the House Committee on Military Affairs.

15 Bartlett with his oldest daughter Doris Ann, on the campaign trail in the early 1950s.

16 Throughout his political career, Bartlett proudly pointed to his mining experience. Here he holds a gold bar in the nearly deserted mining community of Flat, Alaska.

17 Bartlett with Adlai Stevenson in Juneau in 1954, during Stevenson's tour of Alaska at the invitation of the state's Democratic party leadership.

18 Ernest Gruening, center, and Bartlett, right, proudly display the 49-star flag after Alaska was admitted as a state in 1958.

17

15

16

19 Anchorage citizens greet Bartlett after final passage of the Alaska Statehood Act in 1958, admitting the territory as the 49th state.

20 In 1958 Bartlett campaigned for one of Alaska's two new U.S. Senate seats.

21 1966 St. Patrick's Day luncheon with, left to right, Robert Byrd, Bartlett, Frank Moss, Eugene McCarthy, Edmund Muskie, Ernest Gruening. (Man at head of table unidentified.)

22 Alaska native health and housing were two of Bartlett's concerns. Left to right, unidentified woman, Charles Blomfield, Bartlett, Eben Hopson, Emil Notti and Charles Edwardsen, 1964.

23 President Harry S. Truman and Senator Bartlett. Truman was the first President to endorse statehood for Alaska.

19

20

23

22

21

24 Much to his joy, Bartlett was made
    marshal of the 1959 Rose Bowl Parade.
    Bartlett, daughter Susan, wife Vide
    head the procession.

25 Doris Ann Bartlett Riley, Vide and
    Susan Bartlett holding Doris Ann's
    children.

26 Edward McDermott showing map of
    area affected by 1964 earthquake to
    Governor William A. Egan, Lt. Gen-
    eral Raymond J. Reeves and Senators
    Ernest Gruening and Bob Bartlett.

27 Bartlett, McDermott, Gruening
    and Lt. General Reeves, Alaska
    commander-in-chief, inspecting
    earthquake damage in Anchorage,
    1964.

28 Gruening, Bartlett and McDermott at
    4th and C Street, Anchorage, 1964.

26

27

28

29 Natalie Gottstein, Vide Bartlett, Barney Gottstein and Bob Bartlett at reception honoring Bartlett as Alaska's 1966 "Man of the Year."

30 Senator Bartlett, Mrs. Johnson, President Lyndon B. Johnson and Mrs. Bartlett at the White House, May 1965.

31 Senator Edward Kennedy testifies at Senate Commerce Committee hearings on Bartlett's 12-mile off-shore limit bill.

32 Senators Warren G. Magnuson and Bartlett. Magnuson chaired the Senate Commerce Committee, Bartlett chaired the Subcommittee on Merchant Marine and Fisheries. The two men worked closely on many issues.

33 Anchorage honors the Bartletts on Bob's 61st birthday in 1965.

29

30

31

32

35

39

36

34 Senator Bartlett and his staff answered
   many questions about Alaska.

35 Mary Lee Council, Margery Smith
   with Senator Bartlett. The two women
   were the backbone of his office staff.

36 Mary Lee Council and Margery Smith,
   both from Alaska pioneer families,
   worked with Bartlett throughout his
   political career.

37 Bartlett in his Washington, D.C. office,
   1967.

38 Bartlett with native friends at his Anchorage election headquarters, 1966.

39 A rare shot—Bartlett on a bicycle in
   Anchorage.

37

38

40 Bartlett as Alaska's senior U.S. Senator.

41 Vide Bartlett as a member of the
    Board of Regents of the University of
    Alaska, 1975.

42 Congressman Howard Pollock,
    Senator Ted Stevens, Mrs. Bartlett,
    Senator Mike Gravel, Senator Warren
    Magnuson at ceremonies dedicating
    the E. L. Bartlett Memorial Audito-
    rium in Washington, D.C., May 6, 1969.

42

0

41

The Statehood Issue

N o OTHER ISSUE demanded so much of Delegate Bartlett's attention and energies as did statehood. Yet the struggle for Alaska statehood is not the story of one man's unremitting efforts alone but rather the complex interaction of many interest groups and individuals, some opposing and some favoring the cause, in Congress, in Alaska, and in the United States at large. The successful achievement of statehood was closely interwoven with congressional political processes that, more often than not, had little or nothing to do with the merits or demerits of the cause. Despite the complexities of the political issues, it is possible to isolate, analyze, and describe the particular motivations and the efforts undertaken by some of the personalities and interest groups involved.

It is always a temptation to pursue the antecedents of any particular movement as far into the misty past as the materials available will permit. It is sufficient in this instance, however, to note that Alaska's third delegate to Congress, James Wickersham, introduced the first statehood enabling act in Congress on March 30, 1916, supported in Alaska by a small statehood club and a weekly newspaper, the *Forty-Ninth Star,* both located in Valdez.[1] Congress did not act on the measure.

Wickersham's effort had been merely a symbolic one, a token assertion of a continued striving for fuller self-government. Alaskan politicians and newspaper editors, however, continued to discuss the question of self-government intermittently in the years following World War I.

In June 1942 U.S. Senator William L. Langer, a maverick Republican from North Dakota, perhaps induced by Wickersham's successor, Delegate Dimond, announced to the press that he was drafting an enabling bill for Alaska.[2] On April 2, 1943, Senator Langer introduced his measure, cosponsored by conservative U.S. Senator Pat McCarran from Nevada.

Delegate Dimond subsequently discussed the statehood question over radio station WWDC in Washington, D.C. The delegate optimistically asserted that statehood for Alaska was assured. He declared that the territory was ready, and was entitled to it, although the military might prefer to put off any change in the governmental structure until after the war. Opposition, he predicted, would come from absentee-owned fishing and mining industries fearful of high taxes. Dimond argued that further economic development and statehood were interdependent, and this represented the traditional rhetoric on the subject.[3]

Several Alaskan organizations and newspapers responded to the issue. The Juneau Bar Association endorsed statehood, while the city's Chamber of Commerce voted negatively.[4] The Alaska Miners Association concluded that statehood efforts during the war would be ill-considered, and the Fairbanks Chamber of Commerce suggested that any action be deferred until more information became available, a recommendation *Jessen's Weekly* also endorsed. The *Anchorage Daily Times* hesitated to take a stand without more information but pointed out that the war had focused a great deal of attention on the North, which would present an excellent opportunity for a statehood campaign.[5] Dean Sherman, a statehood advocate and the editor of the territorial magazine *Alaska Life*, published in Seattle, solicited opinions from a broad cross-section of northern citizens. He reported that the main concern was the possibility of increased taxes, a concern he decried, because Alaskans were the most lightly taxed "free men" in the world.[6]

The idea of statehood was in the air, being discussed in Alaska and in Congress as well. Although Delegate Dimond had expressed himself in favor of the proposition, he had not yet introduced his own legislation. On his way home after the 1943 congressional recess, he announced his intention to introduce his own enabling measure in the fall because of his dissatisfaction with the Langer bill.[7] While in Juneau, the delegate undoubtedly conferred with Secretary of Alaska Bob Bartlett, and it may be assumed the subject matter included statehood.

Back in Washington, Dimond submitted his companion measure to the Langer-McCarran bill. Although not fundamentally different from that bill, Dimond's provided that the federal government convey to the future state "all public property and all vacant and unappropriated lands, including lands reserved or withdrawn from entry," with the following exceptions: all land and property possessed and actually used by the United States for some governmental purpose; all lands, including adjacent waters and other property, reserved for Alaska's natives; lands already reserved for the support of common schools and the University of Alaska; Mount McKinley National Park, Glacier Bay National Monument, and Naval Petroleum Reserve Number 4 (Pet. 4); the Pribilof Islands and whatever portions of the Aleutian Chain west of the 172nd meridian might be required for military purposes. Alaska, however, would receive Mount Katmai, Sitka, and Old Kasaan national monuments, wildlife refuges, and reserved oil land other than Pet. 4. In addition, the measure provided that fur and game resources and all federal property used for the conservation and protection of the fisheries also become state property. Excluded would be the research facilities dealing with fisheries and wildlife, which would only add to the costs of state government.[8] Obviously, such far-reaching demands for vast lands and extended authority over resources would complicate the situation tremendously. In effect, the nation would be asked to give up great potential wealth to the new state.

Dimond's bill zeroed in on those issues that had always rankled Alaskans most—the federal propensity to withdraw vast acreages at the slightest excuse and the difficulty of obtaining title to lands. Dimond and territorial residents also objected to the establishment of native reservations in Alaska. Between April 20, 1942, and May 22, 1944, Secretary Ickes, under the authority of the Indian Reorganization Act of 1934 and its Alaska amendments of 1936, had created five reservations in the territory, comprising some 1,537,270 acres. The thought behind the establishment of these reservations was to enable native groups to pursue traditional life-styles based on sufficient resources. The secretary's reservation policy had provoked a storm of protests from most Caucasian Alaskans and from many natives as well. Proposed state ownership of most of the public domain, Dimond reasoned, would foreclose further reservations. But as a lawyer steeped in the importance of precedent, Dimond also knew that Congress would convey only a portion of the public domain.[9]

In response to the statehood discussion, Secretary Ickes soon asserted that statehood ultimately was desirable but only after further economic development had brought a certain amount of stability to Alaska. Similarly, the departments of the Interior and War thought wartime inopportune for admission to the Union.[10]

This is where the issue of statehood stood in 1944 when Bartlett decided to run for Dimond's seat. He remembered Dimond's 1943 statement "that the goals and dreams and aspirations of Alaskans could never be realized unless and until statehood was achieved." Dimond had reminded his listeners that efforts to liberalize the Organic Act of 1912 had failed. The Organic Act of 1912 had made Alaska officially a territory. Among other things, it had created a territorial legislature of limited powers but had continued federal management of the North's game, fur, and fishery resources. Dimond suggested that since attempts at amending the Organic Act had failed, "why not try for the big one, for statehood, which would wrap it all up at one time." Bartlett remembered this well and recalled that "it was this declaration that really excited me, and interested me, and, I guess, converted me." When embarking upon his campaign for delegate, Bartlett decided "that I was going to emphasize statehood. I thought whether I won or lost I ought to point out that my belief corresponded with Dimond's, that it was futile to go along and seek improvement of the Organic Act by one amendment after the other," each of which was unlikely to be approved by Congress.[11]

Governor Ernest Gruening delivered his annual message to the Alaska territorial legislature early in 1945. The governor reminded his listeners that the platforms of territorial Republicans and Democrats, as well as the two candidates for the position of delegate in Congress, had favored statehood in 1944. Since most Alaskans accepted statehood in principle, differing only on the timing of admission or on the conditions, the time clearly had arrived to hold a referendum on the question. First, however, the voters needed impartial information which, the governor suggested, should be published in pamphlet form and widely distributed.[12] The legislature, after some false starts, complied with the governor's request for a referendum, with the vote to be taken in the 1946 general election. During the same session the territorial House of Representatives sent a memorial to Congress. This document pleaded dramatically for the extension to Alaska of the "Four Freedoms" proclaimed in the Atlantic Charter, which supported the right of small nations and minorities to choose their own form of government and to control their own destinies. The memorial was followed shortly by a request to admit Alaska as the forty-ninth state.[13]

As Alaskans deliberated the statehood issue, several congressional groups toured the territory. Often such groups traveled to Alaska during the summer and combined sightseeing and fishing with meetings, hearings, and inspections. Sometimes described unkindly by the press as junkets, these trips nevertheless did give congressmen the chance to combine business with pleasure and learn a great deal in the process. The visitors often became more aware of Alaskan problems, later cooperating closely with Delegate Bartlett on territorial legislation.

The first congressional group to come to Alaska during this period was the House Subcommittee on Appropriations for the Department of the Interior, led by its chairman, Jed Johnson of Oklahoma. Back in San Francisco after his tour, committee member John Rooney of New York declared that Alaskans were not ready to assume the burdens of statehood, citing the fact that they allowed the fishing industry to take some $60 million from the territory and return only $1 million. Furthermore, he asserted, absentee fishing and mining interests controlled the territorial legislature. Congressman Johnson essentially agreed and observed that Alaskans would have to start paying for such things as roads, schools, and hospitals and not rely on the federal government to provide the funds. He concluded that, in general, old-timers opposed statehood because of their unwillingness to pay taxes, while newcomers favored immediate statehood. In their report the committee members agreed with the views of congressmen Johnson and Rooney.

These assessments were substantially accurate. Whatever little revenue the territory collected was derived from the excise tax on liquor, taxes on the taking and canning of salmon, and mercantile and license fees. It was a wholly inadequate and inequitable system of taxation, not in harmony with the generally accepted principle of taxing wealth rather than people. As early as the late 1930s, then-

Governor John W. Troy had commissioned the territorial planning council to make a tax study, but the research was not completed until Gruening replaced Troy as territorial governor. The authors of the report had concluded that an annual revenue of $10 million was entirely feasible with the adoption of a modern tax system. In 1941 Governor Gruening had presented a tax reform plan to the territorial legislature, which had soundly rejected it. Gruening had worked hard in subsequent years for tax reforms, without success. Evidently the legislature and, indirectly, the people, were not yet ready to bite the hand that seemed to feed them. The exploitative resource industries still held the threat of total withdrawal of livelihood over many Alaskans.[14]

Another group of congressmen visiting Alaska at this time were members of the House Committee on Territories, led by Chairman Hugh Peterson of Georgia. At the first committee meeting of the year, Delegate Bartlett had requested such a visit, anxious for members of Congress to see the North and gain an appreciation of its needs. The House Committee on Territories toured the area for two weeks, taking testimony at Ketchikan, Juneau, Anchorage, and Fairbanks. Both Bartlett and Governor Gruening had planned the group's itinerary carefully. It was designed to make the guests aware of northern problems, needs, and opportunities and included trips to scenic places and good salmon fishing spots.

In the course of their travels, the twelve congressmen heard opinions about the federal land withdrawals and delays in patenting land, the merits of using fish traps versus purse seines for commercial salmon fishing, the native reservations and title insecurity due to aboriginal claims, the dire need for lower transportation tariffs and a highway network, and the inadequacies of the Organic Act and sundry statehood bills.

While the House Committee on Territories held hearings, William Baker, the editor and publisher of the *Ketchikan Alaska Chronicle,* conducted a telephone poll on the statehood question. The results surprised Baker: of the residents he contacted, 106 favored statehood, 40 opposed it, and 51 were undecided or had no opinion.[15] The statehood opponents had cited higher taxes as their main concern. Others had suggested that self-government be considered only for the populous regions, or that statehood be preceded by a territory-wide tax program or by a transitional period lasting anywhere from five to ten years. In any event, a majority definitely favored statehood, though an overwhelming number appreciated the problems involved.

In Juneau and Anchorage, the committee heard strongly voiced opinions both against and in favor of statehood. In Fairbanks, the center of the territory's mining industry, the committee encountered the largest number of statehood opponents. Glenn Carrington, an equipment dealer and vice-president of the Alaska Miners Association, which included producers of gold, coal, and other minerals, summed up his group's opposition. He stated that out of 40,000 persons employed in Alaska, some 6,600 were miners who paid taxes. Such a small number of individuals could not be expected to carry the major tax burden and develop the country. Furthermore, discounting the transient defense workers, Alaska's population consisted of approximately half Caucasians and half natives, with the natives controlling the votes. Carrington did not believe that this ratio allowed Alaska's development to reflect the wishes of the Caucasian population.

The committee also heard the Fairbanks Chamber of Commerce express itself ambivalently on the statehood question. A majority of that group's members favored self-government, but some thought that more than one state should be carved from the North.[16]

The territorial attorney general, Ralph J. Rivers, testified before the House Committee on Territories in Juneau. If the statehood referendum failed, he proposed, Congress should grant the territory powers to establish its own judicial, police, and penal systems, elect its own governor, and pay the cost of its own legislature, among other items. This would give Alaska nearly all the responsibilities of statehood together with nearly all the costs. Rivers therefore suggested that the federal government return a certain portion of the approximately $20 million of corporate and individual income taxes collected in the territory every year. At the end of five years, federal aid could be withdrawn, Rivers believed, and Alaska made a state.

Much of the testimony heard by the committee was poorly prepared. It was clear that opponents of statehood generally feared increased taxes, while proponents argued that representation in Congress would offset any disadvantages, such as increased costs. The testimony gave the congressmen thousands of facts and many impressions — but no agreement as to how soon the territory should seek admission to the Union. Early in 1946 the committee submitted its report to the full House. It mentioned that statehood had been discussed often and earnestly at most hearings and meetings with citizens, but the committee made no recommendation either for or against it. The committee based its decision on the almost unanimous opinion of the members that statehood would be granted to Hawaii and that any decision on Alaska should be postponed until the outcome of the plebiscite on the issue had become known.[17]

As a result of their hearings in Alaska, the committee did consider changes in the Organic Act. It recommended that Congress extend the powers of the territorial government, such as conveying jurisdiction over the fish, game, and fur resources.[18] Such changes had been discussed often in Alaska, and delegates had submitted measures with regularity over the years, always unsuccessfully. In 1945, for example, the territorial House had recommended some twenty specific changes in the Organic Act. The Division of Territories and Island Possessions had drafted a measure incorporating many of the suggested changes and added provisions for the election of the governor and secretary of Alaska and for redistricting the territorial Senate on the basis of population.[19]

Delegate Bartlett released the proposed bill for amending the Organic Act to his constituency for review. Although committed to statehood, Bartlett knew that, among many old-timers in particular, there was a strong sentiment against statehood but a desire for changes in the Organic Act. Therefore, the hostility with which the Alaska Miners Association received the proposed amendments surprised the delegate. The association rejected the provision for redistricting the territorial Senate on the basis of population. Its members had no intention of giving up equal Senate representation in the Second and Fourth judicial divisions, which, in effect, gave them veto power over territorial legislation.

Actually, Bartlett knew that attempts at amending the Organic Act had proven fruitless in the past. As a consequence, he had decided earlier to press for statehood instead. Furthermore, if Congress by chance should amend the Organic Act, statehood probably would be delayed, because Congress would insist that Alaskans live with an amended Organic Act for a number of years. The delegate, therefore, informed the miners that he would not introduce the bill, because it would confuse the statehood referendum. If Alaskans voted to reject statehood on that occasion, he would then work for amendments to the Organic Act.[20]

In the meantime the federal departments most concerned with Alaska's administration had to take an official stand on statehood. Secretary of the Interior Ickes had opposed statehood in 1943, primarily because of what he considered excessive land grants for the new state contained in the enabling act. But Jack B. Fahy, acting director of the Division of Territories and Island Possessions, persuaded Ickes to change his mind. He told the secretary that most department agencies approved Alaska statehood, with the exception of the Fish and Wildlife Service and Geological Survey. Fahy also reassured the secretary that statehood did not mean that ownership of all public lands would be vested in the state. As a matter of fact, he reminded Ickes, past enabling acts had granted certain acreages for schools, roads, and other public purposes, while title to the bulk of the lands had always remained with the federal government. Perhaps it was this argument that won over the "Old Curmudgeon," or perhaps it was the influence of wartime idealism. Whatever the reason, Acting Secretary of the Interior Abe Fortas announced on August 11, 1945, that statehood was now a part of the department's policy for Alaska and had the blessings of Secretary Ickes.[21] A positive recommendation from the Department of the Interior was of utmost importance to Alaska, because it had jurisdiction over most federal activities in the territory.

In his 1946 State of the Union message, President Harry S. Truman boosted Alaska statehood by recommending its prompt admittance as a state as soon as the wishes of its citizens had been determined. This presidential endorsement kept national attention focused on Alaska. In the fall of 1946 Julius A. Krug, the new secretary of the Interior, visited Alaska to determine, among other things, the sentiment for statehood. *U.S. News and World Report* predicted that Alaska would soon become the forty-ninth state and said that it expected Alaska to be America's most important defense frontier in the age of long-range planes and guided missiles. In September pollster George Gallup reported that 64 percent of the American voters favored Alaska's admission to the Union, 12 percent were opposed, and 24 percent were undecided. Gallup stated that Americans favored admission for two main reasons: the territory was vital to national defense, and its citizens deserved equal representation.[22] These forecasts encouraged optimism, but Bartlett and others realized that there was a long way to go before statehood would be achieved.

Although the territorial legislature had authorized a statehood referendum, it had not provided for the preparation, publication, or circulation of an informational pamphlet. Eventually, journalist George Sundborg prepared the desired analysis. Some 31,600 copies of the Sundborg analysis were printed as a newspaper supplement and distributed widely.[23] Combined with meetings, speeches, debates, and radio broadcasts, they served to stimulate interest and educate the voting public.

When Alaskan voters went to the polls in the general election in October 1946, many had read or scanned the Sundborg report. Amidst much publicity and campaigning, they reelected Delegate Bartlett over his Republican opponent, Almer Peterson. They approved statehood by a margin of three to two, or 9,630 to 6,822 votes.[24] Even if the total vote in the territory had not been large, the referendum clearly had been a victory for the statehood leadership provided by Delegate Bartlett and Governor Gruening.

Although three statehood bills had been submitted to Congress between 1943 and 1946, the exigencies of war had helped prevent their consideration. By 1947, however, Alaska's role in that conflict and in the cold war had generated support for statehood among numerous Americans in the continental United States and members of Congress.

On January 3, 1947 Delegate Bartlett introduced a statehood bill. This measure was substantially identical to the one he had introduced in 1945 and to the Dimond bill of 1943, except that Bartlett now enlarged the public land grant to the prospective state. He proposed to withdraw the federal land reserves and give to Alaska the Aleutian Islands west of the 172nd meridian, the Pribilof Islands and all the lands with adjacent waters, and other property set aside or reserved for the use or benefit of the Indians, Eskimos, and Aleuts.

Hearings on the Bartlett measure were scheduled in Washington in the spring of 1947. It was a different kind of Congress then, for Republicans controlled both houses for the first time since 1933. Furthermore, legislative reorganization in 1946 had reduced the number of standing committees in each house and had strengthened the powers of those that remained. The House Committee on Territories had been absorbed into the House Committee on Public Lands, and its Senate counterpart had been absorbed into what was to become known as the Senate Committee on Interior and Insular Affairs.[25] Delegates Bartlett and Joseph Farrington of Hawaii were the only members of the old House Committee on Territories to sit on the new Subcommittee on Territories and Insular Possessions of the House Committee on Public Lands.

Statehood hearings on Hawaii preceded those on Alaska, which were held between April 16 and April 24, 1947, in Washington. On the first day of the proceedings, Secretary Krug strongly endorsed Alaska statehood but criticized the land provisions of the Bartlett bill. Acting Secretary of the Interior Warner W. Gardner also endorsed statehood, but specifically objected to sections 3, 4, and 5 which, with few exceptions, would have transferred title to practically all public lands to the new state. This, he stated, was contrary to the traditional practice followed throughout the American west. Specified lands had always been granted for schools and internal improvements, while the federal government had retained the bulk. Gardner proposed to grant Alaska about 21,000,000 acres for schools, about 438,000 for the University of Alaska, and another 500,000 acres for various internal improvements. Gardner also proposed that the state and its people forever disclaim both the right and title to all land retained by, or ceded to, the federal government by the statehood bill and to all land owned or held by natives or native tribes, the right or title to which had been acquired from the United States or any previous sovereignty. Until the United States disposed of, or extinguished title to, such land, it would remain within the exclusive jurisdiction of the federal government and be nontaxable by the state. These guarantees for native claims were sought by both the Department of the Interior, which was the trustee of native American claims, and by Washington attorney James Curry, who was representing the National Congress of American Indians and the southeastern-based Alaska Native Brotherhood.[26]

During the hearings Assistant Secretary of Agriculture Charles Brannan asserted that the Tongass and Chugach national forests should remain under federal jurisdiction. He did propose that Alaska receive the average gross receipts from four out of every thirty-six sections of national forest land per year.

In addition to eight congressmen who appeared, numerous Alaskans had flown to Washington to testify. Among them were Anthony Dimond, William Baker, Ralph Rivers, George Sundborg, who was then manager of the Alaska Development Board, Robert Atwood, editor and publisher of the *Anchorage Daily Times*,

Governor Gruening, chambers of commerce representatives, small businessmen, sourdoughs, and federal and territorial officials. In addition, some non-Alaskans who favored statehood appeared.

Bartlett, as a member of the subcommittee, made full use of his privilege of questioning the witnesses. He skillfully used the friendly witnesses to strengthen the statehood case. Among those less friendly, there were some who said they approved of statehood in principle but contended that Alaska was not yet ready. One of these was Herbert L. Faulkner, an attorney and longtime resident of Juneau. He praised the Bartlett bill but then introduced a formidable array of statistics and detailed information designed to totally demolish the case for statehood. The gist of his argument was that Alaska would be financially unable to afford statehood. Under Bartlett's questioning, Faulkner admitted that, as a lawyer, he represented some of the canneries, a large mining company, a few lumber concerns, a bank, and a telephone business—all Alaskan establishments—but he asserted that on this occasion he was representing only himself. Sundborg undertook to rebut Faulkner's arguments and accused the Juneau attorney of having vastly inflated the costs of statehood.

Congressman Arthur L. "Doc" Miller of Nebraska suggested that Alaska be partitioned. He proposed to admit only the southern third to the Union. Most individuals queried disliked the suggestion, with Atwood stating that such an idea was "a bad thing in principle to start with. Alaska has always been one."[27]

Governor Gruening said he had no aversion to partition and thought that any division should occur either along the Yukon River or the 64th or 65th parallel, with the understanding that at some future time the rest of the territory could join if it were desirable and appropriate. Bartlett reluctantly decided to go along with the idea if the only way statehood could be had was by partition.[28] A few days after the end of the hearings, committee members voted to postpone reporting the measure until they visited the territory to gather additional information.

In the meantime, Hawaii's statehood measure was faring much better. The House of Representatives passed it by a vote of 195 to 133 on June 30, 1947, encouraging Alaska statehood enthusiasts.[29]

Bartlett and four other members of the House Subcommittee on Territories and Insular Possessions went to Alaska in the early fall of 1947. In Seward, the ocean terminus of the Alaska Railroad, they heard relatively little about statehood as such. Instead, the witnesses concentrated on denouncing the Seattle shipping monopoly and the outrageous prevailing freight rates. In Anchorage they found the sentiment for statehood overwhelmingly favorable. In Fairbanks Al Anderson, executive secretary of the Alaska Miners Association, stated his fears of the high costs of statehood. Norman Stines, a Fairbanks resident, complained that the hearing seemed to be packed with statehood advocates. Why, he asked, were advocates assumed to be objective, while opponents were considered as paid agents of the absentee owners?[30]

Perhaps most notable was the testimony given by James Wooten, the new president of Alaska Airlines, who talked at length about the neglected territory. Within a few days after his appearance, some six individuals communicated to him the canned salmon industry's displeasure with his position. They indicated that the industry's cannery travel business during the fishing season, worth in excess of $400,000, might well be at stake. Undeterred, Wooten persisted. Shortly before he was to speak to another congressional group, Winton C. Arnold, managing director of the Alaska Salmon Industry, Inc., a trade organization, approached Wooten and pointed out that his position on statehood might jeopardize the airline's standing with the industry. Wooten nevertheless went ahead and testified, stating that the salmon industry paid only a small part of its large income in taxes to the territory. Shortly thereafter, Loren Daley, Jr., of the Bristol Bay Packing Company and Doug Sherrif of the Alaska Packers Association told Wooten bluntly that if he expected "to get any of the canned salmon industry business, you sure in hell had better change your position and keep your mouth shut."[31]

After taking testimony in Fairbanks, the subcommittee made short trips to Barrow, Nome, Kodiak, and Cordova and then flew to Juneau, where Delegate Bartlett and attorney Mildred Hermann critically examined the statehood cost estimates of attorney Faulkner and Juneau insurance agent Allen Shattuck. Hermann's figures were drawn up by economist George Rogers of Juneau. Together with information given by territorial Senator Victor Rivers regarding Governor Gruening's proposals for a modern tax system, they gave the congressmen a more balanced picture of statehood fiscal matters.

The subcommittee members stopped at Petersburg, Wrangell, and Ketchikan, where Governor Gruening delivered a most eloquent and persuasive address. Gruening complimented the subcommittee members for their diligent efforts to learn about Alaska. He pointed out examples of discrimination and neglect against Alaska and concluded that both the nation and the North would gain from Alaska's admission into the Union.[32]

Bartlett and Sundborg accompanied the subcommittee on most of its travels, while Governor Gruening divided his time between that subcommittee and other groups of congressmen touring Alaska, among them Senator Hugh Butler and three members of the Senate Public Lands Committee. Butler, who had become a millionaire in the flour-milling and grain business in Omaha, Nebraska, was touring the territory to get acquainted with Alaska's problems, not to hold official hearings. Although the senators did hold short hearings at times, no record of them was made.[33] While in Anchorage, Butler refused to commit himself on the statehood issue, preferring to judge an enabling act at the time that it came before his committee. After leaving Alaska, the senator stated that the territory would gain statehood in ten years or less if the legislature enacted an adequate tax system.[34]

The 1947 hearings on the statehood measure were important because they placed the issue squarely before Congress. Anderson and Arnold had represented the opposing view ably, but the pro-statehood cause had gained new strength and dimension. The *Anchorage Daily Times,* the *Ketchikan Alaska Chronicle,* and *The Alaska Weekly* of Seattle supported the cause. Many private citizens worked for it as well. Mildred Hermann, who was president of the Alaska Women's Club, one of the few female lawyers in Alaska, and an ardent feminist of the old school, assumed a leadership role in Juneau. Ralph J. Rivers and William A. Egan, territorial senator from Valdez, spent even more time and effort than before. Several prominent Tlingit Indian families in southeastern Alaska and many other respected Alaskans, too numerous to mention, joined the movement.[35]

In Washington, Delegate Bartlett was elated to learn that Fred Crawford of Michigan, the chairman of the House Subcommittee on Territories and Insular Possessions, had been converted to a statehood crusader by his fall trip to Alaska. When Congress reconvened in January 1947, Crawford met with the three colleagues with whom he had toured Alaska. They decided to recommend statehood to the full committee.[36]

The House Subcommittee on Territories and Insular Possessions met in Washington in February 1948 to discuss Alaska statehood. It soon became apparent that the subcommittee disagreed with the departments of the Interior and Agriculture in regard to land grants to the new state. Representatives of the Department of the Interior insisted on two sections for each township, while the subcommittee and Delegate Bartlett held out for four. An impasse developed, and Bartlett was instructed to meet with interior and agriculture officials to work out a compromise, which, together with subcommittee amendments, would be incorporated into a new bill. Negotiations took place in Bartlett's office. The representative of the Bureau of Land Management feared that granting Alaska more than two sections per township would bring demands from existing public land states to seek additional grants of their own. He refused to compromise, and Bartlett, equally adamant, told the group that he would let the statehood bill die before agreeing to less than four sections of land per township. The delegate prevailed.[37] On March 2, 1948, Bartlett submitted a revised statehood bill, which the subcommittee approved a few days later.

When the full membership of the House Committee on Public Lands met in April, the subject of aboriginal rights threatened to delay action. The upshot of that issue was that the status of native property rights was left unaltered. Also at this meeting, Bartlett proposed that Alaska be granted 1,000,000 acres rather than

500,000 acres of land for the support of public institutions and, in addition, that section grants and lieu land selections be allowed to reach 50 percent rather than 25 percent in any one township. This provision was designed to enable Alaska to obtain large blocks of section grants. The committee accepted this and other amendments and unanimously approved the delegate's bill.[38]

The measure was then to go to the House Rules Committee, which had set no date for a hearing. Delegate Bartlett and two of his colleagues arranged a meeting with Speaker of the House Joseph Martin, Jr., an "old guard" Republican from Massachusetts, to learn the leadership's legislative priorities. They found that Alaska statehood was not a priority goal, which, in effect, doomed the measure. Bartlett then pressed Martin for consideration of his elective governor bill, which he had introduced in 1947. House action on such a measure would be ineffective if the Senate did not cooperate, but Bartlett found little help from Senator Butler on the matter, and he decided to try for passage of his statehood measure again in 1948. If it failed, then Bartlett was determined to call for an elective governor bill effective in 1950, even with the knowledge that Congress would insist that Alaskans live with the new system for a time before returning to lobby for statehood.[39]

Despite a special message from President Truman and a resolution introduced by California's Senator William F. Knowland on behalf of Hawaii, Senator Butler, chairman of the Senate Interior and Insular Affairs Committee, still refused to allow either the Alaska or Hawaii statehood bills to come up for discussion and debate.[40]

This killed the possibility of Alaska statehood for that session, but the setback was not a decisive or even a major one. Bartlett's bill had been debated in various committees and had been shaped to conform with the desires of the executive departments, matching the pattern of earlier statehood acts. It had been given wide circulation in Alaskan newspapers and through Bartlett's newsletter to his territorial constituents. The delegate had traveled widely in the territory, discussing the details of the matter. Hearings on Alaska statehood had been held for the first time, and a statehood measure had been approved unanimously by one committee of Congress. Reasons for optimism existed.

The national elections of November 1948 brought a substantial majority of Democrats to both houses of Congress and gave Truman the presidency for the coming four years. This was important for Alaska, inasmuch as the Democratic platform had pledged immediate statehood for Alaska and Hawaii, while the Republicans had promised only eventual admission.[41]

While President Truman had been campaigning against the "do-nothing Eightieth Congress," Governor Gruening was taking his dissatisfaction with the performance of the 1947 territorial legislature to Alaska's voters in a special report. The long-standing paralysis of the territorial legislature had reached a climax in the 1947 session. In the face of the territory's mounting needs for schools, hospitals, a new physical plant for the University of Alaska, expanded health services, more assistance for the aged, and legislation to make airport construction possible, the legislature had provided revenues of only $6,500,000 for a budget request of $10,500,000. Gruening had appealed to the voters to elect a legislature that would run the territory for its citizens rather than for special interest groups.

The electorate responded in 1948 and the Democrats won control of the House, while the Senate was split eight to eight between the parties. Bartlett was returned to Congress by the decisive margin of 17,520 to 4,789 votes over his Republican challenger, R.H. Stock. For the delegate, this election was an affirmation of the leadership he had provided on the issue of statehood.[42] It was also a turning point for Alaska, because it indicated to special interests that they would confront demands for changes and reforms.

The 1949 legislature set the territorial house in order and helped to prepare Alaska for statehood by adopting a comprehensive but moderate tax program. Still another important achievement of the 1949 legislative session was the creation of the official Alaska Statehood Committee — this in recognition of the popular demand for statehood. As early as 1947, efforts to create such a body had been made, unsuccessfully, to replace the inoperative Alaska Statehood Association and to lobby Congress to enact an enabling measure. In 1949 Senate Bill 49 — the number a symbol of the hope that the territory would become the forty-ninth state — was introduced by Senators Frank Peratrovich of Klawock, an outstanding Tlingit legislator, and Victor C. Rivers of Anchorage. Together with an $80,000 appropriation, it passed both Alaskan legislative houses.

Under provisions of the bill, the Alaska Statehood Committee was to consist of eleven Alaskans nominated by the governor and approved by the legislature. As an indication of its bipartisan character, not more than six of the members could belong to the same party. In addition, Governor Gruening, Delegate Bartlett, and former Delegate Dimond were to be ex-officio members. Among the committee's tasks were the research and preparation for a constitutional convention and a plan for the transition from territoriality to statehood.[43]

In the meantime, Bartlett's new statehood bill, which was identical to the one which the House Committee on Public Lands had amended and approved in 1948, was receiving congressional attention. Now the Subcommittee on Territories and Insular Possessions included only ten members in addition to the delegates from Alaska and Hawaii and Puerto Rico's resident commissioner. While all of the subcommittee's Republicans were veterans of the statehood issue, the Democrats were newly appointed and unfamiliar with the subject.[44]

Chairman Monroe Redden of North Carolina felt that the 1947 hearings had made prolonged investigations unnecessary in 1949. Redden held perfunctory hearings before his Subcommittee on Territories and Insular Affairs of the House Committee on Public Lands in Washington, D.C. on March 4 and March 8, 1949. At that time, the secretaries of the interior and agriculture and a representative of the Department of Defense gave testimony favorable to statehood. Arnold for the Alaska Salmon Industry, Inc., and Anderson of the Alaska Miners Association submitted written statements in which their objections, oddly enough, centered on the inadequacy of the land provisions in Bartlett's 1949 statehood bill and the fact that aboriginal claims to Alaskan lands clouded any future title by the state. They insisted that the 1947 hearings had been confined almost exclusively to the merits or demerits of statehood and had not dealt with the quality of the bill itself. If Alaska were to be admitted to the Union, they insisted that most of the land go to the state and no recognition be given aboriginal claims.[45]

Despite these objections, the subcommittee reported the Bartlett measure favorably, and on March 10 the full public lands committee recommended that the House pass the statehood bill. As the weeks passed without action, the public lands committee assigned six of its members to persuade the House Rules Committee to clear both the Alaska and the Hawaii statehood bills for floor debate and action. More weeks passed without action, and the committee finally authorized its acting chairman, J. Hardin Peterson of Florida, to file a discharge resolution under the twenty-one-day rule. (This was a reform procedure which barred the rules committee from holding for more than twenty-one days a measure which had been approved by one of the other committees. After the specified time period, the chairman of such a committee could move for a bill's consideration on the floor.) On March 14 Peterson filed bypass resolutions for the statehood bills, while Bartlett continued to seek a decision from the rules committee, feeling that chances of achieving statehood would thereby be enhanced.[46]

On May 16 President Truman and House Democratic leaders selected ten bills meriting special efforts, among them the Alaska statehood bill but not Hawaii's measure. On May 18 the rules committee debated the measures. Republicans on the rules committee told chairman Adolph Sabath of Illinois that they would block Alaska's bill unless he also acted on Hawaii's, which Sabath refused to do. Southern House members, opposing admission of either territory, participated in these maneuvers in order to kill both measures. And since southerners would not commit themselves to report Hawaii's bill, Republicans did as they had warned, blocking action on Alaska's bill.[47]

Bartlett believed that the eight negative votes in the rules committee had come primarily from Republicans and southern Democrats. Both Bartlett and Peterson now told Speaker of the House Sam Rayburn that they would like to file a discharge resolution again. Speaker Rayburn concurred on condition that they obtain the cooperation of Joseph W. Martin, since Republican votes were necessary for passage. Martin refused but promised to examine statehood in 1950. At that point Peterson gave up further efforts, since forcing a vote then might further jeopardize the statehood bill.[48]

After it had become apparent that an Alaska statehood act would not pass Congress in 1949, Governor Gruening decided to call a meeting of the Alaska Statehood Committee to consider future strategy. In late August 1949, members met in Juneau to organize and plan. Robert Atwood became chairman, William Baker vice-chairman, and Mildred Hermann, secretary. Subcommittees on education and public relations, legislation, constitution, and state organization were appointed. All ex-officio members were granted full committee privileges.

Bartlett informed committee members that Alaska's statehood bill, buried in the rules committee, stood an excellent chance of House passage in 1950. He cautioned, however, that the four House leaders adamantly opposed Alaska's admission and would have to be won over to the statehood cause. These four were Sam Rayburn of Texas, Charles Halleck of Indiana, and Joseph W. Martin and John McCormack, both of Massachusetts. Bartlett also urged the committee to organize better writing campaigns in the home states of those members of Congress who were opposed to statehood.[49]

Members realized that the main task of the committee would consist of publicizing and educating the people on statehood, both in Alaska and in the States. In addition, the committee would have to mobilize expert witnesses for future congressional statehood hearings. The committee, however, did not hire an executive officer-researcher or follow Governor Gruening's suggestion that a public relations firm be employed in Washington to do lobbying on behalf of statehood.[50]

Individual committee members also utilized their associations with national organizations to advertise Alaska statehood. Mrs. Hermann, for instance, gained the support of Mrs. Leslie B. Wright, legislative chairperson of the General Federation of Women's clubs, who promised to put her organization squarely behind the Alaskan campaign. The success of these efforts became evident at the 1950 Senate hearings, when numerous national groups, fraternal organizations, labor unions, newspaper editors, and even state governors testified in favor of the cause.

Additional assistance developed through Gruening's establishment of a committee of distinguished Americans who lent their names and support to the movement. Capitalizing on his broad national experience and connections, Gruening recruited a "committee of one hundred" prominent Americans favoring Alaska's aspirations. This national committee, broadly representative, included famous personalities ranging from Eleanor Roosevelt to Rear Admiral Richard E. Byrd and from famed arctic explorer Vilhjalmur Stefansson to philosopher Reinhold Niebuhr and historian Arthur M. Schlesinger, Jr.[51]

When Congress reconvened in 1950, Hawaii and Alaska statehood bills were still blocked in the House Rules Committee. On January 23, 1950, Speaker Rayburn recognized Hardin Peterson, who asked that the House discharge the rules committee from consideration of the Alaska statehood bill. After a great deal of discussion, the House voted 373 to 25 to approve the resolution. Peterson then moved that the Hawaii bill also be discharged, a move the House approved.[52]

Republican Congressman Frederic Coudert, Jr., from New York, who opposed discharge, raised arguments that were to be repeated often over subsequent years. Coudert objected to the fact that the two prospective states would have four U.S. senators whose powers and influence would be far out of proportion to the populations of the two areas. Unmindful of the Connecticut Compromise of 1787, which established the principle that states be represented in the House on a population basis and in the Senate equally on a geographic basis, Coudert introduced a joint resolution for amending the Constitution, allowing Congress to allot one, two, or no senators to a new state based on its population. Coudert also feared that admittance of Alaska and Hawaii would eventually open the door to Guam, the Virgin Islands, and various other insular possessions. He complained that the reason Alaska and Hawaii statehood bills were being considered at all was due to the fact that both were represented by two very "persuasive, genial, and distinguished gentlemen" who could wrap the House membership around their fingers.[53]

The House majority leader finally scheduled the bills for debate in March. Before it began, Bartlett appealed to his colleagues for their votes, reiterating the various restrictions that lack of statehood imposed on the territory's government and economy.

Debate started on March 3, 1950, and lasted for two hours. As expected, southerners opposed the statehood measure, and representatives from some of the populous northern states did as well. They pointed to Alaska's small population and the significant number of military personnel, federal employees, and natives. Melvin Price of Illinois favored Alaska statehood and pointed out that if statehood opponents had been in the majority after the founding of the nation, there probably would be many independent nations today instead of one nation united.[54]

Peterson reported the amendments of his committee, which were all approved at the conclusion of the debate. At that point Congressman Miller offered an additional amendment that would grant Alaska every even-numbered section of the public domain, substantially increasing the land grant. Bartlett, although sympathetic to Miller's amendment, pointed out that the executive branch would strongly oppose such a provision. The amendment failed. The House then passed the measure 186 votes to 146. While westerners supported Alaska statehood, most southerners and New Englanders opposed the bill. Aside from regionalism, partisanship obviously played a role as well, since Democrats voted 125 to 66 in favor of the measure, while Republicans cast 61 positive votes and 80 negative ones. On March 7 the House also approved the Hawaii statehood bill by the more ample margin of 262 votes to 111.[55]

Optimism prevailed in Alaska. The full House had passed the statehood bill. The next hurdle was the Senate, where statehood for either territory had not yet received even committee approval. Bartlett was aware that vast difficulties lay ahead there.

Senate hearings on the Alaska measure were scheduled to begin in April 1950 before the Senate Interior and Insular Affairs Committee in Washington. Senator Butler, a foe of statehood, had introduced bills granting voting privileges to the Hawaiian and Alaskan delegates in the House of Representatives a year earlier, in January 1949. He did so without informing either Bartlett or Farrington. If this measure were to pass, Congress would ask the territories to try the new scheme, thereby postponing statehood for the lengthy trial period. A few weeks later, in another attempt to delay passage of a statehood bill, Butler also introduced an elective governorship measure for both territories to take effect at the 1950 general elections.[56]

Finally, in March 1950, Senator Joseph O'Mahoney's committee scheduled hearings on Alaska's statehood measure. O'Mahoney had told Bartlett that he harbored doubts about Alaska statehood and would have to be convinced that the enabling act would prevent big business from controlling the new state.[57]

Opponents as well as proponents organized for the hearings. Delegate Bartlett advised Secretary of the Interior Oscar L. Chapman that the Alaska Salmon Industry, Inc., would be represented at the hearing by Arnold, who was "a smooth operator, intelligent and with a pleasing personality." Bartlett cautioned the secretary that Arnold was the industry's chief lobbyist and that he had "fought and is fighting against every liberal and progressive proposal ever made" for Alaska. Bartlett also informed him that a couple of publicity men from McWilkins, Cole, and Weber, a Seattle advertising firm handling the salmon industry account, would be in Washington to smooth press relations for Arnold.[58]

The Anchorage Chamber of Commerce chartered a plane to take interested Alaskans to Washington. The territorial group consisted of mostly older, established residents, including lawyers, businessmen, ministers, representatives of labor, spokesmen for chambers of commerce, officials from veterans groups, and newspaper editors. A day after their arrival, the group met with Bartlett for a pre-hearing briefing. There the delegate warned them that opponents would propose extensive amendments that would make the bill more desirable from the

Alaskan viewpoint but that would make the measure unpalatable to the senators, ultimately retarding its progress. Bartlett felt that the strategy, therefore, must be to urge the Senate to pass the House bill in its present form.[59]

On the first day of the hearings, April 24, Secretary Chapman made a very strong and impassioned plea for Alaska statehood. Chapman had worked closely with Gruening in the Department of the Interior during the 1930s, and Bartlett earlier had favored him for the secretaryship over Julius Krug, Truman's choice. After Chapman had been nominated for the post of secretary of the Interior, he had told Bartlett that he was ready to "pull out all the stops" to obtain statehood for the territories in 1950. Bartlett had faith in the new secretary's decisiveness and influence. That faith was reaffirmed when Chapman summarized the arguments for admission and quickly disposed of the case against statehood. Coached by Bartlett, the secretary also cautioned the Senate committee to beware of the economic interests represented by various witnesses. In particular, the secretary noted the presence of Arnold, whom he described as a registered lobbyist in Alaska for the salmon-packing industry. Chapman did propose an amendment, namely to exclude the Pribilof fur seals from Alaska state jurisdiction, since they were the subject of an international agreement among the United States, Russia, and Canada. Chapman likewise proposed to exclude all wildlife refuges or reservations from state jurisdiction. The secretary proposed, however, that Alaska be given 50 percent of the net income from the sale of fur seal pelts.

Among others to testify was Judge Albert Maris, chairman of the Judicial Conference Committee of the Chief Justice. He suggested that the bill be brought into conformity with the structure and wording of the "Judiciary and Judicial Procedure" title of the *United States Code*. Maris also asked that the ban against appointing anyone but bona fide territorial residents to various federal positions in Alaska be eliminated.

Governor Earl Warren of California spoke eloquently for admission, and General Nathan F. Twining of the U.S. Air Force, then commander-in-chief of the Alaska Command, testified that statehood for Alaska would strengthen the defenses of America. However, the Reverend Bernard R. Hubbard, S.J., of Santa Clara, California, well known for his Alaska studies and travels, expressed doubt that the territory could bear the added costs of statehood.[60]

On the second day of the hearings, April 25, Senator Clinton P. Anderson of New Mexico, who chaired the proceedings, indicated that most senators were sympathetic to the idea of Alaska statehood but that the House version of the measure should be examined carefully. Several Alaskans then appeared before the committee in support of the territory's cause and urged that the House bill not be substantially altered, lest it be defeated on the floor or lost in the haste for adjournment. Mrs. Hermann probably gave the most effectiver pro-statehood testimony. In commenting on the added costs a state government would entail, she stated that $4,242,000 per year above current expenditures would suffice. This amount, she concluded, could be raised from Alaska's resources.

On the third day of the hearings, representatives from various national organizations, such as the Veterans of Foreign Wars and the Order of Railway Conductors of America, presented resolutions in favor of statehood.[61] On the fourth day, however, Arnold appeared before the committee with an elaborate exhibit of charts and graphs, maps and tables, all designed to demonstrate the inadequacy of the statehood bill under discussion. His brilliant testimony captured the interest of the senators, many of whom had been given a preview at a private luncheon in the Vandenberg Room of the Capitol, hosted by Senator Butler. There the senator had introduced his "friend Judge Arnold, who knows much about Alaska and can give us facts concerning statehood." On that occasion Arnold had given the attending senators leather-bound copies of his testimony.[62]

Arnold's arguments before the committee ranged widely. They included the threat of impairment of international treaties, the fact of noncontiguity, and questions concerning federal land policies in Alaska and their relationship to the transfer of public lands to the proposed state. Arnold reminded the senators of his earlier warnings of the confusion that would result from aboriginal land claims. He criticized the Department of the Interior for the erratic policies it had pursued in the territory for years. He pointed out that since the state could only select its lands from the vacant, unappropriated public domain, this automatically excluded approximately 27 percent of Alaska, because various federal agencies, over the years, had created withdrawals and reserves amounting to some 98,596,862 acres. Out of the remaining acreage, the state would be able to select some 42,000,000 acres of section grants but initially receive title to only about 250,000 acres, since only 1 percent of Alaska's land area had been surveyed between 1867 and 1950. At that rate, it would take thousands of years before enough land would be measured to transfer title of the acreage granted in the statehood bill.[63]

On April 28, the second day of his testimony, Arnold introduced two witnesses whom he had brought to Washington at industry expense. No Alaskans had accepted Arnold's offer to go to Washington at industry expense against statehood, so he had settled instead on retired Rear Admiral Ralph Wood, who had served in Alaskan waters during the Second World War, and Edward W. Allen, a Seattle attorney and chairman of the International North Pacific Fisheries Commission. Wood denied General Twining's testimony that statehood would enhance the national security or help substantially in the defense of Alaska. Allen opposed giving the new state control over its fisheries and other sea resources, insisting that such a transfer would be detrimental to international obligations because of uncertain jurisdiction and dual responsibility arising out of federal and state participation in the management of this resource. Allen also worried about the possibility of imprudent exploitation of these assets under a lax state administration.[64]

On the sixth and final day of hearings, Governor Gruening had two hours to speak. Clearly put on the defensive by Arnold's testimony, particularly regarding land grants, Gruening admitted many of the bill's shortcomings and suggested that, since surveying was dependent on appropriations, the Senate should make funds available for that purpose. Delegate Bartlett, clearly frustrated, asserted that the salmon industry did not care how much or how little land the state received but simply opposed statehood.[65]

The responses to Arnold's thorough presentation varied. In Alaska various anti-statehood papers, such as the *Fairbanks Daily News-Miner,* gave broad coverage to the hearings and space for a series of articles by Robert N. De Armond, an avowedly anti-statehood historian and free-lance writer.[66]

Despite the negative intent of this coverage in Alaska, it served to educate residents and alert them to the importance of the content of any statehood legislation. In Washington, Arnold's testimony raised questions in the minds of many senators about the adequacy of the statehood bill under discussion and the applicability of the Western land state model in the case of Alaska. Expressing this concern, Senator Ernest McFarland of Arizona asserted that the committee wanted to write a good bill. He told Governor Gruening that the problems which had been brought up during the hearings should be worked out now, saving Alaska years of difficulties later.

Many pro-statehood Alaskans blamed Arnold above all others for the delays and difficulties being encountered in Congress. To them he appeared as an obstructionist giant, with tremendous forces behind him that were able to thwart the desire of a majority of the territory's citizens. Although this was an oversimplification, Arnold was a very dedicated and skillful advocate for the industry he represented. Whatever his motives, he did show senators the inadequacies of the statehood bill under consideration and thereby made a significant, if unintentional, contribution to Alaska statehood. He educated his congressional audience on Alaska's problems and potentials, and his arguments stimulated positive discussion and action.

The Senate hearings ended on April 29, 1950. Early in May, President Truman again gave his support to Alaska and Hawaii statehood and urged the speedy admission of both territories. Both possessed greater human and natural resources than many states at the time of their admission. Without equal representation in the upper house for large and small states alike, Truman stated, there probably would have been no United States.[67]

On June 29 the Senate Interior and Insular Affairs Committee completed its revision of the Alaska statehood bill and reported it favorably. The most important achievement of the committee was a changed land-selection formula. Instead of requiring the new state to accept sections 2, 16, 32, and 36 in each township regardless of where they happened to be located, the proposed new state was granted the right to select from the public domain twenty million acres of vacant, unappropriated, and unreserved lands best suited to its particular needs five years after being admitted as a state.[68]

Bartlett and Atwood feared that the federal government would utilize the five-year waiting period to withdraw the most desirable land, although Bartlett also thought that the delay would allow the state to carefully select its acreage. Senator Anderson, who inserted the five-year waiting period, however, might have done so because he feared that Alaska, like many earlier states, might squander its land resources for a pittance in return for badly needed funds.[69]

Senator Butler raised questions about native reservations, which he wished to see rescinded. Instead of reservations, he wanted the secretary of the Interior to issue patents for various lands to tribes, villages, or individuals. Both Bartlett and Gruening favored the offered amendment but feared that the Department of the Interior would resist it. The compromise, reached at Senator O'Mahoney's urging, provided that no further native reservations be created until final action had been taken on the statehood bill. This compromise was rejected by the National Civil Liberties Clearing House, Oliver LaFarge, president of the Association of American Indians, John Rainer of the National Congress of American Indians, former Secretary of the Interior Harold L. Ickes, and the *Nation.* All strongly objected that native property rights were being denied. Bartlett disputed that this was the case and maintained that many of the organizations protesting the clause had not studied it at all. Furthermore, Bartlett believed that many of the organizations devoted to protecting minority rights had been misled by a few individuals who desired to blanket Alaska with reservations. Bartlett felt that a disclaimer inserted in the statehood bill was more than adequate to protect asserted native land claims. In any event, he felt, the statehood bill was not the place to resolve native claims; rather, that was a separate issue to be considered by Congress at a later date. Bartlett argued that those opposing Alaska statehood because of the reservation clause did so because they desired the territory to be enclosed in one huge reservation where, he concluded, "there could be little progress, little room for happiness, no room for development, and the only ones who would be satisfied would be the hired attorneys."[70]

Nevertheless, the Senate had fashioned a bill which had the potential of making Alaska an economically viable state. On June 28 the Senate committee voted to approve the amended Hawaii and Alaska bills. The struggle now was to get the bills onto the floor of the Senate, which would prove as difficult as it had been getting them onto the floor of the House.

On June 25, 1950, before the bill had time to reach the floor of the upper house, North Korean Communist forces invaded South Korea across the thirty-eighth parallel. A month after the invasion, the Gallup Poll reported that 81 percent of Americans favored Alaska's admission to the Union, 8 percent opposed it, and 11 percent were undecided. This represented a massive shift in public opinion, which, Gallup believed, had been brought about by the war. In a March 1948 poll, the comparable figures had been 68 percent favoring admission, 7 percent opposing it, and 25 percent undecided. Obviously, the public considered Alaska to be an important link in America's defense system.[71]

At Bartlett's prompting, President Truman promised early in July to do all he could to get Senate Majority Leader Scott Lucas of Illinois to expedite the statehood measure. Senator Lucas indicated his support of the Alaska measure but revealed that Senator James Eastland of Mississippi had told the leadership that if either statehood bill were brought up, Eastland would try to displace it by promoting the Mundt-Ferguson anti-communist bill. If that happened, Lucas feared, one of the senators might try to attach a civil rights amendment to the anti-communist measure. Such action, according to Lucas, held the prospect of a prolonged debate on the Mundt-Ferguson bill and a filibuster on the civil rights amendment. This would indefinitely delay the recess of Congress before the fall elections — and Lucas, up for reelection, was eager to campaign at home.[72]

On August 24 Senator Warren G. Magnuson of Washington accused the Senate of stalling on the statehood bills because there were members who opposed adding four new senators to the upper house and diluting a voting bloc, namely the southern-Democratic conservative-Republican coalition.

In the face of these complications, Lucas abandoned the statehood legislation. Bartlett complained that this was the first time in his experience "that a majority leader in the Senate has failed to carry out the direct command from the President on a piece of administration legislation." Although Bartlett did not know the source of Lucas' resistance, he suspected that it was somehow connected with the Alaskan salmon industry, because Libby, McNeill, and Libby, important in the industry, was headquartered in Chicago.[73]

While the war in Korea increasingly demanded American attention, newspapers and members of Congress still found time to discuss various aspects of statehood for the territories, some of which only clouded the main issue. One such occasion occurred on September 5, 1950, when Senator Andrew Schoeppel of Kansas, a former governor of that state, addressed his Senate colleagues. While saying that he favored statehood for both territories, Schoeppel launched an abusive attack on Secretary of the Interior Chapman and one Randolph Feltus, accusing both of Communist sympathies. Feltus, the senator revealed, had been employed by the Alaska Statehood Committee as a lobbyist. In his capacity as a public relations man, Feltus had also advised the Polish Embassy from October 16, 1946, to July 1, 1948. Senator O'Mahoney responded by announcing that he would call a hearing on the charges, at which he would "welcome the cooperation of the Senator from Kansas . . . and let the chips fall where they may." Senator Murray added that it was unfortunate that the Senate, in view of the Korean war emergency, had to devote "so much of our time to wild pursuits of this kind."[74]

The *Washington Post* reported that the Republican Policy Committee had dis-avowed the charges of Senator Schoeppel, "the bumbling Senator from Kansas, after he tried to smear the red brush on Secretary of the Interior Oscar Chapman."

Five days of hearings soon followed Senator Schoeppel's original verbal bar-rage. Schoeppel indicated that Frank Bow, his legislative assistant, had written the inflammatory speech. Bartlett immediately suspected that perhaps Arnold and William Strand, the anti-statehood managing editor of the *Fairbanks Daily News-Miner,* had cooperated with Bow; and Bow did admit that he had consulted Arnold's testimony before the Senate Interior and Insular Affairs Committee. Although he said he did not know Arnold personally, he had contacted him for information about the activities of Feltus and the Alaska Statehood Committee. In response to his queries, Bow had received an airmail special-delivery envelope with no return address, containing photographic copies of statehood committee warrants sent to Bartlett, as well as the vouchers for them. Bow also told committee members that he had talked with Strand, but only about the alleged mismanage-ment of territorial affairs by the Gruening administration. The *Anchorage Daily Times* suggested that Albert White, the Alaska Republican party's self-appointed general counsel, had been involved in the Schoeppel charges.[75]

The information about Feltus showed that as early as 1946, he had contacted both Bartlett and Gruening about possible employment as a lobbyist for the statehood cause. In the summer of 1949, several statehood committee members and Department of the Interior officials had met in Bartlett's office to talk with Feltus. Although they were impressed with the man, he was not hired, because the $3,000 to $6,000 per month fee Feltus wanted was expensive, and his influence lay in the Senate and not the House, where all major statehood efforts then centered.[76]

Early in 1950 Bartlett and Gruening had met again with Feltus and still were impressed with him, particularly with his knowledge about U.S. senators. At the time, Bartlett had feared that if the statehood bill did not pass in 1950, its failure would cripple Alaskan hopes for some time to come. This feeling, plus Chapman's recommendation of Feltus, had convinced the delegate that the statehood committee should retain the lobbyist after House passage of the statehood bill.[77]

When Feltus received his contract from the statehood committee, Bartlett had made it clear that it would be difficult to change the minds of Senators Hugh Butler, Guy Cordon, and others. "If motivated at all in changing their course for Senate action at this session," the delegate had advised, "they are going to have to be persuaded by personal contact from those who know what makes them tick." It was especially important for Feltus to convert senators on the Senate Interior and Insular Affairs Committee, most of whom apparently opposed statehood. Feltus seemed to know a great deal about individuals "close to opposition Senators who live in their home states and who might be approached and won over to getting their men to act in our behalf." After lobbying for a time, Feltus had reported to Bartlett that he had discussed the statehood issue with some thirty-five senators and the administrative assistants of a dozen others. He had also met with various other individuals and groups and had attended strategy meetings with the delegate and his associates.[78]

Yet despite Feltus' ostensible activity, both Gruening and Bartlett had felt uneasy about him. The governor had complained as early as May 29, 1950, that Feltus "has had two months to work on the members of the committee and as far as I can see he hasn't gained a single adherent." Bartlett had observed that the lobbyist had failed to accomplish anything constructive at all. Feltus had talked of getting Senator Richard Russell to favor statehood, proposing to do so through a connection with Russell's brother-in-law, but would need about $750 "to sweeten" the man and wished to collect expense money to use for such a payment. Bartlett wanted to terminate Feltus but had feared "that if we cut him off he would become embittered and might work against us — and then we could be in the unhappy position of discovering he had a bigger following than we now give him credit for."[79]

The governor had wanted to fire Feltus primarily because of the expense, but Bartlett had made an informal five-month contract with Feltus, which was to terminate only if Congress should adjourn sooner than anticipated. During the contract period, Feltus was to have received $1,500 per month if Congress enacted the statehood legislation during that session. Bartlett finally concluded, however, that Feltus would have to be fired when Senate Minority Leader Robert Taft of Ohio told him that the lobbyist had once worked for the Polish Embassy to boost Polish-American trade. Bartlett had professed surprise at the news, but this should not have been the case, because he had examined the Feltus references. Nevertheless, the possible significance of the Polish connection should have occurred to the delegate earlier. When Bartlett at last confronted him with the matter, Feltus had offered to sever his relations with the statehood committee if his association with it might prove to be an embarrassment. The delegate had accepted the offer effective July 25. Although Feltus had worked only four months, Bartlett paid him $7,500 for five months, as their agreement had stipulated. Feltus had received $500 for expenses which, he had estimated, had amounted to at least $1,600.[80]

Although the hearings on the Schoeppel charges ranged widely and did embarrass the statehood committee, they did not uncover the reasons for the hiring of Feltus nor Bartlett's and Gruening's disappointment with his performance. Witnesses testified with discretion. The hearings cleared Chapman and Feltus of Schoeppel's accusations and innuendos, and the senator stopped attending the hearings. He told a reporter that perhaps his speech on the Senate floor should have been checked more carefully and requested that the committee conduct the remaining hearings behind closed doors — a request which was denied. Bartlett observed that Senator Schoeppel's charges had been completely discredited. Every effort to prove Chapman a Communist sympathizer had failed, and "every effort to prove [that] Randolph Feltus, formerly retained by the Alaska Statehood Committee, is a Communist or a Communist sympathizer, has flopped." Even Bow, Schoeppel's legislative assistant, had refused to state under oath that either Chapman or Feltus "is red or sympathetic to the red cause." Bartlett was particularly annoyed that "after Senator Schoeppel attempted to blast my reputation by planting the idea I might have misused territorial funds, he told newspapermen he couldn't understand my concern because he hadn't made charges against Bartlett."[81]

It is not clear why Senator Schoeppel leveled his charges. Perhaps Schoeppel wanted to damage the Truman administration. There is no evidence that Schoeppel, although unfriendly to the statehood cause, wanted to block the legislation with his speech. Nor is there any evidence that Arnold and the Alaska salmon industry were in any way involved. It is more probable, however, that Bow, seeking election for a first term in the House from Canton, Ohio, was using Schoeppel to gain publicity. Bow obviously had decided to exploit American fear of Communist subversion for his political ends. For his part, Schoeppel, a foe of public development of hydroelectric power resources, had used his vantage point to attack not only Chapman, but Michael Strauss, the commissioner of the Bureau of Reclamation and a protagonist of public hydroelectric power development.[82]

Even before engaging the services of Feltus, Bartlett felt that it might not meet with universal approval in Alaska. Feltus' accomplishments had certainly not been worth the $8,000 expended. Senator Zales Ecton of Montana did not comprehend the necessity for a lobbyist at all, when Alaskans delivered the best reasons for granting statehood to the territory.[83] The best that can be said about the Schoeppel affair is that it further publicized statehood. It certainly paid off for Bow, who handily won a seat in Congress over his Democratic opponent.

Congress reconvened late in November. Senator Lucas, who had been defeated in Illinois by Everett McKinley Dirksen, proposed to bring up the Alaska bill. This action touched off a lengthy debate on the merits of statehood for both Alaska and Hawaii. Continual speech-making and objections blocked attempts to obtain a vote on the motion. Senator Butler stated that he did not want to "thrust statehood upon the helpless Alaskans." The political immaturity of the territory and its citizens, he declared, was amply demonstrated by the fact that the Gruening administration "ruthlessly" controlled the voters of Alaska and perpetuated its own powers. The territory could not afford statehood because its two major industries, gold mining and salmon fishing, were declining. This left only the gigantic defense expenditures, which one day would have to come to an end and upon which a stable society could not be built.

Despite Butler's contributions to anti-statehood arguments, the actual leader of these forces in the Senate was John Stennis of Mississippi, who claimed shock at learning that of the 586,400 square miles in Alaska, the federal government owned 99.7 percent. Privately owned land amounted to roughly fifteen hundred square miles, he said, the equivalent of one large county in Minnesota or two in Mississippi. Yet such an area was to be represented by two U.S. senators. The real danger, Stennis remarked, was that the addition of four senators might curtail the privilege of unlimited debate. In addition, those four new senators would come from areas not attached in culture, ideals, or ideas. Alaska's admission to the Union, he feared, would lead to Hawaii's as well, and he wondered what then would stop the admission of the Virgin Islands, Puerto Rico, Guam, and Okinawa.[84]

The southern-Democratic conservative-Republican coalition managed to prevent both the Alaska and Hawaii bills from coming to the floor of the Senate during that session. A few weeks later President Truman told Bartlett that, had he been majority leader, "I would have kept them in continuous session until they had broken. It would not have taken more than seventy-two hours." The president admitted that, "of course, Lucas was really always against statehood." Bartlett informed the president that Rayburn had warned Secretary Chapman that his opposition to statehood would change from passive to active resistance in 1951. The president advised Bartlett that he already knew this, for "during my last talk with him before the recess, Sam told me I had better get these statehood bills through now because they wouldn't go through next year."[85]

Although the outlook for 1951 seemed dim, a considerable amount actually had been accomplished. The House had passed a statehood bill for the first time, and the Senate Interior and Insular Affairs Committee, also for the first time, had considered and approved a measure leading toward that end.

CHAPTER **13**

The Capstone of
a Delegate's Career

WHEN THE ALASKA STATEHOOD COMMITTEE met early in 1950, many state-hood proponents demanded positive, even militant, action. Delegate Bartlett shared these sentiments and particularly felt that Alaskans as well as friendly members of Congress and supportive national organizations needed to be informed more adequately. Bartlett requested and received committee approval for funds for the printing and distribution of five thousand copies of pro-statehood speeches made by various senators in the previous Congress.[1]

Although it had committee approval, the informational program did not materialize, and a progress report was published instead.[2] In effect, the Alaska Statehood Committee slumped into a moribund condition.

Other statehood proponents became increasingly impatient with congressional delays, however, and in the 1951 territorial legislature, a House memorial, later withdrawn, asked that Alaska be granted statehood without delay. If this could not be done, the memorialists asked for permission to declare independence and form a Republic of Alaska.[3]

Action had to occur in Washington, but the Korean War was delaying such proceedings. While awaiting floor consideration in 1952, Delegate Bartlett, Governor Gruening, and Alaska Statehood Committee members Robert Atwood and Lee Bettinger asked U.S. senators of their political parties (Atwood and Bettinger were Republicans) to make pro-statehood speeches. Many agreed to do so. In addition, Bartlett engaged public relations consultant Emil Hurja and ex-Congressman Hardin Peterson as lobbyists.[4]

Early in 1952 Bartlett told members of the Alaska Statehood Committee that he had received firm assurances that the Alaska bill would receive favorable consideration in the Senate. The Hearst papers and the Scripps-Howard chain had promised editorial support, and all the national organizations which so far had supported the cause had promised to do so again. Bartlett surmised that if the Alaska bill came to a vote in the Senate, it would gain a safe, though small, margin

142

of victory. The delegate accurately predicted that the anti-statehood forces in Congress would try to prevent such a vote so that they would not be forced to go on record against a popular measure. One way they could accomplish this objective, he contended, would be to send the bill back to the committee for further study; another would be to filibuster it to death.[5]

Debate on the Alaska statehood bill opened on February 4, 1952, but it soon became apparent that a majority of Republicans and Democrats would vote to recommit the measure. Both delegates Bartlett and Farrington supported each other's causes in the Senate. To that effect, Bartlett wrote to Senator O'Mahoney, chairman of the Senate Interior and Insular Affairs Committee, that he wanted Hawaii to be admitted in 1952. "I should hope for that result even if by some mischance Alaska's hopes were not to be realized. We Alaskans want statehood for ourselves," he stated, "but we want it for Hawaii too." Delegate Farrington echoed these sentiments, stating that he hoped "the Senate will adopt the bill reported by your Committee for the admission of Alaska to the Union as a state without regard to what may be done with the bill to give statehood to Hawaii."[6]

While newsmen and visitors watched from the crowded galleries, eighty-nine senators answered the roll call on February 27, 1952. Senator Estes Kefauver, who had been campaigning in Iowa, returned to the Capital, and Senator Butler flew to Washington for the occasion. Senator Thomas Hennings, Jr., of Missouri even left his sickbed, accompanied by his physician, to vote against recommittal. The vote was tied three times, but in the end recommittal passed by one vote — forty-five votes to forty-four.[7] As in 1950, a coalition of conservative Republicans and southern Democrats had successfully killed Alaska statehood for another session of Congress. Under those circumstances, the House saw no need to act at all. Bartlett was bitterly disappointed.

When Republican Dwight D. Eisenhower won the presidency in 1952, the delegate expressed his conviction that Alaska statehood chances looked dim for the next four years of Republican rule. Senator Butler, soon to be chairman of the Senate Interior and Insular Affairs Committee, had already told the delegate that, because of its narrow economic base, he did not favor the admission of Alaska. The senator thought that the issue would not even be debated. Hawaii, on the other hand, would certainly be considered, Butler told Bartlett, even though he was not personally committed to the island territory's cause. Despite these dire predictions, however, half a dozen Alaska statehood bills were submitted in the new Congress early in 1953.[8]

In the meantime, the Alaska Statehood Committee met in Juneau and declared that Alaskans would have to quit complaining about congressional stinginess in various statehood bills and show a willingness instead to assume the expenses of self-government. On the second day of their deliberations, members of the Alaska

Statehood Committee met with members of the legislature. Bartlett explained that he would try to double the land grant and include a $50 million cash grant in the measure, but he emphasized that he and others felt that the approximately 23 million acres contemplated were adequate. Governor Gruening, for instance, considered 23 million acres to be a generous land grant, believing any more than that would only impose administrative burdens on the state. Just a few months earlier, Bartlett reminded his listeners, he had discussed with Senator Butler the possibility of turning over all public lands to the state. Butler had maintained that such a measure would never pass, since it would encounter the opposition of conservationists, eastern congressmen, and the Department of the Interior.[9]

A day before the Alaska Statehood Committee met, newly-elected territorial representative Howard Pollock of Anchorage had introduced a bill providing for the dissolution of the committee and the creation of a new one. The responsibilities and makeup of the new group implied a strong criticism of Bartlett and the existing committee. The bill was not passed, and the old group was retained.[10]

The new president's attitude toward statehood quickly became apparent. In his 1953 State of the Union address, Eisenhower urged speedy admission of Hawaii but neglected to mention Alaska. At a news conference on February 25, 1953, the president stated that Alaska was more a dependent than a self-supporting region. The chief executive undoubtedly hoped to bring two Hawaiian Republicans into the United States Senate without balancing this with two Alaskan Democrats.

From the perspective of Alaskans, the second most important federal office was that of secretary of the Interior. Eisenhower's appointee to that post was Douglas McKay, the former governor of Oregon. McKay had voted for statehood at four national governors' conferences, supporting the principle of admission, though not any particular bill. As secretary, however, McKay probably would follow the president's leadership.[11]

Hearings on the Alaska statehood measure finally were to begin on April 14, 1953. As the date approached, Secretary McKay expressed his reluctance to appear before the committee, apparently reasoning that since Alaska statehood was not a part of the administration's program, the hearings would be a waste of time. Chairman Miller, however, quickly apprised the secretary of the political realities—namely, that without hearings on the Alaska bill, Republicans would be unable to get the Hawaii bill out of the House committee.[12]

The House hearings opened on April 14, 1953, as scheduled. The usual cast of witnesses testified, including members and friends of the Alaska Statehood Committee. On the second day of the hearings, Secretary McKay made a noncommittal statement, simply affirming that Alaska should become a state "when it is ready and under a proper bill so that it can develop, pay its taxes and support itself."[13]

Hearings and investigations into the matter of Alaska statehood had occurred with regularity since 1947, and not much new material was added on this occasion. Consequently, the committee was able to report the measure favorably, along with a number of amendments, in June 1953. The most important of the amendments increased the proposed land grant from 40 million to 100 million acres, to be selected within twenty-five years, and reduced a projected federal transitional grant from $50 million to $15 million. In addition, Alaska would receive 2,550,000 acres for internal improvements and some 400,000 acres of public land for community expansion as well as for recreational areas. These 103,350,000 acres of land represented approximately 28 percent of Alaska's land mass. Most importantly, the committee report characterized the amended statehood bill as the "equitable enabling act" called for in the 1952 Republican platform.[14]

In the meantime, the Senate Interior and Insular Affairs Committee was considering the Hawaii measure that had been passed by the House. Democratic committee members soon realized that the Senate's Alaska bill would not even be reported out of committee. To force action, the seven committee Democrats, led by Clinton P. Anderson, proposed to add the Alaska measure to the Hawaii bill. The motion passed in subcommittee eight votes to seven on an almost straight party-line vote. The exception was Senator George W. Malone, a Republican from Nevada, who opposed statehood for either territory but believed both should get the same chance and who therefore voted with the Democrats. The Democrats were simply telling the administration that there would be no admission of Hawaii without reciprocal action for Alaska. Realizing the futility of getting combined bills passed, the Senate Interior and Insular Affairs Committee refused to report the twin measures.[15]

In his 1954 State of the Union message, President Eisenhower renewed his request for the immediate admission of Hawaii but again did not mention Alaska. Under these circumstances, Senator Anderson moved in committee to attach Senator Murray's Alaska statehood bill to a Hawaii bill introduced by Senator Guy Cordon of Oregon.[16] The motion passed, and the senators then unanimously agreed to report the linked measures to the Senate.

Senator Cordon's Subcommittee on Territories and Insular Affairs set about perfecting the Alaska statehood bill, holding hearings from January 20 through February 4. Officials from the departments of Interior and Defense appeared and were asked to justify their land withdrawals. Subcommittee members wanted to know whether an unspecified land grant of 100 million acres would benefit the state, and Senator Anderson wanted to make sure that Alaska did not merely receive the leftovers after various federal agencies had preempted the choicest lands. Alaskan Governor B. Frank Heintzleman, Gruening's successor, also appeared and stated that an unspecified land grant of 100 million acres would ensure Alaska's survival as a state.[17]

When the full committee met on January 26, 1954, it changed its position, deciding to consider the two statehood bills separately. It then reported the Hawaii measure and voted to report the Alaska bill no later than February 4. On that date, the full committee approved the generous Alaska bill, which was very similar to the House measure of the previous year.[18]

Still, the Eisenhower administration had no intention of seeing Alaska admitted to the Union. As early as January 1953 reports on the Alaska bill had been requested from the Bureau of the Budget, the agency which determined whether or not a piece of legislation was consistent with the president's program, and from the departments of the Interior, State, and Commerce—but as of March 11, 1954, no replies had been received. Senator Anderson voiced the apprehension of many of his colleagues when he remarked that the only chance the House would have to vote on Alaska statehood would be in the event the Senate passed a combined Hawaii-Alaska measure. The Senate agreed. Once again it joined the two statehood bills, passing the twin measures on April 1, 1954, the first time the Senate had passed the two statehood bills.[19]

In the House, the bill confronted Speaker Martin, who was unfriendly to statehood, and a rules committee majority that was blatantly hostile to the concept, drawing strength from their knowledge that President Eisenhower shared their attitude. At that critical juncture, Governor Heintzleman wrote a letter to the Speaker in which he suggested that Alaska be partitioned, with only the populated areas to be incorporated within the boundaries of the new state. This would have excluded most of rural native Alaska. The governor's plan, presumably made to mollify the president's objections that Alaska could be defended more easily as a territory, would have made a state out of the roughly 250,000 square miles that contained the larger population centers. To allow military forces free movement, northern and western Alaska would have remained a territory, to be called Frontier Alaska or Alaska Outpost, until it could be absorbed into the new state. The Pribilof Islands with their fur seal herds, Bristol Bay with its rich fishing grounds, Seward Peninsula with its minerals, and the North Slope with its oil-bearing geological strata would have been part of the excluded area.[20]

The governor's letter produced an uproar throughout Alaska. Delegate Bartlett commented that the governor's suggestion was "a nicely calculated effort to hurt the statehood cause. It will give statehood foes opportunity to urge further study of the whole statehood matter, thus making available from the Alaska governor himself a convenient excuse to try to hold up the combined Alaska-Hawaii bill . . . ." The delegate especially resented the fact that Heintzleman had not seen fit to discuss the matter with him or with Alaska Statehood Committee Chairman Atwood.[21] Most Alaskans also opposed partition.

President Eisenhower, asked whether he favored statehood under the Heintzleman plan, replied that he did not know: "It certainly is a different problem; and I would look at it with an entirely different viewpoint than I would if we had all those outer reaches, barren outer reaches, that are lying on the Bering Sea and the Arctic Ocean, included. It would be a different problem in my mind." The *Fairbanks Daily News-Miner* thereupon speculated, probably correctly, that Heintzleman had proposed a statehood plan he knew would be endorsed by the president, a proposal that obviously had originated with the administration.[22]

At the end of 1954, while talking with Congressman Miller, Bartlett was told that one of the reasons that the administration opposed statehood was because of resistance of the military, which reputedly felt that territorial status allowed for greater flexibility in times of emergency. Bartlett, however, was not convinced. He remembered that Nathan Twining, an air force general and the commander-in-chief of the Alaskan Command in 1950, had strongly endorsed statehood as leading to economic development and an influx of population, which, in turn, would ease military supply problems, reduce construction costs, and provide for a stable Alaskan government. Bartlett suspected that Miller had used the excuse merely to justify a deal he had made for considering statehood.[20]

On April 27 Miller again talked with the delegate and told him that Heintzleman's partition proposal had been inspired by the White House out of a real concern for Alaska's defense. Bartlett informed Miller that neither he nor Atwood had been able to uncover any objections to statehood at the Pentagon and that since 1949, the strategic concept of the "heartland defense" had prevailed. Under this scheme, large bases had been constructed at Anchorage, Fairbanks, and Big Delta, from which U.S. forces would repel an enemy attack. The Aleutians and the Arctic were left undefended. After hearing Bartlett's response, Miller shifted ground and stated instead that Eisenhower was probably concerned about the large wasteland acreage becoming part of the state. Bartlett suggested that, whatever Miller's reasons, it still might be wise to consult Bartlett and his constituents about partition proposals. Furthermore, he said that he doubted that Alaskans would accept a compromise—certainly they would reject the Heintzleman line. That angered Miller, who told Bartlett that "you must be ready to compromise. That is the trouble with you Alaskans. You always come here demanding. You should come hat in hand begging. You are only a territory."

On May 17, Bartlett, Heintzleman, and a delegation of fifteen other Alaskans saw the president. Territorial legislator John Butrovich, a Fairbanks Republican, and Walter Hickel, the new territorial Republican national committeeman, spoke for the group. Butrovich told the president that the group felt that he was "a great American, but we are shocked to come here and find a bill which affects the lives of more than 150,000 Americans bottled up in a House committee when a nod from you could bring it out and allow it [to] be passed or killed by the House of Representatives of the United States." Butrovich banged his fists on the president's desk for emphasis as he spoke. Eisenhower, who is said to have reddened, replied that he wanted to extend full citizenship to as many Americans as possible but that Alaska statehood posed many problems which would first have to be resolved. The president denied that partisanship played any role in the Alaska statehood issue.[24]

After a week of making the rounds in Washington, the weary Alaskans returned home, expressing the belief that their visit, if nothing else, had added to the pressure for statehood. All were thoroughly confused about the partition proposal. On July 14, A. Robert Smith, a northwest regional news reporter and friend of Bartlett, asked the president at a news conference about military considerations that might be affecting Alaska statehood. Smith noted that the Department of the Interior had expressed certain apprehensions in this regard, but not the Pentagon, and that both had suggested that the White House felt strongly about the matter. After some verbal exchange, the president finally stated that a territory was not easier to defend but "easier to use, because, in one case, it is under the absolute control of the central government, and in the other it isn't." The *Anchorage Daily Times* concluded that administration representatives had acted under White House orders which had been extremely vague.[25] Vague or not, the result had been one more failure of a statehood measure to pass Congress, which, on August 21, adjourned so that its members could devote time to campaigning.

In his 1955 State of the Union message, the president again strongly recommended the admission of Hawaii. For the first time in such an address, he mentioned the possibility of Alaska statehood, but only dubiously. He expressed hope that "as the complex problems of Alaska are resolved. . ." it might eventually achieve that goal.

Statements of that nature served only to frustrate further many citizens in the territory. Various people began considering the possibility of holding a constitutional convention prior to Alaska's uncertain admission to the Union. Most also rejected various alternatives to statehood that were suggested from time to time.[26]

One of these alternative suggestions was the idea of an elective governorship. Bartlett had introduced various bills over the years to accomplish this end, but his feelings about them had been ambivalent. Politically, it was unrealistic to refuse alternatives, Bartlett had realized, but an "elective governor bill would not suffice if statehood must be postponed. That would be an acceptance of practically nothing on our part for voluntarily joining in giving statehood the heave-ho." If there had to be a compromise, Bartlett had argued, it had to be a new organic act that would transfer control over the fisheries to Alaska and give the territory greater powers. "If we are going to accept serfdom as a semi-permanent position, then the federal government ought to treat us exactly as it does Puerto Rico with respect to taxes." Within a short time, however, Bartlett had decided that an elected governorship was merely a delaying tactic and hurtful to statehood. He had refused to sponsor such bills, particularly since statehood opponents such as Senator Butler and Congressman Miller, among others, had pushed similar legislation.[27]

Another alternative to statehood was the repeated proposal that Alaska and Hawaii become commonwealths. Senator Mike Monroney of Oklahoma was the chief proponent of this idea, first suggesting it in 1952 when Puerto Rico officially assumed that status. He had revived it in 1954, joined by Senators George Smathers, William Fulbright, and Price Daniel, all southerners.[28] Commonwealth status, as its backers had envisioned it, would have granted Alaska exemption from the internal revenue laws of the United States, but not much else. In 1954, Senator Cordon had effectively destroyed the arguments for a commonwealth when he submitted a report from the Library of Congress which indicated that no incorporated territory had ever been exempted from federal taxes.[29] Nevertheless, various small groups in Alaska had supported the concept, still lured by the faint possibility of tax exemption. Delegate Bartlett and Chairman Atwood of the Alaska Statehood Committee had evaluated the Alaska commonwealth movement in testimony before a congressional committee in 1955. They had observed that the subject had seemed to come up in the territory only when statehood was being discussed before Congress and there was a possibility of its success. Once statehood legislation had failed in a particular session, talk of commonwealth also quickly had subsided.[30]

On the national level, statehood did not fare well in 1955, although four statehood bills were introduced—one in the Senate and three in the House. The new Democratic-controlled House and Senate Interior and Insular Affairs committees prepared joined Alaska-Hawaii statehood bills, aware that it was important to satisfy the president on this issue. The House again held hearings, primarily for the benefit of its new members. The hearings and discussions ranged widely, from topics dealing with the size of the land grant to a proposal by John R. Pillion of New York to grant Senate representation to a new state proportional to its population.

How to satisfy the president on statehood was a problem committee members faced. Secretary McKay testified, favoring Alaska statehood with a "proper bill." The secretary wanted to exclude northern and western Alaska from the proposed state. Asked if a military reservation should be inside or outside the state, McKay stated that it made little difference.[31] Committee chairman Miller subsequently had an amendment prepared meeting McKay's requirements. Bartlett knew nothing of this until Congressman John Saylor of Pennsylvania alerted him that he would introduce "something about military reserves." The amendment empowered the president to issue an executive order or proclamation prior to admission, setting aside one or more special natural defense withdrawals in Alaska. The United States would exercise exclusive jurisdiction over each such withdrawal, but all federal and territorial laws operable in such an area prior to admission would continue to be valid unless the president objected.[32]

Bartlett disliked the amendment, pointing out that neither the Department of Defense nor the president had indicated that it met their objections. The amendment was complicated. Bartlett did not understand the basis for the boundary, particularly the inclusion of the Aleutian Islands, since their military importance had been downgraded since the Second World War. Even without such an amendment, the president already had the power to claim land for military purposes. Above all, Bartlett had been given no opportunity to analyze the provisions of the amendment. Bartlett urged the omission of the amendment, and the committee went along with him and voted it down.[33]

Soon thereafter the committee received the long-awaited report on the twin statehood measures from the Defense Department. It raised no objection to Hawaii's admission but cautioned that no change be made in Alaska's status at that time. Bartlett concluded that nothing had been lost by rejection of the defense withdrawal amendment.[34]

Delegate Bartlett had spent additional time studying the controversial amendment, and by February 16 he had concluded that it meant little. Therefore, he was willing to compromise and had worked out an acceptable amendment. The committee approved the Bartlett amendment and Congressman Claire Engle's twin bill by votes of nineteen to six.[35]

In the Senate, Senator James Murray and twenty-five of his colleagues had reintroduced essentially the same bill the Senate had passed nine months earlier. Senator Henry Jackson's Subcommittee on Territories and Insular Affairs dealt with the measure. The Defense Department informed Jackson, as it had the House, that no changes should be made in the political status of Alaska, while the State Department asserted that admission of both territories would comply with the United Nations charter. According to the State Department, it would also reflect America positively in the eyes of the underdeveloped nations of the world and contrast favorably with the Soviet denial of political freedom.[36]

The high point of the hearings undoubtedly was the testimony of the undersecretary of the air force, James Douglas, Jr., who was at a loss to specifically pinpoint Defense Department objections to Alaska statehood.[37]

Unprepared to answer several questions put to him, Douglas tackled them later in a letter. He stated that Secretary McKay's ideas on defense withdrawals were less objectionable than the Bartlett amendment. A few days afterward, the Department of the Interior formally presented these ideas to Jackson's committee. The amendment that they proposed would allow the president to establish one or more special national defense withdrawals, covering any amount of the withdrawal area prior to admission. This area would encompass the Aleutian Islands and the region north of the main channels of the Porcupine, Yukon, and Kuskokwim rivers and be included within the state.[38]

Senator Jackson and Congressman Miller next wrote to the chief executive asking what sort of statehood legislation he would accept for Alaska. Eisenhower's answer was ambiguous. "I am in doubt," he wrote, "that any form of legislation can wholly remove my apprehension about granting statehood immediately. However, a proposal seeking to accommodate the many complex considerations entering into the statehood question has been made by Secretary of the Interior McKay, and should legislation of this type be approved by Congress, I assure your subcommittee that I shall give it earnest consideration." The president at last had indicated that he would at least consider Alaska statehood.[39]

The House sent its version of the twin bills to the rules committee. Congressman Howard Smith of Virginia, the new chairman, was implacably opposed to statehood for either territory. After lengthy hearings it granted a "closed rule," under which no modifications would be permitted except for the fifty-six amendments reported by the House Committee on Interior and Insular Affairs. On May 10, 1955, after two days of debate, the House recommitted the tandem bill by a vote of 218 to 170. The Senate, waiting for the outcome in the House, did not act at all.[40]

After recommittal, Congressman Saylor introduced separate statehood bills, one for each territory. The one for Alaska contained the McKay proposal. Bartlett and Gruening now believed that the admission of Hawaii would be followed by that of Alaska. They tried, unsuccessfully, to persuade Senators Jackson and Anderson to let Hawaii be considered first.[41]

After adjournment, Congressman Leo O'Brien of New York and seven members of the House Subcommittee on Territories and Insular Affairs arrived in Alaska. They conducted hearings which dealt with such topics as statehood, mental health, fisheries, justice, and transportation. The subcommittee traveled widely in Alaska and had heard some 234 witnesses in more than eighty hours of testimony by the time they finished their three-week tour in Ketchikan. During most of that time Bob Bartlett acted as chairman.[42]

Meanwhile, the sentiment for holding a constitutional convention to boost Alaska's sagging fortunes found expression in measures introduced in the 1955 territorial legislature. Such a convention finally was convened, and after seventy-five days of labor, delegates had produced a document which experts considered a model constitution.[43]

The delegates first assembled for the convention on November 8, 1955, at the

University of Alaska, where Bartlett delivered the keynote address, at which he stressed the democratic processes that must underlie the writing of the constitution. Drawing parallels with the federal constitutional convention of 1787, Bartlett pointed out precedents from that earlier convention which would benefit the delegates, but he suggested to them that they had to perform pioneering work to lay the foundations for natural resources policy and management, a key for statehood. He reminded the delegates that they would "write on a clean slate in the field of resources policy. Only a minute fraction of the land area is owned by private persons or corporations. Never before in the history of the United States has there been so great an opportunity to establish resources policy geared to the growth of a magnificent economy and the welfare of a people." Bartlett concluded his remarks by stating that "the convention can demonstrate to the Congress and the people of the United States . . . that Alaska's resources will be administered, within the bounds of human limitations and shortcomings, for the benefit of all the people."[44]

During their deliberations the delegates attached a so-called Alaska-Tennessee Plan ordinance to the constitution. The idea originated with George H. Lehleitner, a public-spirited businessman from New Orleans who had become an advocate of Hawaii statehood. Finding that Hawaii could make no progress, Lehleitner then made the achievement of statehood for Alaska a personal crusade. During his research into American history, Lehleitner had discovered that a number of territories had departed from the conventional procedures for seeking admission to the Union as states. The first of these was an area west of the Carolinas. Its people, envious that Kentucky had been admitted in 1792 and displeased that the first three congresses had not done likewise for them, called a constitutional convention, drafted a state constitution for Tennessee, and elected two senators and sent them to the nation's capital. Four months later, they acquired statehood. Michigan, California, Minnesota, Oregon, and Kansas had each employed a similar procedure.[45]

Gruening urged the convention to adopt Lehleitner's plan. Bartlett was far more cautious, and it is unlikely that the convention would have adopted the Alaska-Tennessee Plan if the delegate had not finally given his endorsement. While admiring Lehleitner, Bartlett was concerned about the possible negative effects upon the Congress if the Tennessee Plan were put into effect by Alaskans. Shortly after the Congress met early in 1956, Bartlett made his decision, advising the delegates to proceed with the plan. Bartlett explained that his reluctance had been due in part to a desire to evaluate statehood attitudes in Congress as well as to determine the effects of the president's 1956 State of the Union message. He also had wanted to evaluate the Tennessee Plan's chances for success in mid-twentieth-century America. Attaining statehood by traditional means had looked bleak, and Bartlett felt that the Tennessee Plan could provide a stimulating factor —"its impact could jar the nation and the Congress from lethargy." Electing and sending a congressional delegation to Washington "might provide the fulcrum needed to jar statehood from dead center."[46]

From the outset, Lehleitner applied enormous pressure on Bartlett to run for one of the three offices under the Alaska-Tennessee Plan, preferably that of representative, because he was best known in the House, where he enjoyed excellent relationships with his colleagues. Lehleitner told the delegate that "there is not even a remote doubt in my own mind that it is your clear duty to accept a Tennessee Plan office and to give it everything you've got." Without Bartlett's participation, the plan would not have much of a chance in succeeding, because Alaskans would be unenthusiastic toward a scheme which "would retire from office their most popular public servant. Congressional reaction would be similar." But Bartlett refused to run, citing among his reasons the fact that he could not do justice to both jobs. Most importantly, however, he basically lacked faith in the efficacy of the Alaska-Tennessee Plan and did not want to work with Gruening on it. Bartlett stated that he had "a hunch [that] those mixed up in it are going to seal their political doom." And although he had high regard for the ex-governor, he hated "to be ordered around all day long, every day, to find myself obliged to dissent at least a half dozen times a day from some of his cockeyed ideas which would spring full blown without thought. [The very idea] is more than I can contemplate at the age at which I now find myself."[47]

Bartlett's personal misgivings did not prevent him from working hard for the plan's success. He had pledged to support Gruening even before the constitutional convention had adopted the plan, and he backed the nomination of strong candidates by his party.

When voters went to the polls in the general election on October 9, 1956, they elected all three Democratic candidates for the Alaska-Tennessee Plan positions— Ernest Gruening, William A. Egan, and Ralph J. Rivers.[48]

Bartlett, Lehleitner, Atwood, and Ernest Bartley earlier had begun the necessary planning to get the most benefit from the Alaska-Tennessee Plan. Bartley, a professor of political science on leave from the University of Florida, had been engaged by the Public Administration Service as a consultant to the Alaska constitutional convention. He had agreed to tabulate the voting records of all members of Congress on statehood and related issues. Those who had voted consistently against it were written off, while those whose records were erratic or those who were new in Congress were investigated extensively. This included obtaining information about their personal backgrounds, views, activities and associations, and the social and economic characteristics of their districts. Thus armed, the newly elected delegation was in a better position to lobby Congress for support of the statehood measure.[49]

As soon as the election was over, Gruening flew to Washington, ready to go to work. Egan and Rivers had been persuaded, because of its public relations effect, to drive to Washington. On December 9, 1956, the Egans and the Riverses were honored at a farewell ceremony held in the gymnasium of the University of Alaska. The following afternoon, with the temperature at -47°F, they left for Washington in white cars that boasted Alaska's flag—eight stars of gold on a field of blue — painted on each door, the name of the car's occupant, and a sign proclaiming, "Alaska, the 49th State."[50] After a long and difficult journey, they arrived in Nashville, Tennessee, where they were joined by the Gruenings and honored by Tennessee's governor.

Despite news coverage and an official introduction by Florida's Senator Spessard L. Holland, Congress did not officially recognize or seat the Alaska-Tennessee Plan delegation.[51]

For his part, Bartlett was not impressed by the performance of the delegates. Rivers, for instance, could not "introduce Bill Snedden to a single member of the Rules Committee on the Democratic side," so Bartlett had to make the introductions. Bill Snedden was the editor and publisher of the formerly anti-statehood *Fairbanks Daily News-Miner.*

Until the spring of 1957, the three Alaska-Tennessee Plan delegates had no office, since Gruening refused to rent one until the legislature appropriated the necessary funds. In the meantime, Rivers occupied a corner of Bartlett's office, which irked Bartlett considerably. Several weeks after an office was finally rented, "Egan broke with Gruening and moved his office to the basement of his home. Thereafter his contacts were largely confined to senators' staff members." Above all, Bartlett remarked, Egan "spent practically all of his time in my office and instead of taking some member of Congress out to lunch . . . almost invariably he would slip away by himself and have lunch alone in one of the joints in the now demolished block called Ptomaine Row." Gruening alone was vigorous and continually active. He entertained influential legislators, as all members of the delegation should have done, but many senators told Bartlett that "he was too persistent, demanded too much time, talked too much" and generally got on people's nerves.[52]

The statehood outlook brightened in 1956. In March of that year Secretary of the Interior McKay resigned to run against Senator Wayne Morse in the fall election, and President Eisenhower appointed Fred Seaton to replace the Oregonian. Seaton, a publisher and broadcasting executive from Hastings, Nebraska, had served in the Nebraska legislature from 1945 to 1949. Upon the death of Senator Kenneth Wherring in 1951, the governor appointed him to fill the vacancy. On February 20, 1951, Senator Seaton delivered his maiden speech in support of Alaska statehood. He had been persuaded to support Alaska's cause by Ernest Gruening, who also wrote the speech for him.[53] Seaton did not run for election in his own right in 1952, but in 1953, President Eisenhower appointed him assistant secretary of defense for legislative and public affairs, and in 1955 he became a presidential assistant. During his confirmation hearings, when asked by Senator Neuberger how he stood on the question of Alaska statehood, he replied that he favored it. Seaton also pledged to have the administration-requested defense withdrawals defined so that Alaska could join the Union.[54]

Seaton was true to his word, for in the summer of 1956 when the Republican party adopted its national platform, Seaton went before the resolutions committee to support an affirmative plank on Alaska statehood that also recognized the president's concern. While Republicans, as in previous years, once again recommended immediate statehood for Hawaii, they also advocated "immediate statehood for Alaska, recognizing the fact that adequate provision for defense requirements must be made."[55]

On the territorial level, Heintzleman resigned as governor some three months before the expiration of his term and was replaced by Fairbanks attorney Mike Stepovich. The new governor told Alaskans in his inaugural address that the time had come to close ranks on the statehood issue and work toward the admission of the territory, since that was what the majority wanted.[56] If Stepovich had been fairly indifferent toward the statehood issue as a private citizen, he now worked vigorously to promote it.

In 1957, at the request of Bartlett and Delegate John Burns of Hawaii, Senator James Murray introduced separate statehood bills for the territories, and each delegate introduced separate measures in the House.[57] The new Alaska statehood measures differed somewhat from previous ones in that they considered the Alaska constitution an accepted fact and thus became admission rather than enabling bills.

In March the House Subcommittee on Territories and Insular Affairs held ten days of hearings on the topic. The Senate Interior and Insular Affairs Committee, presided over by Senator Jackson, devoted two days to the subject. In general, the two hearings were perfunctory, because many members of the House and Senate committees felt that nothing much that had not already been said could be added to the record.

At the end of the hearings, the subcommittee put the statehood bill into final shape. It adopted, practically intact, the amendment for special national defense withdrawals as the price of administration approval of the bill. Bartlett requested, and the subcommittee agreed, to move the line from the main channels of the Porcupine, Yukon, and Kuskokwim rivers to a line five miles north of their right banks, thereby excluding five river settlements from the withdrawal area. Since

Congress was economy-minded, the subcommittee, much to Bartlett's sorrow, also eliminated the $78 million authorization for highway construction and mainte- nance that Senator Anderson had included in the 1954 statehood bill and that had been included in the 1957 measures. The subcommittee also eliminated a $15 million provision for constructing and improving harbors and for surveying the land grant.[58]

Bartlett proposed, and the subcommittee approved, an increase in the state's share of the net proceeds from the sale of seal skins and sea otter skins from 50 percent to 70 percent. The state also would be given 90 percent of all royalties and rentals from federal coal lands, which previously had all gone into the federal treasury. In addition, Alaska was to receive 90 percent of the revenue collected from the mining of coal, phosphate, sodium, oil, oil shale, and gas on the public domain.[59]

As finally reported to the House, the bill provided the state with some 182,800,000 acres of vacant, unappropriated, and unreserved land to be selected within a period of twenty-five years after admission. The aboriginal land claims were left to be dealt with by future legislative or judicial action.[60]

In August the Senate committee reported its Alaska statehood measure favor- ably. It gave the new state the right to select 103,350,000 million acres from the vacant, unappropriated public domain within twenty-five years after admission to the Union.[61]

In July 1957, Speaker of the House Rayburn, hitherto a foe of Alaska statehood, finally changed his mind at Bartlett's urging and promised to give the territory "its day in court." The hopes for statehood soared. Rayburn advised that the Alaska measure not be brought to the floor of the House in the last days of the session when it might be defeated in the rush to adjourn. His advice was accepted.[62]

In January 1958, President Eisenhower, for the first time, fully supported Alaska statehood and again urged Hawaii's immediate admission. But shortly after his message, Eisenhower again dimmed the hopes of Alaska statehood proponents when he advocated that the Hawaii bill be brought up simultaneously with the Alaska measure. The implication was obvious — tying the two measures together had resulted in their failure before. At this critical point, however, Delegate Burns of Hawaii helped the Alaska cause when he asserted that "nothing should interfere with success in the consideration of [the] Alaska" statehood bill. He promised to remove the Hawaii measure from the Senate debate if that were necessary to insure the success of the Alaska measure. The two bills were not combined.[63]

Toward the end of January 1958, Bartlett again visited Rayburn. The Speaker told him that he did not oppose Alaska's admission even though it was outside of the continental United States, stating that "Alaska is part of the mainland, a part of the North American continent." He did not object to Alaska's natives either: "I don't have any feeling against Alaska, and the reason I'm against Alaska is because if Alaska is admitted to the Union inevitably Hawaii will be too, and I'm strongly against Hawaii, very strongly against Hawaii, and the reason I'm against Hawaii is not because a minimum of the population is composed of races other than Caucasian but because it offends my sense of what is right that a group of islands removed by over 2,000 miles from our western coast should be permitted in the Union. I think this is wrong." Rayburn added that he did not believe that the founding fathers had intended to extend the system of states in this manner. He concluded that "it will be a distortion of the American scheme of things if Hawaii is to come in." Despite all that, he had decided to help Alaska. Not long after his talk with the Speaker, Bartlett "had a long, long talk with Lyndon Johnson. Lyndon told me then that he was ready. He was ready to permit Alaska statehood to come to the floor of the Senate for action there."[64]

At about the same time, Rayburn told Congressman Howard Smith, the chairman of the House Rules Committee, that he wanted a ruling on the statehood bill. Bartlett was elated. He was even more pleased when Lyndon Johnson told him that the Alaska bill would be brought to the floor of the Senate soon and would be passed as well. Johnson claimed that southern senators would not even filibuster it, although some might talk lengthily to protect their records with their constituents at home. Liberal Democrats and friendly Republicans had also agreed not to make the Hawaii statehood bill title II of the Alaska measure.[65]

At that point, however, the drive in the Senate stalled when Senator Knowland of California, the minority leader, revealed that he did not regard consideration of the Alaska bill by itself advisable. Bartlett immediately had another talk with Senator Johnson. This time the majority leader waffled on his support for Alaska statehood, remarking that he had received a great deal of mail from Alaska that was opposed to statehood. He might have to vote against the bill, he said, yet, ambiguously, he remained willing to bring it to the floor. Pressed directly, Johnson admitted that Alaska would not gain statehood in 1958. Bartlett was depressed once again.[66]

In the House, Congressman Smith had not changed his mind. Congressman Clair Engle of California, chairman of the House Interior and Insular Affairs Committee, warned Smith that unless the Alaska bill was given the green light by the middle of March, he intended to bypass the House Rules Committee by employing a little-used device under which statehood and a few other types of legislation were deemed as privileged. This procedure required the Speaker of the House to recognize the chairman of the committee concerned, and it permitted each member of the House to speak for one hour.[67]

In the meantime there were demonstrations for statehood in Anchorage and

Fairbanks, and early in March the American television public saw an Alaska and Hawaii statehood debate on the CBS program "See It Now," hosted by Edward R. Murrow. Bartlett, Governor Stepovich, and Robert Atwood spoke in favor of Alaska statehood, while Winton C. Arnold, John Manders, and Senator George Malone spoke against statehood. Malone was particularly worried that if noncontiguous Alaska were admitted, then Hawaii, Puerto Rico, Taiwan, and the Philippines would soon follow. This, he said, would result in free immigration, free trade, and assorted other evils.[68]

Soon afterward, Congressman John Pillion of New York demanded and received prime time to fulminate against statehood for the territories. In essence, he predicted that as soon as statehood was granted, Harry Bridges of the Pacific Coast Longshoremen's Union would send his organizers to Alaska, take over its politics, and that soon Communist tentacles would reach into the very halls of Congress. If that itself were not horrible enough, Alaska's and Hawaii's admission also would give their residents disproportionate representation in the Senate.[69]

Meanwhile, Bartlett's friend Congressman O'Brien announced that he would support four amendments to his bill. One would retain federal jurisdiction over Alaska's fish and game resources until the secretary of the Interior certified that Alaska could adequately administer, manage, and conserve these resources in the broad national interest. The others provided for a statehood referendum, a reduction of the land grant from 182,000,000 to 102,550,000 acres, and permission for the Federal Maritime Board to retain control of Alaska's seaborne trade with other states.[70] Bartlett agreed to the other concessions but was unhappy with the federal retention of fish and game management. For years he had fought hard to have control transferred to Alaska only to see it slip away now.

Howard Smith and the rules committee still continued to stall, holding intermittent hearings. Finally the leadership decided to employ the bypass procedure. On May 21, 1958, Wayne Aspinall brought the Alaska statehood measure up as a privileged matter. Speaker Rayburn overruled various objections, and the debate was on. Under the House rules, each congressman could talk for one hour, although debate could be curtailed by unanimous consent or by a majority vote. Opponents soon realized the futility of extending the discussion to the maximum 431 hours, and all agreed to a unanimous consent resolution to end the debate at 5 P.M. on May 26.[71] The House accepted the four amendments and, after some anxious moments, passed the Alaska statehood bill by 210 votes to 166. Although Bartlett had predicted passage by only seventeen votes, the final count was still a narrow margin.

Except for the likelihood of amendments being added to the bill, prospects looked bright in the Senate. However, if the Senate bill did differ in important particulars from the House version, Bartlett worried, the statehood forces would "be catapulted into a morass." Bartlett therefore set up a meeting with Senator Jackson, floor manager of the bill. Among others who attended the meeting were Bartlett himself, O'Brien, and Gruening. All tried to persuade Jackson to abandon the Senate bill and take the House measure instead. Much to their amazement and relief, Jackson agreed.[72]

The Senate debated the measure in the latter half of May and throughout June. Southerners, realizing the futility of resistance, agreed to make only token speeches in opposition, and on June 30, the Senate passed the Alaska statehood bill sixty-four votes to twenty.[73] The long struggle finally had ended in victory.

Bartlett had slept badly the night before the vote, sensing that June 30 would bring the culmination of long years of hard work. On that day, his office filled early with Alaskans who had come to town for this climactic occasion, disrupting the office routine: "We weren't answering any letters that day; we weren't telephoning any department that day; our thoughts and actions were directed toward one thing and one thing only, that which was to occur in the Senate that afternoon." Bartlett wanted to be prepared and be "armed with every last bit of available information so that if a statehood advocate in the Senate during the course of the day needed ammunition of any kind I would have it readily available for his use." Many Alaskans sat in the visitor's gallery in the Senate, among them Atwood, Governor Stepovich, the Alaska-Tennessee Plan delegates and their wives, Bill Snedden, and Ada and Noel Wien, members of a pioneering Alaska aviation family. Bartlett remembered that when the vote was about half over, "people began to talk. They began to see that we had it, and well, we did." There was spontaneous applause from the galleries and also from the floor. The time at which the roll-call vote ended was 8:02 P.M. EST. Not only the spectators but the senators themselves were jubilant. It became very noisy, and Senator Neuberger, who presided, halfheartedly called for order. Soon after the vote, many of the Alaskans who had been sitting in the galleries all day long headed for the Senate chapel to give thanks for the fulfillment of their hopes and aspirations — the Alaska statehood bill had at last received congressional approval.[74]

For Bartlett, the hours after the vote were anticlimactic. Alaskan friends had asked him to phone immediately after the statehood bill passed. He had consented and "darted back to the office and started to phone Alaska. I was on the phone for hours, since the lines were busy, and I should have realized that the AP [Associated Press] and UP [United Press] had beat me there anyway, but I'd made these promises."

Those who had gone to the chapel soon returned to Bartlett's office and had a big party that went on for hours. The Alaskans were joined by many others: "The place was bulging."[75]

Both O'Brien and Bartlett believed that, had Congress not passed the bill in

1958, the matter would have been as good as dead for a generation. Bartlett explained: "A cause, no matter how noble it is, no matter how deserving it is, can be prosecuted only so long; then the people at home weary and they need a lull, a spell in which to regroup. More importantly, I sensed that Congress was not disposed year after year to go through the motions of rejecting Alaska statehood. It would simply have said to us when we came knocking at the gate next time, we have too much other business. Every year we've taken so much time out . . . in discussion and voting on Alaska statehood and it always gets licked, so we're not going to do it again."[76]

The struggle had been a long one, involving many people in Alaska, in Washington, and throughout the nation. Bartlett, summing up the long fight, stated that "it took fifteen years for fruition, and I think that given the nature of the opposition, the size of the project, the fact that no state had been admitted since 1912, that actually it was a pretty successful campaign."[77] He might well have decided that it was fortunate that statehood had not come earlier under the meager bills then under discussion.

Soon after the achievement of statehood, squabbling broke out among participants as to who had been the major figure in the movement. A short time after the bill had passed, the *Fairbanks Daily News-Miner* published a number of editorials praising everyone even remotely connected with the statehood cause, with the exception of the Alaska-Tennessee Plan delegation. Gruening was "so agitated and so concerned and so childishly hurt," Bartlett observed, "that I continue to feel very sorry for him despite a few invisible (I hope) bobbings of my Adam's apple as I sat across from him at the coffee table and heard him declare himself as Mr. Statehood."[78]

Although many participated in the effort, it is Bartlett who truly deserves the title of architect of Alaska statehood. For some thirteen years the delegate had made congressional friends and had worked strenuously and steadily in promoting statehood in Alaska and in the Congress. Although Bartlett long resented not receiving due credit for his role in the struggle, he nevertheless made no efforts to publicize his many achievements. This did not keep him from complaining long, loud, and repeatedly to friends and associates about those who constantly hogged the spotlight, Gruening foremost among these. Important parts indeed were played by other participants, including Gruening, Atwood, Snedden, Secretary of the Interior Fred Seaton, and House Speaker Sam Rayburn. Statehood truly was a cooperative effort — and now Bartlett was determined to make it work.

CHAPTER 14

At Last a Vote

O N JULY 7, 1958, President Eisenhower, without having invited any of the key personalities to attend the ceremony, signed the measure admitting Alaska into the Union as the forty-ninth state. Democratic Senator James E. Murray complained to Gruening that the president did not want to have his picture taken with all the Democrats who had been so instrumental in bringing about the passage of the statehood bill. Instead, Eisenhower "chose to handle this momentous matter as though he were merely signing a private bill for the relief of Mr. 'X'. Lord knows where he's going to find two Republicans who were sufficiently important in bringing about statehood for Alaska to whom to present the two pens he used in the signing."[1] Murray was correct in his assessment. Except for Republicans John Saylor of Pennsylvania in the House and Thomas Kuchel and William Knowland, both from California, in the Senate, Republicans had been, at best, indifferent to the measure. Secretary of the Interior Fred Seaton, on the other hand, had been the major proponent within the Republican administration.

The statehood act required that Alaska's governor call primary and general elections to select state officials and the congressional delegation. On July 16 the governor decided that candidates for office had to make their intentions known no later than July 28 and that the primary election would be held on August 26, 1958.

As part of the primary election, Alaska's voters were asked either to approve or disapprove three referendum propositions which had been inserted in the statehood bill. They were: (1) Shall Alaska immediately be admitted into the Union as a State? (2) Shall the boundaries of the new State be approved? (3) Shall all the provisions of the statehood act, such as those reserving rights and powers to the United States, as well as those prescribing the terms and conditions of the land grants and other property, be consented to? The last proposition dealt with the special national defense withdrawal and the nettlesome fish and wildlife amendments. If all three were approved, the state constitution would be deemed amended accordingly, as prescribed by the admission act. But if even one was

161

defeated, the statehood act would become null and void. Naturally, many Alaskan organizations, officials, and most candidates for office strongly urged an affirmative vote.[2]

In the meantime a great deal of soul-searching occurred among various Alaskans intending to run for public office. Among Democrats, Delegate Bartlett was perhaps the key to the problem of who was to be running for what position. He had been Alaska's delegate in Congress since 1944, and many of his Washington associates automatically assumed that he would run for one of the two seats in the United States Senate.

In the spring, when the House had passed the Alaska statehood bill amidst hope that the Senate would as well, Delegate Bartlett seriously considered the future. Bartlett felt that perhaps all Democratic hopefuls would stand aside and support the election of the Alaska-Tennessee Plan delegation. Although Gruening obviously would make a capable U.S. senator, Bartlett thought that Ralph Rivers should not represent Alaska in the House of Representatives, because he simply was not qualified for the position. Bartlett was also disappointed with Bill Egan: "Much as I like him, I must concede he hasn't measured up to our expectations. He has become petty in his hatred of Ernest, aided and abetted by Neva [his wife]." Bartlett had watched Mike Stepovich and Ted Stevens lobby members of Congress; in contrast "Ralph and Bill sit through the sessions and do nothing else! God go with them." He felt that Gruening, on the other hand, worked "like a Trojan," but the delegate predicted that Gruening's many strong stands on various issues when he had been territorial governor had created too many enemies. Bartlett urged his son-in-law, Burke Riley, to aim for one of the top spots, presumably the Senate, because of his competence and his previous residence in the Fourth Judicial Division.[3]

Bartlett knew that it would be exceedingly difficult to establish the new state. Whoever was elected the first governor would set the all-important precedents molding the new political entity. He was convinced that certain personalities in the Democratic party "must be kept out, or chaos will come." Robert Ellis, former territorial legislator and airline president, had expressed an interest in the governorship, but the delegate believed that his lack of administrative experience might be "a powerful strike against him." Bartlett considered his friend Hugh Wade to be fully qualified for the gubernatorial post.[4]

Editorials in the *Fairbanks Daily News-Miner* praising everyone even faintly connected with the great victory, from President Eisenhower to novelist Edna Ferber — but totally omitting the Alaska-Tennessee delegation — undoubtedly were the work of publisher Bill Snedden. It was also Snedden who persuaded *Time* magazine to publish a cover story about Governor Stepovich that appeared on the newsstands on June 2, 1958. This neglect deeply hurt both Gruening and Egan.[5]

Egan wrote "a long mournful letter" to Snedden complaining about the omission, but he later thought better of it and destroyed the epistle without sending it.

Egan talked matters over with Bartlett in Washington. He confided his indecision concerning his political future while biting "his fingernails at a furious rate." Bartlett advised him to "try for something," because he certainly could not go back to his Valdez grocery store. Later that afternoon Egan called Bartlett. He had made up his mind to run, "win, lose, or draw," for the Senate, even if he had to run against Gruening. Bartlett was puzzled by Egan's sudden decisiveness and wondered what had helped Egan make up his mind. Apparently a friend of his wife's had called, denouncing the *Time* cover story, which also had omitted mention of the Alaska-Tennessee Plan delegates. Vide shared her surmise with Bartlett that Egan probably had gone home and relayed his indecisiveness to his wife, Neva, who immediately had "set him straight," explaining to him that his contributions to Alaska had been great and that she did not want to return to Valdez.[6]

Bartlett mused that "very frankly, personal desires, for a multitude of reasons, would take me to the Senate," but he had announced in 1957 that he would not run against his friends Gruening, Egan, or Rivers. In retrospect that seemed to have been "a damned fool gesture on my part," because it greatly limited his options. In the meantime the three had been telling him what a great governor he would make, but the possible candidacies of Wade or Ellis faced him in that direction. Bartlett gloomily concluded that "I'm forestalled from anything if my theory that I don't want to run against a friend is followed."[7]

In the final analysis, all who were potential candidates seemed to be miffed at his indecision. Bartlett pointed out that he found it difficult to "take the announcements from EG [Ernest Gruening] and Bill [Egan] these last few days, direct to me, that statehood is where it is because of them." As the delegate saw it, the $186,000 which the territorial legislature had appropriated in 1957 for the operation of the Alaska-Tennessee Plan had been wasted. Neither Egan nor Rivers had expended the necessary effort, and they had rubbed too many members of Congress the wrong way.[8]

Bartlett could not decide what to do, and it was not because of lack of advice or of mounting pressure. George Sundborg, who a year earlier had become the editor of the *Fairbanks Daily News-Miner,* apprised Bartlett that "any number of people are available to heed the call to high duty." Warren Taylor, veteran territorial legislator, considered running for governor, as did Richard Greuel, Steve McCutcheon, Victor Rivers, Bob Ellis and Wendell Kay, also territorial lawmakers. Hugh Wade, territorial official, also desired the governorship. All would probably run unless Bartlett did, Sundborg predicted, because "nobody wants to run against you." On the Republican side Walter J. Hickel, Anchorage hotel owner, sought the governorship, while Elton Engstrom, territorial Senator, hoped to be secretary of state. Mike Stepovich, Alaska's governor, and Paul Robison, Anchorage attorney, each wanted one of the United States Senate seats, and John Butrovich, veteran territorial legislator, had his sights set on the governorship. The list of possible candidates was endless among both Democrats and Republicans. In short, Sundborg concluded, "an epidemic is let loose in the land. Higher service is calling insistently, and any number are willing to sacrifice personal gain and give their all for the people of the great state." The same number, Sundborg assumed, felt they very likely deserved it, because, "after all, didn't I write a letter to the editor about statehood back in 1953?"⁹

A short time later Sundborg volunteered to Bartlett his view that Alaska needed the best man it had for the governorship. The Democratic party should rally around the candidate for governor not only because he would determine the formation of the state, but also because he would have several thousand jobs, "including a bunch of judgeships and all the top department appointments, at his command." Since the governor was limited to two terms, the first successful occupant of that office very likely could run for the U. S. Senate and be retained by a grateful electorate until he died in office. Sundborg concluded that "it would be a sacrifice" for Bartlett not to run for the Senate just yet, "but it may be a sacrifice you should make. If you don't, Bill Egan must."¹⁰

Early in July, Ralph Rivers announced his candidacy for the House. Bartlett was appalled. Although he had known Rivers for a long time, it was not until Rivers' performance as Alaska-Tennessee Plan delegate that he had realized how really incompetent the man was. Bartlett wrote: "It is shocking. It is terrible. It is galling to think that Alaska will first be represented in the House of Representatives by a man devoid of ANY capacity. He is nice and kind. If the voters knew Ralph as we know Ralph, Ralph would have an opportunity to resume the practice of law in Fairbanks, or wherever."¹¹

Pressures were mounting. Paul Butler, the chairman of the Democratic National Committee, and numerous colleagues and friends in Washington, D.C. wanted the delegate to run for the Senate. Among these was Scripps-Howard journalist Douglas Smith, husband of Margery Smith, who had worked on Bartlett's staff. Smith claimed, "I have never known a man to work so hard, over a period of so many years, in what often has been a thankless endeavor. I don't believe I have known anyone else to be so reluctant to take credit for them." Smith advised Bartlett to run for the Senate, because it would give him the "opportunity to have relatively few decisions to make and to have ample time to reflect upon even those few, while others did the chores." The journalist concluded that Bartlett had served the party and his constituents above and beyond the call of duty and that they owed him "whatever office you choose to seek. . . ." Bartlett was still in doubt about the course of action to take, because some party leaders in Alaska wanted him to run for the governorship. While Bartlett hesitated, Egan announced his candidacy for the Senate on July 7, the day President Eisenhower signed the statehood measure.[12]

Bartlett knew that Gruening's ambition also was to win a U.S. Senate seat from Alaska. He realized that the former governor would not hesitate long to announce his candidacy. Still, Bartlett was no closer to a decision. "I wake up at night. And roam the house. Without constructive results," he confided to his daughter and son-in-law. "I turn to Vide for advice. She won't give it. Says it is my decision. Closest she came to advising me was this morning when she said the rug is about worn out." The delegate favored running for the Senate, and colleagues had urged him to file. On the other hand, both he and Vide had a longing "of sorts" to go back to Alaska. But the governor's job, Bartlett worried, would leave no spare time. His Washington job, though, hadn't left any free time either. He continued to vacillate in this manner, but he knew that he had to decide soon what to do and wondered what that decision was going to be.[13]

Vide, in the meantime, was convinced that her husband would run for the governorship, believing it to be his duty but also being convinced that the state's first chief executive would "be ruined politically forever" because of the many precedent-setting decisions he would have to make. She felt that Bob ought to be in the Senate, "but I know in my heart he will do the other. I will not say boo either way — ever," Vide concluded. On July 14 Gruening hesitated no longer and announced his candidacy for the U.S. Senate.[14] Bartlett now felt himself even more boxed in than before.

Among the Republicans, territorial Governor Stepovich experienced many of the same pressures as Bartlett. A political novice, he had ineptly remarked that Alaskan voters probably would choose three Democrats for Congress. He himself apparently wanted to run for the governorship, and the territorial Republican leadership supported him in that desire. Soon, however, Secretary of the Interior Seaton and various other prominent Republicans on the national level pointed out the need for more Republicans in the U.S. Senate. Although Stepovich later tried to cover his mistake, the *Anchorage Daily Times* counseled him to sit tight until Bartlett had announced his own plans, lest he get "his political head cut off."[15]

The *Anchorage Daily Times* finally became impatient with Bartlett's continuing indecision and suggested that perhaps he was too sensitive and loyal to his party and friends — to the detriment of himself and Alaska. The newspaper indicated that if Bartlett chose the governorship, good and well; otherwise he should be in the U.S. Senate.

At a Juneau dinner honoring him, Bartlett told the large crowd that all his Washington experience made him inclined to run for the Senate. Yet he was not unmindful of how important the office of governor was going to be. His audience shared in his uncertainties, for when some cried "Senator Bartlett," others replied no, they needed "Governor Bartlett."

Egan, apparently troubled by a story in a Washington paper that accused the Alaska-Tennessee delegation of trying to squeeze Bartlett out of Congress, told the delegate that whatever his decision would be, it would be fine with Egan.[16]

On July 18 Bartlett made up his mind—tentatively. At a dinner in Fairbanks he announced his intention to run for the Senate but added that if Stepovich filed for the governorship, he, Bartlett, would withdraw from the senate race and run for the governorship. His audience cheered the decision, but not so the *Anchorage Daily Times.* It ran an editorial entitled "A Hero's Armor Takes on Tarnish," in which it stated that Delegate Bartlett had fallen off his lofty perch as beloved statesman and leader of Alaskans. The editorial opined that, in announcing a two-pronged political program for himself, he had been talking "out of both sides of his mouth. On the one side he was the statesman that Alaskans have long admired. On the other he was an ordinary gut-cutting politician." In case Stepovich ran, the editorial continued, then Bartlett intended to foresake Alaska's interest and become a politician primarily interested in seeking power and controlling the governor's office. For whatever reasons, the *Times* expected loftier standards of acceptable behavior from Bartlett than from all other politicians. Moreover, on the same day the delegate announced his intentions, a number of Democrats declared their determination to seek the office of the governor, suddenly feeling the urgent call to higher duty.[17]

A number of motivations influenced Bartlett's announcement. Perhaps he thought that he alone could defeat Stepovich. Furthermore, from his viewpoint, Egan and Gruening had made premature announcements that had certainly limited his choices. But most importantly, perhaps, Bartlett felt that "the man in the street" desired him to run for the governorship.

In any event, Bartlett felt extremely uneasy after his Fairbanks announcement. He rose early the next morning and typed a revised statement of his intentions. A few hours later he boarded a plane for Ketchikan. Upon landing in Juneau en route, Bartlett gave his statement to a reporter, who informed him that Egan had just announced that he would run instead for the governorship. A short time afterward, Stepovich also arrived at the airport, and he and Bartlett talked privately. Bartlett told Stepovich of his revised intentions, which were to run for the Senate without any strings attached. Although relieved that he had committed himself, Bartlett was still troubled when he left for Ketchikan. With Bartlett pledged to run for one Senate seat, Stepovich declared himself a candidate for the other Senate seat. Not only did he thereby satisfy the desires of various Republican leaders, but he also avoided a contest with Egan, who, many thought, would be a more formidable opponent than Gruening.[18]

Although now committed to the Senate race, Bartlett was unconsolable, because he believed that he had let his friends down by his decision. "If he hadn't been pushed so hard there at the last," Vide believed, "he would have made a different choice." In any event, the choice had been made, and "hindsight is horrible—just as at bridge." Vide wondered at times "if a swift kick would do [Bartlett] any good." Her husband, she concluded, would soon have to shed his agonies "so he can come back to the hustings his own self."[19]

Various friends reassured the delegate that he had made the correct choice and should pay no attention to the politicians, office seekers, so-called friends, and antagonists who had chastised him for his Fairbanks announcement. One of Bartlett's friends had tired of the party leaders who continually placed Bartlett into debt to the "people [who] got behind you and put you into office." The friend believed that they were fooling no one, for it was the delegate's own superb record which had won him the elections every two years since 1944. If, this friend concluded, there indeed was a debtor-creditor relationship, it was Alaskans who owed the delegate for his leadership and accomplishments.[20]

Bartlett appreciated the moral support friends gave him at a time when he "needed to have [his] hand held." He was puzzled, however, at the fact that "people just don't expect me to be political; and I guess I can't be." Yet it galled him that "the boys in the Interior Department" and Bill Snedden, the publisher of the *Fairbanks Daily News-Miner,* "get the national magazines to give the Republicans all the credit for statehood . . ." while Democrats and Republicans alike seemed to expect him to stand above the fray.[21]

On August 9, 1958, Mike Stepovich resigned from the governorship after 428 days in office. Secretary of Alaska Waino Hendrickson once again became the acting governor, as he had been after Heintzleman's sudden resignation.[22]

The campaign now swung into high gear. Unopposed in the primary and slated to run against each other in the November 25 general election for Alaska's so-called U.S. Senate Term A were Bartlett and Republican R.E. Robertson, a lawyer and former mayor of Juneau, who had been a delegate to the Alaska constitutional convention. Gruening ran unopposed for his party's nomination to U.S. Senate Term B and would oppose Republican Stepovich in the general election.

Two Democrats, Ralph Rivers and Raymond Plummer, an Anchorage lawyer, vied with each other for their party's nomination for the single seat in the U.S. House of Representatives. The winner of that contest would run against Republican Henry Benson of Juneau, the territorial commissioner of labor.

In the Democratic primary for governor, Bill Egan was opposed by J. Gerald Williams of Juneau, the territorial attorney general, and by Ralph Rivers' brother Vic Rivers, an Anchorage engineer and president of the last territorial Senate. The winner in this three-way contest would face Republican John Butrovich of Fairbanks, a territorial legislator of long experience.

Democrats Hugh J. Wade of Juneau, the territorial treasurer, and Richard J. Greuel of Fairbanks, the speaker of the 1957 territorial House, both ran for nomination for the position of secretary of state. The winner in this contest would oppose Republican Karl Dewey of Juneau, the former territorial tax commissioner.[23]

Before the passage of the Alaska statehood bill in June 1958, it was estimated that approximately a third of Alaska's voters opposed statehood. After passage of the measure, however, many voters who formerly opposed it jumped on the bandwagon. If not overjoyed, they at least were determined to make the best of the new situation, even though many uncertainties and anxieties remained. Some feared additional taxes, while others fretted about problems in the fishing industry. Still others were uneasy about possible elimination of federal employees' cost-of-living allowances or the end of existing native welfare payments. Delegate Bartlett attempted to quell some of these fears by having the chairman of the United States Civil Service Commission declare that admission would not affect the cost-of-living allowances of federal employees. In addition, the secretary of the army reassured military personnel that statehood would not affect duty tours and special pay of servicemen stationed in the North.[24]

More vicious were rumors spread among the Eskimos in arctic villages which asserted that, with statehood, they would be placed on reservations and be restricted to small geographical areas for subsistence hunting and trapping. Similar stories cropped up among the Athapascans of the interior region, who were also told that they would be taxed heavily, that native hospitals would be closed, and that welfare payments would be stopped. Secretary Seaton responded to these rumors, emphatically stating that natives, as American citizens, possessed all the rights and privileges inherent in that status. When visiting Alaska to give a boost to Republican candidates on the eve of the primary election, he asserted that the Interior Department did not want any more reservations.[25]

On August 26, 1958, Alaskans went to the polls in record numbers. Many polling places ran out of ballots and had to use sample ballots or have new supplies flown in to them. On the question, "Shall Alaska immediately be admitted into the Union as a State?" some 40,452 persons voted affirmatively and only 8,010 voted negatively. The other two propositions fared similarly well. Support for the propositions was lowest in southeastern Alaska and highest in southcentral Alaska. Some 48,462 voters exercised their franchise, a considerable increase from the 1956 all-time high of 28,903.[26]

Bartlett and Robertson had run unopposed for Senate Term A. For Senate Term B, Gruening emerged from the primary as underdog, receiving 5,721 fewer votes from the Democratic voters than Stepovich, his rival, had from the Republicans. Rivers emerged victorious over Plummer, the former Democratic national committeeman, by a slim margin of 630 votes. Butrovich was unopposed for the Republican gubernatorial nomination, together with his running mate, Brad Phillips, an Anchorage businessman. Democrat Egan defeated Williams and Victor Rivers, while Wade defeated Greuel to become Egan's running mate.[27]

While Alaskans listened to the oratory of the victorious primary candidates of both parties, Americans in the other forty-eight states went to the polls and gave the Republicans a sound drubbing. Congress, which was to convene on January 7, 1959, would have 62 Democrats and 34 Republicans in the Senate, 282 Democrats and 153 Republicans in the House. That was without the Alaska delegation, which was not to be elected until November 25.[28]

Although not seriously threatened by Robertson, Bartlett campaigned extensively, urging the election of fellow Democrats, particularly of Gruening, who faced a hard struggle to close the gap between himself and Stepovich. Gruening had appealed for Bartlett's help, and together they ran a well-organized campaign that blanketed the state.

For the first time, national figures ventured north to help candidates. It is debatable whether outsiders helped, because northerners were not especially interested in national and international affairs. For the most part, however, the visitors did not speak on national or international issues anyway but rather utilized their personal charms and political magnetism. Senators Frank Church and John F. Kennedy campaigned for the Democrats. Secretary of the Interior Seaton came north on behalf of the Republicans. Voters knew the important part he had played in helping achieve Alaska statehood, and his department had always loomed large in territorial affairs. Campaigning and promising projects of various sorts for the new state, Seaton captured the attention of Alaska's voters and perhaps even overshadowed his party's candidates. Vice-President Richard M. Nixon also came to the new state to campaign and, like Senator Kennedy, drew curious crowds but probably changed no votes.

In the race for U. S. Senate Term B, septuagenarian Gruening had campaigned with energy, flair, and determination, making known to the electorate his great abilities and accomplishments and pointing, in contrast, to Stepovich's conservative voting record. An excellent public speaker, Gruening always determined beforehand the type of audience he would be addressing and then molded his speech to appeal to that particular group. When he came to Fairbanks, for example, the Tanana-Yukon Historical Society had invited the candidate to give a speech. A member of the group, sourdough Forbes Baker, detested Gruening and had told his neighbors angrily that the candidate "will do nothing now but promote his candidacy for the Senate. And I'm against it." Instead, Gruening had begun his talk by stating that Alaskan history had always interested him, and that this interest originally stemmed from an experience his father, an ophthalmologist, had related to him. The account dealt with the time in 1875 when Dr. Emil Gruening was called across the continent to San Francisco to perform an eye operation on former Major General John Franklin Miller. Miller was then president of the Alaska Commercial Company, which had received a twenty-year lease on the fur seal fisheries of the Pribilof Islands. Having linked himself to Alaska through his father, Gruening then had given his own background. At the end of the talk, Gruening had presented the territorial guard flag to Forbes Baker for the society museum. On leaving, Baker had remarked to his neighbor: "You know, that man, he is a pretty good man."[29] As a result of this type of approach, on election day, November 25, Gruening more than overcame his handicap from the primary, polling 26,045 votes to his rival's 23,464.

A record 50,343 Alaskans out of an estimated 65,000 eligible residents went to the polls in this election. To no one's surprise, in the race for U.S. Senate Term A, Bob Bartlett received 40,939 votes compared to Robertson's 7,299, or approximately 83 percent of the votes. Rivers won handily over Benson, 27,948 votes to 20,699 for the seat in the U.S. House of Representatives. Egan and Wade easily outpolled Butrovich and Phillips by 29,189 votes to 19,299. With the election of Bartlett, Gruening, Rivers, and Egan and Wade, Alaska voters had handed the state's top four offices to Democrats. In the state Senate the Democrats won seventeen seats to only three for the Republicans, while in the House they captured thirty-three seats to the Republicans' five. Independents won the remaining two seats.[30]

A number of factors probably were responsible for the Republican debacle. High on the list were the competing factions within the GOP, which for more than two decades had fought each other as bitterly as they had the Democrats. Furthermore, most party-affiliated voters in Alaska were Democrats. The Democrats were better organized, and their candidates were well known and politically experienced. They had campaigned vigorously for the entire slate, while the Republicans had concentrated on their star candidates, Stepovich and Butrovich.

Both Democrats and Republicans had stressed conservative fiscal views, realizing that the first few years of statehood would be expensive and difficult. They also had agreed that the new state government should carefully select and wisely utilize Alaska's land grant of over 100 million acres. With candidates expressing essentially identical views on the basic issues, the election revolved very much around personalities, and here the Democrats had the more colorful and experienced campaigners in men such as Gruening, Bartlett, and a number of others. In addition, it was a year of GOP defeats nationwide, and GOP candidates in Alaska were caught in that trend.

On January 3, 1959, President Eisenhower signed the proclamation officially admitting Alaska as the forty-ninth state of the Union. Representing Alaska at the noon ceremony were Bob Bartlett, Ernest Gruening, Ralph Rivers, Waino Hendrickson, Mike Stepovich, and Robert Atwood. Also attending were Secretary Seaton, House Speaker Sam Rayburn and Vice-President Richard M. Nixon. Alaska officially became the forty-ninth state at the brief ceremony.

While official procedures existed for determining the length of Bartlett's and Gruening's first terms in the Senate, there was no established procedure for determining who would be addressed as the senior senator. Each considered the matter vital and had been maneuvering for weeks trying to get the other to yield voluntarily. Gruening was senior in terms of age, had held many important public offices, had been territorial governor for thirteen years, and early in their relationship clearly had been the acknowledged leader. Bartlett, on the other hand, had been elected delegate to Congress seven times by Alaskans and finally had been elected overwhelmingly to the U. S. Senate. Neither man could understand why the other did not come forth and make the obviously correct offer to stand aside in the matter of address. Finally they agreed to toss a coin in Gruening's drab, temporary office in the Old Senate Office Building.

The first coin toss would resolve who would draw lots first on the Senate floor to determine the length of the respective terms. A second toss would determine who would be the senior senator. Gruening tossed, Bartlett called heads. It came up tails. The coin was flipped again, and this time Gruening called out heads. The coin rolled on the floor, and everyone bent down to peer at it. Since tails was up, Bartlett became the senior senator. To give photographers a chance at a good picture, Associated Press correspondent Frank Vaille and the two senators repeated the ceremony several times, getting down on their knees and examining the coin. The posed photograph looked "like a three-cornered crap game," observed one of the reporters.[31] On the Senate floor on January 7, Gruening drew a four-year term, while Bartlett received a two-year term.

Alaska's congressional delegation soon had the opportunity to exercise its voting power, when a number of measures of particular importance to them came up. The first was the admission bill for Hawaii and the second the omnibus bill for Alaska. As late as December 1958, observers were unsure of how difficult it might be to enact the Hawaii statehood measure. Southern senators had not filibustered the Alaska statehood bill, but feelings on the Hawaii measure ran higher, since Japanese- or Chinese-Americans might be elected to Congress. Neither Sam Rayburn nor Lyndon Johnson favored the measure, but both believed that the new Congress would enact it because of the tremendous support it enjoyed in both parties.

As early as February 4, 1959, the House Interior and Insular Affairs Committee approved the Hawaii measure with amendments. After four days of hearings, the House Rules Committee voted to send the bill to the floor under an open rule. On March 11 the debate in the House began.[32]

On February 25 the Senate Subcommittee on Territories and Insular Affairs, chaired by Senator Jackson, had held a hearing on the Hawaii measure. The next day the subcommittee had voted unanimously to report it, and the full committee had followed suit on March 5. On March 11 both houses took up Hawaii statehood. The Senate debate was brief, perhaps because fifty-two of the ninety-eight senators had sponsored the Hawaii measure. When the debate began, Senator Gruening presided, and when it ended, Senator Bartlett did. The Hawaii statehood bill passed the same day, seventy-six votes to fifteen. All opposing votes came from southern or border-state senators, while all seventeen of the absentees voted in the affirmative.[33]

On March 12 the House abandoned its version of the measure and substituted the Senate bill, passing it 323 votes to 89. One week later the president signed the bill into law.[34]

A short time after the Hawaii measure was enacted, the Alaska omnibus bill was introduced in both houses of Congress. The measure intended to regularize relations between the new state and the federal government and put the new state on an equal footing with the other states. Precedent existed because similar, if much simpler, measures had been enacted after the admission of Oklahoma, New Mexico, and Arizona.[35]

The proposed measure endeavored to enable Alaska to participate in a number of federal grant-in-aid programs and proposed revisions in the apportionment and matching formulas of various others. It terminated special federal programs for Alaska, authorized measures for an orderly transition (property transfers, transitional grants, etc.), clarified the applicability of certain laws to Alaska, and changed references in federal statutes from "Territory" to "State of Alaska."[36]

To gather data that would help in developing the omnibus bill, the Bureau of the Budget had studied Alaska's relationship to the federal government in the post-territorial period. In May 1959 it presented its findings to the House and Senate Interior and Insular Affairs Committees. All of the changes that the legislation proposed, predicted a spokesman for the Bureau of the Budget, would amount to no more than $100,000 annually in extra spending, excluding plans for the restoration of sport fishes and wildlife. In that area, equal treatment as a state would make a substantial difference in Alaska's favor. Since 1950 Alaska had received $75,000 for each of these activities, financed from hunting and fishing license receipts under the Pittman-Robertson and Dingell-Johnson acts. Had Alaska been included on an equal footing in fiscal year 1957, for example, it would have received $811,800 under the Pittman-Robertson Act and some $241,300 under the Dingell-Johnson Act. Alaska now would also be required to match every three federal dollars received with one of its own, something it had not had to do up to then.[37]

In order to ease the transition from territoriality to statehood, the Bureau of the Budget recommended that Alaska be given $27,500,000 in federal aid on a declining scale over a five-year period, ceasing in 1964 with a payment of $2,500,000. The bureau fully realized the difficulties the new state would have in assuming functions previously performed by the federal government. By 1964, bureau personnel reasoned, the state would be generating enough revenue from its natural resources to dispense with further federal transition monies.[38]

Although Bartlett would have preferred to have the Federal Aviation Agency remain in charge of the Anchorage and Fairbanks international airports, the state had to assume the expensive responsibilities for their operation and maintenance in addition to that of seventeen intermediate airports. The state estimated that these management responsibilities would necessitate substantial subsidies for the foreseeable future.[39]

Of perhaps even greater concern to Alaska's political leaders was the state assumption of road construction and maintenance. Alaska had not come under the provisions of the Federal Aid Highway Act until 1956; and even then a special formula had allowed the territory to compute only a third of its land area for fund apportionment purposes. In exchange, Alaska had been able to use federal monies for road maintenance, an authority no other state possessed. Under the omnibus bill, the bureau proposed to have Congress give Alaska the highways, including rights-of-way, as well as whatever other real estate and equipment the government owned and used for their construction and maintenance. The bureau excluded roads in Mount McKinley National Park and the national forests because they remained a federal responsibility. In addition, the bureau recommended grants of $4 million for each year between 1960 and 1962 and Alaska's inclusion under the Federal Aid Highway Act on the same basis as other states.[40]

The donations of equipment and particularly property were meaningful for Alaska, because in 1949 the Bureau of Land Management had reserved a right-of-way 600 feet wide along the Alaska Highway; 300 feet wide for other through roads; 200 feet for feeder roads; and 100 feet for other roads.[41] Delegate Bartlett had futilely protested these withdrawals at the time because they prevented construction of businesses and residences close to the roads and entailed considerable extra costs for the construction and maintenance of access roads.

Hugh Wade, Alaska's acting governor when Governor Egan became seriously ill, worried about the state's financial future, particularly after the exhaustion of the transitional grants. He was particularly concerned about the effects of Alaska's change in status under the Federal Highway Act. Although Alaska was to receive

$37 million in federal funds requiring only some $6 million to be matched by the state, federal monies could not be used for maintenance, a very big item in Alaska's highway budget. But despite a request for special treatment, the Bureau of the Budget insisted that Alaska receive no special consideration in the matter.[42]

Other states had proposed from time to time that federal funds be used for maintenance. All had been turned down. Because of its enormous area in federal ownership, Alaska would receive more matching funds than any other state. The bureau was convinced that within five years state revenue would increase to the point where Alaska could easily afford the cost.[43]

The omnibus bill dealt with many other subjects designed to ease Alaska's transition to statehood. In order to avoid any interruptions in service while the state staffed its agencies, the measure enabled Alaskan officials to use part of the transition monies to finance continued federal operation of various activities. Another alternative allowed the state to contract with federal agencies on a reimbursable basis, a preferable course of action because federal agencies would then be operating as state agents. The omnibus bill also authorized the president to convey or lend to the state federal property which had become surplus because of the cessation or curtailment of federal activites.[44]

There were a number of exceptions from the uniformity rule, justified on the grounds that they did not confer special benefits nor affect federal-state relationships. One example concerned the National Housing Act. Because of higher construction costs for housing in Alaska, Hawaii, and Guam, the federal housing commissioner could exceed the usual maximums on the principal obligations of federally insured mortgages by as much as 50 percent. Without that exception, residents of those areas would have been denied participation in the program.[45]

Following the brief hearings on the omnibus bill, the committee reached a compromise with Congressman Rivers, adopting an amendment which added $1 million to the transition grant, to be used primarily for the expansion of airport facilities in Anchorage and Fairbanks.[46]

With the approval of this and various other amendments, a clean bill was introduced in the House on May 14, 1959. After a brief debate, the House passed the measure by a voice vote, and the Senate passed the bill soon thereafter. On June 11 and June 12, the slight differences between the House and Senate versions were revised to conform to each other, and the president signed the bill into law on June 25, 1959.[47]

The Alaska Omnibus Act supplemented the statehood act, changing the language in various federal laws and statutes to recognize Alaska's new status. It provided federal funds to help ease the transition from territoriality to statehood, emphasizing the important role which the federal government continued to play in Alaskan affairs.

CHAPTER 15

Expanding Horizons

BEING ELECTED UNITED STATES senator from Alaska probably fulfilled a dream long nurtured by Bartlett. His lengthy apprenticeship in the House as voteless delegate had shaped the style of operation he would take with him to the Senate — one which depended on his persuasiveness and his ability to convince others of his point of view. During his fourteen years in the House, he had developed firm friendships with congressmen, senators, and federal bureaucrats and had become a superb and shrewd politician. A longtime associate recalled that "Bob was a political animal. He became adept at protecting his flanks. But he remained a warm, likable human being." Bartlett loved his job, and could not understand why he had ever toyed with the idea of running for the governorship in Alaska, an office considered to be the most "thankless, tiresome, tiring job [to which anyone] in his right mind" could aspire. The United States Senate suited him, for there "one is stimulated by good company among one's peers. There is the chance to meet such ladies as Zsa Zsa Gabor. Every now and again a gift is received from the President of the United States in the form of a fountain pen. If the weather becomes too warm, a Senator can always take a cooling ride on the subway." But perhaps best of all, "where else in the world can a person be assured that if he gets up and utters some words, however trivial, he will be able to read them in print within twenty-four hours." In jest, Bartlett remarked that "if a good, honest draft were ever to come my way for Congress, I might bow to popular demand."[1]

Although Bartlett was joking, the sentiments he expressed were heartfelt. He stated them more seriously when he wrote: "My ambitions are entirely satisfied. I am at my personal summit. I consider membership in the United States Senate to be the very ultimate for me. To sum it up, here I am where I want to be!" Election to the Senate had liberated Bartlett. Although as delegate he had been interested in many issues of international and national importance, he always had felt constrained to keep his opinions to himself on such matters, for fear of alienating congressional friends. Under no circumstances had he wanted to do anything that might adversely affect any Alaskan cause. Now he was freer to speak his mind fully.

Although Bartlett responded quickly to the new opportunities, his constituents continued to lag behind him. Alaskans seemed to ignore the fact that statehood had given them rights equal to those long enjoyed by citizens of the contiguous forty-eight states. Among these was the opportunity to participate, through their congressional representation, in helping to shape American domestic and international policies. Instead, Alaskans continued to be primarily interested in purely Alaskan matters. Bartlett speculated that this parochialism probably had its origin in their peculiarly restricted territorialism with its lack of home rule. In addition, Alaska's sheer physical size, isolation, and difficult living conditions had forced residents for so long to look to Congress and the federal government for aid. Even statehood, he mused, had not made up the "deficit" entirely: "The Alaska people in Congress will have to offer special bills of one kind and another for a long time to come and to the extent they are required to specialize, [they] will have less time and opportunity to swim in the ocean instead of in the lake."[2]

Bartlett's first dive into the broader political ocean concerned the extension of the military draft. Debate on the draft bill was to be held before the Senate Armed Services Committee, chaired by Senator Richard B. Russell, of which Bartlett was a junior member. A few days before the debate was to begin, Bartlett's aide, Joe P. Josephson, introduced Allard Lowenstein to Bartlett. Lowenstein, a friend of Josephson's from college days, worked for Senator Hubert Humphrey at the time. Lowenstein had prepared a speech against the proposed four-year extension of the draft, but since Humphrey was out of town, he wondered whether Bartlett might want to give the speech. "Well," the senator replied, "you know I'm a freshman member of the committee and I've already given my word to Chairman Russell that I would support the bill." Nevertheless, rather than express outright opposition to the draft, Bartlett was willing to give the speech in the form of a series of questions that should be addressed by Congress. After appropriate changes had been made, Bartlett delivered the speech.

At the outset, he praised Senator Russell, under whose able leadership he had been able to work on the legislation under discussion. Bartlett explained that he fully realized that, at present, there was no alternative to such an extension of the draft, but he expressed doubts whether the manpower policies then in effect gave the United States "true security in the missile age—or the illusion of security only." Bartlett reiterated his commitment to vote for the four-year extension, although he would have preferred a shorter period of two years, tied to "an honest-to-goodness, down-to-earth study" of American military manpower needs. Bartlett then submitted his thirty-one widely ranging questions about the draft, which he urged Congress to consider. Should conscription be a permanent feature of

American defense policy? Was it possible to train personnel in the use of complex modern weapons within the two-year mandatory service period? Did the armed services use appropriate incentives to attract and retain competent and motivated personnel? Besides issues such as these, Bartlett questioned the efficacy of conscription in filling manpower needs, in view of the fact that three-fourths of all enlistees left the armed services after the first term of enlistment.

Josephson, who had accompanied Bartlett to the Senate floor to listen to his maiden speech, was well aware of the tradition which demanded junior senators keep a low profile. Josephson "saw Richard Russell across the floor and I sort of shuddered to myself, thinking, my God, what have I gotten Bob into?" Russell listened politely to Bartlett, and at the end of the speech he rose and expressed his delight in having Bartlett as a member of the Senate Armed Services Committee. Russell admitted that many members, having dealt with military problems for a long time, had become somewhat set in their views and opinions. Russell appreciated having a junior member asking new questions and generating new thinking. The chairman promised to utilize Bartlett's talents fully and welcomed him as a new member. Russell, a powerful senator, could easily have rebuked Bartlett. This he did not do. Russell and Bartlett had been friends for years. The senior senator knew and trusted his new colleague. Josephson was relieved about the outcome. Russell had not tried to answer any of the thirty-one questions, and "he didn't get angry, he didn't call Bartlett over and chew him out."[3]

Bartlett was willing to tackle controversial issues as well. Few remember today that he and Mike Mansfield were the first senators to call for a negotiated settlement in Vietnam. In a speech given to the Johnson Foundation Education Conference Center at Racine, Wisconsin on March 7, 1964, Bartlett reiterated and clarified points he had made a few weeks earlier in the Senate. The Senate statement, he admitted to his audience, had "caused a good deal of heated controversy. This controversy has been not a little aided by the fact that most of those engaging in it have not had the time nor the opportunity to read what actually we said." Bartlett and Mansfield had been accused of calling for a policy of passive surrender. That, however, was far from the truth, Bartlett asserted: "It is neither passive nor surrender. It is more an attempt to combine active hope with cool realism."

Bartlett then summarized the situation in Vietnam, the succession of coup upon coup weakening army morale and the deterioration of the military situation in general. "Some have suggested that to save the situation we must take the war to North Vietnam. I fail to see that our national security is endangered enough by happenings in South Vietnam to warrant the risk of a major war. Selective bombings of North Vietnam," Bartlett warned, "could be but the beginning of a very grave and hazardous game" which eventually would cost the United States dearly.

Although supported by the North Vietnamese, the war was a South Vietnamese affair. Bartlett reminded his listeners that guerrilla warfare was extremely difficult to combat. He pointed out Mao Tse-Tung's saying that guerrillas "were fish who could swim in the sea of the people. When guerrillas are not fighting, they fade into the landscape." Bartlett maintained that a guerrilla movement, supported by the people, "has yet to be beaten." Americans could not fight the war for the South Vietnamese, he said, but could only arm, train, and equip them: "We must at all costs avoid being cast in the role of an imperialistic, colonial power. If, through misadventure or folly, we should allow the struggle in Vietnam to become one of Asian versus white intruders, we have lost a good deal more than South Vietnam."

Bartlett proposed a series of changes in the government and the conduct of the war that were designed to give the South Vietnamese soldiers and peasants cause to believe that there was real hope for economic and social reforms. Above all, Bartlett urged that American policy makers consider the possibility of negotiating in order to achieve "something like a settlement in the Indo-Chinese Peninsula." Bartlett concluded that America should attempt to obtain a diplomatic solution to the Vietnam problem: "Let us be rational, let us be flexible. We can no longer afford in men, in money, in wisdom, to do otherwise."[4]

Turmoil continued in South Vietnam. Some months later, Senator Bartlett again addressed his colleagues on the situation in Southeast Asia. Once more there was a crisis in Indochina, he told his colleagues—but that should evoke no surprise, for "the situation in South Vietnam is not much different in kind from what it was last month, or last year, or even ten years ago." Bartlett pointed out that the policies of the late Secretary of State John Foster Dulles, who had attempted to build a noncommunist alliance on the mainland of Asia, had failed. China had gradually reasserted her continuing interest in the Indochina Peninsula, and the people of the region were more interested in their own problems than in participating in the cold war. Bartlett urged negotiations to end the conflict. He believed that the time was right, because China felt vulnerable on its 4,500-mile frontier with Siberia and therefore needed stability on its southern border.

Russia, Bartlett maintained, was unwilling to tolerate "the advance of China's interests in any place where they can possibly be stopped." The senator urged that the United States attempt to reconvene the signatory nations of the 1954 Geneva accords, which he hoped would produce a reaffirmation of the independence and integrity of the nations of Southeast Asia. Most importantly, any such reconvening would have to include the Communist Chinese; and, Bartlett concluded, American policies toward Red China "are in serious need of review. . . ."[5]

There had been few attempts to discuss American policy toward China rationally. Bartlett made another attempt on the floor of the Senate on February 19, 1964, when he asked that Communist China be defused as a domestic policy issue:

"We must be able to discuss Red China as we discuss other nations, communist or free. We must be able to examine our policies toward Red China in terms of our own self-interest and the interests of the free world, not in the terms of emotional display and political abuse." Historically, Bartlett stated, recognition of a new regime involved no moral judgment. Even more important, perhaps, was the fact that any peaceful resolution of conflict in Southeast Asia had to involve China. Above all, Bartlett concluded, America needed to regain the flexibility in its Asian policies which it once had possessed: "We cannot allow ourselves to be frozen forever with a rigid policy hoary with age." The United States had "no need to fear Red China and no need to fear negotiations."[6]

The American government soon proved to be neither rational nor flexible in its response to the situation in Vietnam. In the summer of 1964 there occurred a historic encounter in the Gulf of Tonkin between American and North Vietnamese forces. The public was told that American vessels had been the target of an act of unprovoked aggression in international waters. President Johnson responded by ordering warplanes from the carriers *Ticonderoga* and *Constellation* to attack four North Vietnamese torpedo-boat bases and an oil depot. The president asked Congress to give him a free hand in dealing with the North Vietnamese pirates. The so-called Tonkin Gulf Resolution passed the Senate after eight hours of debate, with only two negative votes — those of Senators Wayne Morse of Oregon and Ernest Gruening of Alaska. It passed the House of Representatives after a mere forty minutes of discussion on a vote of 414 to 0.[7]

Bartlett's reasons for approving the resolution were wholly pragmatic. Although opposed to the widening conflict, he did not want to offend the administration, particularly President Johnson, who often had been very helpful in Alaskan matters and with whom he had maintained an excellent relationship over many years.

Nor did Bartlett want to offend his southern friends who were "hawks." "I am in a terrible fix," he had admitted. "My age on reaching the Senate was such that it was quite obvious that I could not climb up the long ladder of seniority and obtain a position of place and prominence of power." It was obvious to Bartlett that Alaska would need special legislation for years to come, and he wanted to "assist in every way possible in placing the new state on an even keel. In all of this the southerners have been of tremendous assistance to me. Their help has been needed. After all, they do have that seniority; they do occupy those positions of prominence and power." Bartlett wanted to preserve the warm and cooperative relationship with members of the Senate he had enjoyed as a delegate: "I was not searching and am not searching for a place in the history books."

The nation also seemed to approve the Tonkin Gulf Resolution, and President Johnson signed the document the day it passed, August 7, 1964. Less than a year later, on March 8, 1965, two marine corps battalions, 3,500 strong, waded ashore near Da Nang. America was committed on a scale its people did not yet realize.[8]

On April 7, 1965, President Johnson delivered a speech at Johns Hopkins University outlining the administration's attitude toward the war. He said that America had become involved for "purposes of freedom, not of conquest; and of construction, not destruction. We seek the security of our freedom through the security of others, not by the domination of others."[9]

With other senators, Bartlett responded to the president's address. He reiterated his earlier belief that it was useless for the United States to attempt to establish permanent borders in Southeast Asia, for there were none: "We must recognize this and we must not cast our lot and the lot of the free world in a quixotic attempt to preserve a stability which does not exist." Fortunately, Bartlett believed, the president had pledged the United States only to maintain the right of self-determination for the South Vietnamese: "We are not obligated to preserve a particular government in power or to support one clique over another." Above all, Bartlett urged the warring parties to settle their many differences at the bargaining table, because there was "no point to the fighting if we are not willing to confer."[10]

Foreign policy had become one of Bartlett's broader interests, and the relationship between Congress and the scientific community was yet another. Bartlett's interest in research and development stemmed from a meeting that he attended shortly after his appointment to the Senate Appropriations Committee in 1963—a meeting in which more than a billion dollars in research and development monies for programs in health, education, and welfare were approved by the committee in just thirty seconds. That upset Bartlett and he began trying to find out what in the maze of research requests was redundant or unnecessary and what deserved top priority. He quickly discovered that there was little, if any, expert advice available. If representative government were to prevail, Bartlett felt it was necessary that Congress understand the importance of the decisions that funded scientific research and that it have something other than a rubber-stamp role in making those decisions. Therefore, on August 13, 1963, Bartlett introduced a measure designed to give the Senate and House scientific advice through the creation of a congressional Office of Science and Technology in each chamber.

In 1948, Congress had appropriated only $900 million for research and development, while in 1962 the amount had risen to $14.5 billion, and further increases could be expected. While the president, in requesting these monies from the Congress and formulating a consistent federal science policy, had the counsel of the whole scientific community marshalled by his Office of Science and Technology and his Science Advisory Committee, Congress groped in the dark. Congress had no independent scientific advice, and frequently congressional committees relied for expert advice upon the testimony of the very scientists who had conceived a particular program under review. Due to congressional ignorance, Bartlett felt that too often scientists, rather than elected officials, were formulating public policy. Consequently, Congress was in no position to ascertain whether requested research projects were necessary, which ones should have priority for public funding, and whether such funds were spent in an efficient and effective fashion. Without adequate scientific advice, there loomed the dangers of uncontrolled growth of federally sponsored research and choices involving critical decisions made by scientists rather than by elected representatives.[11]

Others shared Bartlett's concerns. The magazine *Science* acknowledged that the educational background of members of Congress was heavily weighted toward the legal profession, with little scientific representation, yet the magazine doubted "that a man trained in science would bring as much wisdom to Congress as one trained in the law. Some of the most narrowminded, uncompromising, chauvinistic individuals in this world are scientists." The editors of *Science* endorsed Bartlett's proposal to make available to Congress a special group of scientific advisors, for to "make good decisions it is not necessary to digest all the facts. It is necessary to be well advised." The *National Observer* echoed Bartlett's apprehensions and endorsed his call for the creation of a congressional Office of Science and Technology.[12]

Others disagreed with Bartlett's concerns. One administrator, in particular, insisted that any member of Congress who really wanted to check testimony could contact several eminent experts in the field in question in a very short time and receive the necessary answers. Among the resources available were the Office of Science and Technology, the National Academy of Sciences, the National Science Foundation, and various civilian counterparts. Of more consequence was the real question of whether scientists could survive the political atmosphere within Congress.[13]

Bartlett's measure did not pass, but in 1964 Congress appropriated additional funds to the Library of Congress legislative reference budget allowing for the employment of senior scientists to assist the Congress. If not enough, Bartlett considered this at least a step in the right direction.[14]

As early as 1962, Bartlett had become concerned about radioactive contamination in the arctic food chain. That year Dr. William A. Pruitt, Jr., a scientist formerly on the staff of the University of Alaska, published an article in *Beaver,* the magazine of the Hudson's Bay Company, pointing out that caribou and reindeer in the circumpolar countries had been contaminated by radioactive fallout, primarily by the radionuclides strontium 90 and cesium 137. The contamination came from the fallout generated by atmospheric nuclear explosions. Lichens and sedges, the two most important caribou foods, showed particularly high levels of radioactive contamination, which was a result of their peculiar physiology.

A lichen consists of a combination of two types of plants—a fungus and an alga. Living together, they form a lichen that receives its nutrients directly from the air, from dust, and other windblown material. A lichen thus feeds on a kind of natural fallout. Before the atomic age began in 1945, that fallout had been harmless. After 1945, however, lichens absorbed increasing amounts of man-made radioactive fallout along with natural nutrients. Since lichens have evolved very efficient mechanisms for retaining natural fallout, they also retain virtually 100 percent of the radioactive particles falling onto them. Lichens grow very slowly, and while a blade of grass may contain fallout particles deposited on it during a two-to-three-month growing season, a lichen fragment of similar size may contain fallout particles deposited over many years. The mechanism whereby sedges are contaminated is not well understood, but plants from tundra-wet meadows generally contain more radioactive material than plants from other tundra habitats.[15]

It was noted that since circumpolar residents eat a great deal of caribou and reindeer meat, they show much higher whole-body radiation counts than those who do not eat caribou and reindeer meat. Alaskan Eskimos who used caribou as a staple in their diet were found to have four times the average strontium 90 content of the world population of the North Temperate Zone.[16]

Senator Bartlett found a bright and interested researcher in the Library of Congress, Warren Donelly, who supplied him with the material he needed. Radiation safety turned out to be a highly complex and technical subject, but Bartlett mastered it well. "We kept putting a series of articles and speeches in the record. There was nobody interested in that then, there is nobody interested in it now," recalled John M. Cornman, a Bartlett staff member at the time.[17]

In the spring of 1963, Bartlett alerted his colleagues to the dangers of radioactive contamination in arctic caribou meat. Bartlett explained the highly technical and scientific nature of the problem and, although admitting he possessed no expert knowledge, he stated that as a senator, "it is my responsibility to speak out when the health and safety of the people of my state are threatened. I am not an expert, but I will become one if it is necessary in order to get action and attention on this subject." Bartlett explained that strontium 90 found its way into the bones, lodging there for many years. Concentrations could cause leukemia or bone cancer. The danger of cesium 137 was that, after a time, it caused mutation of the gene structure "leading to deformities in children yet unborn."[18] Bartlett complained that the United States, unlike other governments, had shown little interest and had taken even less action in this area of worldwide concern.[19]

A month later, Bartlett became worried by the exceptionally high fallout levels of iodine 131, a radioactive isotope, reported in Salt Lake City, Utah and in Palmer, Alaska the previous year. Although the period of fallout was of short duration, it substantially raised the yearly total level of radiation in individuals living in those areas. Children drinking one liter of milk per day in Palmer for the previous year had received 38,220 micromicrocuries of iodine 131. The guide established by the Federal Radiation Council for a twelve-month intake of iodine 131 set 36,500 micromicrocuries of iodine 131 as an acceptable health risk for large population groups for a lifetime. Young children were particularly vulnerable to this intake, because practically all the iodine 131 settled in the thyroid gland which, in very high levels, caused cancer of the thyroid. Since that organ is much smaller in children than in adults, children's tissues received a far higher concentration of contamination per gram of tissue than would an older person.

Bartlett complained that the radiation protection guide recommended by the Federal Radiation Council was wholly inadequate, while the nation's radiation surveillance and control program constituted no more than an ineffective gesture. Americans were confused and uneasy. The time had come, Bartlett concluded, "to stop treating radiation as once we treated cancer"—by not speaking of it in polite society. Radiation exists; "it threatens us." Congress, he said, had the responsibility to initiate a program of research and development on public health policy to insure adequate national safeguards.[20]

During the debate on the Nuclear Test Ban Treaty in the fall of 1963, Bartlett supported the treaty. He emphasized the importance ratification would have on diminishing the dangers caused by radioactive contamination, since the end of atomic atmospheric testing in time would end fallout. And the hazards of radioactive fallout, Bartlett continued, had been underestimated consistently from 1945 until the present: "[The] residue from atomic blasts which poisons the air we breathe, the ground we walk, the food we eat, are still largely unknown to science and to civilization . . . are not understood . . . and largely ignored." Bartlett cited numerous studies which lent emphasis to his contention that radioactive fallout constituted one of the gravest hazards to the health of modern man throughout the world.[21]

In the year following the adoption of the Nuclear Test Ban Treaty, no atmospheric nuclear tests occurred, but underground testing continued. Unfortunately, seventeen cases where radioactive debris had escaped into the atmosphere from underground explosions had been documented since September 15, 1961. These accidents continued, and alarming amounts of iodine 131 had been released across Nevada and Utah.[22]

In light of this situation, on August 31, 1964, Bartlett reminded his colleagues that for eighteen years the scientific community had expanded its knowledge of nuclear explosions and its ability to produce them. Important knowledge about the somatic and genetic effects of radiation on large-scale population groups had not similarly increased. Furthermore, despite the Nuclear Test Ban Treaty, levels of radiation in the Arctic had continued to increase. What, if anything, Bartlett asked, did the government intend to do about the mounting hazards in the Arctic?[23]

The federal government was doing very little in that regard, Bartlett complained, because while spending over $7 billion in 1965 to develop and perfect nuclear weapons and their delivery systems, an appropriation of only $20 million for radiological health all but crippled that program. Although in May 1965 the Federal Radiation Council had released its staff report setting protective action guides for strontium 89, strontium 90, and cesium 137 for the first time, Bartlett contended that these guides only added to the existing confusion.[24]

In May 1966 Bartlett decried the proliferation of nuclear weapons. Fallout, he observed, knew no nationality. He used as examples the citizens of tiny Anaktuvuk Pass in Alaska's Brooks Range, who continued to receive more than eighty times as much radiation in their daily diets as did citizens of other states; the children of Utah, who continued to receive radiation from accidental venting of underground atomic blasts; the people in Colorado, who drank radium-polluted water; and the Japanese population, who bore the brunt of fallout from Chinese atmospheric blasts.[25]

Bartlett's inquiry into radiation safety had awakened latent fears. Dangers lurked everywhere. The American Academy of Pediatrics warned against the use of the fluoroscope. The British Medical Journal *Lancet* cautioned against unnecessary diagnostic x-rays. Columbia River oysters were found to be contaminated by radioactive materials from the tailings of uranium mines. "No one denies that excessive radiation is dangerous," Bartlett stated, "and that inherent in some of its uses is possible destruction of life on this planet. No one denies these facts, yet our government has not responded with the effort needed to solve the problem."[26]

On July 10, 1967, Bartlett culminated several years of hard work with the introduction of a Radiation Health and Safety Act, cosponsored by nine of his colleagues. It authorized the secretary of HEW to increase research efforts in radiological health and safety and to develop and administer standards for the control of radiation emissions from electronic products. On August 28 of that year, Senator Bartlett opened hearings on his measure before the Senate Committee on Commerce. The bill had acquired new urgency with the recent discovery that over 100,000 color television sets that emitted radiation in excess of safe levels had made their way to dealers and into homes. Television, however, was only one aspect of a much broader problem. The hearings which Bartlett conducted in August 1967 and in May 1968 were designed to gain an overview of the wide and growing range of devices utilizing or giving off ionizing or other types of radiation. The hearings also were concerned with the health hazards they posed and with effective methods of surveillance and control.[27]

In the spring of 1968, Senator Lister Hill of Alabama introduced a measure to provide for the protection of the public from radiation emissions from electronic products. In the early summer, Congressman Paul L. Rogers of Florida sponsored similar legislation—an amendment to the Public Health Service Act to provide for the protection of the public health from radiation emissions from electronic products. Although neither measure was nearly as comprehensive as Bartlett would have liked, he was a master in appraising the mood of Congress, and he thought the Rogers bill had a good chance for passage. Consequently, he decided to strengthen the bill and offered a series of amendments. They defined advisory standards for licensing x-ray technicians and established a technical committee to document performance standards and procedures for notifying the public and recalling devices found to emit radiation in excess of the standard. On October 2, 1968, the Rogers measure passed the Senate. It incorporated most of Bartlett's amendments. A few days later House and Senate conferees reached agreement, and the president signed the Radiation Control for Health and Safety Act shortly thereafter.[28] After the passage of this act, Bartlett continued to speak on the dangers of radiation until his own deteriorating health preoccupied him more and more.

Senator Warren G. Magnuson perhaps best summed up Bartlett's contributions during Senate consideration of the Rogers bill. Magnuson stated that the "Senate is in essence paying tribute to the senior Senator from Alaska, Mr. Bartlett, who more than any member of Congress has led the fight for radiation safety." And although it was the report on the emissions of radiation from color television sets exceeding the generally accepted standard which prodded congressional action in the field of radiation safety, it was Senator Bartlett who, alone for many years, had been vitally concerned with other potential sources of radiation. "With one exception," Magnuson concluded, "the amendments being considered by the Senate today are the result of Senator Bartlett's extensive knowledge in this area."[29]

CHAPTER **16**

Bartlett and the Senate Commerce Committee

MMEDIATELY UPON COMING to the Senate in 1959, Bartlett had received an appointment to the Senate Commerce Committee, his first choice. Warren G. "Maggie" Magnuson of Washington, the chairman of the committee, was one of the most powerful men in the Senate. As territorial delegate, Bartlett had often turned to Magnuson for help in putting measures through the Senate, and Magnuson had rarely refused him. Bartlett, however, had worried about Senator Magnuson's operating style from time to time. As a Bartlett staffer put it, the senator always waited until the last minute before ambling onto the Senate floor when some piece of Alaskan legislation was before that body. Just before the bill "would be called up for consideration, Maggie showed up from the chamber. Maggie would just pare [the measure] down to the barest, just to the bone structure, and we had more legislation scooped through the Senate with Maggie masterminding it."[1]

Magnuson and Bartlett shared similar interests in the fishing and shipping industries and in oceanography. Bartlett's primary area of concern, however, was the fishing industry, which had long been one of the main props of the Alaskan economy. Many of the financial woes of the new state could be traced to the steady decline of the fisheries, which Alaskans, characteristically, blamed on federal mismanagement.

Bartlett quickly realized that Senator Magnuson's interest in fishing had diminished over the years and that, instead, he was giving much more attention to the shipping industry, which was well organized and represented by an effective lobby. The shipping industry was one of the first to receive federal assistance. Whenever it had felt a need, it traditionally had gone directly to Congress, generally with quite specific proposals. Members of Congress, as well as staff personnel, sometimes questioned the efficacy of proposals and called for new approaches and fresh ideas, but the industry usually obtained what it wanted.

A number of factors reinforced the tendency of the shipping industry to bring its proposals to Congress, among them the careful attention they received there, the character of the Maritime Administration, and the relative lack of concern of the president. The shipping industry was localized and specialized, and its economic difficulties, though severe, were of limited public concern. The Maritime Administration, a small bureau in the Commerce Department, had never been organized, staffed, or oriented as a center for the generation of policy proposals. This made it difficult for the president to respond to the rising demands for a national maritime policy. The Maritime Administration concentrated on the administration of construction and operation-differential subsidies. Congress and the shipping interests viewed it as a lackluster organization, neither inclined nor equipped to play a policy role. Moreover, the industry's day-to-day dealings with the agency discouraged the development of a client-advocate relationship. Despite the reorganization in 1961 which entrusted the enforcement of the various shipping and merchant marine acts to an independent Federal Maritime Commission, the Maritime Administration's subsidy programs continued to involve regulation as well, and this introduced a certain distance into industry-government relations.[2]

The context in which a senator championed the interests of the fishing industry was different from that of shipping. Fishing involved fewer companies, a smaller workforce, and much less capital. Federal regulation had traditionally lagged far behind the utilization of the resource, and strong and politically potent vested interests in the maintenance of the status quo were well entrenched before the federal management program could even be launched. Actually, the federal management of commercial fisheries was unique to Alaska. Elsewhere, this was the primary responsibility of the state or the territorial government, with the federal government merely providing supplementary research and guidance. Furthermore, the federal commercial fisheries programs had moved among the various federal bureaus fairly frequently, making for considerable instability.

A 1945 report of the Department of the Interior on the status of the aquatic resources of the United States perhaps best summed up the shortcomings of the national program: "The Federal Government has never done justice to these functions because its fishery conservation agency [formerly Bureau of Fisheries, now Fish and Wildlife Service] has never been given broad enough direction by the Congress to permit it to carry out a unified program to suit the needs of the country as a whole. Without a fundamental plan, the Service has evolved by a process of tacking on projects one by one, which have generally been thrust upon it to meet particular crises, often as the result of pressure by special groups. The appropriations to the Service are based principally on the support of these projects. Thus the Federal Service is helpless to execute a dynamic program based on national needs; instead, it can only carry on with its agglomerate of activities inherited from the past, and wait for further crises which its timely services would otherwise have averted."³

It was not until the 1956 creation of the Bureau of Commercial Fisheries (BCF) in the Department of the Interior that a separate governmental bureau was organized around the commercial fishing interests. It soon saw itself as a promoter of the industry, and several of its officials developed various legislative ideas toward that end. But the BCF was small, inadequately funded, and barely able to make its voice heard in administration councils. As a result, the bureau found it wise to develop a harmonious working relationship with the appropriate committees in Congress.

Bartlett quickly realized that championing the fishing interests would benefit Alaska economically and himself politically. He realized that no strong pressures would be exerted on him from either the industry or the executive branch. It would be politically profitable to develop legislation to promote the industry, to publicize his programs, and to activate support. And Bartlett would find in the BCF an agency amenable to his efforts, willing to establish cooperative ties which, while aiding the senator and increasing his chances of success, would at the same time increase the bureau's leverage in the executive branch.

Senator Bartlett moved quickly to take advantage of the situation. He was helped by William Foster, a bright and personable individual who had become his staff attorney in the fall of 1961 and who later became counsel to the Senate Commerce Committee. Between 1963 and 1966, Bartlett pushed a plethora of fishing legislation through Congress. The measures included bills to define the territorial waters of the United States and prohibit foreign vessels from fishing within this limit; to establish a twelve-mile fishing zone forbidden to foreign vessels; to authorize BCF research to develop a high-grade fish protein concentrate and to undertake experimental production of it in pilot plants; to liberalize the construction subsidy program for fishing vessels; to include fish products in the Food for Peace program; and to establish a new program of matching grants to the states for fishery research and development.

The formulation of these proposals generally followed a uniform pattern. Fishing interests rallied behind the bills after they were proposed, but they did not exert decisive pressure or even come to Congress with specific proposals of their own. Officials of the Bureau of Commercial Fisheries were generally helpful and supportive, especially in furnishing needed statistics and other information, although they at first felt uncomfortable with the fish protein concentrate and twelve-mile limit proposals. The White House paid little attention to Bartlett's fishery bills; the Bureau of the Budget refused to release funds for the purchase of fish products for the Food for Peace program and did not allow adequate budget requests in the case of matching grants for state research and development, thus torpedoing some of the programs.

It was in this context that Bartlett also proposed the creation of a new agency to conduct a program of marine exploration and continental-shelf resource development. Foster developed the bill in close cooperation with Edward Wenk, who, as head of the Science Policy Research Division, had led the Library of Congress' Legislative Reference Service into substantial information-gathering efforts. The proposal was not yet another organizational scheme but rather an effort to shift the focus of the projected program from pure research to resource development. This was designed to solicit the support of industry in general, which was interested in the minerals beneath the floor of the continental shelf. The fishing industry was partial to the legislation because Bartlett had written it to include the species that clung to the seabed. Bartlett's bill was notable in that it made clear the relevance of oceanography to industry and to the fishing interests, and it also was the first measure relating to that subject which any senator besides Magnuson had offered.

Bartlett's move into fisheries and oceanography represented an encroachment on Magnuson's field of interest, and the chairman felt slightly uncomfortable with Bartlett's role. Bartlett, however, had always taken pains to let Magnuson know what he was doing, and he freely shared the credit with the chairman for whatever was accomplished. The result was that an impressive percentage of Bartlett's proposals became law and that they were praised by the press as "Magnuson bills."

Still, Magnuson's discomfort increased with Bartlett's new role, and he became increasingly sensitive to rumors that he was no longer looking after the fishing interests. Jerry Grinstein, Magnuson's staff man on the Senate Commerce Committee, thought he had solved the problem when he offered Foster a position on the committee staff. Grinstein hoped that this would remove the center of initiative from within Bartlett's office and once again place the whole area firmly within Magnuson's control. Bartlett concurred with the shift, thinking it might increase his voice in committee affairs. Foster moved to the Commerce Committee early in 1964. Fishing measures continued to be developed by Foster, but he still worked them out in consultation with Bartlett, who introduced them under his own name. Foster was very loyal to Bartlett and used his staff position to further the Alaska senator's involvement in shipping and oceanography as well.

Magnuson, though generous with members of his committee, was uncertain as to how far this magnanimity should apply to the areas of merchant marine and fisheries, which had been more or less his personal domain. At the staff level, tension soon developed between Foster and Grinstein. In 1966, as soon as the legislative calendar was relatively clear, Foster left the staff. At the same time Magnuson formed a new Consumer Subcommittee and left Bartlett with the chairmanship of the Subcommittee on Merchant Marine and Fisheries.[4]

When Bartlett was originally appointed to the Senate Commerce Committee, one of his first concerns relative to the fishing industry centered around a measure designed to strengthen the hand of the federal government in forbidding foreign vessels to fish in American territorial waters. As early as 1793, Secretary of State Thomas Jefferson took the position that the United States should consider territorial waters as extending outward from shore for one sea league or three geographical miles. A provision of American law, in effect since the days of George Washington, barred foreign fishing vessels of over five tons from fishing in American territorial waters, but its enforcement provisions were weak. In most cases, it only authorized federal agents to apprehend and expel the offending vessels from the offshore United States territorial sea area. No fines, confiscation, or other sanctions were stipulated.[5]

On September 28, 1945, President Truman took an important step when he claimed United States jurisdiction over the natural resources of the subsoil and seabed of the continental shelf. Subsequently, Congress affirmed the president's claim with the 1953 passage of the Outer Continental Shelf Lands Act, which extended "the Constitution and laws and civil and political jurisdiction of the United States" over the outer continental shelf.[6]

American fishermen had been concerned about foreign incursions into fishing grounds they considered their own. After the Second World War, foreign fishing fleets in increasing numbers appeared off the Pacific and Atlantic coasts. Well financed, with large boats and modern processing equipment, they soon competed effectively with the American fleet, which quickly complained about the foreign competition and demanded federal protection.

This protection was not forthcoming, but many experts realized that the whole fishery problem could only be solved on the basis of international agreements. As early as 1956, the International Law Commission, in its final report to the United Nations, had submitted draft recommendations of seventy-three articles, including commentaries, dealing with the territorial high seas. The commission recommended the convening of an international conference of plenipotentiaries to examine the law of the sea and to embody the results in one or more international conventions. The United Nations General Assembly considered the commission report and on February 21, 1957, adopted a resolution calling for a U.N. Conference on the Law of the Sea. The first conference was held at Geneva, Switzerland from February 24 to April 27, 1958.[7]

On March 17, 1960, another Conference on the Law of the Sea convened in Geneva. This prompted a Senate discussion dominated by two important subjects — the rights of high sea fisheries and the rules and regulations governing them, and what the territorial limits of the coastal states should be. Senator Magnuson pointed out that the Soviet Union and her satellites had demanded a twelve-mile limit for all nations attending the 1959 Conference on the Law of the Sea. "At first blush, that sounds pretty good," Magnuson stated, "but then somebody discovered that to give Russia and her satellite countries a twelve-mile territorial limit would add three million square miles to the Russian and satellite territories because of the tremendous coast lines." The senator considered the adoption of a twelve-mile limit to be disastrous for the United States, because it would potentially close a total of 116 strategic straits throughout the world's oceans to American civilian and military navigation. Furthermore, such an extension would not solve problems of fishery depletion. Only an international agreement on conservation practices could restore rapidly dwindling stocks of some major species.[8]

Senator Magnuson, although worried about the declining fisheries, was more concerned with freedom of the seas. He was careful to separate the matter of ownership of the mineral resources beneath the ocean bottom from the twelve-mile limit. The senator was particularly annoyed with the State Department's desire to compromise at a six-mile limit, which was obviously not in the best interest of the American fishing industry. "I am not so sure, some days," Magnuson declared, "that we should not appropriate about $1 million and hire about fifty Greyhound buses and take the State Department on a Cook's tour of the United States." The nature of their duties prevented these specialists from being close to the electorate, as were members of Congress. Yet officials of the State Department always seemed to say that "this cannot be done. We have to make this compromise." Perhaps the United States did not have to compromise: "I have watched other countries. Brother, they stick to their guns."[9]

Both Senators Magnuson and Bartlett agreed that a twelve-mile limit would not benefit American fishermen. It probably would further harm the important salmon runs, because the Japanese might decide to renounce the 1952 treaty of abstention. This agreement specified that the Japanese would not fish for salmon east of a dividing line drawn at the 175th meridian. Although imperfect, it was the best treaty that could have been worked out, because Americans had no idea where the Asian and North American salmon intermingled on the high seas. The 175th meridian was as good a guess as any.[10] In addition, Bartlett warned American fishermen that unless they exercised their fishing rights in the Bering Sea, where a large and modern Soviet fishing fleet had been operating for more than a year, they would surely lose their claimed historic rights."[11]

Alaskans had long been concerned about protection of their fisheries from foreign exploitation and depletion. Ironically, they always thought that they utilized the fishery resources wisely, while only foreigners depleted and exploited them. The truth was that Americans, historically, had not been very concerned with the proper utilization of the fishery resources. The prevailing industry philosophy seemed to be to make a few bucks while the resources lasted.

In any event, this foreign competition was felt not only by Alaskan fishermen but also by the lobster fishermen of Maine and the shrimp fishermen of the mid-Atlantic and Gulf Coast states. Early in 1962 Alaska took unilateral steps in protecting its resources when it arrested three Japanese vessels found fishing in Shelikof Strait near Kodiak. Governor William A. Egan, charging that the United States State Department was unresponsive to American needs, proposed that Congress pass legislation which would delineate territorial and inland waters. The governor also proposed that Congress unilaterally claim as its territorial sea a band of twelve miles for fishery regulation and six miles for all other purposes. The United States had suggested these boundaries at the 1959 Geneva conference but had been rebuffed. Governor Egan reminded Senator Bartlett that the extent of territorial waters had been changing for the last few years. For example, Iceland, Ecuador, and the Soviet union claimed twelve miles, while Norway had recently extended its original four-mile claim to twelve miles, subject only to certain pre-existing fishing rights of various nations which were to expire within ten years. Several South American countries had extended their territorial waters to an expansive two-hundred-mile width. The governor concluded that he shared Bartlett's frustration in "attempting to impress the urgency of the problem we face upon those presently entrusted with our relations with foreign countries" and promised to place the state government's skills at the senator's disposal in helping draft a measure along the suggested lines.[12]

In the fall of 1962 Governor Egan reiterated his concerns before the National Governor's Conference and stated that unless Congress acted promptly to extend the United States territorial sea, the nation would soon see the extinction of bottom fish, salmon, and other fisheries resources, as well as foreign exploitation of the mineral riches below territorial waters. This would result in the loss of untold billions of potential dollars to the nation, he warned.[13]

Senator Bartlett soon considered introduction of appropriate legislation to solve the problem. He asked experts if an extension of United States territorial waters would protect Alaskan fish resources. The information that he received revealed that if fishing rights were extended to twelve miles, Alaskan herring, king crab, and shrimp would be afforded some additional protection. But whether or not such a unilateral extension of territorial fishing rights to twelve miles would be beneficial in the long run was problematical. Japan, for example, had agreed not to fish for salmon east of the 175th meridian, but provoked at a United States extension to twelve miles, it might retaliate by ceasing to honor that agreement. Mexico might also extend its fishing protection to twelve miles, thereby effectively limiting American shrimp fishermen on its coast. The twelve-mile limit would not affect Japanese and Soviet fishing, since those nations operated vessels generally from about twenty to fifty miles offshore in the Bering Sea and off the Aleutian Islands.[14]

Sometime late in 1962 Senator Bartlett decided that it was imperative that the United States extend the limits of its territorial waters. He realized that such a step would not save the fishing industry, but he hoped that it would force fishing nations to work more seriously on reaching agreements on comprehensive conservation laws at law of the sea conferences.

On May 15, 1963, the senator alerted his colleagues to the fact that Great Britain had proposed an international meeting for the fall in which the European Common Market and free trade countries were to consider the extension of their territorial waters. Canadian Prime Minister Lester Pearson had also announced that Canada might be forced to take similar steps. Bartlett felt that it was necessary to take action, because the waters off the United States coast had been subjected to increasingly heavy fishing pressure from foreign fleets, particularly those of Russia and Japan. In 1962 Russian trawlers had entered the Gulf of Alaska for the first time and had severely damaged American king crab fishing gear. Appeals to the State Department had been of no avail, Bartlett stated, despite the fact that the United States was a signatory to the International Convention of the High Seas, which included a provision reserving creatures of the continental shelf, such as king and dungeness crab, for utilization by Americans.[15]

Soon thereafter Bartlett learned that the Danish parliament had decreed a twelve-mile fishing zone for Greenland, to become effective on June 1, 1963, and that the Canadian parliament had acted in an identical fashion, its twelve-mile fishing zone to be enforced starting in May 1964.[16]

In the fall of 1963 Senators Bartlett and Magnuson urged extension of exclusive fishing rights beyond the traditional three-mile limit. Both men expressed alarm at the huge Russian and Japanese fleets found off American coasts. They also urged the imposition of $10,000 fines and one-year jail sentences for poachers invading United States territorial waters.[17]

On October 1, 1963, the Senate passed Bartlett's measure designed to strengthen the federal government's hand in forbidding foreign fishing vessels to fish in United States territorial waters. Bartlett pointed out that his bill claimed no new jurisdiction. It merely provided sanctions against foreign violators and prohibited fishing for American continental shelf resources unless such utilization was permitted by an international treaty to which the United States was a party.[18]

Bartlett did not support a measure which his Alaskan colleague, Senator Gruening, had introduced, calling for the establishment of a twelve-mile fishing zone. Bartlett felt that the president should be given an opportunity to move on foreign fishery violations, especially "since actually no legislative action is required." Bartlett indicated that the twelve-mile fishing zone was the next logical step, but only after the United States had completed pending negotiations with Mexico and Canada on fishery matters.[19]

Neither the State Department nor the Department of the Interior was happy with Bartlett's provisions for the protection of continental shelf fishing resources. The State Department particularly worried that Bartlett's bill would encourage other nations to make similar unilateral proclamations and would stimulate public demand for action to force the Japanese and Russians out of the Bering Sea. Enforcement would pose other problems. Was it necessary, for example, to consult a foreign government before boarding and arresting vessels ignoring United States claims, or could the United States act first and open discussions afterwards?[20]

Senator Bartlett realized that no arbitrary extension of the fishing zone would solve America's problems in the ocean fisheries off the United States and throughout the world. Only international agreements on conservation and sustained yield harvests promised a permanent solution. Bartlett only hoped that unilateral action would force nations to gather around the conference table for talks.

On May 4, 1964, the House considered, debated, amended, and passed the Bartlett bill, and the Senate concurred in the House amendments several days later. On May 20 the president signed the Bartlett measure into law. It expressly forbade foreign vessels from fishing within the territorial waters of the United States and its possessions; forbade them from fishing within waters in which the United States had the same fishing rights as it had within its territorial waters; and forbade them from fishing for continental shelf resources of the United States. In all three cases, fishing permitted by international treaty to which the United States was a party was excepted. Foreign vessels in violation of these laws were subject to forfeiture, and any fish illegally taken were also forfeited. The legislation further provided for a $10,000 fine and imprisonment of up to one year for violators. Under certain conditions, the Treasury could authorize a foreign vessel to fish for designated species in United States territorial waters. This would be permitted if both the State and Interior departments agreed; if the involved state or territorial governments agreed; if Congress received sixty days' notice; and if U.S. fishermen were given similar privileges by the foreign nation involved.[21]

The fruitful relationship between Senator Bartlett and his legislative assistant William Foster had been responsible for the success of this measure and of many others that Bartlett had sponsored. After the signing ceremonies for this most recent bill, both men were jubilant. Bartlett considered the measure the most significant fishery bill he had steered into enactment since he began his Senate tenure.

He had been successful in spite of a great deal of pressure by the Japanese embassy on the House Committee on Merchant Marine and Fisheries. For a while, the Japanese believed that the bill had been bottled up in the House committee, "and its emergence therefrom and subsequent approval by the House of Representatives came, we are told, as a great blow to them." Subsequent to House passage, the Japanese ambassador (Ryuji Takenehi) repeatedly lobbied the State Department, seeking a White House veto. Bartlett was told that this was a most unusual procedure: "Bill Foster and I had to sweat this one out . . . Despite assurances from both the State Department and the White House staff, we had a continuing fear that a veto might be possible, that the State Department might have gone behind our backs and told the President that in the larger interests of comity between the U.S. and Japan the bill should be nixed." On May 20, the final signing deadline for the measure, Bartlett telephoned the bill clerk on the measure at intervals all day long: "No signature. No signature at 6 P.M. At 6:10 I called Walter Jenkins [a presidential aide] at the White House and expressed my anxiety." Jenkins told the senator to hold the line for a few minutes and then reported that "the magic words 'Lyndon B. Johnson' had been placed on the bill at 6:07. That evening was a delightful one."[22]

Bartlett was happy and relieved after the signing. The measure had been his from inception to passage: "I introduced it. I fought for it. I succeeded in getting it through the Senate." Despite the fact that the departments of State and Interior and the Coast Guard had testified unfavorably on the continental shelf provisions of the bill, Bartlett was able to change their minds after "they had met with me in meetings which I hastily called. So I think I can claim almost unilateral credit for pushing this bill through."

The senator thought that the Japanese were unduly apprehensive, because the bill provided only "proper protective measures after the king crab has been declared a creature of the continental shelf and the property of the United States insofar as the shelf off our shores is concerned. And I hope that such declaration will soon be made."[23]

The Japanese, understandably, were upset by the provisions of Bartlett's bill, for they feared that the new legislation would keep their crabbers from fishing on grounds they had developed as far back as 1930. Not only would Japanese king crabbing be impaired in the Bering Sea, but most likely also along the coast of Kamchatka if Russia, which had ratified the continental shelf convention, followed the precedent set by the United States. The White House, however, quickly assured the Japanese that, since the waters over the continental shelf were part of the high seas, efforts would be made to work out in advance with foreign countries procedures for enforcement in the area, and the United States would fully consider Japan's long-established Bering Sea king crab fishery.[24]

Bartlett soon moved to extend the fishing limit to twelve miles. While in Anchorage in December 1964, he promised his constituents that he would introduce an appropriate measure no later than the spring or early summer of 1965. Senator Gruening moved first, however, and on January 6, 1965, introduced a twelve-mile measure, cosponsored by five of his colleagues. Bartlett, who claimed expertise in matters pertaining to shipping and fishing, was angry at Gruening's precipitous action. The senior senator also considered Gruening's bill inadequate, for under its provisions the twelve-mile fishery zone could not be established unless an independent board recommended to the president that foreign fishing operations within twelve miles of the coast of a state were of such intensity that the resources were in danger of depletion. Bartlett staunchly maintained that the United States should not wait until such a time and that the twelve-mile limit should be established on all coasts at the same time by an act of Congress.[25] Clearly, Alaska's two senators were working at cross-purposes.

On June 29, 1965, Senator Bartlett introduced his twelve-mile limit legislation, cosponsored by Senators Magnuson and Edward M. Kennedy of Massachusetts. Subsequently seven other senatorial colleagues joined as cosponsors. The Merchant Marine and Fisheries Subcommittee, chaired by Senator Bartlett, held hearings on the measure from May 18 through May 20, 1966, in Washington, D.C. All of the governmental agencies involved supported the bill. Fishery interests in the United States also supported the proposed legislation, but some felt the bill did not go far enough and therefore promoted an extension beyond the 12 miles to 200 miles or to the edge of the continental shelf. During the hearings the legal advisor of the Department of State testified that, although the 1958 Geneva Conference on the Law of the Sea had adopted four conventions, it left unresolved the extent to which a coastal state could claim exclusive fishing rights in the high seas off its coast. The witness pointed out that there had been a definite trend toward the establishment of a twelve-mile fisheries rule in international practice in recent years. Furthermore, the twelve-mile fishery zone would not be contrary to international law. Representatives of the Department of the Interior pointed out the advantages and disadvantages in extending United States jurisdiction over fisheries out to twelve miles. Although seeing no clear need for it, they did not object to the legislation. The Department of the Navy and the Department of the Treasury expressed no opposition to the measure.[26]

The American Tunaboat Association of San Diego, California and the Van Camp Seafood Company of Long Beach, Calfornia opposed Bartlett's bill. They argued that the proposed legislation was premature; that a twelve-mile fisheries zone would not significantly benefit U.S. coastal fishermen; that it would encourage further expansion of fishery jurisdiction; and that finally, if an extension were made at all, it should be to 200 miles, not a miserly 12 miles.[27]

Bartlett was mad at the "tuna boys," particularly at W.M. Chapman of Van Camp. Bartlett believed that the twelve-mile zone would not hurt the tuna interests "one little, tiny bit, and why they have become so terribly agitated about this [was] beyond [his] comprehension." But they effectively blocked the bill. Undeterred, Bartlett decided to launch a counter-lobby of his own and do some bargaining. Congressman John Dingell of Michigan appeared to be the key to the bill's passage, and the tuna advocates had convinced him of the validity of their arguments. Bartlett knew that an endangered species bill, which was "dear to Dingell's heart," had already passed the House and was awaiting Senate action. Bartlett's plan was "to put a 'hold' on it so the Senate will take no action until the efforts to swing Dingell into line have been made."[28]

Apparently Bartlett's scheme succeeded. On September 26, 1966, the House favorably reported its companion bill to the Bartlett measure. On October 3, after a short debate, the House passed the measure, and the president signed the bill into law on October 14, 1966. The new law established a fisheries zone contiguous to the territorial waters of the United States. In this area, the United States exercised the same exclusive fishing rights as it had in its territorial sea. The legislation also provided for the continuation of such traditional fishing by foreign states within the new zone as the United States wanted to recognize; defined the new zone as a strip of water extending nine nautical miles beyond the existing three-mile-wide territorial sea; authorized the president to change the established limit if he found that a portion of the fisheries zone conflicted with the territorial waters or fisheries zone of another country; and stipulated that states would continue regulating fisheries within the three-mile limit but that the federal government would regulate the new nine-mile zone.[29]

Closely tied to the expansion of exclusive American fishing rights was Bartlett's long-standing interest in the utilization of bottom fish and fish waste from canneries. As early as the 1940s, both Gruening and Bartlett had taken a keen interest in the fishing industry and were appalled at the waste they encountered in fish processing alone. They found that about a third of the weight of the total fish catch was not utilized in any form at all. By 1945 the Fishery Products Laboratory in Ketchikan had developed a product it named "cannery loaf." Manufactured from salmon waste, it was an appetizing paste suitable for a sandwich spread, but the Food and Drug Administration (FDA) objected to it on the grounds that using fish eyes, among other parts, was "disgusting." Gruening and Bartlett were angry and considered the decision to be a wholly unscientific one. "What is disgusting to some people," Gruening asserted, "may not be to others. I know people who refuse to eat kidneys, although I happen to consider them a particularly desirable delicacy. Tripe or animal intestines is highly prized and, I believe, is not barred by the FDA. One could go on almost indefinitely listing articles that, from the standpoint of a squeamish person, might, even after being cooked, be objectionable." If not allowed on the domestic market, Gruening concluded, at least "the starving masses of Europe and Asia would consider cannery loaf as manna from heaven. So, I am sure, would the Puerto Ricans. As a matter of fact, the Bartletts and the Gruenings would probably enjoy it."[30]

The fish flour or protein issue was not revived again until the 1950s. At that time, Ezra Levin, president of the Vio Bin Corporation of Monticello, Illinois, developed a processing method utilizing the whole fish, including the head, tail, and internal organs. This method was more efficient and less costly than previous techniques using only parts of the fish.

Upon inquiries from Levin, in early 1961, the FDA issued an informal opinion that fish protein concentrate made from the whole fish was unfit for domestic consumption. The FDA based its decision on the grounds that use of the whole fish was aesthetically undesirable. Senator Bartlett recalled the frequent complaint of his colleague, Senator Paul Douglas of Illinois that a "society that permits canned bees and canned rattlesnake meat and canned other oddities to be sold on the open market ought to be able to bear up under fish concentrates."[31]

After the informal decision in 1961, the National Fisheries Institute, in an action backed by Levin, sought a formal opinion from the Food and Drug Administration on the subject. On September 15, 1961, it filed a proposed standard-of-identity order that would have permitted use of the whole fish in fish flour production for domestic consumption. On January 25, 1962, the FDA, responding to pressure, amended the proposed order, approving production of fish flour from fillets of fish only. Although the amended order never became effective, it nullified the proposed order filed by the institute.[32]

In 1966 proponents of the product took a new approach when they requested FDA approval of a food additive petition that would declare fish protein concentrate produced from the whole fish—but in a certain manner for certain purposes only—safe for domestic consumption. The Department of the Interior filed one such petition in February. Its Bureau of Commercial Fisheries had begun research on fish flour in 1962, attempting to develop a process using the whole fish that would win FDA approval. In April 1966 Levin filed the other petition for approval of his process, developed some fifteen years earlier. By the end of 1966 the Food and Drug Administration had taken no action on either petition.[33]

Late in the fall of 1965 Senator Bartlett, joined by his colleague Senator Magnuson, introduced a measure which directed the secretary of the Interior to promote the development of fish protein concentrate through an accelerated research program, including the construction of five demonstration plants. Bartlett pointed out the world need for an inexpensive process to produce fish protein from the sea. The government, industry, and universities would participate in this accelerated research program, and the American fishing industry would benefit because it would increase its catch fivefold by making a vast market available.[34]

Early in 1966 various senators interested in fish protein concentrate supported Bartlett's demand for FDA approval for the product. The senator once again pointed out that the export of fish protein concentrate would not only improve immensely the starchy diet of millions of human beings in the underdeveloped world but also would provide a tremendous boost to the American fishing industry.[35] He estimated that the American catch would increase from some five billion pounds to approximately twenty-five billion pounds annually through the utilization of bottom fish so far not taken by the American fleet.

On June 27, 1966, the Senate considered Bartlett's measure. After defeating an amendment reducing the authorized plants from five to one, the Senate passed the bill. Later that month Bartlett discovered that a section of the American dairy industry had launched a lobbying campaign in the House against the fish protein concentrate measure, stating, among other things, that a New Zealand physician had found that fish flour caused stomach cancer. The actual industry fear was that fish flour would cut into the powdered milk market.[36]

In early Sepember the *Washington Post* reported that "fish flour enthusiasts' upstream efforts to gain an official blessing for their high-protein wonder food are stalled in a new bureaucratic eddy." The Food and Drug Administration this time objected to fluoride residues in the fish meal. If children ate large amounts of the flour, the Food and Drug Administration contended, it could discolor their teeth. This allegation drew replies from advocates who pointed out that in the fight against malnutrition, "mottled teeth are better than no teeth at all — and certainly a small price to pay for staving off starvation." Fluorides, however, were involved in many emotional battles in the United States, such as the controversy over the fluoridation of public water supplies as a means of reducing tooth decay. Furthermore, there could be no export of fish flour unless it received FDA approval for domestic consumption, because the federal government undoubtedly would be accused by Communist propagandists of foisting on other peoples a product deemed unusable at home.[37]

On October 3, 1966, Congressman Dingell asked for unanimous consent for considering the House version of the fish protein concentrate measure. A few House members objected to the bill, maintaining that, for example, one could "take a bucket of sewage and make it safe by bringing it to a high enough temperature, but it still would not be wholesome." Strong support for the measure, however, resulted in its passage. While the Bartlett bill had authorized the construction of five plants, the House followed the lead of the Senate and reduced them to one.[38]

As finally enacted, Bartlett's bill authorized the secretary of the Interior to make grants to, and contracts with, public and private agencies for studies, research, and experiments to develop production methods for fish protein concentrate and to conduct similar research within the department. It further enabled the secretary to construct one experimentation and demonstration plant for the production of fish protein concentrate and to lease one other plant for the same purpose. It specified, however, that no construction or leasing of any plant could take place until after the Department of Health, Education, and Welfare certified that fish protein concentrate produced from the whole fish was safe for human consumption and complied with the provisions of the Food, Drug, and Cosmetics Act. Although the Food and Drug Administration no longer objected on aesthetic grounds, it now opposed the amounts of isopropyl, alcohol, lead, and fluoride residues remaining in the finished product. Nevertheless, the senator's efforts were finally crowned with success when President Johnson, while visiting Anchorage, used the occasion to sign the Bartlett bill into law.[39]

Because of foot-dragging on the part of bureaucrats responsible for the implementation of the Bartlett bill, by 1968 no plant had been constructed or leased. By that time, construction costs had increased considerably. The Senate, therefore, provided the needed $900,000 in additional funds to launch a pilot plant, but the House reduced the number of plants from two to one.[40]

By late 1966, Senator Bartlett's health had deteriorated and William Foster had left the staff of the Senate Commerce Committee. Although by then Bartlett had assumed chairmanship of the Subcommittee on Merchant Marine and Fisheries, he had decided to retrench in the field of innovative fishery legislation. He knew that he had already accomplished a great deal in that area, in spite of the bureaucratic stupidity in the name of public health that he had encountered.

CHAPTER 17

Father and Son

T HEY MET FOR THE first time in 1934 in the office of Alaska's territorial delegate, Anthony Dimond. Gruening had recently been appointed director of the Division of Territories and Island Possessions, a New Deal agency within the Department of the Interior that was designed to supervise federal relations with America's outlying and dependent areas and assist them in every way possible to compensate for their lack of voting representation in Congress. Certainly neither man suspected then how intertwined their lives would become in subsequent years. Bob Bartlett did not record any impressions of the first meeting, while Ernest Gruening simply stated: "I liked Bob Bartlett exceedingly."[1] Although part of the account of their relationship already has been recorded here, the full story bears retelling.

In background, as in a number of other matters, Bartlett and Gruening were very dissimilar men. Bartlett, the younger of the two by seventeen years, was the son of working people who grew up in Alaska. Gruening grew up in a bilingual upper middle-class family that had a solid cultural standing.

President Roosevelt appointed Gruening Alaska's territorial governor in 1939. Gruening, who was fifty-two years old when he assumed his new duties in December of that year, already had a distinguished career behind him. He was born on February 6, 1887, in New York City, the son of Dr. Emil Gruening, a prominent eye and ear physician who had immigrated to the United States from East Prussia in 1861 at the age of nineteen. After serving in the Union Army during the Civil War, Emil Gruening had been graduated from the Columbia University College of Physicians and Surgeons and did postgraduate work in Paris, London, and Berlin.

Ernest Gruening grew up in New York City. He attended school in France for a year to learn the language and traveled widely in Europe with his family on several occasions. After graduating from Sachs's Collegiate Institute in 1902, he attended Hotchkiss School in Lakeville, Connecticut for a year preparatory to entering Harvard University in 1903. There he became acquainted with many of the individuals who later became America's intellectual and governmental leaders.

Gruening attended Harvard Medical School, but he became interested in journalism and did a stint as a cub reporter on the Boston *American* between his junior
and senior years in medical school. He returned to Harvard to receive his M.D.
degree in 1912.

Instead of following in his father's footsteps in the practice of medicine, Gruening chose to go into journalism. In 1921, after several jobs on various papers, he
became the managing editor of *The Nation,* a weekly intellectual and liberal
magazine. Gruening's journalism blossomed into a writing career with the publication of his highly acclaimed volume *Mexico and Its Heritage* in 1928, followed by
five other books later in his life. After Gruening had held several other journalistic
jobs, President Roosevelt appointed him to serve as an advisor to the United States
delegation at the Seventh Inter-American Conference at Montevideo. There he
had a hand in fashioning the New Deal's policy toward Latin America, which at
that point became known as the Good Neighbor Policy.

In his position as director of the Division of Territories and Island Possessions,
Gruening, an energetic and forceful man, soon came into conflict not only with his
superior, crusty Secretary of the Interior Harold L. Ickes, but also with Rexford G.
Tugwell, who was setting up Puerto Rican development programs. Gruening
embarked on a similar program in his division. At that point the president
apparently decided to avoid further conflict between Tugwell and Gruening by
promoting Gruening to the governorship of Alaska in September 1939.

Gruening, who had visited the territory in his capacity as the director of the
Division of Territories and Island Possessions, arrived in Alaska in December 1939
to take up his new duties. Although Alaska was remote and off the beaten path,
Gruening was looking forward to service in the territory and decided to devote his
considerable energies and great talents wholeheartedly to his new job. The new
governor arrived in Alaska at a propitious time, because before long the outbreak
of the Second World War and the Japanese invasion of Kiska and Attu in the
Aleutian Islands set vast changes in motion. As governor, Gruening played an
instrumental part in many of these changes.

The same year that President Roosevelt appointed Gruening governor, he
appointed Bartlett secretary of Alaska. Although second only to the governorship,
it was a position which actually had few duties. When Bartlett assumed his new job,
he did very little; nobody expected or wanted him to do much. George Sundborg,
the editorial writer and government reporter for the *Juneau Daily Empire,* met
Bartlett early in 1939, when he included the secretary on his "daily rounds of the
Federal Building beat. He never produced any news. But he was a pleasant fellow.
Never any particular ambition, so far as I could detect."[2] Bartlett was an affable
and easygoing individual, who probably desired nothing more than a little financial security after the succession of jobs he had held, none of which had amounted

to much. Thirty-five years old, he felt reasonably secure in his new position and promptly settled into family life and the routines of a small Alaskan town.

When Gruening arrived to assume his new position in Juneau, Alaska's capital, on December 5, 1939, he was greeted at the dock by about a dozen Democratic office holders, Bartlett probably among them. Since the official swearing-in ceremony was not to take place until later in the evening, the group suggested that they all walk up the hill to the governor's mansion, which, Gruening mentally noted, would subsequently be referred to more modestly as the governor's house. There the mayor presented the new chief executive with the key to the city of Juneau. Gruening took the oath of office, inwardly bristling at being introduced as the "Democratic governor of Alaska." Not wanting to start his tenure with a controversy, Gruening again noted mentally that he would emphasize the fact that he was the governor of Alaska, period.[3]

After the ceremony he asked Bartlett to stay for a private talk. Gruening wanted to discuss the organization of the governor's office and have Bartlett assume a considerable share of the work. Gruening liked Bartlett, thought him to be capable, and had decided to use his talents, inasmuch as he knew that the secretary of Alaska's "actual work now could be performed in perhaps an hour a week. I told him what I hoped of him, and asked him how he felt about it and found him very enthusiastic."[4]

From that day onward, Bob Bartlett's leisurely work schedule changed abruptly. Every day the governor conferred with Bartlett, discussing current problems and searching for solutions. All of Gruening's official letters went to Bartlett for suggestions before being sent, and within a very short time the governor and Bartlett had established an excellent working relationship. Gruening almost immediately recognized that the "Governor has really very little power; that he may be able, if he handles himself correctly, to exercise a good deal of influence and leadership which apparently has been lacking." Gruening determined to supply that leadership. There was no question at all that a man of his talents, ability, determination, drive, and ego would throw himself into his work and lead Alaska superbly. It was equally clear that in the process he would disrupt established relationships, generating both intense dislike and admiration.[5]

Gruening soon discovered a number of Alaskan realities with which he had to deal. The first, and perhaps most important, was the fact that Alaskans considered him an "outsider."

Although few Caucasians had been born in the territory up to that time, Alaskans carefully reminded each other of their length of residency in the North. The longer the stay, most believed, the more genuine was the honored term "pioneer" or "sourdough." Alaska's Indians, Eskimos, and Aleuts were collectively known as natives but apparently could not become sourdoughs or pioneers, on the assumption, perhaps, that an individual could not be either one on his native ground. More basically, most white Alaskans shared American racial attitudes of the day, considering natives to be inferior to them.

The governor also quickly discovered Alaska's regionalism, fostered by vast distances and different modes of making a living. Gruening determined to do his part in breaking down this regionalism. He discovered that until his arrival, most governors, either by necessity or by choice, had been contented to stay in Juneau. Gruening decided to make the governor's office a highly visible one throughout the territory. He traveled widely and incessantly. He also encouraged Bartlett to travel all over Alaska, and both men came to know Alaska well.

Temperamentally, Gruening was like a "trip hammer. He broke up everything that was in his way; he bored through. He had the determination of sixteen men and a mind that was sharp and quick and ruthless, ruthless, egotistical, but a fine humor. Loved to call himself—rather with a sort of humorous attitude—the 'Little White Father'" of Alaska. Once he had made up his mind, he seldom changed it. He was a very athletic individual, who at times exerted himself physically to the point of collapse, almost as if to show his strength to prospective opponents.[6] Gruening's swimming stunts in cold mountain lakes, his hiking expeditions with a string of panting and exhausted bureaucrats trying to keep up with him, and his fast tennis matches soon became legend in Alaska.

Although Bartlett and Gruening quickly became a smoothly working team, Bartlett was totally unlike the governor in terms of character and style of operation. He "liked to sit back in an easy chair and . . . didn't give a damn whether anybody thought he was an athlete or not." Powerfully built but physically lazy, he preferred riding and sitting to walking. Intellectually, Bartlett was a very inquisitive man with an excellent, though not formally trained, mind. He was basically shy, but he projected a warmth in his relationships with others, understanding human nature and what made different people tick. While Gruening was flamboyant, Bartlett was quiet but persuasive, a man whom people trusted instinctively. Above all, Bartlett soon acquired a sense of the possible, knowing when to compromise and to soothingly stroke a wounded ego.[7]

There was no question in anybody's mind that Gruening provided the leadership, but it was equally clear that Bartlett complemented the governor ideally and did an excellent job representing him. Bartlett learned fast and well. His travels on the governor's behalf soon made him known in areas of Alaska he normally would never have visited. Gruening's extended absences from Alaska—at such times, he was usually in Washington, D.C., lobbying the various federal agencies on behalf of Alaska's problems — put Bartlett into the position of acting governor. This enabled him to acquire some executive experience to add to his rapidly expanding administrative skills.

Gruening interested himself in Alaska's problems and opportunities — and he saw plenty of both. A few days after his arrival in Juneau, he asked Bartlett to accompany him on a walk around town so that he might get a feeling for the community. The two stopped at the newly completed Baranof Hotel, and Gruening introduced himself to the manager, Robert Schoettler. The governor was impressed with the facility and the fact that the necessary capital for building it had been raised locally by subscription. "This seems to me a very definite example of native enterprise and initiative and definitely a refutation to the allegations of Ickes that nobody would do anything here," the governor commented. On the other hand, the performance of a community choral group singing Christmas songs evoked critical comments from Gruening, who remarked that their efforts "were extremely feeble and without any leadership whatever. A chorus of four persons able to sing would have made a better showing."[8]

Small problems as well as large ones caught the governor's attention, and he tackled all with singular gusto and enthusiasm. Gruening strongly disagreed with the discriminatory hiring practices of navy defense contractors who secured their labor from Seattle unions to the virtual exclusion of resident Alaskans. He carried his complaint to Secretary of the Navy Charles Edison, an old friend, who ordered that contractor employment managers visit Alaskan centers at six-week intervals and hire Alaskans on the same basis as men from Seattle. Gruening then successfully persuaded the army to forego discriminatory practices in its defense construction program, but, as he noted later, such battles for priority employment for Alaskans would have to be fought over and over again.[9]

The governor looked at Alaskan municipal government management and financing and found both to be lacking. He persuaded the Juneau City Council to contribute reluctantly $2,400 in matching funds for the construction of a municipal swimming pool financed by the Works Progress Administration. He counseled the Sitka municipal government to reassess all property adequately to stave off financial collapse. He also advised them to purchase the city light and water services, a private monopoly which charged exorbitant rates but did not meet expanding needs.[10]

The chief executive lobbied Congress for appropriations for the construction of military bases. The German bombing of Rotterdam and the seizure of the Netherlands and Belgium—more than Gruening's persuasive power—moved the Senate and House committees to restore the Alaskan appropriations. Concerned about freight rates to Alaska, he had the Maritime Commission hold hearings in Alaska in 1940. They revealed that rates were needlessly high and that further increases were unjustified, but the commission still took no action.[11]

One of the governor's chief concerns was the overhaul of the outdated and inadequate Alaskan tax system. John W. Troy, Gruening's predecessor, had asked the territorial planning council to make a tax study in the late 1930s, but the research was not completed until the fall of 1940. The authors of the report concluded that an annual revenue of $10 million was entirely feasible. They recommended the adoption of a modern tax system and urged that the revenue obtained be invested in a soundly planned and economically executed program of permanent improvements, such as roads, schools, hospitals, and public buildings.[12] The members of the territorial planning council transmitted the tax proposal through the governor to the legislature but made neither a positive nor a negative recommendation.

Bartlett, who was a member of the planning group, realized that Gruening enthusiastically endorsed the tax reforms and intended to push them through the legislature. Although agreeing with many of the proposals, Bartlett knew that the mining and fishing interests would "oppose with all the vigor at their command any change whatsoever in tax laws." He also expected that the opposition forces "may lick us, as they generally have done in the past, notwithstanding the active and aggressive campaign Governor Gruening will wage."

Gruening decided to dispatch Bartlett to the western and northern regions after the Christmas season of 1940 to lobby for the tax program among territorial legislators before they convened in Juneau in early 1941 for their biennial session. But Bartlett grew wary. He sought advice from his mentor, Delegate Dimond: "[Would it be] proper for me to go only so far as to cover the points with which I am in thorough harmony? . . . I gravely fear the governor is terribly inept politically . . . and between you and me, strictly, I shouldn't be too surprised if he takes a terrific drubbing from the Legislature. And well as I like him and as much as I believe in most of his programs, I have no real desire to crash at the same time."[13] Despite Gruening's earnest efforts and Bartlett's lobbying, the 1941 territorial legislature defeated the governor's tax reform proposals.

Although he admired and generally agreed with the governor, by 1943 Bartlett had become visibly worried about his identification with Gruening in the public mind. His efforts to act as a conciliator between Gruening and Alaskan politicians had been to no avail. Instead he had been "branded as a hundred percent Gruening man [and had] to withstand onslaughts which the opposition crowd did not have nerve enough to launch against the governor of Alaska."

Bartlett felt that he had "not followed Ernest Gruening slavishly." He criticized the governor's operating style as one without any political 'feel': "He chooses to barge into a situation head on when a more cautious approach would serve him better." Despite this, Bartlett felt that Gruening had "one great virtue which recommends him very highly indeed to me and that is he is, with all his ability, trying to help Alaska and Alaskans." His opponents, Bartlett observed, had no program of their own. They assailed the governor personally as "a carpet bagger and as a Jew and as a good many other things entirely unrelated to the problems at hand."[14]

When Gruening pushed Bartlett into the delegate race in 1944, the governor had a variety of reasons for doing so. Among them were his high regard for Bartlett's abilities and the excellent working relationship they had developed since 1939. Gruening expected this relationship to continue, and he was not disappointed. While Bartlett settled into his new job and acquainted himself with its dimensions, the two stayed in close contact.

Gruening kept Bartlett informed on the progress of the enlarged legislature meeting in Juneau in 1945, at which the governor again presented a comprehensive program of social and economic reforms together with the proposed comprehensive tax reforms. Unhappily, only a part of the governor's program was adopted. The chief executive reviewed the performance of the legislature in his message to the people of Alaska, discussing important measures enacted and those that had been rejected. He also praised those legislators who, in his opinion, had labored in behalf of Alaska's best interests, and he named those he thought had been derelict in carrying out their duties and responsibilities as elected representatives. Gruening was aware then that any extension of his term would be in jeopardy. He had incurred the hostility of the canned salmon industry, and the campaign against him, supported by many Alaskan papers, would be intense. But in 1944 he had been reappointed to a second term without difficulty,[15] and he knew that he would not have to fight for renomination and confirmation until 1949.

At the end of the 1945 legislative session, Gruening reported to Bartlett that he was pleased that the legislature had raised the salaries of territorial employees by 15 percent, a move long overdue. For that session, the governor awarded the booby prize in the House to Fairbanks Representative Mrs. Alaska Linck, "whose entire performance was one of attempted obstruction and sabotage of every worthwhile move." A memorial calling for fundamental changes in the Organic Act had passed the territorial House, and Gruening urged Bartlett to attempt to get Congress to enact some of these proposals. The governor felt that "public opinion will support them," and most importantly, "we may not get Statehood for several years, but if these changes can be made they would help us definitely in the direction of self-government."

Bartlett fully realized the restrictions the Organic Act placed on the territorial legislature. For years his predecessors had regularly attempted to persuade Congress to revise Alaska's basic legislative document, always unsuccessfully. Bartlett continued this tradition, introducing measures designed to give his constituents a greater degree of self-government. Among others, these included bills for electing the territorial governor and for giving Alaskans a greater responsibility in the management of game, fur, and fishery resources.[16] Bartlett also elicited ideas from friends and constituents on ways in which a new organic act might be drafted, intending to introduce such a bill that same year.

By July 1945 however, Gruening had changed his ideas on the desirability of introducing a new organic act. The governor counseled Bartlett to wait until two congressional groups, the House Subcommittee on Appropriations and the House Committee on Territories, both slated to visit Alaska, had done so and returned to Washington. The introduction of a new organic act would then come about as a result of the congressional visits. By November 1945 Gruening told the delegate not to introduce a new organic act at all, because members of the House Committee on Territories had indicated that such a measure, if passed, would postpone statehood indefinitely. Alaska's problems could not be solved without statehood, Gruening stated, and therefore all energies should be dedicated to that end.[17]

While Bartlett slowly established himself in his new office, Gruening kept him supplied with a steady stream of Alaskan news, good advice, and requests for actions or help. For example, when the governor learned that the House had slashed the Interior Department appropriation and eliminated the entire Alaskan program, he advised Bartlett to approach the president directly for help. Truman might feel impelled to aid Alaska, Gruening reasoned, "not merely because FDR made a pledge to that effect but because of its national importance, both from an ultimate military and strategic standpoint, nearness to Russia . . . but also because many discharged servicemen would want to settle in Alaska." Bartlett did not believe it possible to have the funds restored and asked Gruening to come to Washington and help in the lobbying effort. The governor pointed out that it would be nearly impossible for him to come to Washington at that time but added that he would if it were really necessary. Gruening encouraged the delegate, however, by stating that "you can accomplish what needs to be accomplished without me."[18]

Over the years his enemies in Alaska and Washington had criticized Gruening for his incessant travels. Such criticism had little effect, however, because Gruening knew many government leaders on a personal basis from his years at Harvard and from his work as a newsman and government bureaucrat. Secretary of the Interior Ickes, Gruening's superior, had no special love for the governor and had been particularly unhappy with Gruening's style of operation. Ickes finally had ordered Gruening to stay in Alaska and channel his requests through the Department of the Interior. Much to the imperious Ickes' dismay, he had concluded that "Governor Gruening considered that he was a law unto himself. He never hesitated to shortcut me when he thought that he could advantage himself. He was the only member of my staff who would insinuate himself into the White

House without my knowledge or consent. It was not only disloyal, it was highly reprehensible for the governor of Alaska to be running from door to door in Washington" and lobbying busy cabinet officers and members of Congress for special Alaskan projects.[19]

Undeterred by this criticism, early in February 1946 Gruening and Bartlett called on President Truman and submitted a memorandum to him dealing with the development of Alaska. Their plan included massive outlays, amounting to approximately $56.5 million, for a public works program in most Alaskan towns. They discussed the necessity for such a program with a sympathetic president but received no formal commitment.

In the meantime, Gruening's adversaries had been at work. A few days after his meeting with the president, Gruening came into possession of a telegram that Allen Shattuck of Juneau had sent to Governor Mon Wallgren of Washington. The telegram indicated that an anti-Gruening campaign to influence the new Truman administration should concentrate on the theme that a fresh slate of officials in Alaska was needed for the young administration. The writer urged that either the president or Secretary of the Interior Julius Krug ask Governor Gruening for his resignation. Ickes' previous resignation, the author of the telegram stated, had removed one of the great barriers of Alaskan development; "the second great barrier would be gone when Gruening quit or was fired."[20]

Late in March 1946, before overflow galleries, the territorial Senate discussed Senate Memorial Number 1 — impeaching Governor Gruening. All kinds of charges against the governor were made, ranging from serious to ridiculous. Of the more serious ones was an allegation that Gruening had pressured J.G. Shephard, the former head of the Public Works Administration in Alaska, to refuse Lanham Act funds for the construction of a much-needed water system in Anchorage. Gruening allegedly told Shephard that the people in Anchorage did not cooperate with him—therefore the punishment. Shephard, according to this story, had resigned rather than follow political dictates. He was succeeded by Earl McGinty, under whom the Anchorage grant was rescinded.[21]

One of the more absurd charges concerned the governor's direct political interference in territorial politics. Gruening allegedly had written to Grace Coulter, former teacher at Point Hope School, directing her to work for the election of Bartlett to succeed Delegate Anthony J. Dimond.[22]

There were ringing speeches in Gruening's defense, citing his many accomplishments. The governor was his own best spokesman, however, when he addressed the territorial Senate before packed galleries that included the full House membership, friendly to him, which had recessed in anticipation of hearing Gruening's reply. Although he did not disappoint his followers in his able defense, Gruening personally thought that the whole show had "been somewhat nauseating." The opposition, he confided to Bartlett, were "going to do everything to smear [him] in Washington," but the territorial House would "adopt a long memorial praising [him] unqualifiedly" and send it to the president, the secretary of the Interior, and the Congress. He hoped that it would offset the impact of the anti-Gruening Senate memorial, which also had been sent to Washington. In the meantime, Gruening reminded Bartlett, "don't forget that dirty work is afoot with all the vigor and venom at the disposal of this gang," which consisted of Senators Walker, Shattuck, Green, Coffey, Collins, Rogge, Scott, Cochran, and Whaley.[23]

Bartlett counseled Gruening not to be perturbed by the Senate memorial, because it would have no influence in Washington at all. Above all, he told the governor, do not come to Washington now because, "the gang up there might say you were afraid and were coming back here to attempt to nullify the Senate memorial. Since we are convinced that the memorial won't count . . . it would be just as well not to give them an opportunity to squawk."[24]

Gruening's Senate enemies persisted, however, and Senator Walker wrote directly to the president, asking him to remove Gruening. In July of that year Secretary of the Interior Krug told the delegate that Seattle cannery operator and Alaskan power figure Nick Bez had complained to the president and the secretary about the governor. Slowly, Bartlett now feared, Gruening's enemies were making headway in Washington, and rumors about Gruening's imminent political demise gained such circulation that reporters on the Hill were almost daily questioning Bartlett about it. Surreptiously leaking news is a time-honored device to test the general reaction for a change in personnel and policies; and it was obvious that somebody in the Interior Department was sending up these trial balloons to test the mood, because Doc Watkins, an Associated Press reporter, "had been given reason to believe, somewhere in the Department of the Interior, that a change was impending."[25] Rather than telling the governor directly what to do, Bartlett recommended to the Department of the Interior that Gruening be advised "to remain at his desk at Juneau and be Governor of Alaska for awhile instead of trotting all over the country," not to come to Washington so often, and not to participate in the forthcoming political campaign in any supporting role whatsoever.[26]

The Bartlett-Gruening relationship was changing subtly at this point. The delegate had gained a great deal of self-confidence in his abilities to fill his job competently. He had been in Washington for more than a year and in that time had made many contacts within the bureaucracy concerned with Alaskan matters and among his congressional colleagues. Bartlett no longer was the "country boy" he had been when he first came to Congress.

Bartlett was fortunate that the work load in his office was relatively light. He was also lucky that he had Mary Lee Council as his secretary and Margery Neil to staff the office. Council, in particular, provided important continuity, because she had come to work for Dimond in 1940 and remained when Bartlett took over the delegate's position. Dimond had left the bulk of his office files for his successor—an additional boon to continuity.[27]

Bartlett had further advantages as well. With other than his own family, he was warm and outgoing, so people warmed to him quickly. Furthermore, in the eyes of many, Alaska was considered a very glamorous, if distant, area. Americans were interested in the North and listened readily to its Washington representative.[28]

The two leading Alaskan politicians disagreed openly for the first time early in 1949, when the governor proposed to establish a Washington office of the Alaska Development Board. This agency, created in 1945 by the territorial legislature, was to handle the matter of postwar planning, industrial development, tourism and settlement promotion, and long-range studies of needs and opportunities.

Gruening considered Bartlett his political protégé and viewed him almost as a son. There comes, of course, the time when any son stands on his own two feet and does not accept the counsel of his father, no matter how well meant. Although Gruening's feelings were hurt, Bartlett now asserted his independence, refusing even to entertain the idea of a Washington office of the development board. The delegate insisted that he had "been elected to represent the people of Alaska before Congress and the various federal bureaus." Bartlett was unwilling to tolerate a territorial official, with personnel not elected by Alaskans, who would essentially duplicate many of his own efforts. "I can see too much trouble ahead. . . so I think the time to announce my position is right now," the delegate wrote. Gruening was utterly surprised that Bartlett did not see the wisdom in creating such a position, which, after all, was designed specifically to help the delegate. Furthermore, Bartlett would be able to name his own man. "For the first time in an increasingly intimate association of over nine years," Gruening asserted, "I cannot recall that we ever failed to have a meeting of mind on issues large and small." Bartlett quite readily agreed with that assessment but modified it when commenting "that before unity was achieved, there was sometimes a terrific beating of the gums."[29]

Bartlett, it is clear, had become increasingly irritated with the governor, particularly with his frequent trips to Washington. On those occasions Gruening made Bartlett's office his headquarters, commandeering secretarial services and monopolizing the telephone. Bartlett kept his displeasure to himself or shared it only with his friend Hugh Wade, so on the surface the Bartlett-Gruening relationship remained close and cordial. Increasingly, however, Bartlett went his own way instead of following Gruening's suggestions.

Although the governor fully intended to serve another term, Bartlett briefly considered the possibility of promoting his friend Wade for the governorship in case Gruening fell from presidential grace. On March 12, 1948, however, the president, at the urging of Secretary of the Interior Krug, sent Gruening's name to the Senate for reappointment. Bartlett was happy, telling Krug that "I won't forget ever that you went to the White House today and successfully urged President Truman to reappoint our friend, Ernest Gruening, as governor of Alaska. It was a noble stroke of work. I believe that not only because of personal friendship with Ernest, but because I am convinced it is best for Alaska and best for the Nation to have him continue in office." To Wade, Bartlett confessed that Gruening's renomination, "all things considered . . . is for the best . . . I really do like him as a man although at the same time I do reserve the privilege of becoming provoked . . . life up there would be pretty dull without him."

The Republican Congress did not act immediately upon Gruening's renomination. They expected to elect a Republican president that November who, undoubtedly, would nominate a Republican governor. But Truman was reelected, and Gruening's renomination was finally taken up in April 1949, when Senator Joseph O'Mahoney, the new chairman of the Senate Committee on Interior and Insular Affairs, decided to hold a hearing on the renomination. Gruening opponents in Alaska were jubilant and planned to field witnesses in Washington.

Bartlett learned that the governor and his wife were coming to Washington to be present at the confirmation hearings. "If I wore a belt," Bartlett remarked nervously, "I would start to tighten it." The delegate did not relish the idea of yet another visit, and the planeload of pro-Gruening people who were expected to testify on his behalf in Washington would flood his office. "God save the mark, we'll have them on our hands," Bartlett complained. "We were consoling ourselves with the thought that if the anti-Gruening people came down they wouldn't be bothering us much at 1029 House Office Building." But Bartlett also worried about Gruening and thought that the governor should not submit himself to harrassment at the hands of a possibly unfriendly committee.[30]

As Bartlett had hoped and expected, the Senate Interior and Insular Affairs Committee unanimously confirmed the governor for another term. Vindicated before the eyes of his Alaskan detractors, Gruening lost no time tackling northern problems with his usual enthusiasm and energy. Both men increasingly devoted more time to the statehood issue. Gruening worked in Alaska with the statehood committee that the legislature had created in 1949 and toured the forty-eight states, where he lectured audiences on the issue of Alaska statehood. Bartlett, in the meantime, publicized the matter in Congress, trying to convert opponents and telling his colleagues about Alaska and its promises and problems. In addition, he and his congressional friends bombarded Congress with statehood bills session after session.

After expending so much energy, both men had become discouraged by late

1950. Bartlett's relations with the Department of the Interior had become strained, primarily because the department often did not consult with him before making important decisions affecting the territory. Both men had expected the appointment of their old friend Oscar Chapman as secretary of the Interior in late 1949 to represent "the advent of the millennium." Chapman, a very cautious administrator, disappointed them both. Frustrated, Bartlett asked Gruening if he could possibly "arrange for my appointment as the governor of the very smallest Pacific Island. I am desirous of getting away from it all." Gruening sympathized with Bartlett and admired the fact that the delegate could "stand so much with such good nature and equanimity." He counseled Bartlett to take a long vacation with a change of scene and no telephones, strongly recommending Hawaii.

Gruening confessed that he, too, was "pretty well fed up with the kind of smearing and knifing that is going on in return for merely an honest and conscientious effort to do a job for Alaska." He was pessimistic about Alaska's chances of achieving statehood. Gruening had planned to file for some elective office should Alaska eventually enter the Union as a state, but now he had almost made up his mind to retire at the end of his gubernatorial term: "It would give me a far clearer sense of freedom and independence to feel that the fight for statehood is in no way bound up with any personal ambitions."[31]

Such feelings of dejection did not last very long. Both men were politicians and as such were certainly accustomed to the ebb and flow of fortune in public office. They continued with their work, glorying in occasional victories and complaining about the lumps they were taking.

On the eve of the November 1952 general elections, both men were apprehensive that the Republicans would sweep to victory nationally, as they already had on the territorial level one month earlier. Bartlett, dispensing with his customary reserve, told Gruening that "our association which has gone on for thirteen years, minus only a single month and two days, had been for me exceedingly pleasant and highly educational and most useful." Bartlett praised the governor's Alaskan policies and concluded, "I want you to know beyond all doubt that my feeling toward you transcends esteem, and that stands for the future as well as the past."[32]

As they had feared, the Eisenhower-Nixon team won the nation's top elective offices in 1952. The national Republican victory meant a change in leadership at all the top levels of the federal bureaucracy, and it also meant that Governor Gruening had become Alaska's lame-duck chief executive.

The new secretary of the Interior, Douglas McKay, a former governor of Oregon, decided to keep Gruening as governor until his term expired in April 1953. The secretary also decided that neither Albert A. White of Juneau, long considered the Republican boss of Alaska, Walter Hickel, a young contractor from Anchorage, nor Elmer Rasmuson, president of the National Bank of Alaska at Anchorage, were suited to fill Alaska's governorship. McKay favored the appointment of B. Frank Heintzleman, regional forester of the U.S. Forest Service in Juneau.[33]

With no immediate decision forthcoming, the Republican party in Alaska, in power once again but internally divided, could not agree on a gubernatorial choice. Instead, literally dozens of Republicans, both inside and outside Alaska, heard the urgent call to higher office and declared themselves willing and ready to serve. In that confusion, Gruening encouraged the candidacy of various individuals, among them Lee Bettinger of Kodiak, a member of the Alaska Statehood Committee. Bartlett was miffed that Gruening had not informed him of his activities. "Since I am supposed to be the leader of the Democratic party in Alaska," Bartlett observed, "he could have at least consulted me about it." Although Gruening's connection with political affairs in Alaska would soon draw to a close, Bartlett concluded that the governor typically was still "trying to mastermind the future. . . ."[34]

Gruening's term ended on April 10, 1953, after an unprecedented thirteen years and four months in office. The governor was nostalgic on his last day, observing that he had made many good and loyal friends in Alaska and modestly admitting that he had also made some enemies. On reflection, Gruening was grateful for the many good, if difficult, years he had been able to work in the territory. He was very disappointed with the 1953 legislature, however, which was dominated by Republicans and "old guard" conservative Democrats and which "did not wait long to turn the clock back." The first House bill to pass repealed the property tax. Gruening vetoed it but was overridden. That set the tone of the legislature, which consistently overrode the governor's vetoes — except for some bills that reached his desk on the last day of the session so that his vetoes could not be returned to the legislature.[35] The territorial House also created a McCarthy-type investigating committee whose purpose was to find evidence of any malfeasance in office by the government that had been led by Gruening.

The speaker of the House during that legislative session was George Miscovich, a Fairbanks miner who was fairly notorious for his drinking habits. One observer watched him "drunk on the speaker's stand in the last few days of the session, watched him pour whiskey into his coffee cup from a desk drawer up on the speaker's stand." The session ended in "a terrible atmosphere. The House never formally adjourned; it only walked off in the middle of the night without any formal action. It was a drunken and irresponsible array."[36]

Gruening had requested the privilege of appearing before the territorial Senate to make a farewell address. The Senate, which had been meeting all night, had stopped the clock in order not to exceed the statutory limit of sixty days for the session. Gruening was finally called to make his speech. Senator Howard Lyng, a conservative Democrat of Nome who heartily disliked Gruening, exercised a very substantial influence in that session. As Gruening entered the chamber to speak, Lyng rose and moved that the governor be denied the privilege of addressing the Senate. Thereupon Senator Paul Robison, a young Republican lawyer from Anchorage and no friend of Gruening, "got up and made a very gentlemanly but rather impassioned plea that this would be a most improper thing to do to a man who had served as governor for thirteen years and that the body could not indulge in such a tactic." The Senate voted once again to allow Gruening to speak, and the governor thereupon gave a "somewhat emotional but as usual very literate statement closing his years" as governor of Alaska.[37]

Gruening left the governorship with few, if any, regrets. His departure was cheered by the gift of a Chrysler automobile from anonymous donors. It was Bartlett who originated that idea, having written to numerous friends after Eisenhower's election, suggesting that Gruening be given a suitable gift expressing appreciation for his long and dedicated service to the territory. In addition, Robert B. Atwood, editor and publisher of the *Anchorage Daily Times*, ran a full-length editorial entitled "Alaska's Greatest Governor" in honor of Gruening.[38]

Gruening had been most fortunate in recruiting collaborators who had worked hard and loyally as a team for the improvement of the territory. But in his last days as governor, Gruening singled out for the highest praise Delegate Bartlett, his close associate for many years. "I want to try to express how very greatly I have enjoyed our friendship," he wrote to Bartlett, "how much I have benefitted from it, how stimulating and heartwarming it has been at all times. There never has been and will, in all probability, never again be, quite such a relationship, both in the matter or duration, cooperativeness, and understanding as has existed between Secretary and later Delegate, and Governor since we became associated officially. . . [so many years ago.] I would say in all modesty. . . that I think Alaska has benefited by the similarity of our views on almost every question, large and small, and by our ability to work together with complete harmony for the good of Alaska." Gruening had highest praise for Bartlett's service as delegate: "I can say unreservedly that you are the best delegate that Alaska has ever had, and that when a better delegate is elected than the one who has served Alaska for the last nine years, his name will still be E.L. 'Bob' Bartlett." The governor concluded that their relationship would continue but that he had felt it only appropriate to try to express a matter "on which I feel so deeply — what I have long felt and always will feel."[39]

Gruening was dispirited about the tapering off of the statehood movement after its apparently promising start in the early 1950s. He was troubled that his successor as governor, Heintzleman, opposed statehood for Alaska. Gruening therefore decided to set down Alaska's case and the record of its long neglect in a scholarly volume, in the hope that such a book would help the cause of statehood. Various publishers had expressed interest, and soon Gruening signed a contract with Random House. He and his wife moved to their cabin at Eagle River outside of Juneau, where the ex-governor set to work. A year later *The State of Alaska* appeared.[40] Bartlett had helped Gruening's effort by procuring government documents from the Library of Congress and from his own collection, as well as by having his staff research various questions posed by the ex-governor.

Gruening continued to act as Alaska's spokesman, touring the continental United States on lecture engagements where he advocated statehood and extolled Alaska's physical beauties and economic promise. He also wrote articles which appeared in such national magazines as *Harper's* and *Atlantic,* urging Alaska's admission as the forty-ninth state.

Making a living from lecturing and writing was not easy. Receiving only a small retirement income, Gruening soon found himself in straitened economic conditions. Bartlett was aware of the ex-governor's financial plight and arranged for Gruening's employment by the Alaska Statehood Committee as researcher and writer. The committee allocated $3,000 for the project, a sum which was to include stenographic services as well. After deducting services, Gruening was to receive fifty dollars a day until the money was gone. The ex-governor still was, and would remain, a very controversial figure in Alaskan politics, and Bartlett knew that giving him a job might elicit criticism. "No publicity will be given Gruening's employment," Bartlett noted, "in the hope that there won't be any public comment prior to the adjournment of the legislature. After that, Neil Moore [auditor of Alaska and a bitter enemy of both men] may choose to make a *cause célèbre* of it, but by then he will have little but the *Empire* [Juneau's paper] as a sounding board." In any event, the delegate concluded, there would not "be much room for a contention that the treasury has been ruined by this operation," and he was prepared to "defend the arrangement without a single blush."[41]

Late in 1955 tragedy stalked the ex-governor. Word reached him that his son Peter, general manager of United Press in Australia and New Zealand, was missing in Australia. Gruening called his son Hunt, an airline captain in Juneau, who at once flew to Australia. On arrival he was told that Peter's body had been found in his car on a little-traveled road some miles from Sydney. He had taped a tube to the car's exhaust and taken his life, apparently despondent over the dissolution of his second marriage. In 1931 the Gruenings had lost their eldest son, Ernest, Jr., who had died of an infection. The Gruenings were in anguish, deepened by the incredibility of it all. Peter's marriage had clearly been a mistake, but his many Australian friends had assured them in the months preceding the tragedy that he had recovered from the experience.[42]

Always a hard worker, Gruening became even more deeply involved in his many projects, in part to forget his sorrow. Earlier he had aspired to become Alaska's Democratic national committeeman after many friends had approached him and urged that he become a candidate. Bartlett opposed this for a number of reasons, among them the fact that the ex-governor was such a controversial figure and that he had stated his intention to operate from Washington, D.C. Above all, Bartlett was afraid that Gruening would antagonize the various factions within the party rather than pull them together.[43]

Gruening was terribly hurt and offended when he discovered Bartlett's opposition and the fact that Bartlett supported Alex Miller of Fairbanks for the position. Miller won the post, and Gruening suspended all communication with Bartlett. Early in January 1956 the delegate felt as low in spirits as he could ever recall: "I am distressed. No word has come to me from Ernest whatsoever during all the time he has been in Alaska. This is one of those times when I could crawl underneath a dachshund without his knowing it."[44]

In mid-January 1956 Gruening returned to Washington but did not pay his customary visit to Bartlett's office. Instead, the delegate found that Gruening had asked Congressman James Roosevelt to insert a speech he had made to the Alaska constitutional convention, entitled "Let Us End American Colonialism," in the *Congressional Record*. Bartlett was very apprehensive "that a friendship, no less, which has been so long in existence, may be on the point of dissolution. Out of all the tribulations of all the years in politics and in government, none has come close to making my heart so heavy."[45]

A few days later, after repeated entreaties by his wife and office staff, Bartlett called Gruening. Following an exchange of the usual pleasantries, Gruening informed the delegate coolly that he was "as well as he could be considering the fact that he had lost his boy and his best friend in Alaska, [who had] stabbed him in the back." The two met that afternoon in Gruening's house and talked for two and a half hours. Gruening was terribly disappointed that Bartlett had never told him of his sentiments regarding the Democratic national committeemanship. Gruening asserted that he had wanted the position principally because it was a top spot and would have given him an opportunity to work on Alaska's behalf in Washington. He was shocked when he had called Bartlett in Anchorage and discovered that the delegate did not endorse his candidacy. During the afternoon, Bartlett learned that he had also been badly misquoted, when, for example, Gruening was told that if he ran and won, Bartlett would "see to it he is never seated by the National Committee." If not completely reconciled, at the end of their talk the two had at least established the framework for making such reconcilement possible. "It was not easy for me to march into the Gruening home," Bartlett concluded, but he had made the effort and had prevented their long friendship from disintegrating.[46]

Small incidents soon after their reconciliation served to irritate Bartlett again. Basically, Gruening continued to regard Bartlett as his protégé and son, never realizing that the delegate had long since molded his own identity. In the early summer of 1956, for example, Bartlett complained that since leaving Washington, D.C., Gruening had "fired a series of letters to me telling me what to do in respect to certain matters in such detail that he failed only to instruct me as to what color necktie I should wear on my visits to the people he told me I should see on various subjects." Bartlett observed that he now was fifty-two years old, "not thirty-five as I was when Ernest and I started our association." Bartlett was absolutely unwilling to tolerate Gruening's desire to exercise total control in their relationship. Furthermore, the delegate considered Gruening to be as politically naive as when the ex-governor had begun his career.[47]

Nevertheless, after the achievement of Alaska statehood, Bartlett worked hard and loyally to have Gruening elected to the United States Senate in 1958. Bartlett realized that Gruening had great obstacles to overcome in his quest for the Senate seat, among them his age, seventy-one years, and his lack of funds. In his favor were his enthusiasm, vigor, intellectual stature, and aggressiveness. Bartlett staunchly supported his friend, writing potential supporters to channel any monies they raised to Gruening rather than to himself.[48]

As previously related, both Gruening and Bartlett won election to the United States Senate, and the two men started their Senate careers together—but with a difference. Bartlett had served as Alaska's delegate in Congress for fourteen years and had just successfully completed his eighth campaign for national office. He had an established Washington operation that functioned smoothly and was staffed by experienced personnel. Bartlett had inherited many of his predecessor's office files and had generated extensive ones of his own over these many years. His training in the House had been very broad, and his fellow senators had known him when he had served there. Bartlett had been cultivating congressional relationships for many years: "He had a very good basic understanding of human nature. . . . Fourteen years as a delegate—that is a lot of years getting things done without a vote—and that is because you learn to know people very well and how to state your case and how to develop it." In short, his colleagues had come to trust him; he was a real professional, an ardent student of Congress.[49]

Gruening, on the other hand, had held only appointive office, except for his position as a delegate under the Alaska-Tennessee Plan, and was not as experienced politically as Bartlett. His election as a United States senator had been the fulfillment of a cherished dream. George Sundborg, who had managed his uphill campaign and subsequently was named his administrative assistant, set up the Gruening office and did the hiring. But there were no files, no continuity, not many experienced staff members.

There was also a lot to the job that was new to Gruening, who, perhaps for the first time, was meeting Bartlett on his home turf. Here Bartlett had developed his own unique working style—smooth, conciliatory, but willing to fight for important principles. Bartlett preferred to settle many of the routine problems at the Washington bureaucratic level, where he knew many individuals well. Never particularly aggressive, his role as a delegate without a vote had reinforced a belief in the efficacy of persuasion and cooperation, and being senior senator from Alaska did not change his operating method.

In contrast, Gruening had always been a scrappy fighter, a man who had tackled problems head-on. Finding himself the junior senator from Alaska at the age of seventy-one did not change a style acquired over a lifetime.

Two such different men, both Democrats, both working for Alaska, were bound to come into conflict. Bartlett, ever the realist with an eye on the possible, was appalled, for instance, at a Gruening scheme to introduce legislation that would have retroactively given Alaska all the money it would have received under the Federal Aid Highway Act had it been a member of the federal system from its inception in 1916. Bartlett considered the proposal frivolous because Congress simply would not do such a thing. Furthermore, Alaska never would have been able to put up the required matching funds had it been a member of the federal system since 1916. In the fisheries field, Gruening proposed federal funds for the rehabilitation of Alaska's depleted stocks. Bartlett found the idea sensible, since Alaskan fisheries had been depleted under federal management. Gruening, however, harped upon the fact that foreign aid monies had helped restore the fisheries of eighteen foreign countries, but that in the meantime, Congress and the administration were dragging their feet in providing funds for Alaskan fisheries rehabilitation. Gruening suggested, therefore, that foreign aid funds be used for that purpose. Bartlett was opposed. Gruening's proposal, he believed, would automatically earn the antagonism of all supporters of foreign aid in Congress and not accomplish his purpose. Bartlett resignedly concluded that "I have more trouble with him than I do with any Republican opponent."[50]

There were other problems, among them one common to any state represented by two senators from the same party: who should get the credit for congressional accomplishments benefiting the home state? The question soon arose in reference to two measures featured in Senator Gruening's newsletter to his constituents. Bartlett objected to the junior senator's wording which stated that the bills in question had been "pushed to successful passage" by Senators Gruening and Bartlett. Bartlett wanted to set the record straight. Both measures, he griped to friends, had been passed over on the calendar the previous week. Only Bartlett's intervention with the Senate leadership resulted in a promise that both would be passed. Unfortunately, Bartlett explained, the consideration of the bills conflicted with a luncheon sponsored by the Alaskan congressional delegation in honor of Miss Dorcas Brower, a young Eskimo from Barrow who had played a minor role in a Hollywood movie based on Edna Ferber's Alaskan novel *Ice Palace*. Bartlett protested that "while the junior senator was introducing this very nice girl to the guests and while he was mugging for the photographers, I returned to the Senate floor and put through the two bills, and he didn't know a damn thing about it until I returned and told him. So, I guess it is more humorous than distressing to learn that the bills were pushed to successful passage" by Senators Gruening and Bartlett. It was a minor matter—yet it irritated Bartlett immensely.[51]

Bartlett became progressively annoyed with Gruening, more and more considering him simply a grandstander, adept at grabbing headlines. Actually, it was again a matter of their different operating styles. Gruening dealt with the Senate business at hand as conscientiously as Bartlett and, in addition, devoted his considerable talents to favorite causes of national importance. He was a man who had strong opinions on national issues and actively sought positions of leadership with respect to them, cherishing a good fight and quickly becoming controversial. Gruening was not a sensitive person but superbly self-confident, forceful, and possessed of a brilliant mind: "He was big league always. He could perfectly well have been senator from New York or senator from Pennsylvania or Massachusetts. He always had all the skills and all the accomplishments it required."[52]

Bartlett, on the other hand, was not a dominant personality. He avoided open controversy and solved problems by persuasion and compromise. He was far too sensitive a person for being a politician; he was a chronic worrier: "He was always insecure. He was insecure...even though he would win by 70 or 80 percent of the vote...he always worried [about the remaining 20 percent of the vote he had not received.] He was always worried about what people were thinking—what support he had." Bartlett was a man of the people who had a tremendous rapport with his constituency. He also had a personal charm and magnetism which Gruening lacked, and he was well liked and trusted by most people with whom he came into contact.[53]

Both men were dedicated to strengthening Alaska economically, and both believed that the federal government had a continuing responsibility to aid in this process. Because of their different styles, they complemented each other beautifully, reaching and influencing a broad variety of politicians and administrators.

In the early years after statehood, the Alaskan congressional delegation held periodic meetings to discuss common problems and approaches. It was in these meetings where the Gruening-Bartlett differences perhaps appeared most sharply. Gruening's immediate reaction to a problem was usually to "get a press release out" or "I'll send a wire down to the secretary." Bartlett generally responded in the vein of "wait a minute, I know Mr. X, a civil servant, and if I call him

I think he can talk to so-and-so and get this straightened out. Or let me talk to the chairman of the committee because I think he'll give us time to do the necessary things." Bartlett, in short, had excellent relationships with Congress, the administration, and the bureaucracy and knew how to utilize these ties to his advantage.[54]

It was not long before Gruening had angered not only assorted top bureaucrats but also the Senate leadership. In the fall of 1960, for example, he asked Bartlett for help in getting a measure through the Senate granting mineral rights in certain homestead lands to their owners. Bartlett soon substantiated what Gruening had suspected, namely that Senate Majority Leader Lyndon B. Johnson's attitude was that "[Gruening] isn't for me; why should I be for him?" The measure did pass, however, in amended form, applying only to the Kenai Peninsula. The following spring Gruening met with the director of the Bureau of Land Management, attempting to have the bureau do administratively what Congress had refused to do legislatively in respect to mineral rights for Alaskan homesteaders. The official refused, which angered Gruening. Bartlett, in turn, was upset with Gruening's action, because he wanted to maintain good relations with the Bureau of Land Management.[55]

In the spring of 1961 Bartlett had a major disagreement with Gruening. The dispute centered around a measure which Gruening had introduced the previous year to rehabilitate the fishing industry. Bartlett had found the bill so deficient technically that he had refused to cosponsor it. During the winter of 1960 and the spring of 1961, a member of Bartlett's staff and Don Greeley, who worked for Congressman Ralph Rivers, devoted a great deal of time and energy to refining and redrafting the Gruening fishery bill. With a draft ready, the two informed Herb Beaser, Gruening's legislative assistant, what they had done. Beaser immediately "wanted to take it over lock, stock, and barrel for the benefit of E.G." Gruening subsequently informed Bartlett that their staffs had had a misunderstanding about his fishery bill. He intended to introduce it and felt that Bartlett should defer to him because Gruening would be up for reelection in 1962. Bartlett remembered the disagreement: "I lost my temper completely. This I regretted two minutes later and still regret. He demanded that I be 'civilized.' I remained 'barbaric.'" Bartlett quickly decided to give up the bill. Gruening promptly introduced the measure, getting as cosponsors other senators not including Bartlett, who was mightily miffed. The two stopped talking with each other. On reflection, Bartlett thought that Beaser probably had told Gruening that the bill was a joint effort, in which case Gruening had been correct in assuming he should introduce the bill, since he had offered the original one. Bartlett also concluded that his temper tantrum "was not primarily actuated by the fishery bill at all. It was that I had been engaged in too many conferences in the days and weeks immediately before then when he and I and generally Ralph [Rivers], too, would meet with some administration official. These meetings uniformly resulted in Ernest taking over, conducting a monologue, delivering the colonization story [a speech Gruening had delivered at Alaska's constitutional convention in 1955, in which he had compared the territory's plight to that of the American colonies before the revolution against Great Britain in the 1770s] all over again and repeating accounts of other episodes in which he always is the hero and which over the years I have heard so often that I am ready to scream — literally — when the familiar words start to roll out."[56]

A week later Gruening called on Bartlett, ostensibly to discuss the Alaskan member of the North Pacific Fisheries Commission. Soon they began to talk about the fishery rehabilitation bill. "I have been expecting you to come to see me," Gruening stated. Bartlett insisted that it would have to be the other way around. Gruening thereupon stated that Bartlett probably did not like him very well anymore — a sentiment which the senior senator confirmed. But no matter, Gruening asserted, despite all this he retained his affection for Bartlett, whom he practically considered to be his son. Twice recently he had experienced dreams, he told Bartlett, in which "we have had words" and Bartlett was bitter to Gruening, who then awakened on each occasion "deeply troubled."[57]

Their talk did not settle the differences between them, and Bartlett finally concluded that Gruening never intended him to be a full partner. Bartlett certainly had outgrown the role of a son long ago. And although he did not specifically state it, Bartlett assuredly resented Gruening's intrusion into an arena which he had long considered his own, namely, the Congress. In years past, when Gruening had been in Alaska or just visiting in Washington, it had been bearable to have him give advice and generally try to run Bartlett's life. Bartlett always could ignore the advice, and Gruening's visits eventually ended. Now that they served together in the Senate, there was no escape. Bartlett was plainly jealous. Perhaps he resented the older man's fame, his ability to generate favorable publicity, his highly visible profile. Bartlett unjustifiably felt that Gruening did not produce, that all substantial work was performed in his own office. Bartlett clearly resented the fact that Gruening reaped so much of the glory while the senior senator, he felt, did most of the work.

The two soon staked out their major areas of interest. As early as 1959 Gruening suggested that the Army Corps of Engineers construct a huge hydroelectric dam at Rampart Canyon on the Yukon River. When finished it would boast an installed capacity of nearly five million kilowatts, making it the largest hydroelectric project under the American flag. This was a project that Gruening unsuccessfully pursued throughout his Senate career. In international affairs, the junior senator became a highly vocal critic of American foreign aid and the deepening involvement of the United States in the Vietnam quagmire. Gruening also became an effective spokesman for birth control on a large scale. In addition, he was a strong congressional proponent of special appropriations to speed Alaskan economic development.

Bartlett's main preoccupation consisted of making statehood work, of making Alaska a viable state, which meant continuing to ask Congress for special Alaskan programs and appropriations. But Bartlett quickly branched out and became an effective proponent of a strong American merchant marine, an effective coast guard, a comprehensive American fisheries policy, and radiation safety, among others. Unlike Gruening, Bartlett felt that the United States, as the richest nation on earth, had a moral responsibility to help underdeveloped countries develop economically. Bartlett essentially felt that each aid program should be justified on its merits.

Bartlett had drawn a two-year Senate term in 1959, while Gruening had won a four-year tenure. In 1960 Bartlett won a full six-year term by a comfortable margin, defeating his Republican opponent, Palmer dentist Dr. Lee McKinley.

Gruening ran for reelection in 1962 against Republican Ted Stevens, an able young attorney from Anchorage. Unlike Bartlett, who was widely admired, loved, and respected in Alaska, Gruening, though respected, did not communicate the warmth or elicit the wide support Bartlett did, and he worked hard to get elected.

Nevertheless, on November 6, 1962, Alaskans returned Gruening to the Senate, giving him 58.1 percent of the vote to Steven's 41.9 percent. The campaign had centered around the relative merits of Republican versus Democratic policies in Alaska. The voters decided they preferred the Democrats.[58]

Gruening's energy always astounded and irritated Bartlett. "His Honor," "His Worship," or "Nibs," as the senior senator had begun calling his colleague, arrived back from "those strenuous days in Alaska, all filled with ginger and pep, and looking marvelous after flying all night," Bartlett reported to a friend. He theorized that "the only reason he [Gruening] was ever elected to anything is that he hasn't met every Alaskan and hasn't had opportunity to berate and insult every Alaskan." What particularly galled Bartlett was the fact that their mutual friend Oscar Chapman, former secretary of the Interior during the Truman administration, had raised $16,000 for Gruening, with more money in sight. Although Chapman had promised to help Bartlett in his 1960 campaign, he had managed to raise a mere $550.[59]

From early 1963 onward, Bartlett's attitude toward Gruening worsened rapidly, although Gruening probably was not even consciously aware of this. Bartlett put undue emphasis on irritations associated with Gruening's style, and his increasing dislike of Gruening was mainly the result of tensions within himself—his chronic worrying and lack of self-confidence — rather than with actual events and incidents occurring in their Senate work.

Bartlett's ambivalent feelings toward Gruening undoubtedly went back many years. He confided much later to an aide that Gruening had treated him as a staff person as early as 1939. Even though Bartlett had been appointed secretary of Alaska in his own right by President Roosevelt, Gruening, after assuming the governorship a few months later, would phone and tell him, "Bob, get in here, I need to see you." Retrospectively, Bartlett resented having been taken for granted by the governor and treated in a routine manner.

Bartlett did not feel he was as worldly as Gruening. He knew no languages besides English and envied Gruening's ability to make eloquent speeches in German and French. He was jealous of Gruening's Harvard education, intellectuality, oratorical skills, social smoothness, and cosmopolitanism — it all made him feel like a country cousin. "He needn't have been," a former aide recalled, "because he had common sense and a gift of language and read a lot and was a very smart person." Furthermore, unlike Gruening, whom some Alaskans never really accepted, Bartlett was widely loved and considered a friend.[60]

It was uncharacteristic of Bartlett to be petty and small in his relationships with others, but that was not his stance toward Gruening. Bartlett became more and more exasperated with his colleague. In correspondence with friends, he grumbled about "His Honor" and "Your Worship" and "The Senator" from Alaska. Bartlett complained: "It is beyond his tolerance to permit me to become a specialist in any field. He must move in, he must seek to take over. He was born this way. Nothing will change him."[61] Bartlett exaggerated and, in his anger, forgot the many advantages he possessed over Gruening. His staff had handled Alaskan affairs for a much longer time, so constituents often came to them first because they knew them and had dealt with Bartlett for many years: "Often times there was nothing for Gruening to do but try to hop in when he could. Sometimes, perhaps, he hopped in when Bartlett . . . should have gotten the credit." But whether Gruening stole any of the headlines made no difference, because it did not make him any more popular with the Alaskan electorate. Former Bartlett aide John M. Cornman recalled that the "people seemed to understand that you were the guy who was doing it, even though the headline didn't say it." Individuals working in the Bartlett style "don't get many of the headlines."[62]

Nevertheless, most Alaskans realized and appreciated Bartlett's many achievements in the Congress. His continued lopsided victories at the polls certainly reflected this. Some constituents, however, were obviously not quite so cognizant of his accomplishments, as Bartlett was reminded from time to time. A Seldovia constituent, writing a pleasant letter to the senior senator, asked him "to convey his profound thanks to Senator Gruening for everything he has done to help Alaska's fishing industry and the Alaskan fisherman." Bartlett confessed that the sentiments the Seldovian had expressed "caused me to stagger, reel and fall back; for the good senator, as you well know, has done nothing except to introduce a bill to establish a twelve-mile fishing zone, a bill which will never see the light of day."

Yet Bartlett did admire Gruening for his skill in handling the news media and for skillfully planning his speaking engagements ahead of time. Gruening, for example, was scheduled to speak in Anchorage under the sponsorship of the Chugach Electric Association in celebration of National Electric Week. Bartlett praised the advance preparations Gruening had made. "He is much more agile at this sort of thing than I," Bartlett admitted. "He always arranges for these appearances before leaving here, as anyone with sense would do. Then he has an audience when he arrives instead of wandering aimlessly around without rhyme or reason as I too often do."[63]

Although Bartlett usually refrained from reading the junior senator's "misnamed newsletters" because it raised his blood pressure too much, he could not resist taking a peek from time to time. Predictably, whenever he did he was angered. Gruening's most recent newsletter, Bartlett once railed, was "the tops, the worst, the stinkingest newsletter they have ever put out." It concerned the Alaska omnibus bill designed to aid southcentral Alaska after the devastating earthquake of March 27, 1964, which had registered 8.6 on the Richter scale. All of the liberalizing amendments to the measure had been proposed by Senator Gruening, the newsletter claimed. That was "an outright lie," Bartlett angrily observed. Gruening indeed had proposed three amendments, but they all had been defeated. Perhaps even more upsetting was the claim that Gruening had stood alone for weeks insisting that Alaskans be treated generously by the federal government after the devastating earthquake. Not to have mentioned the name of the senior senator in the common effort had been like sinking a knife "into my vitals — and in the abdominal region," where it had penetrated deeply. Bartlett concluded that Gruening indeed was "a stinker of the first order."[64]

By early 1967 Gruening realized that running for reelection in 1968 would be difficult. His age — eighty years — would undoubtedly be made an issue. He also knew that he had many enemies in Alaska who wanted to deny him another term. Gruening turned to Bartlett: "I'm going to have a hard time in 1968. I realize it. I need all the help you can give me. In the past I've been willing to help you at every opportunity, but you never needed my help the way I need yours now. I only want one more term." He then asked Bartlett to let him have all the press releases for the next two years and also to allow him to introduce a measure amending the Maritime Act of 1920, known as the Jones Act after its senatorial sponsor, Wesley Jones of Washington. Alaskans long had objected to section 27 of that measure, which, in effect, had made Alaskans dependent on Seattle shipping by prohibiting their use of British Columbia ports closer to the state. "As too often in the past," Bartlett stated, "I surrendered on one point. I told him to go ahead and introduce the Jones Act bill but also made it clear that I simply could not drop out of sight for two years to accommodate Gruening." Actually, Bartlett admitted, "I should have told him to go jump."[65]

Mary Lee Council, who had retired from Bartlett's staff in 1966, advised Gruening against seeking another term. His wife, Dorothy, was crippled by arthritis and confined to a wheelchair. A move to a sunny and warm climate would have helped her. Council, who had known the Gruenings for years, recalled that she told him, "Ernest, you're an absolute ass to run, you know Dorothy is so sick; why don't you think of her for a change, think of your family for a change." She observed further that "he doesn't think of people; he's a strange man. He's got these great visions, these great liberal ideas, and yet his relationship with people is terrible." Gruening officially announced in the fall of 1967 that he would seek another term. His schedule for a two-week Alaskan trip, Bartlett observed, "would put a less vigorous man in the hospital. It makes me tired just to look at it."[66]

By 1967 Bartlett's physical condition was deteriorating. He had suffered a series of heart attacks and was in continual pain. His physical strength was gradually ebbing away. His hair whitened, wrinkles appeared in his skin, and hollows deepened beneath his eyes. Bartlett was beginning to die, and he knew it. Yet he attended and spoke at a massive fund-raising dinner in Washington on Gruening's behalf.[67]

As Gruening began his preparations for the primary campaigns, rumors began seeping out of Anchorage that Mike Gravel, a former speaker of the state House and the unsuccessful 1966 Democratic candidate for the U.S. House of Representatives, was thinking about challenging Gruening in the August 1968 primary. Party officials were chagrined, because such a turn of events would lead to a division within the party when unity was badly needed. It also nullified an unvoiced understanding that once Gruening had decided to run again, he would be unopposed. Candidates for various offices had filed, but those desiring the Democratic nomination for the U.S. Senate seat had deferred to Gruening. On the last day for filing, with the field clear of any opponents save Gruening, Gravel announced that he would seek the Senate position.

The primary campaign was uneventful until its closing days. Gravel moved about the state swiftly, leaving the suggestion that he was everywhere, an impression heightened by Gruening's absence due to a lengthy congressional session. Gravel's quick movements from place to place and Gruening's continued absence as well as the lethargy of his campaign accentuated Gravel's youthful thirty-eight years and his opponent's age of eighty-one. As political analyst Oliver Quayle had pointed out in a poll and survey of the state's political climate, which the Gruening camp had financed, age was Gruening's most vulnerable point. Only personal campaigning could dispel this, but when Gruening finally did arrive and undertook such stunts as swimming in the Arctic Ocean off Barrow just before the end of the campaign, it was already too late.

By that time Gravel had saturated the state's television stations with a thirty-minute campaign film, entitled "A Man for Alaska." The film, which cost approximately $50,000, had been made by Shelby Storck, a St. Louis film producer, and was the brainchild of Joseph Napolitan of Springfield, Massachusetts, whom Gravel had hired as his campaign director. The film was a Madison Avenue spectacular of Gravel's life. It was shown on Alaskan television stations twice a day for one week before the election and then four times a day for the last two days prior to voting. The Gravel campaigners also went into the bush areas, where they treated residents to an evening of free entertainment that usually featured a full-length film, free popcorn, and of course the Gravel film. It was impressive, and the votes showed it. While early polls had favored Gruening by a margin of two to one or better, Mike Gravel beat Gruening by 1,694 votes.[68] The Vietnam War was an unspoken issue of the campaign. Many Alaskans still favored pressing the war to a successful conclusion, and were tired of Gruening's continued opposition.

Gruening was bitter over the defeat, and Bartlett was "really bowled over." While in Chicago attending the Democratic National Convention, he had predicted that Gruening would win by a margin of almost two to one. "It merely goes to show that my record as a political prophet remains close to zero," Bartlett later wrote. Soon a movement to run a write-in campaign developed, initiated by Anchorage furrier David Green, who first cleared the idea with Senator Gruening in Washington. Green then contacted individuals on the campuses of Alaska Methodist University in Anchorage and the University of Alaska in Fairbanks, who launched the write-in campaign. Bartlett told Gruening that such an effort would only result in the election of the Republican candidate, Elmer Rasmuson of Anchorage, and also would seriously harm the Democratic party as a whole. When asked, Bartlett told his colleague that he would oppose the write-in "as strongly and vigorously as [he] could." But unless there was tremendous pressure against Gruening, Bartlett knew that he would plunge ahead anyway: "He will not go lightly on anyone who is against him. We can look forward to a ghastly seven weeks."[69]

Bartlett, as he had said he would, endorsed Gravel. As a loyal party man, he rejected write-in efforts: "There is just no chance whatsoever that a United States Senator can be elected by such a method. And there is no reason why there should be. He had a fair chance, a democratic chance, in the primary, and he lost and he should take it gracefully. It seems impossible for him to do so." Bartlett supported Gravel's bid in a cover letter to his many supporters and also on the radio. "The crowning blow to Ernest Gruening," recalled one friend, "was when Bob Bartlett came out for Gravel on the radio." By that time the senior senator was close to death.

In the November general election, Gruening ran third, receiving 14,118 votes compared to winner Gravel's 36,527 votes and Rasmuson's 30,286 votes. Voters had cast their ballots on November 5. On December 11 Bartlett was dead.[70]

Gruening was about to depart for Puerto Rico for a vacation when Bartlett died. He proceeded with his plans: "He did not go to Fairbanks for the funeral. Puerto Rico was the excuse. He really did not want to go."[71]

In time, Gruening even came to believe that Bartlett had actually connived with Mike Gravel to get into the primary race against him in 1968. There was, however, no basis to these suspicions.

Some years earlier Bartlett had vowed that "I have made a firm determination to serve in public office at a more advanced age and for more years than a certain someone." Bartlett had served twenty-nine years, as had Gruening. Virtually at the same time, death ended Bartlett's career, and political defeat ended Gruening's.[72]

But Gruening had the last word. In evaluating a proposal which had come to the National Endowment for the Humanities for writing a biography of Bob Bartlett, he recommended against it. "My adverse recommendation to the application," Gruening stated, "is based on the subject. E. L. Bartlett was not, in my opinion (based on a third of a century of close association with and friendship for Bartlett, and likewise the active participation in the struggle for Alaskan statehood) 'the architect of statehood.' He played an important role, as did others. Neither he nor any other individual can be nominated as statehood's architect. Neither is there any evidence that Bartlett was a humanist. He was an assiduous worker for legislation in behalf of Alaska, both as delegate and as senator, carrying out. . .the prescribed function of a member of Congress. His activity in public life was essentially limited to those efforts, which he carried out devotedly and untiringly. But beyond this activity his career is bare of any unusual or special distinction."[73]

Gruening outlived Bartlett by six years and succumbed to cancer on June 26, 1974, at the age of eighty-seven.

Bartlett, The Private Man

I N HIS EARLY LIFE, while scratching for a living as a reporter, as a miner, and in various low-level governmental jobs, Bartlett spent abundant time with his wife and friends. He paid a great deal of attention to his first-born child, Doris Ann, who was pretty and very intelligent. Doris Ann recalls the 1937 mining season at Independence Creek: "I remember sleeping in a tent with my grand-mother and coming out and seeing Bob and Vide coming out of a stable. I was sure that they had spent the night in the stable." Her father would take her along on the Caterpillar tractor, and "I thought I was driving it. I suspect I may not have been." She recalls the hydraulic operation, "great big enormous hoses and great big spurts of water." During the 1938 mining season, Doris Ann and Vide stayed in Seattle, because it was cheaper, while Bartlett once again mined Independence Creek: "I missed him very much. I remember cutting pictures out and sending them to him. I could not write yet!"[1]

In 1939 Bartlett was appointed secretary of Alaska, and the family moved to Juneau. Vide was expecting another child, and Doris Ann remembers her father calling her on the phone in December 1940 and telling her to hurry over to the hospital. He met her at the door and took her to Vide's room, where she saw Vide holding up her baby sister, Susie.[2]

The Juneau school district then had a policy of dismissing students on the rare sunny days. On such occasions, the Bartletts and their friends the Wades would drive from Juneau to Tee Harbor and rent a row boat to go fishing for the day. Doris Ann views that period as "a wonderful time. I used to go and see Bob in his office. The museum was in the same building, so when he was busy I could go into the museum."[3]

The Bartletts did quite a lot of casual entertaining during their years in Juneau. High-ranking federal and military officials passed through Alaska's capital during the war years. Many of these spent an evening with the Bartlett family, and even though there never was much money, "they would entertain and served baked beans rather than not have people to the house. There always were lots of people around... He and Vide had an enormous number of real close friends. But it did not take from the family. The family was even closer. We would entertain, maybe five nights a week. But after the people had gone we would all be doing the dishes together and talk about what had gone on that evening, share our impressions of people, discuss." For Doris Ann, the Alaska years were happy ones, shared with her parents and her grandmothers, Lulu and Babbi, who lived with the family.[4]

Moving to Washington, D.C. was hard for Doris Ann. She had just turned eleven years old, "which is a bad age for children, a hard age" to adjust to a new environment. She particularly disliked the fact that her father no longer had much time to spend with her, since he was almost immediately caught up in the frenzy of life on Capitol Hill. She soon began to dislike Washington and yearned to return to the Alaska of her memories. She did, however, greatly enjoy the times her father paid attention to her: "Bob took me on the floor of the House when Roosevelt had just died and Truman gave his maiden speech." She visited the galleries often and "went on a regular basis to the office and worked at least once a week when Mary Lee [Council] put out the newsletter. I put in the physical labor required."[5]

In 1946 the Bartletts sent Doris Ann to Juneau, where she stayed with family friends, the Nordales and the Wades. It was an election year, and Doris Ann involved herself in the campaign of her father's Republican opponent, Almer J. Peterson: "I was out on the street handing out Almer Peterson pencils because I wanted Bob to lose so we could move back to Juneau." She added that it was a put-on, "it was a joke amongst the Bartlett friends. One time I was decorated with Peterson buttons . . . in the lobby of the Baranof Hotel, and Bob was not pleased. The joke had gone too far. He took all the buttons off me and that was the end of that joke."[6]

Susie, Bartlett's younger daughter, grew up without seeing much of her father. Born in Juneau in 1940, she was five years old when her family moved to Washington. She thrived in the capital's urban environment. She recalls noticing her father for the first time in 1945, seeing "him sitting in his chair, reading a newspaper, talking to Vide and talking to the rest of us . . ." Above all, Susie feels that Bartlett must have been a very ambitious man: "Bigger and better things always. You're not aware of ambitions or driving forces in your own family until you're older and can recognize what makes your father go to work, seven days a week, ten or twelve hours a day. He went to work every Sunday as far as I can remember."

Susie saw her father essentially as a "very homely man which, indeed, he was; a very quiet man. Since I don't have any real recollection of him when I was small, I really don't think I ever saw him as a big man. If I'd been three years old and thinking about my dad he would appear big, but because I was so much older when I do remember him he was just an average-size man."

Her father loved good clothes but was "very sloppy. He could put on a $200-suit and look like he had gotten it out of the thrift shop. Even the most expensive suit looked rumpled on him very quickly. I'd see the ever-present rose in his lapel and his neckties. When he was at home he had some slippers that he wore." Sitting in his chair, "he always had one leg thrown over the arm of the chair, and the arm of the chair was worn off; it had been broken and had to be replaced because he always threw that left leg over the chair while he read."

Bartlett was a chain-smoker all of his life, "a cigarette in his hand. Lucky Strikes for most of his life and then he broke down and went to filters later on, and he smoked Marlboros. Or anything else he could scrounge." He had chronic bronchitis, and attempted to kick the smoking habit from time to time, but it was a losing battle. Early in 1964 he told a friend that "one day surely I shall commence to examine and to start thinking seriously of quitting smoking." A report of the Surgeon General of the United States — prompted by religious fanatics and puritan groups, Bartlett believed—had concluded that cigarettes were dangerous to the smoker's health. The report nevertheless had made him so nervous, he confessed, that "I find myself smoking more than ever."

Senator Maurine B. Neuberger of Oregon, a good friend, alerted Bartlett to a new cigarette called Carlton, which featured "holes in the side to allow the smoke to escape so it doesn't get to your lungs." "Let me know what you think of it," Mrs. Neuberger asked, because "I can still taste the miserable thing." Bartlett already had tried the new cigarette, he reported, and found it a great invention: "The more effort placed in the inhalation process, the faster the smoke jumps out those little holes. The Carlton is, indeed, a cure for everything except total disarrangement of the nervous system."

Bartlett never quit smoking, even late in his life when cigarettes had been strictly forbidden because of his bad heart. A neighbor often observed him walking along Forty-ninth Street, N.W., a beautiful curving, tree-lined street in the Berkeley-Foxhall district, a block off McArthur Boulevard where he lived. As soon as Bartlett was shielded from any observation from his house, he looked nervously back over his shoulder and then lit up the taboo weed.[7]

As did her older sister, Susie liked the frequent Sunday-morning sourdough pancake breakfasts, where "we had some of the hottest shots in town," and the many dinner parties: "Bartlett was at his finest at things like that, a very witty man, just incredibly witty. I can remember being in that dining room, being very little, and watching all these people have a good time listening to the chatter, and Bartlett would entertain them with tall tales."

Both Bartletts insisted that their daughters speak and write proper English: "We spoke precise, proper English in our home. It was a game. Words were always a game . . . and if I'd learn a new one I'd try it out, and he would guffaw and carry on and tell if it was used correctly." Bob had an obsession with the correct use of the

English language: "You could never say 'an Alaskan sunset'— it had to be an 'Alaska sunset.'" Bartlett had an excellent command of the English language and could explain the most complex subject in the sparsest fashion.[8]

Bartlett's command of English and his sense of humor were reflected in his wide-ranging correspondence. On March 1, 1954, as he was about to enter the House chamber, a number of Puerto Rican nationalists started a shooting spree, which wounded five congressmen. "I gave some thought to dashing into the fray and capturing whoever was doing the shooting," he reported to a friend, "but decided to reflect on that a bit further and in order to establish the proper atmosphere for thinking, moved behind a nearby and very thick pillar. I had been there quite briefly when the limited space became extremely crowded and the boys started to shove me aside." The doors of the House chamber "just then opened and numerous House members came galloping out seeking safety. Most everyone who had been in the vicinity later claimed credit for capturing one or more of the shooters," Bartlett recounted, and "I would have been in on the kill too finally if I had not been required to stop and tie a shoelace."

On another occasion, in June 1966, Bartlett attended a White House dinner in honor of the king of Saudi Arabia. All went well until the senator "was making an exit which I thought to be exceptionally stately and almost regal following the conclusion of the whole shebang, when I heard a noise on the floor. Looking down I discovered that my cummerbund had come undone and was lying on the floor in full view of all. Some people would have been distressed. I was."[9]

Alaskans are informal with one another, and Bartlett, as an old-timer, was included in this informality. His constituents addressed him as "Bob," and he cultivated the image of the ex-miner and veteran newsman until it became a part of his political personality. He entertained Washington friends with tall tales of wild gold-mining days with his father in the Alaska hills. These recollections of his mining and newspapering past helped him to maintain his Alaskan roots.[10]

Friends and acquaintances alike characterized Bartlett as "an easy-going fellow, a very human guy, a warm and human personality, so alive with his interest in the people he was with and so able to bring out a sense of humor and good feelings, a really delightful personality, a warm, naturally bright individual."

Bartlett stories abound in Washington and Alaska. A few will serve to illustrate the man's temperament and eccentricities.

One friend recalls having lunch with the delegate while Bartlett was campaigning in Fairbanks. When they met at noon, Bartlett kept chuckling to himself and then recounted the story of his morning breakfast at the Model Cafe. The proprietor of the establishment was known for hiring large and tall waitresses. One of these, "two ax-handles wide and six feet tall," came to greet him and take his order. "Do you think the cook would be able to prepare me a couple of basted eggs?" Bartlett asked hopefully. She looked him in the eyes steadily for a minute and then replied, "Basted, hell, he couldn't cook shit if you gave him a cupful."[11]

At a Washington–Alaska state dinner in the capital, staff member Frank Barton introduced his Georgia-born and -raised wife to the senator just before dinner began. After exchanging a few pleasantries, Bartlett excused himself by saying, "You know, we Alaskans like to go where the grub is" and headed for the dinner table. Mrs. Barton was dumbfounded. The "use of the term 'grub' to a delicate lady from Georgia" was not quite what she had expected.[12]

At one point on the campaign trail, Bob and a party of candidates flew into Cordova to give speeches in the high school auditorium. Before taking his seat on the rostrum, Bartlett made a quick dash to the restroom. After he had taken his seat, he looked into his lap and discovered to his embarrassment that his fly was unzipped. Having a program and a few other papers in his lap, he casually crossed his legs. As the audience listened attentively to the speakers, Bartlett slowly zipped up, glancing at the audience from time to time. He finally got to the top and looked up in relief only to see Mrs. Vic Rivers, a friend and member of the audience, making the V-for-victory sign.[13]

Bartlett liked off-color stories, much to the chagrin of Mary Lee Council, who refused to hear them. Margery Smith, however, did consent to listen. On Monday mornings she would wait for the buzzer, whose sound indicated to her whether Bartlett was in a good mood, a bad mood, or a let's-get-right-with-it mood. The good news buzz was a short one, and when it would sound, "he usually had a story to tell."[14]

Bartlett also collected erotic pictures. One particular Monday morning he could hardly wait to show her the cover of the *New Yorker* magazine, which had appeared with a picture of a fellow going through the jungle, "and if you looked very carefully you could see a great big erection in his pants." Some artist had apparently tricked the magazine. "And it hit the mails, and Bob got it, and he recognized what it was before anybody else did." Soon the story broke in public, and the magazine had to remove the issue with the offending cover from the newsstands.[15]

Among his prized possessions was a tray with a full-length nude picture of Marilyn Monroe, a gift from an oil man. It was inscribed, "With my everlasting love, to Bob [signed] Marilyn." Smith recalls the photo: "It was just a stark nude. It was a tray to serve drinks on. Well, Vide told him he couldn't have that thing around the house." He did keep it around the house, hiding it under the sofa.[16]

In Bartlett's office was a large old desk, a Senate relic, with a wide center drawer that he always kept locked. Mary A. Nordale remembers that sometimes during staff meetings "he'd open the drawer and look in it, and I always figured he was going after a pencil." One day, during a meeting where the senator was absent, she sat in Bartlett's chair behind his desk: "I happened to lean back, and I almost lost my balance. And I grabbed at the drawer, and it started to slide forward, and that drawer [was full of erotic pictures.] I just about choked. I shoved the drawer in, and I straightened up, and everybody thought I was startled because of being tipped over in the chair."[17]

Bartlett attracted a very competent and loyal staff, and he became very involved in the careers of his employees. He liked to take care of them and to draw them into a close family-type relationship. A number of the people working for him attended law school, and not a few owe their subsequent careers to the opportunities Bartlett offered them while they were working for him. William Foster, for example, now a successful lobbyist with a large Washington law firm, made his initial and very important contacts while working for the senator.[18]

For years Bartlett was in the habit of raising the salaries of his male employees whenever their wives gave birth to babies. This rankled the unmarried staff, and soon "the secretaries began muttering. They hadn't had a raise in two years or three, and these guys were newly married and just having children like peas out of a pod." Mary Nordale finally confronted Bartlett and explained to him the injustice of his pay system. If a job performance merited a raise, it should be given, she declared, and not merely because somebody had a new baby. But perhaps Bartlett was hinting to his female employees to get pregnant, she suggested. The senator "blushed and he snorted and he huffed and he puffed," but soon thereafter pay raises were given to all on a regular basis.[19]

Bartlett was a prodigious correspondent, dictating letters into a tape recorder, a machine he could not handle "worth diddly squat," according to Smith, who did much of the transcribing. Often she would type a two-page letter only to discover at the end of the tape that Bartlett had changed his mind, directing her to "scratch the whole thing. I don't want to say a word I have said in this letter."

When in Alaska, Bartlett carried notebooks in which he wrote the name of everybody to whom he talked as well as a summary of the subjects discussed. The names usually were legible, but the substantive notes which followed frequently were not—and the letters to his constituents were based on these notes. His office staff used to despair whenever he was in Alaska, because soon tapes would flood the office. They would find that often Bartlett had forgotten to punch a strategic button on the gadget which indicated he had changed his mind, or he would get away from the microphone and the typist would not be able to hear what he was saying. Sometimes he would decide to comment on little incidents happening along the campaign trail, and the gist of conversations which had taken place. Although entertaining, "it was absolutely chaotic" when the tapes arrived. "It got so bad, I used to just sit and laugh," Smith stated, and tell the secretaries to be patient, because "you might end up with two short letters, but here are six tapes."

After Mary Nordale had just joined the staff, she received a crash course in

Bartlett's ways of carrying on a vast correspondence while accompanying him on a campaign trip to Valdez. Bartlett dictated correspondence to her for a solid six hours: "I thought I was going to die, I was so tired, muscles sore and everything." It took her two weeks, working eight-hour days, to type that particular bundle of correspondence.[20]

The staff was amused about Bartlett's private toilet, which, he made very clear, was for his own use exclusively. None of them would dream of using his toilet, even if they couldn't make it to the one they were to use. The janitors, apparently, had no such scruples. Not only did they avail themselves of the facility after hours, they also threw into the bowl paper cups used in the office during the day. Even if flushed, paper cups did not go down, and Bartlett was annoyed many mornings to find them floating in the toilet bowl. He finally put up a sign which said: "Do Not Put Paper Cups in the John." One day, Jerry Grinstein, an assistant to Senator Warren Magnuson on the Senate Commerce Committee, called on Bartlett. During the course of their conversation he asked to use Bartlett's rest room. The senator graciously gave his permission. Some time later the staff heard Bartlett "laughing his head off." Grinstein had read the sign and penned a little note beneath it which read: "How about apple cores?"[21]

Bartlett had a passion for soft water. This was understandable in a person who had grown up in Fairbanks, where the water is heavily mineralized and quite discolored. Bartlett had to have his soft water, and he went "through a song and dance" every time the salt for the water softener had to be reordered. "Ho, that used to be a pain," Smith stated.[22]

Throughout his political life Bartlett maintained small checking accounts in various Alaskan communities. At one point Bartlett wrote to the banker in Petersburg, Alaska and asked what his balance was. The banker replied that Bartlett did not have any balance at all, that, in fact, he had "been making your checks good out of my own pocket." Bartlett immediately wanted to know how much he owed. The gentleman, however, told him to consider the money a campaign contribution. This willingness to accept small contributions on an informal basis endeared Bartlett to a number of Alaska's small town bankers.[23]

Bartlett went to the limit in rewarding and helping his friends, but he also believed in punishing his enemies. Cliff Cernick was an enemy, as far as the senator was concerned. Cernick had worked in Alaska on the *Anchorage Daily News*, where he wrote many anti-Democratic and anti-Bartlett stories. Most of these were crude, and Bartlett did not forget them. In later years Cernick went to work in California for the Federal Aviation Administration (FAA) as a public affairs representative. One day the Anchorage newspapers announced that Cernick had been appointed regional public affairs representative for the Federal Aviation Administration in Alaska. Bartlett was outraged and called the director of the

FAA and told him that Cernick was personally objectionable and would serve the FAA in Alaska only over his dead body. The director expressed his regret but stated that the appointment had already been made and that Cernick was on his way to Anchorage to take up his duties. Bartlett, by this time a senior and prestigious member of the Senate Commerce Committee, which had jurisdiction over the FAA, was not satisfied. He called the White House, and President Johnson gave the Federal Aviation Administration director appropriate orders. Cernick did not serve in Alaska as long as Bartlett was alive. He was transferred to Anchorage years later.[24]

Katherine Nordale, on the other hand, was Bartlett's friend. Her husband had been killed in an airplane crash, leaving her a widow with two small children to raise. Bartlett became a substitute father to the children. In 1943 he helped Katherine get an appointment as a representative of the United States Treasury, selling war bonds throughout Alaska. In the late 1940s she went to work for the Federal Security Agency, and in 1950 Bartlett was able to have her appointed Collector of Customs for Alaska. In the early 1960s he pushed through her appointment as postmaster in Juneau. Bartlett helped many others in Alaska, if not necessarily with a job appointment, then at least with friendly counsel.[25]

Throughout his political life, Bartlett worried about his weight. As long as he worked physically, he had no problem controlling it. Stocky and powerfully built at 5 feet, 10 inches, he weighed approximately 160 pounds during his mining days, but political life and the lack of physical exercise soon put pounds on his frame. In early 1951 he confessed to a friend that "I am now weighing in at 194½ and am two inches bigger around the middle than a hogshead. For a long time it was possible to argue with a sincere belief that the cleaners were shrinking my clothes, but even I am past that point now." After a physical examination in 1959 disclosed that he had diabetes mellitus, Bartlett went on a diet that restricted his consumption of carbohydrates and his weight thereafter fluctuated between 146 and 155 pounds. He took diabetic pills and became very concerned about the disease. An associate recalled that "he got to be a fanatic on diabetes, and he used to hand out to anyone . . .these little papers that you piddled on, and if it turned a certain color you better watch out; you had diabetes." In fact, Bartlett's health had been deteriorating for a long time. Always very nervous and unable to relax, he smoked too much and suffered many headaches. In 1949, he wrote in jest to a friend that he was getting ready to file an application for the Pioneer's Home because the dentist had just "yanked out the remaining upper teeth I had and slapped in a set of false ones. Everyone who has them tells me I'll be overjoyed soon. I wonder." In 1956, after considerable nagging from "the girls in the office" and after Vide alleged that Bartlett looked as if he were "about to go into a state of decline," he finally made an appointment for a physical examination. All was in order and even his lungs were "clear as a bell. This simply enraged Vide, who was sure that they were filled up with nicotines and tars of various kinds from too many cigarettes. I was a little amazed myself," he confessed, "because I was sure I had four or five cancers growing there."[26]

Besides his smoking, Bartlett also had periodic problems with alcohol. Like so many of his contemporaries who had also grown to manhood during the prohibition era, he associated liquor with machismo, daring, virility, and maturity. Unfortunately, he was allergic to alcohol. Only a couple of drinks would make his eyes puff out and his skin turn blotchy. After he went to Washington, he vowed he would not drink again, and for the most part he kept his promise. Occasionally, however, he would fall "off the wagon" and go on a binge, which at times lasted as long as a week. One staffer recalled receiving a phone call from Chief Powell of the Capitol Police Force. He requested that she take the call in the privacy of the senator's office, and he asked her whether she knew where Bartlett was. Bartlett was supposed to be in the Caribbean, but she was informed that he was in jail in Las Vegas, Nevada instead, having gambled and drunk too much. The matter was covered up.

Although some Bartlett associates knew that he had liked to drink before coming to Congress, few were aware of his later occasional binges. George Sundborg, an old political friend, had heard of Bartlett's problems with alcohol but "never saw Bob take a drink. I was told that he had vowed not to drink while serving in Congress." Instead, reports Sundborg, Bartlett "cheerfully watched me pour drinks for myself from his bottles," while he would drink enormous quantities of Dad's Root Beer. It was not until 1967 that Sundborg, at one of the many cocktail parties for congressional members, noticed Bartlett "sipping from a tall glass something which looked suspiciously unlike Dad's Root Beer." Bartlett cheerily replied that yes, he was having a drink that night, "the first one in a long time."[27]

Even though Vide knew better, she always maintained that Bartlett did not drink. Perhaps drinking did not agree with her image of a public man, or perhaps his occasional lapses were too painful for her.

By and large, however, Bob and Vide maintained a good relationship with each other over the years. Vide was his most trusted political advisor, and she became a very competent politician in her own right.

How can a marriage endure for close to thirty-five years? Bartlett asked himself that in 1965 and observed that until very recently he would have been unable to give a convincing answer. But now an explanation was easy, he claimed, for he had found an old note Vide had written when she thought she would be out when he returned home. The note simply stated, "heat slowly or wait for me." Under those conditions, Bartlett remarked, a marriage could not fail.[28]

CHAPTER

Sickness and Death

F RIENDS HAD COME FROM ALL over the United States to Fairbanks to pay their last respects to Alaska's senior United States senator, E. L. "Bob" Bartlett. But Alaskans and his colleagues from Washington, D. C., where he had served his country, his territory, and later his state so well for twenty-four years, felt his loss particularly keenly.

In Alaska's interior, December 14 is a time of deep darkness, the nadir of the year, with subzero temperatures and less than four hours of daylight. This did not deter Bartlett's many friends. Those who had come, the high and the mighty, the lowly and the humble, all had to be accommodated. The crowd was so large that it was necessary to transfer the funeral services from St. Matthew's Episcopal Church to the larger Catholic Sacred Heart Cathedral. Bartlett had been a nominal Episcopalian and had told Vide that "I should prefer Episcopal services with the Pioneers [of Alaska] present but not participating too actively. And at graveside if possible only recitation of 'Home is the Sailor.'"[1]

Still, it is hard to bury a man like Bob Bartlett simply. Using the facilities of the Catholic cathedral made the ceremony truly ecumenical.

After the services the immediate family and a few close friends buried Bartlett's body in the frozen ground at Northern Lights Memorial Park, next to the grave of Ray Wrede, an old friend and mining partner.[2] Northern Lights Memorial Park is located on the edge of Fairbanks and the northern wilderness that make up so much of the Alaska that Bartlett loved.

Alaska's senior senator had undergone heart surgery on November 21, 1968, in a Cleveland hospital. He had lain critically ill for nearly three weeks after the surgery and finally died of an internal hemorrhage on December 11, 1968, at the age of sixty-four. Bartlett, the son of Klondike gold rush parents, at last had returned to his home town in the state which he had helped fashion and which he had loved and had ably represented.

Although a strapping and healthy individual as a young man, Bartlett was plagued throughout his life by various allergies. His eyes were bad, and as a boy he

238

had undergone surgery to correct crossed eyes. After he quit mining in 1938, he did not take care of his body properly. He never exercised. He smoked three packs of Lucky Strike cigarettes a day for most of his life and only later switched to filter cigarettes, believing they were healthier. He coughed endlessly and had chronic bronchitis and frequent respiratory infections.

Bartlett, as noted, also had a problem with alcohol. If he had "his first drink, that was it. He could not say 'just one drink tonight.' Never could he do that. He could not have a beer, he could not have wine. His first drink started a binge." And although Bartlett controlled his drinking sprees, particularly in later life, they must have taken their physical toll. "He certainly never was the walking insurance man's dream," his daughter Susie, a nurse, recalled. "He's what they call the type A personality" in the field of cardiology — one susceptible to heart problems.[2]

Bartlett had been suspicious about his health as early as 1957. A medical check-up at the office of the Capitol physician and at Bethesda Naval Hospital revealed no organic difficulties but showed a high blood-sugar content, though no diabetes. On August 24, 1959, another examination revealed that he had diabetes mellitus. An electrocardiogram and medical evaluation revealed that he very likely might suffer a coronary attack in the not-too-distant future.[3]

In April 1965, when Bartlett was unable to rid himself of a case of the flu, he again worried about his health. To a friend, he confided that he had "never felt more miserable in my life than I did last week. Terrible in fact. My body was in a deplorable state, and my mind couldn't function at all." At Bethesda Naval Hospital, examining physicians found that his blood pressure was too high. Proper medication brought it down, yet it took Bartlett months to feel like his old self again.

In the spring of 1966 he once again caught the flu. This time he felt extremely tired and worn-out for a period of months. In August of that year the senator again fell ill with a persistent cold. A checkup at Bethesda revealed that sometime between April and August of that year, he had suffered a coronary attack due to arteriosclerotic heart disease. This explained his constant fatigue and low level of energy. Bartlett professed not to be worried, for it had "been a good life, made just as I should have wanted it."[4]

The senator's office announced that he had suffered a "minor heart attack some time ago." Medical tests showed that Bartlett had suffered a coronary occlusion. The attending physician prescribed a period of complete rest for the senator but also stated that "an early release is contemplated." Most important to Bartlett, however, he had been assured that he would be able to resume his Senate duties and go to Alaska to campaign for reelection that fall.[5]

From the fall of 1966 onward, however, Bartlett's health deteriorated rapidly. That December the Bartletts decided to spend Christmas in Europe. They flew to

Madrid, where Bob fell ill. Vide called the hotel physician, who understood little English. Vide remembers: "Between the two of us we had one terrible time trying to make each other understood. Between my poor Spanish and his poor English and the sign language...the doctor and I, in our stumbling way," agreed that Bob had pneumonia. It was then a week before he was able to take a meal in the dining room. Bob, still very weak, and Vide left Madrid and flew to San Juan, Puerto Rico and from there to St. Croix for hot sun and rest.[6]

There were no further problems until the middle of 1967, when Bartlett again entered Bethesda Naval Hospital with heart trouble. After a short time in the intensive care unit, he remained in the hospital under observation. Soon he resumed his work, but he did not feel well.

In December 1967 the Bartletts attended an aviation dinner in Washington. Just after he had started to eat, Bartlett "clutched himself [and turned] as white as death." They left the dinner, and after arriving home, Bartlett had another attack. Vide phoned Dr. Alan Weintraub, a family friend, who called an ambulance that transported the senator to Georgetown University Hospital. There he was treated for pericarditis, an inflammation of the heart lining. Released on January 10, 1968, Bob went home for convalescense and returned to his Senate office in February. On June 6 he again entered Bethesda Naval Hospital for what was diagnosed as lung congestion. After spending ten days under intensive care, he returned home but soon thereafter complained of shortness of breath and was readmitted to Bethesda. Doctors quickly found that he had suffered a coronary occlusion sometime during the previous ten days. Home once again, he suffered another heart attack on June 22 and again was rushed to the hospital, where he stayed in intensive care for some days.

In August Bartlett took a trip on the old Mississippi River passenger paddle-wheeler *Delta Queen,* for which he had pushed through special legislation to allow the boat to operate. While on board he became ill with what a physician among the passengers diagnosed as another heart attack. The problem turned out to be a case of angina. Taken off the boat at East Liverpool, Ohio, he was admitted to the hospital there. The next morning a coast guard plane fetched the senator and flew him back to Washington for tests at Bethesda Naval Hospital.[7]

Friends advised Bartlett to skip the Democratic National Convention opening on August 26 in Chicago, but he was determined to go, although "he looked like death warmed over." Vide accompanied him to Chicago and all went well. At the conclusion of the convention, Bartlett decided to accept an invitation for a flight to Bergen, Norway, and then on to Rome. The invitation had been extended several times before, but Bartlett never had found the time to accept. Vide remembers: "He was determined to go. So we went. We got into Bergen, cold and raining. It was just like Ketchikan at its worst." She was "scared to death to get out of the country, scared to death that something could happen." The weather was horrible and neither had brought along enough clothes to keep warm.

They left Bergen and flew on to Rome. After two days of sightseeing, Bartlett suffered a severe angina attack, "a super duper," as Vide called it. Nevertheless, he was determined to see the poet Shelley's grave and the Sistine Madonna in the Vatican. They found the grave and on a subsequent day went to St. Peter's Cathedral, climbing many steps to get to it. From there they walked and walked to get to the Sistine Chapel: "We'd get maybe a block and then Bob would have to sit down." They reached their destination, and after returning to the hotel Bartlett had another severe angina attack. Vide now insisted that they return home immediately in order to be close to medical facilities.[8]

Back in Washington, Bartlett soon became restless. He and Vide flew to Freeport in the Bahamas in October. Everything seemed fine for four or five days, "and then one day down on the beach . . . he had an extremely bad angina attack, or it could have been a heart attack . . . right there in the chair and he began to get white and the perspiration was rolling off of him . . . ." Vide took him back to the hotel, where he suffered a series of painful attacks. For a few days afterward, everything seemed normal once more. But he was beset by additional attacks at the casino, where he had gone for some gambling, and Vide took him back to the hotel: "I don't know how many nitroes he took, and he went to sleep and he slept finally. I don't know how many times I touched him to see if he was alive." They returned to Washington, D. C. ahead of schedule.[9]

There Admiral R. J. Pearson, Jr., the Capitol physician, recommended that Bartlett undergo testing at a Cleveland, Ohio clinic to determine the degree of hardening of the arteries and to find out whether surgery was indicated. Bartlett was told that since the Cleveland clinic's program had been inaugurated in 1962, more than two thousand patients had been treated with internal mammary artery implants there. He phoned Congressman William St. Onge of Connecticut, who had been through the clinic's standard operating procedure. St. Onge explained that generally the surgeons waited six weeks after the examination to operate but that in his case, he was operated on four days after the tests. St. Onge told Bartlett that he sported a fourteen-inch-long scar. "Some make it, some don't," he cautioned Bartlett, who decided to at least have the tests.[10]

On November 12, 1968, Bartlett underwent the testing in Cleveland. To his office staff, he reported that "an incision is made in the arm and an artery opened. Then a catheter is put through to the heart. X-ray pictures are taken constantly and there is a hook-up made in some way or another beyond my comprehension that enables the doctor performing the job to watch the whole thing on TV." The next day he received the report: "The heart is not too badly scarred. If it is, corrective measures are impossible. But two of the main arteries to the heart are blocked entirely. They have thrown out some branches which take up some of the slack, although not too much. An operation was recommended. I consented." In the surgical procedure, the senator's two mammary arteries were to be implanted into the front and rear of his heart's left ventricle. Even though it involved some risks, Bartlett realized that the operation represented his only hope of ever functioning in a nearly normal fashion again: "If the operation is successful, in time — generally about six months — these arteries will perform a good share of the work originally done by the now-blocked vessels."[11]

The physicians told Bartlett that after coming to after surgery, "I will feel like I'm dying. [The next day] I'll wish that I could die, and on the third day there will be a little bit of personal hope. So here goes!"[12]

The operation was scheduled for November 21. A few days beforehand, the senator informed his staff that he had talked with Dr. Donald B. Effler, the surgeon "who is going to cut me up Thursday. I spoke pretty strictly to him and told him that he was carrying a heavy responsibility in hacking away at me, not because I was a U.S. senator" but because a regrettable change in the law enabled the governor of Alaska, Republican Walter Hickel, to appoint an individual from either political party. "I have a strong feeling, although not the definite knowledge, that the governor of Alaska would not appoint a successor of my political faith." (Bartlett's fears were justified because Ted Stevens, the Republican House majority leader helped push a measure through that body, subsequently also approved by the Senate, which allowed the governor to appoint a member of either party to a vacancy in Congress. Previously, such a position had to be filled by a member of the same party as the incumbent. After Bartlett's death, Hickel appointed Stevens to fill the seat.) Furthermore, the surgeon had the obligation to keep Bartlett alive until the spring of 1970 "so I may have the benefit and enjoyment that comes by reason of lower income taxes upon attainment of age 65. I think Dr. Effler was impressed," Bartlett concluded, because "he promised not to let his knife slip."[13]

A day before the scheduled surgery, the Bartletts arrived in Cleveland. Vide remembers that Bartlett "was feeling real great about it. I'm sure he had a great deal of confidence, real confidence that it was going to be all right, real confidence because I don't think he was trying to boost my morale any because I could put up a front, too. I don't think he knew how scared I was, but he might have." The Bartletts dined at a restaurant overlooking the city. Afterwards they went to the hospital, where the senator checked in. Vide recalls: "I went with him to his room, and we sat and visited and he was trying to get me to go and get him a cigarette, last cigarette before surgery." But Vide did not want to go against the doctor's orders and refused him. Bartlett did have still another wish. "If the Grim Reaper should snatch me, there is one specific request I make relating to my estate," he wrote, and that is "give all the cigarette lighters in the office to MAN [Mary A. Nordale]. If you do this she will have enough to last her for a long lifetime."[14]

Much to their surprise, Stanley McCutcheon, an old friend and political associate from Anchorage, joined them in the hospital that last night before surgery. The talk was light and bantering before Vide and Stanley were ushered out by the nurse on duty. "That's the last time I ever saw Bob in even normal condition," remembers Vide.[15]

Although the physicians predicted a normal recovery, Bartlett suffered a cardiac arrest nine days after the operation. Doctors managed to restart his heart through a combination of external and open chest heart massage. To be effective, external massage requires that considerable pressure be applied, and during the procedure one of his ribs broke, penetrating his left lung, which collapsed. Bartlett apparently was unconscious at the time. When he regained consciousness he wrote a note, asking "What happened, when did this happen, where was I?" Vide told him that the physicians had performed a tracheotomy to help his breathing. In the meantime a coast guard plane flew Dr. Pearson to Cleveland to check on the senator. Pearson reported that it was fortunate that a nurse had been in Bartlett's room when he had suffered the cardiac arrest. Bartlett must have been drifting in and out of consciousness during Pearson's visit, because he wrote a note to Vide asking her: "Was Admiral Pearson here yesterday, or is it my imagination?" On December 2 Margery Smith told the staff, "The boss is tough, and given any type of good fortune, for which he is long overdue, he will be back with us some time next year."[16]

Soon, however, Bartlett suffered a chest infection, then two more cardiac arrests. Doctors put him once again on the operating table to clean out the infection and repair the lung. His condition, however, deteriorated rapidly, and on December 6 he suffered heart fibrillation, a condition in which the heart loses its normal beating rhythm and contracts rapidly without coordination. Once again doctors controlled the situation, but at this point the senator hovered near death. Suddenly, however, the infection cleared up, and Bartlett seemed a bit more alert. On December 8 his doctors expressed cautious optimism.[17]

On the evening of December 11, Vide and her oldest daughter, Doris Ann, returned to their hotel, the Bolton Square, just a few blocks from the hospital. When they arrived at the hotel, they were told to go immediately to the hospital: "And we ran. We just ran all the way over there. And got up to whatever floor it was, and we were waiting out there, and the priest and the doctor walked up toward us together and said, 'It's all over.'" Bartlett had died of an internal hemorrhage at 8:25 P.M. EST. After claiming his belongings, Vide unrolled his clothing and found a package of cigarettes in his robe pocket with one cigarette gone. Bartlett had managed to have his last smoke after all.[18]

Alaskan politics clearly had changed. Even prior to the death of the senator, old-time Alaskan Democratic politician Ralph Rivers was defeated by Republican Howard Pollock in his 1966 bid for reelection to Alaska's lone seat in the U.S. House. Egan, too, was defeated for election to a third term in that year. As noted, veteran Ernest Gruening suffered a primary defeat in his bid for a third Senate term in 1968 and subsequently lost his write-in campaign for the Senate seat in the general elections in the fall of 1968. Two hours before Bartlett died, President-elect Richard M. Nixon appointed Alaska Governor Walter J. Hickel to the post of secretary of the Interior. Keith H. Miller, the secretary of state, took over the governorship, and Hickel appointed Anchorage attorney and state representative Ted Stevens to fill the Senate seat vacated by Bartlett's death.

Bob Bartlett had served his territory and state well for twenty-four years, and editorial writers around the state praised him. *Jessen's Weekly* of Fairbanks characterized him as "rugged, virile, kind, generous, and one of the most honorable of men, [whose] unfailing courtesy and kindly interest endeared him alike to all and created for him a cosmopolitan circle of staunch friends. [His] uncompromising integrity made his name a synonym for square dealing throughout a lifetime residency in Alaska and Washington, DC." *The Anchorage Daily Times,* whose publisher and editor, Robert B. Atwood, had been a close Bartlett associate in the long statehood struggle, stated that "we know of no one who has ever been recognized, trusted, and revered as he was." Alaska's population, the editorial remarked, is known for its "individualism, divisiveness, sectionalism, arrogance, and clannishness. Yet he held them united behind him for 24 years—a longevity in public office that is unequalled. On ten different occasions the stubborn, unmanageable, belligerent and politically erratic populace of Alaska handed him the crown with election returns as much as 81 percent in his favor."[19] The *Fairbanks Daily News-Miner* referred to Bartlett as "Alaska's most revered citizen," adding that it was not often that a politician "can reach the plateau of devotion that Alaskans held for Senator Bob Bartlett. It was a devotion, however, that was well-founded, and returned in kind. For Bob Bartlett was that kind of man. He devoted the last quarter of a century of his life to his fellow Alaskans."[20]

State Senator-elect Joe Josephson, who had worked for Bartlett in Washington from 1957 to 1960, recalled that "Bob Bartlett was a perfect gentleman. He respected everyone as a member of the human family; he labored for everyone— not just friends, or just contributors, or just Democrats." Most importantly, perhaps, was that "he didn't wear intellectuality on his sleeve, and he never strove consciously to impress anyone with bigness or smartness. He was a stranger to pretense or pretentiousness. But he was a reader, a thinker, a mind of breadth and depth, and he could master the fine print in a bill or a budget."[21]

Alaskans grieved at the death of Bob Bartlett, and his many friends and associates, both in Washington and in Alaska, sent their condolences. An Alaskan friend perhaps best summed up Bartlett's qualities as a man and a politician. "He lacked that flamboyance," the writer stated, "so often the handmaiden of insincerity, which makes the person of a man well talked about. Nor did he have that gross incapacity in some particular, which makes a man the butt on a special point. People talked about Bartlett's ideas or what he might do or not do, not about the accidents of his life. He was a whole man. He was also a moderate one, not out of any lack of conviction, for his convictions were unmistakeably vigorous, but from the depth of understanding of his fellow man which kept him from harsh judgments on the frailties of others."[22]

CHAPTER **20**

Epilogue

EVEN A DECADE AFTER HIS DEATH, Alaskans still remembered Bob Bartlett with love and affection. Most recollections begin with a personal anecdote about how the individual recalled frequently seeing Bartlett on the campaign trail, drinking a cup of coffee, smoking a cigarette, head cocked, listening to whomever was talking. Bartlett was always a familiar figure, never a remote politician away in Washington, D.C. He was "just a wonderful friend, and he was very, very kindhearted, and he was good company. He was fun to be around...we loved him very much...he was just a wonderful friend to us—not only to us but to loads of people and certainly to Alaska."[1]

Bartlett was a worldly and sophisticated politician who embodied the cunning shrewdness of the Alaskan frontier of his boyhood. But he deliberately shunned the glamour of life on the Potomac that often separated the successful politician from his humble origins and often, also, from his congressional seat. Well known, liked, and respected in Washington, he never lost touch with his constituents, because he was genuinely concerned for their welfare.

During a long apprenticeship in the House, Bartlett became a master of successfully forging a coalition between competing interests among his own and potential supporters and among his opposition in Congress, who also had to be placated. For example, some of Bartlett's constituents wanted statehood; others desired a continuation of the territorial status but desired to elect their own governor and to control Alaska's fish and game resources; others desired commonwealth status instead of statehood; others wanted statehood with certain qualifications; and still others did not care one way or the other. Bartlett was elected time and again by suggesting that, in regard to these and other matters, he would support all of these people in their aspirations, as diverse as they might be.

Once Bartlett came to Congress and took his seat with other representatives, a range of issues came into view which he had never considered in his dialogue with his constituency. He felt that many of his constituents might conceivably be interested in these new issues, while others would not be. On what points, Bartlett pondered, should he solicit their views, and which opinions, if rendered, should he ignore? Furthermore, on what portions of any one issue should he carefully inform the voters, and on which ones would it be beneficial if they were to remain ignorant? Often issues came up in which Alaskans had no direct interest or opinion. Could he, in such a neutral issue, indulge in his own private views? Clearly he could not, he decided, because he had to secure the future cooperation of men whose constituencies did not care about matters of vital concern to Alaskans but whose support Alaska might desperately need nonetheless. Bartlett, therefore, voted accordingly, representing his constituents on matters unbeknownst to them or in which they had no interest at all.

Bartlett's greatest asset was his wholly undoctrinaire approach to politics. Faced with a legislative problem, he was remarkably free of preconceived ideas, a quality that helped him to attain his political and legislative goals. Bartlett believed in the constitutional tenet that government should promote the general welfare, and he therefore felt that it was the federal government's proper role to fund and expand the economy through political action, to stabilize the social system in which individuals made their own way. In short, Bartlett believed that individualism and freedom were based on each person fully utilizing his or her talents in a stable and expanding American economic system. In this respect, he was neither a unique figure nor an aberration in American politics.

Throughout his entire political life, Bartlett was single-mindedly determined to help fashion the Alaska he loved so well into a modern economic, social, and political community. As a delegate, Bartlett believed that the federal government, acting as Alaska's colonial master, had a responsibility to contribute substantially toward that goal. As U.S. senator, he recognized that Alaska was rich in undeveloped resources that would some day make it a great and prosperous state and a contributor to the national economy. But he felt that such was not the case during its transition from territoriality to statehood and that during this period it needed massive federal assistance to overcome the retardation imposed upon it by past federal neglect and inaction.

Although as a politician, Bartlett had to perform many difficult and unpleasant tasks, public life rewarded him richly. As he rose within the political hierarchy, Bartlett attained certain perquisites, such as power, high visibility, and the personal acquaintance of the movers and shakers in political life. All of this undoubtedly satisfied his considerable ego. Politics was his passion, and he died a fulfilled man.

NOTES

Notes

CHAPTER 1

1 Based on family history documents, Private Papers, Vide Bartlett.

2 Interview with Forbes Baker, November 24, 1974, North Pole, Alaska.

3 Vide Bartlett talking to Tanana-Yukon Historical Society, November 22, 1965, Tape No. 13, University of Alaska Archives, Fairbanks, Alaska.

4 Tanana Directory, 1907, University of Alaska Archives, Fairbanks, Alaska.

5 Duane Koenig, "Ghost Railway in Alaska: The Story of the Tanana Valley Railroad," in *Alaska and its History,* ed. by Morgan B. Sherwood (Seattle and London: University of Washington Press, 1967), pp. 395-396; *Fairbanks Daily News,* December 12, 1907.

6 Interview with Charley Geis, April 15, 1975, Casa Grande, Arizona; Robert Bloom, Interview University of Alaska Archives, H-74.

7 R. Bloom; Interview with Vide Bartlett, April 1974, Fairbanks, Alaska.

8 Interview with C. Geis, April 15, 1975, Casa Grande, Arizona.

9 E. L. "Bob" Bartlett, "An Alaskan Boyhood," in *The Alaskan Quarterly,* summer, 1954, pp. 5–7, 33.

10 Interview with C. Geis, April 15, 1975, Casa Grande, Arizona.

11 *Ibid.*

12 Interview with Mrs. Robert Bloom, October 4, 1961, entitled "Early Life in Fairbanks," tape H-132, University of Alaska Archives, Fairbanks, Alaska.

13 Interview with C. Geis, April 15, 1975, Casa Grande, Arizona.

14, 15, 16, 17 *Ibid.*

18 Margaret E. Murie, *Two in the Far North* (New York: Alfred A. Knopf, 1970), p. 61.

19 E. L. Bartlett, "Alaskan Boyhood."

20 George W. Rogers and Richard A. Cooley, *Alaska's Population and Economy: Regional Growth, Development and Future Outlook* (Fairbanks, Alaska: ISEGR, 1963), Volume 1, Analysis, p. 19.

21 Interview with C. Geis, April 15, 1975, Casa Grande, Arizona

22 E. L. Bartlett, "Alaska Boyhood."

23 Interview with C. Geis, April 15, 1975, Casa Grande, Arizona

24 *Ibid.*

25 Interview with Vide Bartlett, April 1974, Fairbanks, Alaska.

26 Ida Bartlett to Ed Bartlett, April 24, 13, 1917, Private Papers, Vide Bartlett.

27 Interview with Vide Bartlett, April 1974, Fairbanks, Alaska

28 E. L. Bartlett report cards, Private Papers, Vide Bartlett.

29 E. L. Bartlett, "Alaskan Boyhood."

30, 31 *Ibid.*

32 E. L. Bartlett, "Alaskan Boyhood."

33 Interview with C. Geis, April 15, 1975, Casa Grande, Arizona.

34 *Ibid.*

35 Interview with Vide Bartlett, April 1974, Fairbanks, Alaska; Constance L. Edmunds to E. L. Bartlett, June 9, 1921, Private Papers, Vide Bartlett.

36 Interview with Vide Bartlett, April 1974, Fairbanks, Alaska.

37 *Ibid.*

38 High School graduation announcement, 1922, E. L. Bartlett Papers, Personal file, 1935–68, box 17, folder general, 1965, E. L. Bartlett Papers, University of Alaska Archives, Fairbanks, Alaska; Interview with Vide Bartlett, April 1974, Fairbanks, Alaska.

39 *Fairbanks Daily News-Miner,* hereafter cited as *FDNM,* November 13, 1963, Progress Edition; Interview with Vide Bartlett, April 1974, Fairbanks, Alaska.

40 *FDNM,* November 13, 1963, Progress Edition; Interview with F. Baker, November 24, 1974, North Pole, Alaska.

41 Interview with F. Baker, November 24, 1974, North Pole, Alaska; *FDNM,* November 13, 1963, Progress Edition.

42 Interview with Vide Bartlett, April 1974, Fairbanks, Alaska.

43 *Ibid.*

CHAPTER 2

This chapter is based on correspondence and newspaper clippings in Vide Bartlett's private papers, as well as an interview with Vide Bartlett in November 1975 in Fairbanks, Alaska.

CHAPTER 3

1 Claus M. Naske, *An Interpretative History of Alaskan Statehood* (Anchorage, Alaska: Alaska Northwest Publishing Company, 1973), p. 52.

2 *New York Times,* April 25, 1932, 7:4; *Ibid.,* April 28, 3:2; *Ibid.,* October 16, II 6:6.

3 Interview with Vide Bartlett, November 14, 1975, Fairbanks, Alaska.

4 *Ibid.*

5 E. L. Bartlett to Vide, February 16, March 2, 1933, Private Papers, Vide Bartlett.

6 Richard B. Morris, *Encyclopedia of American History,* (New York and Evanston: Harper & Row, Publishers, 1961), p. 341.

7 Interview with Vide Bartlett, November 14, 1975, Fairbanks, Alaska.

8, 9, *Ibid.*

10 William Manchester, *The Glory and the Dream; A Narrative History of America, 1932–1972* (Boston-Toronto: Little, Brown and Company, 1973), I p. 95.

11 Ernest Gruening, *The State of Alaska* (2nd ed.; New York: Random House, 1968), p. 298.

12 *Ibid.*

13 E. L. Bartlett to Vide, February 6, 1935, Private Papers, Vide Bartlett.

14 E. L. Bartlett to Vide, February 12, 1935, Private Papers, Vide Bartlett.

15 Clarence Burglin to E. L. Bartlett, telegram, August 29, 1935, E. L. Bartlett Papers, Personal file, box 11, folder general, 1935–38, University of Alaska Archives, Fairbanks, Alaska.

16 E. L. Bartlett to Vide, August, 1935, Private Papers, Vide Bartlett.

CHAPTER 4

1 Interview with Vide Bartlett, April, 1974, Fairbanks Alaska.

2 E.L. Bartlett interview, October 10, 1965, University of Alaska Archives, Fairbanks, Alaska.

3 Telegram Ed Bartlett, September 15, 1933. Private Papers, Vide Bartlett.

4 Interview with Vide Bartlett, April, 1974, Fairbanks, Alaska.

5 Unidentified newspaper clipping, box 10, E. L. Bartlett Personal file, University of Alaska Archives, Fairbanks, Alaska.

6 Information supplied by Professors Ernest Wolff and William R. Hunt, University of Alaska, Fairbanks, Alaska.

7 CAF-11, $3,800 per annum, E. L. Bartlett Personal file, general, 1939, box 12, University of Alaska Archives, Fairbanks, Alaska.

8 Interview with Doris Ann Bartlett Riley, April 9, 1975, Eugene, Oregon.

9 E. L. Bartlett Personal file, general, 1939, box 12, University of Alaska Archives, Fairbanks, Alaska.

10 E. L. Bartlett to Vide, May 1, 1938, Private Papers, Vide Bartlett, throughout.

11 E. L. Bartlett to Vide, May 3, 1938.

12 E. L. Bartlett to Vide, May 6, 1938.

13 E. L. Bartlett to Vide, May 9, 1938.

14 E. L. Bartlett to Vide, May 10, 1938.

15 E. L. Bartlett to Vide, May 10, 1938.

16 E. L. Bartlett to Vide, May 11, 1938.

17 E. L. Bartlett to Vide, May 15, 1938.

18 E. L. Bartlett to Vide, May 21, 1938.

19 E. L. Bartlett to Vide, May 23, 1938.

20 E. L. Bartlett to Vide, Memorial Day, 1938.

21 E. L. Bartlett to Vide, June 10, 1938.

22 E. L. Bartlett to Vide, June 24, 1938.

23 E. L. Bartlett to Vide, July 26, 1938.

24 E. L. Bartlett to Vide, July 26, 1938.

25 E. L. Bartlett to Vide, August 2, 1938.

26 E. L. Bartlett to Vide, August 19, 2, 1938.

27 E. L. Bartlett to Vide, August 2, 1938.

28 E. L. Bartlett to Vide, August 10, 1938.

29 E. L. Bartlett to Vide, August 19, 1938.

30 E. L. Bartlett to Vide, August 2, 1938.

31 E. L. Bartlett to Vide, August 26, 1938.

CHAPTER 5

1 Victor C. Rivers to Anthony J. Dimond, January 14, 1939, John W. Troy to First Assistant Secretary of the Interior Ebert K. Burlew, January 12, 1939, E. L. Bartlett Papers, Personal file, box 4, folder general, 1939; Governor John W. Troy to Secretary of the Interior Harold L. Ickes, January 31, 1939, E. L. Bartlett Papers, Personal file, box 4, folder Secretary of Alaska, 1939–42, University of Alaska Archives, Fairbanks, Alaska.

2 E. L. Bartlett to Vide, February 9, 1939, Private Papers, Vide Bartlett.

3 Ernest Gruening, *Many Battles: The Autobiography of Ernest Gruening* (New York: Liveright, 1973), pp. 281–284.

4 Interview with Vide Bartlett, April 1974, Fairbanks, Alaska.

5 *Ibid.;* Gruening to Troy, November 17, 1939, E. L. Bartlett Papers, Personal file, 1935–68, box 12, folder general, 1939, University of Alaska Archives, Fairbanks, Alaska.

6 Interview with Vide Bartlett, April 1974, Fairbanks, Alaska.

7 *Ibid.;* Winston S. Churchill, *The Second World War,* II, *Their Finest Hour* (Boston: Houghton Mifflin Company, 1949), pp. 31, 219; Interview with Vide Bartlett, April 1974, Fairbanks, Alaska.

8 Gruening, *Many Battles,* p. 286.

9 William Manchester, *The Glory and the Dream,* I, pp. 277–79.

10 Naske, p. 56.

11 Gruening, *Many Battles,* pp. 307–308.

12 Interview with Vide Bartlett, April 1974, Fairbanks, Alaska; Gruening, *Many Battles,* p. 308.

13 Interview with Vide Bartlett, April 1974, Fairbanks, Alaska.

14, 15 *Ibid.*

16 Reports by T. E. Huntley and R. E. Royall, *Construction of the Alaska Highway* (Washington: Government Printing Office, 1945), p. 5.

17 E. L. Bartlett to Gruening, November 27, 1942, Private Papers, Vide Bartlett, *Alaska Sportsman,* September 1967, pp. 20–24.

18 Russell H. Peters to N. R. Hunt, August 17, 1942, E. L. Bartlett to Gruening, November 10, 1942, E. L. Bartlett Papers, Personal file, 1935–68, box 3, folder censorship, 1942–43, University of Alaska Archives, Fairbanks, Alaska.

19 Gruening, *Many Battles,* pp. 312–314.

20 Members: Hugh Wade, Federal Security Agency; Howard Thompson, Department of Commerce; Secretary Bartlett representing the people of Alaska as an Alaskan resident chosen by the other members; M. D. Williams, Federal Works Agency; Ralph C. Vogel, Department of Justice; Lieutenant-Commander J. S. McKinnon, liaison office for the navy; Colonel Hobart Murphy, liaison officer for the army; B. Frank Heintzleman, Department of Agriculture; *Ketchikan Alaska Chronicle* August 14, 1942.

21 Unidentified newspaper clipping, August 14, 1942; E. L. Bartlett to Gruening, August 31, 1942, E. L. Bartlett Papers, Personal file, 1935–68, box 3, folder censorship, 1942–43, Alaska War Council, 1942-43, University of Alaska Archives, Fairbanks, Alaska.

22 Gruening, *Many Battles,* pp. 314–315.

23 Interview with Vide Bartlett, April 1974, Fairbanks, Alaska.

24 Circular, Hq. Salt Lake City Officer Procurement District, undated, E. L. Bartlett to Dimond, March 15, 1943, E. L. Bartlett to Gruening, April 17, 1943, E. L. Bartlett Papers Personal file, 1935–68, folder correspondence, army, 1943, University of Alaska Archives, Fairbanks, Alaska.

25 Captain H. R. Dowell to E. L. Bartlett, April 15, 1943, E. L. Bartlett Papers Personal file, 1935–68, box 3, folder correspondence, army, 1943, University of Alaska Archives, Fairbanks, Alaska.

26 Gruening to General Lewis B. Hershey, Director, Selective Service System, May 11, 1943, General Hershey to Governor Gruening, May 17, 1943, E. L. Bartlett Papers, Personal file, 1935–68, box 3, folder correspondence, army, 1943, University of Alaska Archives, Fairbanks, Alaska.

27 Interview with Vide Bartlett, April 1974, Fairbanks, Alaska.

28 E. L. Bartlett and Hugh Wade to Delegate Dimond, July 10, 1943, E. L. Bartlett Papers, Personal file, 1935–68, box 3, folder correspondence, War, 1943, University of Alaska Archives, Fairbanks, Alaska.

29 Ruth Hampton to E. L. Bartlett, June 15, 1943, telegram, Ickes to Bartlett, July 2, 1943, telegram, Thoron to Bartlett, August 28, 1943, E. L. Bartlett Papers, Personal file, 1935–68, box 3, folder correspondence, War, 1943, University of Alaska Archives, Fairbanks, Alaska.

30 Bartlett to Dimond, September 22, 1943, Gruening to Chapman, September 22, 1943, Dimond to Chapman, October 9, 1943, E. L. Bartlett to Don W. Hagerty, October 14, 1943, E. L. Bartlett Papers, Personal file, 1935–68, box 3, folder correspondence, War, 1943, University of Alaska Archives, Fairbanks, Alaska.

31 Naske, pp. 56–59.

CHAPTER 6

1 Gruening, *Many Battles,* pp. 297–98.

2 E. L. Bartlett to Dimond, April 7, 1943, E. L. Bartlett Papers, Personal file, box 12, folder general, 1942, University of Alaska Archives, Fairbanks, Alaska.

3 Gruening to Secretary of the Interior Harold L. Ickes, December 10, 1943, E. L. Bartlett Papers, Personal file, box 12, folder general, 1943, University of Alaska Archives, Fairbanks, Alaska.

4 E. L. Bartlett to Gruening, November 25, 1943, E. L. Bartlett Papers, Personal file, box 12, folder general, 1943, University of Alaska Archives, Fairbanks, Alaska.

5 *Ibid.*

6 Gruening to E. L. Bartlett, December 30, 1943, E. L. Bartlett Papers, Personal file, box 12, folder general, 1943, University of Alaska Archives, Fairbanks, Alaska.

7 Memo by Gruening to Secretary Ickes, December 10, 1943; Gruening to E. L. Bartlett, December 16, 1943, E. L. Bartlett Personal file, box 12, folder general, 1943, University of Alaska Archives, Fairbanks, Alaska.

8 *FDNM,* January 17, 1944.

9 E. L. Bartlett to Gruening, January 19, 1944, E. L. Bartlett Papers, Personal file, box 14, folder general, 1944, University of Alaska Archives, Fairbanks, Alaska; interview with Sister Marie Therese, Dimond's oldest daughter, Trinity College, Washington, D.C., April 20, 1975; telegram E. L. Bartlett Papers,University Personal file, box 12, folder general, 1944, University of Alaska Archives, Fairbanks, Alaska.

10 E. L. Bartlett to Hugh Wade, January 21, 1944, E. L. Bartlett Papers, Personal file, box 14, folder general, 1944, University of Alaska Archives, Fairbanks, Alaska.

11 E. L. Bartlett to Gruening, January 22, 1944, E. L. Bartlett to Hugh Wade, January 22, 1944, E. L. Bartlett Papers, Personal file, box 14, folder general, 1944, University of Alaska Archives, Fairbanks, Alaska.

12 *FDNM,* January 24, 1944.

13 E. L. Bartlett to Dimond, January 26, 1944, E. L. Bartlett Papers, Personal file, box 14, folder general, 1944, University of Alaska Archives, Fairbanks, Alaska.

14 Interview with Vide Bartlett, November, 1975, Fairbanks, Alaska, Interview with Mary A. Nordale, April 3, 1977, Fairbanks, Alaska.

15 Interview with Vide Bartlett, April 1974, Fairbanks, Alaska; E. L. Bartlett to Hugh Wade, February 2, 1944, E. L. Bartlett Papers, Personal file, box 14, University of Alaska Archives, Fairbanks, Alaska.

16 Interview with Vide Bartlett, April 1974, Fairbanks, Alaska.

17 *Ibid.;* Gruening to Secretary of the Interior, Harold L. Ickes, February 1, 1944, box 10a, E. Gruening Papers, University of Alaska Archives, Fairbanks, Alaska; interview with Katie Hurley, November 8, 1976, Wasilla, Alaska.

18 Gruening, *Many Battles,* p. 325.

19 *Anchorage Daily Times* (hereafter cited as ADT), February 9, 1944; *Alaska Life,* March, 1944, p. 57.

20 E. L. Bartlett, draft of Wrangell speech, box 13, E. L. Bartlett Papers, Personal file, folder general, 1944, University of Alaska Archives, Fairbanks, Alaska.

21, 22 *Ibid.*

23 E. L. Bartlett appeal to Juneau constituency, April 20, 1944, copy in author's files; *FDNM,* March 8, 1944.

24 Interview with Mary A. Nordale, April 3, 1977, Fairbanks, Alaska.

25 Gruening to Bartlett, March 17, March 22, 1944, E. Gruening Papers, box 10a, University of Alaska Archives, Fairbanks, Alaska.

26 E. L. Bartlett draft of speech, April 20, 1944, E. L. Bartlett Papers, Personal file, box 13, folder general, 1943, University of Alaska Archives, Fairbanks, Alaska; *FDNM,* March 25, 1944.

27 *FDNM,* March 25, 1944.

28 *FDNM,* March 29, April 4, 1944; Interview with Vide Bartlett, November 14, 1975, Fairbanks, Alaska.

29 *FDNM,* April 3, March 21, 1944; A. H. Ziegler to Stanley Nichols of Galena, February 25, 1944, E. L. Bartlett Papers, Personal file, box 13, folder general, 1944, University of Alaska Archives, Fairbanks, Alaska.
30 Handbills, 1944 campaign, in author's files.
31 Interview with K. Hurley, November 8, 1976, Wasilla, Alaska; interview with Vide Bartlett, November 14, 1975, Fairbanks, Alaska.
32 Interview with K. Hurley, November 8, 1976, Wasilla, Alaska.
33 Interview with Vide Bartlett, November 14, 1975, Fairbanks, Alaska; Mary Lee Council to E. L. Bartlett, February 7, 1944, Private Papers, Vide Bartlett.
34 Everett E. Smith to E. L. Bartlett, March 19, 1944, Noel C. Ross to E. F. Jessen, March 18, 1944, John Wiese to E. L. Bartlett, E. L. Bartlett Papers, Personal file, box 13, folder general, 1944, University of Alaska Archives, Fairbanks, Alaska.
35 E. L. Bartlett to Stanley J. Mc Cutcheon, May 2, 1944, E. L. Bartlett to Anthony J. Dimond, May 5, 1944, E. L. Bartlett Papers, Personal file, box 13, folder general, 1944, University of Alaska Archives, Fairbanks, Alaska.
36 Interview with Vide Bartlett, November 14, 1975, Fairbanks, Alaska; E. L. Bartlett to Miss Jessie M. Howard, July 13, 1944, E. L. Bartlett Papers, Personal file, box 13, folder general, 1944, University of Alaska Archives, Fairbanks, Alaska.
37 E. L. Bartlett to Paul Herring, July, 1944, E. L. Bartlett Papers, Personal file, box 13, folder general, 1944, University of Alaska Archives, Fairbanks, Alaska.
38 Interview with Vide Bartlett, November 14, 1975, Fairbanks, Alaska.
39 *ADT,* August 1, 1944.
40 *ADT,* August 8; August 14, 1944.
41 *Daily Alaska Empire,* (hereafter cited as *DAE*), August 10, 1944.
42 *ADT,* August 12, 1944; *DAE,* August 12, 1944.
43 Robert Arnold, *Alaska Native Land Claims* (Anchorage, Alaska: Alaska Native Foundation, 1976), pp. 86–87.
44 *DAE,* August 25, 1944.
45 E. L. Bartlett statement, Juneau, Alaska, November 10, 1944, in author's files.
46 *FDNM,* August 26, 1944.
47 Interview with Vide Bartlett, November 14, 1975, Fairbanks, Alaska.
48 *Ibid.*
49 *FDNM,* August 25, 1944.
50 Interview with Vide Bartlett, November 14, 1875, Fairbanks, Alaska.
51 *Ibid.;* "Alaska General Election, September 12, 1944, Official Returns," copy in author's files.
51 Interview with M. Nordale, April 3, 1977, Fairbanks, Alaska.

CHAPTER 7

1 Burke Riley to author, April 29, 1975.
2 George Sundborg to author, August 19, 1975.
3 Interview with Susie Bartlett Peterson, November 23, 1976, Fairbanks, Alaska; Interview with Vide Bartlett, April 1974, Fairbanks, Alaska.
4 Interview with Mary Lee Council, April 23, 1975, Wash., D.C.
5 Affidavit, January 1, 1944, E. L. Bartlett Papers, 79 Cong., Leg. Bill File 1945–46, box 1, folder H.R. 802, for the relief of Alaska Native Brotherhood, University of Alaska Archives, Fairbanks, Alaska.

6 Dimond to Dan R. McGehee, January 18, 1944, H.R. 3994, Dimond to L. Yaw, February 21, 1944, E. L. Bartlett Papers, 79 Cong., Leg. Bill File 1945–46, box 1, folder H.R. 802, for the relief of Alaska Native Brotherhood, University of Alaska Archives, Fairbanks, Alaska.

7 Henry L. Stimson to D. R. McGehee, November 21, 1944, E. L. Bartlett Papers, 79 Cong., Leg. Bill File, 1945–46, box 1, folder H.R. 802, for the relief of Alaska Native Brotherhood, University of Alaska Archives, Fairbanks, Alaska.

8 E. L. Bartlett to William L. Paul, Jr., January 8, 1945, E. L. Bartlett to L. Yaw, May 15, 1945, E. L. Bartlett to Andrew Hope, July 3, 1945, E. L. Bartlett to A. Hope, December 15, 1945, E. L. Bartlett Papers, 79 Cong., Leg. Bill File 1945–46, box 1, folder H.R. 802, for the relief of Alaska Native Brotherhood, University of Alaska Archives, Fairbanks, Alaska.

9 Statement by Mike Clipper, May 15, 1948, E. L. Bartlett Papers, 81 Cong., 1949–50, Leg. Bill File, box 2, H.R. 584, folder for the relief of Mike Clipper, University of Alaska Archives, Fairbanks, Alaska.

10 W.M. McDade, Capt., U.S. Navy, to M. Clipper, January 3, 1944, E. L. Bartlett Papers, 81 Cong., 1949–50, Leg. Bill File, box 2, H.R. 584, folder for the relief of M. Clipper, University of Alaska Archives, Fairbanks, Alaska.

11 M. Clipper to L.V. Ray, February 8, 1946, Patricia R. Williams to E.L. Bartlett, March 1, 1946, E.L. Bartlett to Patricia R. Williams, March 7, 1946, Bartlett to P. Williams, April 1, 1946, E.L. Bartlett Papers, 81 Cong., 1949–50, Leg. Bill File, box 2, H.R. 584, folder for the relief of M. Clipper, University of Alaska Archives, Fairbanks, Alaska.

12 Kenneth C. Royall to E.L. Bartlett, January 2, 1948, H.R. 584, January 3, 1949, E.L. Bartlett Papers, 81 Cong., 1949–50, Leg. Bill File, box 2, H.R. 584, folder for the relief of M. Clipper, University of Alaska Archives, Fairbanks, Alaska.

13 Gruening, *The State of Alaska*, 2nd ed., pp. 151–52.

14 *Ibid.*

15 Gruening to E.L. Bartlett, March 26, 1945, box 32a, E. Gruening Papers, University of Alaska Archives, Fairbanks, Alaska.

16 E.L. Bartlett to Dimond, July 5, 1945, E.L. Bartlett Papers, Personal file, box 3, folder Organic Act 1933–45, University of Alaska Archives, Fairbanks, Alaska.

17 E.L. Bartlett to W.C. Stump, July 18, 1945, E.L. Bartlett Papers, Personal file, box 3, folder Organic Act, 1933–45, University of Alaska Archives, Fairbanks, Alaska.

18 E.L. Bartlett to John E. Pegues, October 22, 1945, Gruening to E.L. Bartlett, November 7, 1945, E.L. Bartlett Papers, Personal file, box 3, folder Organic Act 1933–45, University of Alaska Archives, Fairbanks, Alaska.

19 M. Council to Dimond, April 30, 1945, Anthony J. Dimond Papers, box 35, folder Council, Mary Lee, Personal, University of Alaska Archives, Fairbanks, Alaska.

20 *Cong. Record,* 79 Cong., 1S, pp. 3887–88.

21 E.L. Bartlett to Vide Bartlett, May 1 to June 14, 1945, Private Papers, Vide Bartlett.

22 Interview with Margery Smith, April 21, 1975, Washington, D.C.

23 *Ibid.*

24 *Ibid.;* Interview with John Cornman, April 17, 1975, Washington, D.C.

25 Interview with M. Smith, April 21, 1975, Washington, D.C.

26 E.L. Bartlett's Washington News-Letter, August 1, 1947, in author's files.

CHAPTER 8

1 Gruening, *Many Battles,* p. 287.

2 Dimond to E.L. Bartlett, November 24, 1945, Wilbur Wester to E.L. Bartlett January 23, 1946, E.L. Bartlett Papers, Personal file, 1935–68, box 14, folder general, 1946, University of Alaska Archives, Fairbanks, Alaska.

3 E.L. Bartlett to Vide, September, 1946, E.L. Bartlett to Vide, September 2, 1946, Private Papers, Vide Bartlett.

4 *ADT,* September 16, September 17, 1946.

5 E.L. Bartlett to Vide, fall, 1946, E.L. Bartlett to Vide, October 3, 1946, Private Papers, Vide Bartlett.

6 *Ibid.*

7 E.L. Bartlett to Vide, October 5, October 8, 1946, Private Papers, Vide Bartlett; general election, and general receipts and expenditures in 1946 election, E.L. Bartlett Papers, Personal file, 1935–68, box 14, folder general, 1946, University of Alaska Archives, Fairbanks, Alaska.

8 Statements of E.L. Bartlett, 1948 campaign, Private Papers, Vide Bartlett; "Official Returns —Territorial Canvassing Board, General Election, October 12, 1948," in author's files.

9 *ADT,* January 6, May 29, July 19, 1950.

10 E.L. Bartlett to Vide, September 5, 1950, Private Papers, Vide Bartlett.

11 E.L. Bartlett to Vide, September 4, September 6, 1950, Private Papers, Vide Bartlett.

12 E.L. Bartlett to Vide, September 12, September 15, 1950, Private Papers, Vide Bartlett.

13 E.L. Bartlett to Vide, no date, 1950, Private Papers, Vide Bartlett.

14 *ADT,* October 9, 1950; "Official Returns—Territorial Canvassing Board, General Election, October 10, 1950," in author's files.

CHAPTER 9

1 Neil F. Moore to E.L. Bartlett, October 11, 1951, Robert Atwood to William Baker, November 13, 1951, E. L. Bartlett Papers, Personal file, 1935–68, box 1, folder Bartlett vs. Moore, 1951–53, University of Alaska Archives, Fairbanks, Alaska.

2 E. L. Bartlett to E. Jensen, February 7, 1952, E. L. Bartlett Papers, Personal file, 1935–68, box 1, folder Bartlett vs. Moore, 1951–53, University of Alaska Archives, Fairbanks, Alaska.

3 Beth Day, *Glacier Pilot: The Story of Bob Reeve* (New York: Ballantine Books, 1973); E. L. Bartlett to A. D. Lawrence, December 27, 1951, E. L. Bartlett Papers, Personal file, box 2, folder campaign 1952, University of Alaska Archives, Fairbanks, Alaska.

4 E. L. Bartlett to Mrs. Luther Brice, August 17, 1965, E. L. Bartlett Papers, Personal file, box 17, folder general, 1965, University of Alaska Archives, Fairbanks, Alaska.

5 E. L. Bartlett to Gruening, January 2, 1952, E. Gruening Papers, box 9, University of Alaska Archives, Fairbanks, Alaska.

6 Frank Barr to E. L. Bartlett, February 14, 1952, E. L. Bartlett Papers, Personal file, box 2, folder campaign, 1952, University of Alaska Archives, Fairbanks, Alaska.

7 Vernon M. Metcalfe to E. L. Bartlett, February 18, 1952, E. L. Bartlett Papers, Personal file, box 2, folder campaign, 1952, University of Alaska Archives, Fairbanks, Alaska; *FDNM,* March 31, April 8, 1952.

8 *DAE,* March 28, 1952; E. Gruening to E. L. Bartlett, March 28, 1952, E. Gruening Papers, box 32a, University of Alaska Archives, Fairbanks, Alaska.

9 *DAE,* March 28, 1952.

10 Kenneth Bowman to Helen Troy Monsen, March 30, 1952, E. L. Bartlett Papers, Personal file, 1935–68, box 1, folder campaign, 1952, University of Alaska Archives, Fairbanks, Alaska.

11 K. Bowman to E. L. Bartlett, March 30, 1952, E. Gruening to E. L. Bartlett, April 10, 1952, E. L. Bartlett Papers, Personal file, 1935–68, box 1, folder campaign, 1952, University of Alaska Archives, Fairbanks, Alaska.

12 E. Gruening to E. L. Bartlett, April 10, 1952, E. L. Bartlett Papers, Personal file, 1935–68, box 1, folder campaign, 1952, University of Alaska Archives, Fairbanks, Alaska.

13 *FDNM,* April 8, April 17, 1952.

14 *Ibid.,* April 24, 1952.

15 "The American Way of Life: A Democratic Achievement—Let's Preserve It!" Address by E. Gruening, Jefferson–Jackson Day Dinner, April 24, 1952, Anchorage, Alaska, copy in author's files.

16 E. L. Bartlett to Louis R. Huber, May 6, 1952, E. L. Bartlett Papers, Personal file, 1935–68, box 1, folder election, 1952, University of Alaska Archives, Fairbanks, Alaska.

17 E. Gruening to E. L. Bartlett, April 21, 1952, Bob Ellis to E. L. Bartlett, May 5, 1952, E. L. Bartlett Papers, Personal file, 1935–68, box 1, folder Bartlett vs. Moore, 1951–53, folder 1952 election, University of Alaska Archives, Fairbanks, Alaska.

18 Mildred R. Hermann to E. L. Bartlett, May 3, 1952, E. L. Bartlett Papers, Personal file, 1935–68, box 2, folder politics, general, 1952, University of Alaska Archives, Fairbanks, Alaska; *Ketchikan Daily News,* hereafter cited as *KDN,* April 21, 1952.

19 E. L. Bartlett to L. Huber, May 6, 1952, E. L. Bartlett Papers, Personal file, 1935–68, box 1, folder election, 1952, University of Alaska Archives, Fairbanks, Alaska.

20 E. L. Bartlett to Burke Riley, May 6, 1952, E. L. Bartlett Papers, Personal file, 1935–68, box 2, folder election, 1952, University of Alaska Archives, Fairbanks, Alaska.

21 E. L. Bartlett to L. Huber, E. L. Bartlett Papers, Personal file, 1935–68, box 1, folder campaign, 1952, University of Alaska Archives, Fairbanks, Alaska.

22 Tony Schwamm to E. L. Bartlett, May 27, 1952, E. L. Bartlett Papers, Personal file, 1935–68, box 1, folder campaign, 1952, University of Alaska Archives, Fairbanks, Alaska.

23 1952 campaign materials, in author's files.

24 Interview with Mary A. Nordale, April 3, 1977, Fairbanks, Alaska

25 E. L. Bartlett campaign material, E. L. Bartlett Papers, Personal file, 1935–68, box 1, folder campaign, 1952, University of Alaska Archives, Fairbanks, Alaska.

26 *Ibid.*

27 Interview with F. Barr, October 17, 1976, Fairbanks, Alaska.

28 E. L. Bartlett campaign material, E. L. Bartlett Papers, Personal file, 1935–68, box 1, folder campaign material, 1952, University of Alaska Archives, Fairbanks, Alaska.

29, 30 *Ibid.*

31 E. L. Bartlett to Helenka Brice, August 17, 1965, E. L. Bartlett Papers, Personal file, 1935–68, box 17, folder general, 1965, University of Alaska Archives, Fairbanks, Alaska.

32, 33 *Ibid.*

34 Wasilla debate transcript, 1952, copy in author's files.

35, 36, 37, 38, 39, 40, 41, 42 *Ibid.*

43 "Official Canvass of Results, Alaska General Election, October 14, 1952," copy in author's files.

44 *Congress and the Nation, 1945–1964* (Washington, D.C.: Congressional Quarterly Service, 1965), p. 19.

45 Interview with M. Nordale, April 3, 1977, Fairbanks, Alaska.

46 Beth Day, *Glacier Pilot,* p. 259; Interview with M. Smith, April 21, 1975, Washington, D.C.

CHAPTER 10

1 E. L. Bartlett office memo, April 21, 1953, E. L. Bartlett to Wilbur Wester, June 26, 1953, E. L. Bartlett Papers, Personal file, 1935–68, box 15, folder general 1953, University of Alaska Archives, Fairbanks, Alaska.

2 *Ibid.*; E. L. Bartlett to Wendell Kay, October 30, 1953, E. L. Bartlett Papers, Personal file, 1935–68, box 15, folder general, 1953, University of Alaska Archives, Fairbanks, Alaska.

3 Peter Wood to E. L. Bartlett, February 1954, Robert Atwood to George Sundborg, February 13, 1954, E. L. Bartlett Papers, Personal file, 1935–68, box 2, folder general, 1954; Bill Egan to E. L. Bartlett, April 11, 1954, E. L. Bartlett Papers, Personal file, 1935–68, box 15, folder general, 1954, University of Alaska Archives, Fairbanks, Alaska.

4 *DAE,* April 28, 1955; Sundborg to E. L. Bartlett, April 30, 1954, E. L. Bartlett Papers, Personal file, 1935–68, box 5, folder correspondence, George Sundborg, University of Alaska Archives, Fairbanks, Alaska.

5 E. L. Bartlett to Katie Alexander, May 4, 1954, E. L. Bartlett Papers, Personal file, 1935–68, box 15, folder general, 1954, University of Alaska Archives, Fairbanks, Alaska.

6 G. Sundborg to author, August 19, 1975; *ADT,* September 11, 1954.

7 *ADT,* September 16, September 21, 1954; "Official Canvass of Results, Alaska General Election, Tuesday, October 12, 1954," in author's files.

8 Peter Wood to E. L. Bartlett, February 4, 1954, E. L. Bartlett primary election results, E. L. Bartlett Papers, Personal file, 1935–68, box 2, folder general, 1954, box 15, folder general, 1956, University of Alaska Archives, Fairbanks, Alaska.

9 *Juneau Independent,* October 14, 1956; "Official Canvass of Results, Alaska General Election, Tuesday, October 9, 1956," in author's files.

CHAPTER 11

1 Thomas G. Smith, "The Treatment of the Mentally Ill in Alaska, 1884–1912: A Territorial Study," *Pacific Northwest Quarterly,* January 1974, pp. 17–24.

2 *Ibid.,* p. 26.

3 "Resolution at regular meeting of Igloo No. 1, Pioneers of Alaska, Nome, February 19, 1936," Edward Cannon to Anthony J. Dimond, July 24, 1935, E. L. Bartlett Papers, 84 Cong., Legislative Bill File, 1955–56, box 4, folder H.R. 6376, Alaska Mental Health, University of Alaska Archives, Fairbanks, Alaska.

4 Harold L. Ickes to Lex Green, Chairman, Committee on Territories, May 20, 1937, E. L. Bartlett Papers, 84 Cong., Legislative Bill File, 1955–56, box 4, folder H.R. 6376, Alaska Mental Health, University of Alaska Archives, Fairbanks, Alaska.

5 E. L. Bartlett Papers, 84th Cong., Legislative Bill File, 1955–56, box 4, folder H.R. 6376, Alaska Mental Health, University of Alaska Archives, Fairbanks, Alaska. The measures introduced in 1940 and their sponsors were H.R. 2963 by Anthony J. Dimond, H.R. 8289 by Congressman Mon C. Wallgren, S. 3415 by Senator Lewis Schwellenbach, and H.R. 9362 by Congressman Homer Angell; in 1941 Dimond submitted H.R. 81.

6 B. W. Thoron to E. L. Bartlett, February 21, 1945, E. L. Bartlett Papers, 84th Cong., Legislative Bill File, 1955–56, box 4, folder H.R. 6376, Alaska Mental Health, University of Alaska Archives, Fairbanks, Alaska.

7 Hospital for Insane in Portland Region, E. L. Bartlett Papers, 79th Cong., Legislative Bill File, box 4, folder H.R. 1412, University of Alaska Archives, Fairbanks, Alaska.

8 Claus-M. Naske, "The Alcan: Its Impact on Alaska," *The Northern Engineer,* Spring 1976, pp. 12–18; George W. Rogers and Richard A. Cooley, *Alaska's Population and Economy: Regional Growth, Development and Future Outlook,* Vol. II (College, Alaska: University of Alaska, Institute of Social, Economic and Government Research, 1963), pp. 5–6.

9 E. L. Bartlett Papers, 89th Cong., Legislative Bill File, 1955–56, box 4, Statistics folder, H.R. 6376, Alaska Mental Health, University of Alaska Archives, Fairbanks, Alaska.

10 Statement of the Honorable Anthony J. Dimond, U.S. District Judge, Third Division, Territory of Alaska, August 23, 1949 at the Public Hearing on Alaska Mental Health Needs, Anchorage, Alaska, E. L. Bartlett Papers, 84th Cong., Legislative Bill File, box 4, folder Mental Health, University of Alaska Archives, Fairbanks, Alaska.

11 *Ibid.*

12 "A Mental Health Program for Alaska," Report and Recommendations of the Investigating Committee designated by the Department of the Interior, E. L. Bartlett Papers, 84th Cong., Legislative Bill File, 1955–56, box 4, folder H.R. 6376, Alaska Mental Health, February 10, 1950, University of Alaska Archives, Fairbanks, Alaska.

13 U.S. Cong., House, *Governing the Hospitalization of the Mentally Ill of Alaska, and for other Purposes,* H. Report 2152 to accompany H.R. 8086, 82nd Cong., 2S., (Washington: GPO, 1952) pp. 1–2; E. L. Bartlett to Dr. C. Earl Albrecht, July 3, 1952, E. L. Bartlett Papers, 84th Cong., Legislative Bill File, 1955–56, box 4, folder H.R. 6376, Alaska Mental Health, University of Alaska Archives, Fairbanks, Alaska.

14 *Alaska's Health: A Survey Report by the Alaska Health Survey Team,* Thomas Parran, Chief (Pittsburgh, PA.: The Graduate School of Public Health, 1954), pp. 56–59.

15 E. L. Bartlett to William L. Baker, April 2, 1954, E. L. Bartlett Memo on H.R. 8009, May 3, 1954, E. L. Bartlett Papers, 84th Cong., 1955–56, Legislative Bill File, box 5, folder H.R. 6376, Alaska Mental Health, University of Alaska Archives, Fairbanks, Alaska; U.S. Congress, House, *Providing for the Hospitalization and Care of the Mentally Ill of Alaska,* H. Report 1670 to accompany H.R. 8009, 83rd Cong., 2S., (Washington: GPO, 1954); Copy, News Release Office of Representative John P. Taylor, May 29, 1954, E. L. Bartlett to Katie Alexander, May 28, 1954, E. L. Bartlett Papers, 84 Cong., 1955–56, Legislative Bill File, box 5, folder H.R. 6376, Alaska Mental Health, University of Alaska Archives, Fairbanks, Alaska.

16 E. L. Bartlett Memo on H.R. 8009, June 8, 1954, E. L. Bartlett Papers, 84 Cong., 1955–56, Legislative Bill File, box 5, folder H.R. 6376, Alaska Mental Health, University of Alaska Archives, Fairbanks, Alaska.

17 E. L. Bartlett memo on mental health to Messrs. Baker, Sundborg, Atwood, August 7, 1954, Private Papers, Vide Bartlett.

18 U.S. Cong., Senate, *Providing for the Hospitalization and Care of the Mentally Ill of Alaska, and for Other Purposes,* S. Report 2486 to accompany H.R. 8009, 83rd Cong., 2S., (Washington: GPO, 1954), pp. 2–5.

19 *ADT,* September 4, 1954, E. L. Bartlett memo to Katherine D. Nordale and Burke Riley, January 4, 1955, E. L. Bartlett to W. M. Whitehead, M.D., January 12, 1955, E. L. Bartlett Papers, 84 Cong., Legislative Bill File, 1955–56, box 5, folder H.R. 6376, Alaska Mental Health, University of Alaska Archives, Fairbanks, Alaska.

20 H.R. 6376, H.R. 6334, H.R. 610, H.R. 5092, H.R. 3991, H.R. 5093, S. 1027, S. 1028; E. L. Bartlett Papers, 84 Cong., 1955–56, Legislative Bill File, box 5, folder H.R. 6376, Alaska Mental Health, University of Alaska Archives, Fairbanks, Alaska.

21 *Care of Alaskan Mentally Ill,* Serial No. 22, 1956, pp. 55–61; *Ibid.,* pp. 62–98.

22 *Ibid.,* p. 125.

23 *Care of Alaskan Mentally Ill,* Hearings, Serial No. 22, pp. 202–04.

24 *Ibid.,* pp. 213–15; *Ibid.,* p. 261–64.

25 *ADT,* June 18, 1955.

26 *Care of Alaskan Mentally Ill,* Hearings, Serial No. 22, p. 298.

27 E. L. Bartlett to Governor B. Frank Heintzleman, July 12, 1955, E. L. Bartlett Papers, 84 Cong., 1955–56, Legislative Bill File, box 5, folder H.R. 6376, Alaska Mental Health, University of Alaska Archives, Fairbanks, Alaska; *ADT,* July 16, 1955.

28 U.S. Cong., House, *Providing for the Hospitalization and Care of the Mentally Ill of Alaska,* H. Report No. 1399 to accompany H.R. 6376, 84 Cong., 1S. (Washington: GPO, 1955).

29 E. L. Bartlett to Byron A. Gillam, July 30, 1955, E. L. Bartlett Papers, 84 Cong., 1955–56, Legislative Bill File, box 5, folder H.R. 6376, Alaska Mental Health, University of Alaska Archives, Fairbanks, Alaska.

30 U.S. Cong., House, *Alaska, 1955,* Hearings before the Subcommittee on Territorial and Insular Affairs of the Committee on Interior and Insular Affairs, pursuant to H. Res. 30, 84 Cong., 1S., Serial No. 27 (Washington: GPO, 1956), p. 159.

31 *Ibid.,* p. 213.

32 *Ibid.,* II, p. 59.

33 *Ibid.,* p. 122.

34 *The Register* of Santa Ana, California, January 24, 1956. See also Ted C. Hinckley, "Alaska as an American Botany Bay," *Pacific Historical Review,* Feb. 1973, pp. 1–19.

35 Marjorie Sharon, "Origin of Opposition to H.R. 6376, and Nationwide Propaganda Channels, an account of Mass Hysteria Affecting Nine States: California, Nebraska, Arizona, Texas, Indiana, Illinois, Vermont, New York, Massachusetts," in E. L. Bartlett Papers, 84 Cong., Legislative Bill File, box 6, folder H.R. 6376, Alaska Mental Health, University of Alaska Archives, Fairbanks, Alaska; Priscilla L. Buckley, "Siberia, U.S.A.: The Rocky Road of H.R. 6376," *National Review,* July 25, 1956, pp. 9–10; the Bricker Amendment, heatedly debated but eventually rejected by the U.S. Senate, would have sharply curtailed the treaty-making power of the executive branch by denying to all treaties the force of law, making their enforcement depend on subsequent action of the Congress.

36 E. L. Bartlett to Senator Henry M. Jackson, January 31, 1956, E. L. Bartlett to Dr. C. Earl Albrecht, February 7, 1956, E. L. Bartlett Papers, 84 Cong., 1955–56, Legislative Bill File, box 5, folder H.R. 6376, Alaska Mental Health, University of Alaska Archives, Fairbanks, Alaska.

37 E. L. Bartlett to Roswell B. Perkins, Assistant Secretary, HEW, February 9, 1956, E. L. Bartlett Papers, 84 Cong., 1955–56, Legislative Bill File, box 5, folder H.R. 6376, Alaska Mental Health, University of Alaska Archives, Fairbanks, Alaska.

38 U.S. Cong., Senate, *Alaska Mental Health,* Hearings before the Subcommittee on Territories and Insular Affairs of the Committee on Interior and Insular Affairs on H.R. 6376, S. 2518 and S. 2973, and also the provisions of S. 1027 and S. 1028, 84 Cong., 2S. (Washington: GPO, 1956), pp. 119–125, 135–170, 269, 287–88.

39 *Ibid.*

40 *Ibid.,* pp. 135–170.

41 U.S. Cong., Senate, *Alaska Mental Health,* Hearings before the Subcommittee on Territorial and Insular Affairs of the Committee on Interior and Insular Affairs on H.R. 6376, S. 2518 and S. 2973, and also the provisions of S. 1027 and S. 1028, 84 Cong., 2S. (Washington: GPO, 1956), pp. 135–170.

42 *Ibid.,* pp. 269, 287–88.

43 E. L. Bartlett to Ernest Gruening, March 28, 1956, E. L. Bartlett to Charles R. Hayman, M.D., Acting Territorial Commissioner of Health, March 2, 1956, E. L. Bartlett Papers, 84 Cong., 1955–56, Legislative Bill File, box 6, folder H.R. 6376, Alaska Mental Health, University of Alaska Archives, Fairbanks, Alaska.

44 U.S. Cong., Senate, *Alaska Mental Health,* 1956, p. 220; Henry W. Coe to E. L. Bartlett, April 11, 1956, E. L. Bartlett Papers, 84 Cong., 1955–56, Legislative Bill File, box 6, folder H.R. 6376, Alaska Mental Health, University of Alaska Archives, Fairbanks, Alaska.

45 U.S. Cong., Senate, *Alaska Mental Health,* Senate Report No. 2053 to accompany H.R. 6376, 84 Cong., 2S., (Washington: GPO, 1956); U.S. Cong., House, *Providing for Hospitalization and Care of the Mentally Ill of Alaska,* H. Report No. 2735, Conference Report to accompany H.R. 6376, 84 Cong., 2S (Washington: GPO, 1956).

CHAPTER 12

1 Naske, pp. 35–37.
2 *ADT,* June 25, 1942.
3 Naske, p. 60.
4 *DAE,* July 9, July 15, July 29, September 2, 1943.
5 *Jessen's Weekly,* hereafter cited as *JW,* October 1, October 15, April 20, 1943; *ADT,* September 27, 1943.
6 Dean Sherman, "Statehood for the Asking," *Alaska Life,* November 1943, pp. 3–7.
7 *DAE,* July 28, September 24, 1943.
8 H. R. 3768.
9 *JW,* January 5, 1945; 48 Stat. 984–988; 49 Stat. 1250–1251; U.S. Cong., Senate, Committee on Interior and Insular Affairs, *Rescinding Certain Orders of the Secretary of the Interior Establishing Indian Reservations in the Territory of Alaska,* report, to accompany S. J. Res. 162, 80 Cong., 2 Sess., S. Rept. 1366 (Washington: GPO, 1948), pp. 5–7; U.S. Cong., Senate, *Alaska Statehood,* Hearings on S. 50, 83 Cong., 2 S. (Washington: GPO, 1954), p. 204; *DAE,* July 29, 1943.
10 Dean Sherman, "The Statehood Question," *Alaska Life,* June 1944, pp. 15–18.
11 Transcript of E. L. Bartlett interview by Val Trimble and Scott Hart, Washington, D.C., August 1, 1965, Private Papers, Vide Bartlett.
12 Alaska House *Journal,* 1945, pp. 46–47.
13 Naske, p. 70.
14 *Ibid.*
15 *Ketchikan Alaska Chronicle,* hereafter cited as *KAC,* August 8–11, August 18, August 22, August 25, 1945.
16 U.S. Cong., House, 79 Cong., 1 S., Committee on the Territories, *Hearings Pursuant to H. Res. 236; To Conduct a Study and Investigation of the Various Questions and Problems Relating to the Territory of Alaska,* (Washington: GPO, 1946) pp. 43–44, 108–109, 160–162, 212–215, 224.
17 U.S. Cong., House, 79 Cong., 2 Sess., Committee on the Territories, *Official Trip to Conduct a Study and Investigation of the Various Questions and Problems Relating to the Territory of Alaska,* House Rept. 1583 to accompany H. Res. 236 (Washington: GPO, 1946), pp. 28, 31; *DAE,* Dec. 5, 1946.
18 *Hearings Pursuant to H. Res. 236,* p. 29.
19 *Ibid.* pp. 233–35; Alaska House *Journal,* 1945, pp. 448, 669.
20 U.S. Cong., House Subcommittee on Territorial and Insular Possessions of the Committee on Public Lands, *Alaska,* Hearings Pursuant to H. Res. 93, Committee Hearing No. 31, 80 Cong., 1 S. (Washington: GPO, 1948), p. 358; *JW,* December 28, 1945.

21 Naske, p. 71.

22 *Ibid.*, p. 72.

23 *KAC,* September 3, 1946.

24 Naske, pp. 72–73.

25 60 Stat. 819, 827–828.

26 Naske, p. 76.

27 U. S. Cong., House, Committee on Public Land, Subcommittee on Territorial and Insular Possessions, *Statehood for Alaska,* Hearings on H. R. 206 and H. R. 1808, 80 Cong., 1 S. (Washington: GPO, 1947), pp. 70, 66, 95, 62, 71, 281, 340); Naske, p. 76.

28 *Hearings on H. R. 206,* p. 424; E. L. Bartlett to Gruening, February 15, 1947, Gruening to E. L. Bartlett, March 15, 1947, E. L. Bartlett to Gruening, March 8, 1947, E. L. Bartlett Papers, Statehood File, box 7, folder Correspondence, general, 1947, University of Alaska Archives, Fairbanks, Alaska.

29 *Cong. Record,* 80 Cong., 1 S., p. 7941.

30 Naske, p. 77.

31 *ADT,* August 30, September 13, 1947; *KAC,* September 13, 1947.

32 *Hearings Pursuant to H. Res. 93,* pp. 29–390.

33 *KAC,* August 1, September 3, 1947; *ADT,* September 5, 1947; *JW,* September 12, 1947.

34 *ADT,* September 5, 1947; *KAC,* September 15, 1947.

35 Naske, p. 78.

36 *KAC,* November 4, 1947, January 12, 1948.

37 E. L. Bartlett to Burke Riley, March 1, 1948, E. L. Bartlett Papers, St. File, box 7, folder Correspondence, general, 1948, University of Alaska Archives, Fairbanks, Alaska.

38 *DAE,* March 26, 1948; *KAC* April 17, 1948; D'Ewart to Felix S. Cohen, March 29, 1948; E. L. Bartlett to friend, April 8, 1948, E. L. Bartlett Papers, St. File, box 16, folder Legislative History, 1948, University of Alaska Archives, Fairbanks, Alaska; *KAC,* April 17, 1948; Frances Lopinski to friend, April 26, 1948, E. L. Bartlett Papers, St. File, box 16, folder Legislative History, 1948, University of Alaska Archives, Fairbanks, Alaska.

39 *Alaska Federationist* (Juneau), June 1948; *DAE,* May 8, 1948, *KAC,* May 18, June 16, 1948; *ADT,* June 1, 1948.

40 Naske, p. 79.

41 Kirk H. Porter and Donald Bruce Johnson, *National Party Platforms, 1840–1960* (Urbana: University of Illinois Press, 1961), pp. 435, 453.

42 Naske, p. 88.

43 *DAE,* January 23, February 14, 20, 1947; *KAC,* February 22, 1947; Alaska House *Journal,* 1947, p. 320; Naske, p. 90.

44 81 Cong., 1 S., H. R. 331, January 3, 1949.

45 Naske, p. 95.

46 *Ibid.,* pp. 95–96; "Report by Delegate E. L. Bartlett…," July 22, 1949, Records of the Office of the Governor of Alaska, General Correspondence, 1934–53, box 520, folder 58-11-Statehood (Alaska), No. 2, Federal Records Center, Seattle, Washington; *Cong. Record,* 81 Cong., 1 S., p. 10.

47 *ADT,* May 17, 1949; *KAC,* May 17, May 18, June 29, 1959; *DAE,* May 27, June 13, 1949; E. L. Bartlett to Dimond, July 20, 1949, E. L. Bartlett Papers, Statehood File, box 7, folder Correspondence, general, 1949, University of Alaska Archives, Fairbanks, Alaska.

48 *KAC,* July 22, July 23, 1949; "Report by Delegate E. L. Bartlett…," July 22, 1949, Records of the Office of the Governor of Alaska…; E. L. Bartlett to Gruening, July 22, 1949,

A. J. Dimond Papers, Personal File, 1904–53, box 34, folder Bartlett, St. Correspondence, University of Alaska Archives, Fairbanks, Alaska.

49 Naske, pp. 91–92.

50 *Ibid.*

51 *Ibid.*, pp. 92–93.

52 *Cong. Record,* 81 Cong., 2 S., pp. 773–785.

53 *Cong. Record,* 81 Cong., 2 S., pp. 777, 784; 81 Cong., 1 S., H. J. Res. 205, March 28, 1949.

54 *DAE,* February 27, March 3, 1950; *Cong. Record,* 81 Cong., 2 S., pp. 2744–51.

55 *Ibid.*, pp. 2771–2781, pp. 2947–2948.

56 *KAC,* January 24, 1949, March 27, 1950; 81 Cong., 1 S., S. 513, January 17, 1949; S. 727, January 31, 1949; S. 2036, June 10, 1949.

57 E. L. Bartlett memo, December 23, 1949, E. L. Bartlett Papers, St. File, box 16, folder Legislative History, 1949, University of Alaska Archives, Fairbanks, Alaska.

58 Naske, p. 97.

59 *Ibid.*, pp. 97–98; *KAC,* April 24, April 27, 1950.

60 *DAE,* November 11, 1949, February 26, 1946; U. S. Cong., Senate, Committee on Interior and Insular Affairs, *Nomination of Oscar L. Chapman to be Secretary of the Interior,* 81 Cong., 2 S., (Washington: GPO, 1950), p. 6; *KAC,* December 1, 1949; Naske, p. 98.

61 Naske, p. 98.

62 *KAC,* April 28, 1950; *DAE,* April 27, 1950.

63 Naske, pp. 98–99.

64 *JW,* May 19, 1950; Naske, p. 99.

65 *Ibid.*, pp. 98–99.

66 *FDNM,* April 24, May 2, June 10–17, 1950; *KDN,* April 24, May 3, June 13–20, 1950.

67 Naske, p. 101.

68 *Ibid.*

69 Alaska Statehood Committee, "Meeting of the Joint Special Committee on Statehood of the Alaska Territorial Legislature, January 29, 1953, pp. 98–94, Alaska Historical Library, Juneau; U. S. Cong., Senate, Committee on Interior and Insular Affairs, *Alaska Statehood,* Hearings on S. 50, 83 Cong., 2 S., (Washington: GPO, 1954), p. 346.

70 80 Cong., 1 S., S. J. Res. 162, Dec. 4, 1947; *Alaska Statehood,* Hearings on H. R. 331, and S. 2036, p. 346; *DAE,* April 25, April 27, 1950, E. L. Bartlett to Victor C. Rivers, December 16, 1950, E. L. Bartlett to Gruening, August 3, 1950, E. L. Bartlett Papers, Statehood File, box 16, Legislative History, August–December 1950, box 8, folder Correspondence, general, July 1950, University of Alaska Archives, Fairbanks, Alaska; "The Shape of Things," *Nation,* 171 (1950), p. 138; *Cong. Record,* 81 Cong., 2 S., pp. 11869–11881.

71 Mildred Strunk, ed., "The Quarter Polls," Public Opinion Quarterly 13 (1949), p. 367; 14 (1950), p. 817.

72 Naske, p. 102.

73 E. L. Bartlett to Atwood, August 2, 1950, E. L. Bartlett Papers, Statehood File, box 8, folder Correspondence, general, July 1950, University of Alaska Archives, Fairbanks, Alaska.

74 *Cong. Record,* 81 Cong., 2 S., pp. 14393–14403; U. S. Congress, Senate, Committee on Interior and Insular Affairs, *Investigation of Charges by Senator Andrew F. Schoeppel,* 81 Cong., 2 S., (Washington: GPO, 1950).

75 *Washington Post,* September 9, 1950; *KAC,* September 14, 1950; *ADT,* September 15, 1950.

76 Memo to Members of Statehood Com. from E. L. Bartlett, February 27, 1950, E. L. Bartlett to Gruening, July 19, 1949, A. J. Dimond Papers, Personal File, 1940–53, box 34, folder E. L. Bartlett—St. Correspondence, University of Alaska Archives, Fairbanks, Alaska.

77 Memo to Members of Statehood Committee from E. L. Bartlett, Feb. 27, 1950, Dimond Papers, Personal File, 1940–53, box 34, folder Bartlett—Statehood Committee, University of Alaska Archives, Fairbanks, Alaska; E. L. Bartlett to Atwood, Feb., 18, 1950, E. L. Bartlett Papers, Statehood File, box 1, folder Alaska Statehood Committee, January–May 1950, University of Alaska Archives, Fairbanks, Alaska.

78 E. L. Bartlett to Baker, February 27, 1950, E. L. Bartlett to Atwood, February 18, 1950, Feltus to E. L. Bartlett, September 22, 1950, E. L. Bartlett Papers, Statehood File, box 1, folder Alaska Statehood Committee, January–May 1950, folder Alaska Committee, June–December 1950, University of Alaska Archives, Fairbanks, Alaska.

79 Gruening to E. L. Bartlett, May 29, 1950, E. L. Bartlett to Gruening, July 13, May 31, 1950, E. L. Bartlett Papers, Statehood File, box 8, folder Correspondence, general, May 1950, University of Alaska Archives, Fairbanks, Alaska.

80 Gruening to E. L. Bartlett, July 10, 1950, E. L. Bartlett to Gruening, July 13, 1950, Feltus to Gruening, July 25, 1949, E. L. Bartlett Papers, Statehood File, box 8, folder Correspondence, general, July 1950, box 1, folder Alaska Statehood Committee, 1949, University of Alaska Archives, Fairbanks, Alaska, *Investigation of Charges,* pp. 54–81.

81 *DAE,* September 8, September 11, 1950; E. L. Bartlett rough draft for UP, September 15, 1950, E. L. Bartlett Papers, Statehood File, box 1, folder Alaska Statehood Committee, June–December 1950, University of Alaska Archives, Fairbanks, Alaska.

82 *Investigation of Charges,* pp. 185–350; *KAC,* September 11, 1950.

83 Investigation of Charges, pp. 50–164; *DAE,* September 16, 1950; *FDNM,* January 11, 1951.

84 Naske, p. 103.

85 E. L. Bartlett Memo, December 21, 1950, E. L. Bartlett Papers, Statehood File, box 16, folder Legislative History, August–December 1950, University of Alaska Archives, Fairbanks, Alaska.

CHAPTER 13

1 "Minutes of the meeting of the Alaska Statehood Committee," January 6–7, 1951, Records of the Office of the Governor of Alaska, Box 668, Federal Records Center, Seattle, Washington.

2 *Statehood for Alaska: A Report on Two Years' Achievement* (Alaska Statehood Committee, 1951).

3 Naske, p. 105.

4 E. L. Bartlett to Alaska Statehood Committee members, Feb. 8, 1952, Anthony J. Dimond Papers, Personal file, 1904–53, box 34, folder Bartlett—Statehood Correspondence, University of Alaska Archives, Fairbanks, Alaska.

5 Naske, p. 105.

6 *Ibid.,* p. 106.

7 *KAC,* March 4, 1952; *Congressional Quarterly Almanac,* 8 (1952), p. 55.

8 Naske, p. 112.

9 Alaska Statehood Committee, "Meeting of the Alaska Statehood Committee," January 28, 1953; Alaska Statehood Committee, "Meeting of the Joint Special Committee on Statehood of the Alaska Territorial Legislature," January 29, 1953, Alaska Historical Library, Juneau.

10 Alaska House *Journal,* 1953, p. 45; Alaska Senate *Journal,* 1953, pp. 886-887.

11 *ADT,* November 21, 1952; *KAC,* December 26, 1952.

12 Naske, p. 113.

13 *Ibid.,* p. 114.

14 U.S. Cong., House, Subcommittee on Territories and Insular Possessions of the Committee on Interior and Insular Affairs, *Statehood for Alaska,* Hearings on H.R. 20, H.R. 207, H.R. 1746, H.R. 2684, H.R. 2982, and H.R. 1916, 83 Cong., 1 S. (Washington: GPO, 1953), p. 64; Naske, p. 114.

15 *Ibid.*

16. *FDNM,* January 28, 1954; *KAC,* January 19, January 25, 1954; *ADT,* January 21, 1954; *FDNM,* January 22, 1954.

17 U.S. Cong., Senate, Committee on Interior and Insular Affairs, *Providing for the Admission of Alaska into the Union,* Report to Accompany S. 50, 83 Cong., 2 S., S. Report 1028, p. 17.

18 *DAE,* January 27, 1954; *ADT,* February 5, 1954; Naske, pp. 119–120.

19 *Ibid.,* p. 120.

20 *Ibid.,* p. 121.

21 *Ibid.*

22 U.S., President, *Public Papers of the Presidents of the United States* (Washington, D.C.; Office of the Federal Register, National Archives and Records Service, 1953–1961), Dwight D. Eisenhower, 1954, p. 386; *FDNM,* April 8, 1954.

23 U.S. Cong., Senate, Committee on Interior and Insular Affairs, *Alaska Statehood: Hearings on H.R. 331 and S. 2036,* 81 Cong., 2 S., pp. 60–61; E.L. Bartlett to Atwood, Dec. 30, 1953, E.L. Bartlett Papers, Statehood File, box 17, folder Legislative History, 1953, University of Alaska Archives, Fairbanks, Alaska.

24 Naske, pp. 125–126.

25 President, *Public Papers,* 1954, pp. 638–639; *ADT,* July 15, 1954.

26 Naske, p. 126.

27 E.L. Bartlett to Gruening, March 10, 1951, E. Gruening Papers, Box 32a, University of Alaska Archives, Fairbanks Alaska; *JW,* February 19, 1953.

28 *Cong. Record,* 83 Cong., 2 S., p. 3501.

29 *Cong. Record,* 83 Cong., 2 S., pp. 4069–71.

30 Naske, p. 123.

31 U.S. Cong., House, Committee on Interior and Insular Affairs, *Hawaii–Alaska Statehood: Hearings on H.R. 2525 and H.R. 2536 and H.R. 49, H.R. 185, H.R. 187, H.R. 248, H.R. 511, H.R. 555, and H.R. 2531,* 84 Cong., 1 S., (Washington: GPO, 1955), pp. 91–98, 111–112.

32 *Hearings on H.R. 2535,* pp. 337–42; E.L. Bartlett memo entitled "Memorandum Seeking to Preserve for the Benefit of History Certain of the Events Which Took Place During the Week Starting February 13 as They Related to Alaska Statehood," February 18, 1955, E.L. Bartlett Papers, Statehood File, box 18, folder Legislative History, January–February 1955, University of Alaska Archives, Fairbanks, Alaska; *Hearings on H.R. 2535,* pp. 337–47.

33 *Ibid.,* pp. 397, 350–55; E.L. Bartlett memo "Seeking to Preserve . . ."

34 *ADT,* February 22, 1955; *Hearings on H.R. 2535,* pp. 395–96.

35 *Ibid.,* pp. 421–32; U.S. Cong., Senate Committee on Interior and Insular Affairs, *Alaska–Hawaii Statehood, Elective Governorship, and Commonwealth Status: Hearings on S. 49, S. 399, and S. 402,* 84 Cong., 1 S., (Washington: GPO, 1955), p. 26; E.L. Bartlett memo "Seeking to Preserve . . .," February 18, 1955, E.L. Bartlett Papers, Statehood File, box 18, folder Legislative History, January–February 1955, University of Alaska Archives, Fairbanks, Alaska.

36 S. 59, January 6, 1955, 84 Cong., 1 S., *Hearings on S. 49, S. 399, and S. 402,* pp. 20–21.

37 *Hearings on S. 49, S. 399, and S. 402,* pp. 28, 67–84.

38 *Ibid.,* pp. 87–88, 27, 36–38.

39 *Ibid.,* pp. 89–90, *Cong. Record,* 84 Cong., 1st S., p. 5880.

40 Naske, p. 138.

41 H.R. 6177, H.R. 6178, May 11, 1955, 84 Cong., 1 S.; *FDNM,* May 12, May 17, 1955; E.L. Bartlett to Payne, May 21, 1955, E.L. Bartlett to Mildred R. Hermann and Robert B. Atwood, May 20, 1955, E.L. Bartlett Papers, Statehood File, box 11, folder Correspondence, general, May–June 1955, University of Alaska Archives, Fairbanks, Alaska.

42 U.S. Cong., House, Subcommittee on Territorial and Insular Affairs of the Committee on Interior and Insular Affairs, *Alaska, 1955: Hearings Pursuant to H. Res. 30,* 5 pt. 84 Cong., 1 S. (Washington: GPO, 1955).

43 For details see Victor Fischer, *Alaska's Constitutional Convention* (Fairbanks, Alaska: University of Alaska Press, 1975).

44 Fischer, *Alaska's Constitutional Convention,* p. 26.

45 *Ibid.,* pp. 52–53; Gruening, *Many Battles,* p. 383.

46 E.L. Bartlett to Egan, January 19, 1956, Private Papers, Vide Bartlett.

47 George Lehleitner to E.L. Bartlett, April 11, 1956, Private Papers, Vide Bartlett; E.L. Bartlett to Hugh Wade, May 10, 1956, E.L. Bartlett to Bill Egan, May 1, 1956, E.L. Bartlett Papers, Personal file, box 25, 7, Correspondence, general, Hugh Wade, 1956–57, Bill Egan, 1952–66, University of Alaska Archives, Fairbanks, Alaska.

48 Naske, p. 146.

49 Atwood's Notes, June 19, 1956, Bartley to Atwood, August 29, 1956, E.L. Bartlett Papers, Statehood File, box 33, folder TP, June 1956, box 2, folder Alaskan Statehood Committee, 1956, University of Alaska Archives, Fairbanks, Alaska.

50 Naske, p. 146.

51 *Ibid.*

52 E.L. Bartlett to Tom Stewart, January 19, 1957, E.L. Bartlett to Mildred Hermann, February 11, 1957, E.L. Bartlett Papers, Statehood File, box 33, folder TP, 1958–67, folder TP, January–February 1957, University of Alaska Archives, Fairbanks, Alaska; *FDNM,* May 8, 1957.

53 Naske, p. 106.

54 U.S. Cong., Senate, Committee on Interior and Insular Affairs, *Nomination of Frederick A. Seaton to be Secretary of the Interior,* 84 Con., 2 S. (Washington: GPO, 1956), pp. 23, 30.

55 *DAE,* August 22, 1956; Porter and Johnson, *National Party Platforms,* p. 553.

56 *Cong. Record,* 85 Cong., 1 S., p. A4651.

57 85 Cong., 1 S., S. 49, S. 50, January 7, 1957 H.R. 50, H.R. 49, January 3, 1957.

58 *FDNM,* April 30, May 8, 1957; E.L. Bartlett to Thomas B. Stewart, May 20, 1957, E.L. Bartlett Papers, Statehood File, box 12, folder Correspondence, general, May 1957, University of Alaska Archives, Fairbanks, Alaska; *DAE,* May 17, 1957; E.L. Bartlett to Alaska Statehood Committee, May 17, 1957, E.L. Bartlett Papers, Statehood File, box 19, folder Legislative History, May 1957, University of Alaska Archives, Fairbanks, Alaska.

59 Interview with Mary Lee Council, April 23, 1975, Washington, D.C.

60 Naske, p. 159.

61. *Ibid.*

62 *Ibid.,* pp. 159–60.

63. *Ibid.,* pp. 160–61.

64 E.L. Bartlett interview by Val Trimble and Scott Hart, August 1, 1956, Washington, D.C., Private Papers, Vide Bartlett.

65 E.L. Bartlett to Snedden, January 28, 1958, E.L. Bartlett Papers, Statehood File, box 13, folder Correspondence, general, February 1958, University of Alaska Archives, Fairbanks, Alaska; *FDNM*, January 28, 1958.

66 E.L. Bartlett confidential memo, February 7, 1958, E.L. Bartlett Papers, Statehood File, box 19, folder Legislative History, January–April 1958, University of Alaska Archives, Fairbanks, Alaska.

67 Naske, p. 162.

68 *FDNM*, March 3, 1958; *Cong. Record*, 85 Cong., 2 S., p. 5041.

69 *Cong. Record*, 85 Cong., 2 S., pp. 18186–18187.

70 Naske, pp. 163–64.

71 *Cong. Record*, 85 Cong., 2 S., pp. 9217–18, 9368.

72 Naske, pp. 164–65.

73 *Ibid.*, p. 166.

74 E.L. Bartlett interview by Val Trimble and Scott Hart, Washington, D.C., August 1, 1965, Private Papers, Vide Bartlett; Naske, p. 166.

75 E.L. Bartlett interview by Val Trimble and Scott Hart, Washington, D.C., August 1, 1956, Private Papers, Vide Bartlett.

76, 77 *Ibid.*

78 *FDNM*, May 29, May 31, July 7, 1958; E.L. Bartlett confidential memo, June 3, 1958, E.L. Bartlett Papers, Statehood File, box 33, folder TP, 1958-67, University of Alaska Archives, Fairbanks, Alaska.

CHAPTER 14

1 Naske, p. 167.

2 *Ibid.*

3 E.L. Bartlett to Burke and Doris Ann Bartlett Riley, early 1958, Private Papers, Vide Bartlett.

4 *Ibid.*

5 *FDNM*, May 29, May 31, 1958; E.L. Bartlett confidential memo, June 3, 1958, E.L. Bartlett Papers, Statehood File, box 33, folder T.P., 1958–67, University of Alaska Archives, Fairbanks, Alaska.

6 E.L. Bartlett to B. and Doris Ann Bartlett Riley, June 5, 1958, Private Papers, Vide Bartlett.

7, 8 *Ibid.*

9 George Sundborg to E.L. Bartlett, July 4, 1958, Private Papers, Vide Bartlett.

10 G. Sundborg to E.L. Bartlett, July 5, 1958, Private Papers, Vide Bartlett.

11 E.L. Bartlett to B. and Doris Ann Bartlett Riley, July 6, 1958, Private Papers, Vide Bartlett.

12 Doug Smith to E.L. Bartlett, July 7, 1958, E.L. Bartlett Papers, Personal file, box 16, general, 1958, University of Alaska Archives, Fairbanks, Alaska; *ADT*, July 2, 1958; *FDNM*, July 7, 1958.

13 E.L. Bartlett to B. and Doris Ann Bartlett Riley, July 6, 1958, Private Papers, Vide Bartlett.

14 *FDNM*, July 14, 1958.

15 *FDNM*, June 18; *ADT*, June 26, July 12, 1958; "Builders of a New State," *U.S. News and World Report*, July 11, 1958, p. 7; "Alaska's Senator?" *Time*, August 14, 1958, p. 16.

16 *ADT*, July 11, 1958; *FDNM*, July 15, July 28, 1958.

17 *FDNM*, July 19, July 28, 1958; *ADT*, July 19, 1958.

18 *FDNM*, July 28, July 21, July 19, 1958; "Alaska's Senator?"; *Time*, August 14, 1958, p. 16.

19 Vide to B. Riley, July 30, 1958, Private Papers, Vide Bartlett.

20 John Dimond to E.L. Bartlett, July 21, 1958, E.L. Bartlett Papers, Personal File, box 16, general, 1958, University of Alaska Archives, Fairbanks, Alaska.

21 E.L. Bartlett to Dimond, August 1, 1958, E.L. Bartlett Papers, Personal file, box 16, general, 1958, E.L. Bartlett to Sundborg, July 24, 1958, E.L. Bartlett Papers, box 5, correspondence, George Sundborg, University of Alaska Archives, Fairbanks, Alaska.
22 *DAE,* August 10, 1958.
23 *DAE,* July 29, 1958.
24 *DAE,* July 6, 1958; Mary Lee Council to E.L. Bartlett, July 12, 1958, E.L. Bartlett Papers, Statehood File, box 2, folder Alaska Statehood Committee, 1958–59, University of Alaska Archives, Fairbanks, Alaska; *FDNM,* July 24, 1958; *ADT,* August 2, 1958.
25 *FDNM,* August 14, August 9, August 25, 1958; Robert Atwood, "Alaska's Struggle for Statehood," State Government, Autumn, 1958, p. 208.
26 *ADT,* August 27, 1958; Alaska, Territorial Canvassing Board, "Official Canvass of Results, Alaska General Election, Tuesday, October 9, 1956"; Alaska, Secretary of State, "Alaska Official Returns of the Special Statehood Referendum Election, August 26, 1958, and the General Election, November 25, 1958," in author's files.
27 "Statehood Primary Election Results," Alaska Historical Library.
28 *Congressional Quarterly Almanac,* 1959, p. 24.
29 Interview with Paul Solka, April 9, 1975, Eugene, Oregon.
30 Alaska, Secretary of State, "Alaska, Official Returns of the Special Statehood Referendum Election, August 26, 1958 and the General Election, November 25, 1958."
31 Sundborg to author, July 15, 1975; *FDNM,* January 5, 10, 1959.
32 *ADT,* February 4, March 9, 1959; *Congressional Quarterly Almanac,* 1959, p. 174; *Cong. Record,* 86 Cong., 1 S., p. 3903.
33 *Cong. Record,* 86 Cong., 1 S., pp. 3828, 2890–3897; *Congressional Quarterly Almanac,* 1959, pp. 173–74; *FDNM,* Nov. 5, 1958.
34 House, *Cong. Record,* 86 Cong., 1 S., p. 4038.
35 86 Cong., 1 S., S. 1541, March 25, 1959; H.R. 6091, March 26, 1959; *Cong. Record,* 86 Cong., 1 S., p. 9472.
36 U.S. Cong., House, Subcommittee on Territorial and Insular Affairs of the Committee on Interior and Insular Affairs, *Alaska Omnibus Bill,* Hearings on H.R. 6091, H.R. 6109, and H.R. 6112, 86 Cong., 1 S., (Washington: GPO, 1959), p. 25.
37 *ADT,* March 25, 1959; U.S. Cong., House, Committee on Interior and Insular Affairs, *Providing for the Admission of the State of Alaska into the Union,* Report to accompany H.R. 7999, 85 Cong., 1 S., H. Report No. 624, pp. 27–28.
38 *Hearings on H.R. 6091,* pp. 27–56.
39 *Hearings on S. 1541,* p. 43; *Hearings on H.R. 6091,* pp. 67–69; *Cong. Record,* 86 Cong., 1 S., p. 9473.
40 *Hearings on H.R. 6091,* pp. 43–49; Hearings on S. 1541, pp. 10–11.
41 U.S. Dept. of the Interior, Bureau of Land Management, Public Land Order 601, "Reserving Public Lands for Highway Purposes," *Federal Register 14* (1949), pp. 5048–5049.
42 *Hearings on H.R. 6091,* pp. 57–59; *Hearings on H.R. 6091,* p. 61.
43 *Ibid.,* pp. 61–63, 78.
44 *Hearings on H.R. 6091,* pp. 27–39; *ADT,* March 25, 1959.
45 *Hearings on S. 1541,* pp. 5–8, 74.
46 *ADT,* May 11, 1959; Hearings on H.R. 6091, pp. 79–80.
47 *ADT,* May 28, 1959; *Cong. Record,* 86 Cong., 1 S., pp. 9470, 9480–9484; *ADT,* June 15, 1959; *Cong. Record,* 86 Cong., 1 S., pp. 10568, 9678–9679, 10594; 73 Stat., 154.

CHAPTER 15

1 George Sundborg to author, August 19, 1975; E.L. Bartlett to Joe Josephson, February 9, 1962, E.L. Bartlett Papers, Personal file, 1935–68, box 13, folder Joe Josephson, 1962–63, University of Alaska Archives, Fairbanks, Alaska.

2 E.L. Bartlett to Stanley J. Erickson, July 24, 1959, E.L. Bartlett Papers, Personal file, 1935–68, box 11, folder voting record, University of Alaska Archives, Fairbanks, Alaska.

3 Interview with Joe Josephson, September 24, 1976, Anchorage, Alaska; *Cong. Record,* 86 Cong., 1 S., pp. 3755–3758.

4 *Cong. Record,* 88 Cong., 2 S., reprint, March 11, 1964, Private Papers, Vide Bartlett.

5 *Cong. Record,* 88 Cong., 2 S., pp. 13366–13368.

6 Text of E.L. Bartlett Senate speech, 1964, Private Papers, Vide Bartlett.

7 William Manchester, *The Glory and the Dream,* II, pp. 1244–1248; E.L. Bartlett to Josephson, June 24, 1963, E.L. Bartlett Papers, Personal file, 1935–68, box 13, folder Correspondence, general, Joe Josephson, 1963–64, University of Alaska Archives, Fairbanks, Alaska.

8 Manchester, II, pp. 1249–1283.

9 *Cong. Record,* 89 Cong., 1 S., p. 7231.

10 *Ibid.,* pp. 7233–7234.

11 *Ibid.* pp. 4426, 4419–23.

12 *Ibid.,* pp. 4423–24.

13 *Ibid.,* p. 4426.

14 *Ibid.,* pp. 4419–20.

15 William O. Pruitt, Jr., "A New Caribou Problem," *Beaver,* Winter, 1962, Private Papers, Vide Bartlett.

16 Copy, Arthur R. Schulert, "Strontium 90 in Alaska—Alaskan Eskimos For Whom The Caribou Is a Dietary Staple Have A High Strontium 90 Concentration," *Science,* April 1962, Private Papers, Vide Bartlett.

17 Interview with John M. Cornman, April 17, 1975, Washington, D.C.

18 Clipping, *Cong. Record,* April 4, 1963.

19 *Ibid.*

20 Clipping, *Cong. Record,* May 14, 1963.

21 Clipping, *Cong. Record,* September 12, 1963, Private Papers, Vide Bartlett.

22 Clipping, *Cong. Record,* June 18, 1964, Private Papers, Vide Bartlett.

23 Clipping, *Cong. Record,* August 31, 1964, Private Papers, Vide Bartlett.

24 Clipping, *Cong. Record,* August 3, 1965, Private Papers, Vide Bartlett.

25 Clipping, *Cong. Record,* May 17, 1966, Private Papers, Vide Bartlett.

26 Clipping, *Cong. Record,* July 21, 1966, March 10, 1967, Private Papers, Vide Bartlett.

27 Clipping, *Cong. Record,* July 10, 1967, Private Papers, Vide Bartlett; E.L. Bartlett statement opening hearings of Senate Committee on Commerce on S. 2067, August 28, 1967, E.L. Bartlett Papers, 90 Congress, 1967–68, Legislative Bill File, box 15, folder S. 2067, Radiation Control for Health and Safety Act, 1968, reports, University of Alaska Archives, Fairbanks, Alaska.

28 Clipping, *Cong. Record,* July 1, 1968, Private Papers, Vide Bartlett; P.L. 90-602, 90 Cong., H.R. 10790, October 18, 1968.

29 Copy "Senator Bartlett: A Fighter for Radiation Safety," Private Papers, Vide Bartlett.

CHAPTER 16

1 Interview with Margery Smith, April 21, 1975, Washington, D.C.
2 David E. Price, *Who Makes The Laws? The Legislative Roles of Three Senate Committees*, Ph.D. Dissertation, Yale University, 1969, pp. 117–118.
3 Lionel A. Walford, *Fishery Resources of the United States of America*, Fish and Wildlife Service, U.S. Department of the Interior (Washington, D.C.: GPO, 1945), p. 132.
4 Price, *Who Makes The Laws?*, pp. 119–122.
5 Virginia Wemyss Brewer, "The Three Mile Limit and the Pronouncement of Thomas Jefferson Concerning It" (Library of Congress, Foreign Affairs Division, April 9, 1958), pp. 1–3, in E. L. Bartlett Papers, Interior, Fish and Wildlife, Fisheries, box 19, folder Fisheries, 12 Mile Limit, 1952–60, University of Alaska Archives, Fairbanks, Alaska. 45 U.S.C. 251, 1958 ed.
6 "Proposed Statutes Defining Territorial Waters of the United States," August 29, 1962, the Library of Congress, in E. L. Bartlett Papers, Interior, Fish and Wildlife, Fisheries, box 19, folder Fish and Wildlife, Fisheries, 12 Mile Limit, 1962, University of Alaska Archives, Fairbanks, Alaska.
7 A. L. Shalowitz to Burke Riley, October 23, 1962, E. L. Bartlett Papers, Interior, Fish and Wildlife, Fisheries, box 19, folder Fish and Wildlife, Fisheries, 12 Mile Limit, 1962, University of Alaska Archives, Fairbanks, Alaska.
8 *Cong. Record,* 86 Cong., 2 S., pp. 4428–4431.
9 *Ibid.,* p. 4434.
10, 11. *Ibid.,* p. 4435.
12 William A. Egan to E. L. Bartlett, July 18, 1962, E. L. Bartlett Papers, Interior, Fish and Wildlife, Fisheries, box 19, folder Fish and Wildlife, Fisheries, 12 Mile Limit, 1962, University of Alaska Archives, Fairbanks, Alaska.
13 "Coastal Boundary Problems," Statement by Governor William A. Egan of Alaska to the Governor's Conference Workshop on "Solutions to Old and New Problems," 1962, in E. L. Bartlett Papers, Interior Fish and Wildlife, Fisheries, box 19, folder Fish and Wildlife, Fisheries, 12 Mile Limit, 1962, University of Alaska Archives, Fairbanks, Alaska.
14 Library of Congress, "Extension of Territorial Waters," August 29, 1962, E. L. Bartlett Papers, Interior, Fish and Wildlife, Fisheries, box 19, folder Fish and Wildlife, Fisheries, 12 Mile Limit, 1962, University of Alaska Archives, Fairbanks, Alaska.
15 *Cong. Record,* 88 Cong., 1 S., p. 8163.
16 Donald L. McKernan to E. L. Bartlett, June 24, 1963, E. L. Bartlett Papers, Fish and Wildlife, Fisheries, box 19, folder 12 Mile Limit, 1963, University of Alaska Archives, Fairbanks, Alaska.
17 *Japan Times,* September 8, 1963.
18 *Cong. Record,* 83 Cong., 1 S., p. 17555.
19 Bill Foster to Gerry Grinstein, October 8, 1963, E. L. Bartlett Papers, 88 Cong., Leg. Bill File, 1963–64, box 11, folder 12 Mile Limit, University of Alaska Archives, Fairbanks, Alaska.
20 Confidential memo, March 12, 1964, E. L. Bartlett Papers, 88 Cong., Leg. Bill File, 1963–64, box 11, folder S. 1988, University of Alaska Archives, Fairbanks, Alaska.
21 S. 1988-P.L. 88-308, May 20, 1964.
22 E. L. Bartlett to David B. Galloway, May 28, 1964, E. L. Bartlett Papers, 88 Cong., Leg. Bill File, 1964, box 12, folder S. 1988, University of Alaska Archives, Fairbanks, Alaska.

23 E. L. Bartlett to A. W. Boddy, June 2, 1964, E. L. Bartlett Papers, 88 Cong., Leg. Bill File, 1963–64, box 12, Folder History of S. 1988, University of Alaska Archives, Fairbanks, Alaska.

24 *FDNM,* May 19, 1964: White House News Release, May 20, 1964, in E. L. Bartlett Papers, Interior, Fish and Wildlife, Fisheries, box 10, folder 12 Mile Limit, 1964, University of Alaska Archives, Fairbanks, Alaska.

25 Memo, Foster to E. L. Bartlett, June 30, 1965, E. L. Bartlett Papers, 89 Cong., Leg. Bill File, 1965–66, box 7, folder 12 Mile Limit, University of Alaska Archives, Fairbanks, Alaska; S. 49, 89 Cong., 1 S., January 6, 1965.

26 89 Cong., 2 S., U.S. Senate, *Twelve-Mile Fishery Zone,* Senate Report No. 1280 to Accompany S. 2218, pp. 1–2.

27 *Ibid.,* pp. 2, 8.

28 E. L. Bartlett to Edward W. Allen, August 13, 1966, E. L. Bartlett Papers, 89 Cong., Leg. Bill File, 1965–66, box 7, folder 12 Mile Limit, University of Alaska Archives, Fairbanks, Alaska.

29 P.L. 89-658, October 14, 1966.

30 Gruening to E. L. Bartlett, April 30, 1945, Private Papers, Vide Bartlett.

31 *Congress and the Nation,* Vol. II, 1965–1968 (Washington, D.C.: Congressional Quarterly Service, 1969), p. 4853; E. L. Bartlett to Stanley J. McCutcheon, January 13, 1966, E. L. Bartlett Papers, 89 Cong., Leg. Bill File, 1965–66, box 11, folder S. 2720, Fish Protein Concentrate, University of Alaska Archives, Fairbanks, Alaska.

32 *Congress and the Nation,* II, 1965–68, p. 485.

33 *Ibid.*

34 E. L. Bartlett news release, May 16, 1966, E. L. Bartlett Papers, 89 Cong., Leg. Bill File, 1965–66, box 11, folder S. 2720, Fish Protein Concentrate, University of Alaska Archives, Fairbanks, Alaska.

35 *Cong. Record,* 89 Cong., 2 S, p. 5427.

36 E. L. Bartlett Washington Report, July 1, 1966, copy in author's files; E. L. Bartlett to Dr. I. A. Parfentjev, July 28, 1966, E. L. Bartlett Papers, 89 Cong., Leg. Bill File, 1965–66, box 11, folder S. 2720, Fish Protein Concentrate, University of Alaska Archives, Fairbanks, Alaska.

37 *The Washington Post,* September 5, 1966.

38 *Cong. Record,* 89 Cong., 2 S., pp. 28910–23914.

39 *Fish Protein Concentrate,* House Report No. 2290, Conference Report to accompany S. 2720, 89 Cong., 2 S. (Washington: GPO, 1966); P.L. 89-701, 89 Cong., S. 2720, November 2, 1966.

40 *Cong. Record,* 90 Cong., 2 S., pp. 8725–8730, 11263; P.L. 90-549, 90 Cong., S. 3030, 82 Stat. 436.

CHAPTER 17

1 Gruening, *Many Battles,* p. 286.

2 George Sundborg to the author, July 15, 1975.

3 Gruening Diary, December 5, 1939, E. Gruening Papers, University of Alaska Archives, Fairbanks, Alaska.

4, 5 *Ibid.*

6 Interview with Doris Stewart, April 6, 1975, Sequim, Washington.

7 *Ibid.;* Interview with John M. Cornman, April 17, 1975, Washington, D.C.

8 Gruening Diary, December 9, December 17, 1939, University of Alaska Archives, Fairbanks, Alaska.

9 Gruening, *Many Battles,* pp. 278–290.

10 *Ibid.,* pp. 288–94.

11 *Ibid.,* pp. 245–297.

12 Herbert Henry Hilscher, *Alaska Now* (Boston: Little, Brown, 1948), pp. 275–77.

13 E. L. Bartlett to Anthony J. Dimond, November 16, 1940, Private papers, Vide Bartlett.

14 E. L. Bartlett to Dimond, May 4, 1943, Private Papers, Vide Bartlett.

15 Gruening, *Many Battles,* pp. 328–35.

16 Gruening to E. L. Bartlett, March 26, 1945, E. Gruening Papers, box 329, University of Alaska Archives, Fairbanks, Alaska.

17 Gruening to E. L. Bartlett, July 16, November 7, 1945, E. Gruening Papers, box 329, University of Alaska Archives, Fairbanks, Alaska.

18 Gruening to E. L. Bartlett, May 4, 7, 1945, E. Gruening Papers, box 32a, University of Alaska Archives, Fairbanks, Alaska.

19 Harold L. Ickes to Wenz, November 20, 1946, E. L. Bartlett Papers, Personal file, 1935–68, box 10, folder Correspondence, general, Ernest Gruening, 1946, University of Alaska Archives, Fairbanks, Alaska.

20 E. L. Bartlett Papers, Personal file, 1935–68, box 2, folder confidential memos of the 1940s, memorandum February 19, 1946, University of Alaska Archives, Fairbanks, Alaska.

21 Clipping from *DAE,* no date.

22 *Ibid.*

23 E. Gruening to E. L. Bartlett, March 29, 1946, E. L. Bartlett Papers, Personal file, 1935–68, box 10, folder Correspondence, general, 1946, University of Alaska Archives, Fairbanks, Alaska.

24 E. L. Bartlett to E. Gruening, April 1, 1946, E. L. Bartlett Papers, Personal file, 1935–68, box 10, folder Correspondence, general, Ernest Gruening, 1946, University of Alaska Archives, Fairbanks, Alaska.

25 E. L. Bartlett confidential memos, July 2, July 11, 1946, E. L. Bartlett Papers, Personal file, 1935–68, box 2, folder confidential memos of the 1940s, University of Alaska Archives, Fairbanks, Alaska.

26 E. L. Bartlett confidential memo, June 26, 1946, E. L. Bartlett Papers, Personal file, 1935–68, box 2, folder confidential memos of the 1940s, University of Alaska Archives, Fairbanks, Alaska.

27 Interview with Mary Lee Council, April 23, 1975, Washington, D.C.

28 *Ibid.;* Interview with Susie Bartlett Peterson, November 23, 1976, Fairbanks, Alaska.

29 E. Gruening to Bartlett, January 25, January 31, February 11, 1949, E. L. Bartlett to E. Gruening, February 22, 1949, E. Gruening Papers, box Z, folder 34, ADB, 1949–52, University of Alaska Archives, Fairbanks, Alaska.

30 E. L. Bartlett to Gruening, March 12, 1948, E. L. Bartlett to "Cap" Krug, March 12, 1948, E. L. Bartlett Papers, Personal file, 1935–68, box 10, folder Correspondence, general, E. Gruening, 1948, University of Alaska Archives, Fairbanks, Alaska; *Washington Evening Star,* April 5, 1949; E. L. Bartlett to Hugh Wade, March 13, 1949, E. L. Bartlett Papers, Personal file, 1935–68, box 25, folder Correspondence, general, Hugh Wade, 1945–51 University of Alaska Archives, Fairbanks, Alaska.

31 E. Gruening to E. L. Bartlett, September 1, 1950, E. Gruening Papers, box 32a; E. L. Bartlett to E. Gruening, January 17, 1951, E. Gruening Papers, box 32a, University of Alaska Archives, Fairbanks, Alaska; E. Gruening to E. L. Bartlett, September 1, 1950, E. L. Bartlett Papers, Personal file, 1935–68, box 10, folder Correspondence, general, Ernest Gruening, 1950–51.

32 E.L. Bartlett to E. Gruening, November 3, 1952, E.L. Bartlett Papers, Personal file, 1935–68, box 9, folder Correspondence, general, Ernest Gruening, 1952, University of Alaska Archives, Fairbanks, Alaska.

33 E.L. Bartlett memo, January 21, 1953, E.L. Bartlett Papers, Personal file, 1935–68, box 2, folder confidential memos of the 1950s, University of Alaska Archives, Fairbanks, Alaska.

34 *Ibid.*

35 Gruening, *Many Battles,* pp. 376–77.

36 Interview with Tom Stewart, March 22, 1976, Juneau, Alaska.

37 *Ibid.*

38 Gruening, *Many Battles,* p. 381.

39 E. Gruening to E.L. Bartlett, April 9, 1953, E.L. Bartlett Papers, Personal file, 1935–68, box 15, folder general, 1953, University of Alaska Archives, Fairbanks, Alaska.

40 Gruening, *Many Battles,* pp. 381–82.

41 E.L. Bartlett to Burke Riley, March 8, 1955, E.L. Bartlett Papers, Personal file, 1935–68, box 20, folder Correspondence, general, Riley, Burke, 1952–55, University of Alaska Archives, Fairbanks, Alaska.

42 Gruening, *Many Battles,* pp. 401, 149.

43 Interview with Mary Lee Council, July 1969, Washington, D.C.

44 E.L. Bartlett to Wade, January 11, 1956, E.L. Bartlett Papers, Personal file, 1935–68, box 25, folder Correspondence, general, Hugh Wade, 1956–57, University of Alaska Archives, Fairbanks, Alaska.

45 E.L. Bartlett to B. Riley, January 11, 1956, E.L. Bartlett Papers, Personal file, 1935–68, box 20, folder Correspondence, general, Riley, Burke, 1956–57, University of Alaska Archives, Fairbanks, Alaska.

46 Confidential memo, January 15, 1956, E.L. Bartlett Papers, Personal file, 1935–68, box 2, folder confidential memos of the 1950s, University of Alaska Archives, Fairbanks, Alaska.

47 E.L. Bartlett to Wade, June 12, 1956, E.L. Bartlett Papers, Personal file, 1935–68, box 25, folder Correspondence, general, Hugh Wade, 1956–57, University of Alaska Archives, Fairbanks, Alaska.

48 Council to C. Girard "Jebby" Davidson, Sept. 12, 1958, E.L. Bartlett Papers, Personal file, 1935–68, box 9, folder Correspondence, general, Ernest Gruening, 1955–62, University of Alaska Archives, Fairbanks, Alaska.

49 Interview with John M. Cornman, April 17, 1975, Washington, D.C.

50 E.L. Bartlett to Wade, January 25, 1960, E.L. Bartlett Papers, Personal file, 1935–68, folder Correspondence, general, Hugh Wade, 1958–60, University of Alaska Archives, Fairbanks, Alaska.

51 E.L. Bartlett memo to Katherine Nordale, Bill Egan, John Dimond, Hugh Wade, Burke Riley, June 11, 1960, E.L. Bartlett Papers, Personal file, 1935–68, box 3, folder confidential memos of the 1960s, University of Alaska Archives, Fairbanks, Alaska.

52 Interview with Joseph FitzGerald, March 25, 1977, Fairbanks, Alaska.

53 *Ibid.*

54 Interview with Joe Josephson, September 24, 1976, Anchorage, Alaska.

55 E.L. Bartlett memo, August 24, 1960, March 28, 1961, E.L. Bartlett Papers, Personal file, 1935–68, box 3, folder confidential memos of the 1960s, University of Alaska Archives, Fairbanks, Alaska.

56 E.L. Bartlett to Wade, April 7, 1961, E.L. Bartlett Papers, Personal file, 1935–68, box 24, folder Correspondence, general, Hugh Wade, 1961–62, University of Alaska Archives, Fairbanks, Alaska.

57 E. L. Bartlett memo, April 15, 1961, E. L. Bartlett Papers, Personal file, 1935–68, box 3, folder confidential memos of the 1960s, University of Alaska Archives, Fairbanks, Alaska.

58 *ADT*, November 2, 1968.

59 E. L. Bartlett to B. Riley, September 6, 1962, Private Papers, Vide Bartlett.

60 Interview with Joseph Josephson, September 24, 1976, Anchorage, Alaska.

61 E. L. Bartlett to B. Riley, June 1, August 19, 1963, Private Papers, Vide Bartlett.

62 Interview with J. Cornman, April 17, 1975, Washington, D.C.

63 E. L. Bartlett to B. Riley, February 7, February 12, 1964, Private Papers, Vide Bartlett.

64 E. L. Bartlett to B. Riley, August 12, 1964, Private Papers, Vide Bartlett.

65 E. L. Bartlett confidential office memo, January 11, 1967, Private Papers, Vide Bartlett.

66 Interview with M. L Council, July 1969, Washington, D.C.; E. L. Bartlett to Al White, October 21, 1967, E. L. Bartlett Papers, Personal file, 1935–68, box 26, folder Albert White, 1967–68, University of Alaska Archives, Fairbanks, Alaska.

67 George Sundborg to author, August 19, 1975.

68 Oliver Quayle and Company, "A Study of the Political Climate in Alaska," Study #1080 (New York: Station Park Building, Bronxville, May 1968), in author's files; *ADT*, October 22, 1968; *ADN*, October 27, November 2, 1968; Gruening, *Many Battles*, p. 510.

69 E. L. Bartlett to White, September 20, 1968, E. L. Bartlett Papers, Personal file, 1935–68, box 26, folder Correspondence, general, Al White, 1967–78, University of Alaska Archives, Fairbanks, Alaska; *ADN*, November 10, 1968; E. L. Bartlett memo to files, September 17, 1968, E. L. Bartlett Papers, Personal file, 1935–68, box 3, folder confidential memos of the 1960s, University of Alaska Archives, Fairbanks, Alaska.

70 E. L. Bartlett to White, September 20, 1968, E. L. Bartlett Papers, Personal file, 1935–68, University of Alaska Archives, Fairbanks, Alaska; Interview with Katie Hurley, November 8, 1976, Wasilla, Alaska; State of Alaska, "Official Returns by Election Precinct, Primary Election, August 27, 1968 and General Election, November 5, 1968," in author's files.

71 Sundborg to author, August 19, 1975.

72 *Ibid.*; E. L. Bartlett to B. Riley, February 12, 1964, Private Papers, Vide Bartlett.

73 Gruening to William R. Emerson, 1972, E. Gruening Papers, box 1A, University of Alaska Archives, Fairbanks, Alaska.

CHAPTER 18

1 Interview with Doris Ann Bartlett Riley, April 9, 1975, Eugene, Oregon.

2, 3, 4, 5, 6, *Ibid.*

7 Interview with Susie Bartlett Peterson, November 23, 1976, Fairbanks, Alaska; E.L. Bartlett to Leonard King, February 1964, Maurine Neuberger to E.L. Bartlett, February 6, 1964, E.L. Bartlett to Maurine Neuberger, February 8, 1964, E.L. Bartlett Papers, Personal file, 1935–68, box 17, folder general, 1964, University of Alaska Archives, Fairbanks, Alaska; George Sundborg to author, July 15, 1975.

8 Interview with S. Peterson, November 23, 1976, Fairbanks, Alaska; Interview with Mary Lee Council, April 23, 1975, Washington, D.C.

9 E.L. Bartlett to Hugh Wade, March 4, 1954, E.L. Bartlett to Burke Riley, June 24, 1966, E.L. Bartlett Papers, Personal file, 1935–68, box 25, folder Correspondence, general, Hugh Wade, 1952–55, box 20, folder Correspondence, general, Riley, Burke, 1966–67, University of Alaska Archives, Fairbanks, Alaska.

10 Interview with John M. Cornman, April 17, 1975, Washington, D.C.

11 Interview with Paul Solka, April 9, 1975, Eugene, Oregon.

12 Interview with Frank Barton, April 23, 1975, Washington, D.C.

13 Interview with Margery Smith, April 21, 1975, Washington, D.C.

14, 15, 16 *Ibid.*

17 Interview with Mary A. Nordale, April 3, 1977, Fairbanks, Alaska.

18, 19, 20 *Ibid.*

21 Interview with M. Smith, April 21, 1975, Washington, D.C.

22, 23 *Ibid.*

24 Sundborg to author, July 15, 1975.

25 *Ibid.*

26 E.L. Bartlett to Katie Alexander, April 21, 1951, E.L. Bartlett Papers, Personal File, 1935–68, box 12, folder Correspondence, general, Katherine Alexander Hurley, 1950–54, University of Alaska Archives, Fairbanks, Alaska; Alan M. Weintraub to E.L. Bartlett, September 25, 1960, Private Papers, Vide Bartlett; Interview with M. Smith, April 21, 1975, Washington, D.C.; E.L. Bartlett to Wade, December 9, 1949, January 3, 1956, E.L. Bartlett Papers, Personal file, 1935–68, box 25, folder Correspondence, general, Hugh Wade, 1945-51, 1956-57, University of Alaska Archives, Fairbanks, Alaska.

27 Interview with M. Nordale, April 2, 1977, Fairbanks, Alaska; Interview with M. Smith, April 21, 1975, Washington, D.C.; Sundborg to author, July 15, 1975.

28 E.L. Bartlett to B. Riley, July 22, 1965, E.L. Bartlett Papers, Personal file, 1935–68, box 17, folder general, 1968, University of Alaska Archives, Fairbanks, Alaska.

CHAPTER 19

1 E.L. Bartlett to Vide, February 14, 1967, Private Papers, Vide Bartlett.

2 Interview with Susie Bartlett Peterson, November 23, 1976, Fairbanks, Alaska.

3 E.L. Bartlett memo, June 27, August 24, 1959, E.L. Bartlett Papers, Personal file, 1935–68, box 2, folder confidential memos of the 1950s, University of Alaska Archives, Fairbanks, Alaska.

4 E.L. Bartlett to Burke Riley, April 5, 1965, final diagnosis causing admission, September 8, 1966, Private Papers, Vide Bartlett, E.L. Bartlett to Hugh Wade, May 11, 1966, E.L. Bartlett to B. Riley, August 31, 1966, E.L. Bartlett Papers, Personal file, 1935–68, box 24, folder Correspondence, general, University of Alaska Archives, Fairbanks, Alaska.

5 "News from E.L. (Bob) Bartlett, Senator from Alaska, September 1, 1966," author's files.

6 Interview with Vide Bartlett, April 1974, Fairbanks, Alaska.

7, 8, 9 *Ibid.*

10 E.L. Bartlett memo November 8, 1968, E.L. Bartlett Papers, Personal file, 1935–68, box 9, folder Health, 1968, University of Alaska Archives, Fairbanks, Alaska.

11 E.L. Bartlett office memo, November 8, November 18, 1968, E.L. Bartlett Papers, Personal file, 1935–68, box 9, folder Health, 1968, University of Alaska Archives, Fairbanks, Alaska.

12 *Ibid.*

13 E.L. Bartlett office memo, November 18, 1968, E.L. Bartlett Papers, Personal file, 1935–68, box 9, folder Health, 1968, University of Alaska Archives, Fairbanks, Alaska.

14 Interview with Vide Bartlett, April 1974, Fairbanks, Alaska; E.L. Bartlett memo to Vide, November 20, 1968, E.L. Bartlett Papers, Personal file, 1935–68, box 9, folder Health, 1968, University of Alaska Archives, Fairbanks, Alaska.

15 Interview with Vide Bartlett, April 1974, Fairbanks, Alaska.

16 Memo to staff from Margery Smith, December 2, 1968, E.L. Bartlett Papers, Personal file, 1935–68, box 9, folder Health, 1968, University of Alaska Archives, Fairbanks, Alaska.

17 *ADN*, December 12, 1968.

18 Interview with Vide Bartlett, April 1974, Fairbanks, Alaska.

19 *ADT,* December 12, 1968.
20. *FDNM,* December 12, 1968.
21. *ADN,* December 13, 1968.
22 John Havelock to Vide Bartlett, December 1968, Private Papers, Vide Bartlett.

CHAPTER 20

1 Interview with Hugh Wade, December 30, 1976, Anchorage, Alaska.

INDEX

Index

Acheson, Dean, 80
Agriculture, Tanana Valley, 4-5
Aiken, Tom, 12
Alaska: during depression, 24; federal control, 75; game resources, 76-7; geography and population, 55; postwar changes, 57, 62; during World War II, 42-6. See also Fairbanks, Statehood
Alaska Constitutional Convention, 151-3
Alaska Mental Health Bill of 1956, 76, 99-114
Alaska Miners Association, 116, 129; on statehood, 119-21, 124. See also Anderson, Al (representative)
Alaska Native Brotherhood, 68-70, 123
Alaska Native reservations, 63, 68-70
Alaska Native rights, opinions on, 136
Alaska Omnibus Bill, 172-4
Alaska Planning Council, 33
Alaska Salmon Industry Inc., 125, 129, 133. See also Arnold, Winton C. (representative)
Alaska Statehood Committee, 81, 128, 130, 137-8, 216. See also Feltus, Randolph (lobbyist)
Alaska-Tennessee Plan, 152-4, 160, 162-3
Alaska, University of, 151-2
Albrecht, Dr. C. Earl, 104, 105
Alcan Highway, 44-45
Allen, Edward W., 134-5
Anderson, Al, 124, 126, 129
Anderson, Clinton P., 133, 136, 145, 151, 156
Angell, Homer, 101, 103
Anti-semitism, 25
Arnold, Winton C., 125, 126, 129, 132-5, 138, 158
Aspinall, Wayne, 158
Attu, 44
Atwood, Robert B., 123, 124, 130, 136, 142, 147, 149, 153, 158, 159, 160, 171, 215, 244

Baker, Forbes L., 15, 169-70
Baker, William L., 81, 119, 123
Barr, Frank, 82, 87, 88-9
Bartlett, Al, 30
Bartlett Doris, 2, 10
Bartlett, Doris Ann (later Mrs. Burke Riley), 28, 31-4, 39, 60, 62, 67, 229, 230, 243
Bartlett, Ed, 1-2, 9, 10, 12, 29, 30
Bartlett, Edward Lewis "Bob," background, 1-2; childhood, 2-7, 9, 10; education, 6, 11-14, 16; courtship, 17-23; marriage, 23; children, 28, 47, (see also Bartlett, Doris Ann and Susie); family life, 27-8, 31-9, 66-7, 229-32; health and death, 231, 236-7, 238-43; early employment, 11-14; newspaper work, 14-7, 24-6, 32, 51, 61; mining, 30-39; political career: secretary to territorial Senator Anthony J. Dimond, 25-8; assistant territorial director of FHA, 28-9; information service representative for Social Security, 32-3; executive secretary Alaska Planning Council, 33; chairman of Alaska's Unemployment Compensation Commission, 33; Secretary of Alaska, 40-9, 202-6; Alaska's territorial Delegate to Congress, 50-174; U.S. Senator, 175-247. Legislative record: comprehensive mental health legislation, 1944-56, 101-14; promotes fishery, 186-8, 223; Radiation Health and Safety Act, 184-5; revise Organic Act of 1912, 70-1; Alaska statehood, 56-7, 115-74; twelve-mile fishery zone, 188, 190-7. Opinions: on Alaska Native rights, 136; on Alaska parochialism, 176; on Alaska-Tennessee Plan, 153; on American merchant marine policy, 223; on elective governor for Alaska, 148; on marriage, 38; on military draft, 176; on Native reservations, 63; on Nuclear Test Ban Treaty, 183-4; on partition, 146; on radiation safety, 223; on radioactive contamination, 181-5; on Red